PLATO'S DIALECTIC AT PLAY

PLATO'S DIALECTIC AT PLAY

ARGUMENT, STRUCTURE, AND MYTH IN THE *SYMPOSIUM*

KEVIN CORRIGAN AND ELENA GLAZOV-CORRIGAN

THE PENNSYLVANIA STATE UNIVERSITY PRESS

UNIVERSITY PARK, PENNSYLVANIA

Library of Congress Cataloging-in-Publication Data

Corrigan, Kevin.
    Plato's dialectic at play :
    argument, structure, and myth in the Symposium /
    Kevin Corrigan and Elena Glazov-Corrigan.
        p.   cm.
Includes bibliographical references and index.
ISBN 978-0-271-02913-9 (alk. paper)
1. Plato. Symposium.
2. Plato-Literary art.
I. Corrigan, Elena.
II. Title.

B385 .C67 2004
184-dc22
2003024817

Copyright © 2004 The Pennsylvania State University
All rights reserved
Printed in the United States of America
Published by The Pennsylvania State University Press,
University Park, PA 16802–1003

The Pennsylvania State University Press is a member of
the Association of American University Presses.

It is the policy of The Pennsylvania State University Press
to use acid-free paper. Publications on uncoated stock satisfy the minimum requirements of American National
Standard for Information Sciences—Permanence of Paper
for Printed Library Materials, ANSI Z39.48–1992.

The Platonic dialogue was the lifeboat in which the ship-wrecked older poetry saved itself, together with its numerous offspring. Crowded together in a narrow space and timidly obeying their helmsman Socrates, they moved forward. . . . Plato has furnished for all posterity the pattern of a new art form, the novel, viewed as the Aesopian fable raised to its highest power.

—Nietzsche, The Birth of Tragedy from the Spirit of Music

The serio-comical genres (especially the Socratic dialogues, and Menippean satire [including the *Satyricon* of Petronius]) were the first authentic and essential step in the evolution of the novel as the genre of becoming.

—Bakhtin, "Epic and Novel: Toward a Methodology for the Study of the Novel"

CONTENTS

Acknowledgments   xi

Introduction   1

1 Apollodorus's Prologue: An Imitation of an Imitation   7
- 1.1 The Historical Frame   7
- 1.2 Apollodorus and Mimetic Narrative   10
- 1.3 The Force of *Hybris*   13
- 1.4 Malakos versus Manikos: Soft or Mad?   15
- 1.5 Anachronisms?   18

2 Aristodemus's Prologue: The Destruction and Transformation of the Factual Frame of Reference   21
- 2.1 The Story   22
- 2.2 Sufficiency and Beauty: Emerging Criteria for Judgment   23
- 2.3 The Spatial Order?   26
- 2.4 Mimetic versus Hubristic: The Destruction and Transformation of the Factual Narrative   28
- 2.5 Sophistic Education in the Context of Other Dialogues: *Protagoras, Phaedo, Republic*   33
- 2.6 Between Religious Observance and the Cycle of Opposites   37
- 2.7 "The Father of the Discourse"   39

3 The Order of the Speeches: Formulating the Problem   43
- 3.1 Eros   44
- 3.2 Encomium   46
- 3.3 The Problem of the Significance of the Early Speeches   46

4 From Character to Speech: The Early Speeches and Their Significance   51
- 4.1 Phaedrus: The Ardent Apprentice, but Confused Mythologue   51
- 4.2 Pausanias: The Sophistic Sociologue   56
- 4.3 Hiccups and Eryximachus, the Homogenic Doctor-Scientist   62
- 4.4 Aristophanes: The Poet as Educator   68
    - 4.4.1 Aristophanes' Speech and Socrates' Criticism of Mimetic Art in the *Republic*   70

	4.4.2 The Possibility of Anachronism and Plato's Vanishing Signature	78
	4.4.3 Aristophanes' Speech as a Parody of Philosophical Dialectic	80
	4.4.4 Aristophanes' Speech and Individual Identity	82
	4.4.5 Aristophanes' Hiccups Revisited	85
4.5	Agathon: The Sophistic Theologue as the "Climax" of an Unselfcritical Tradition	85
	4.5.1 Advance over the Previous Speakers?	86
	4.5.2 Agathon as Theologue Without Need	92
	4.5.3 The Shadow of the "Good": Agathon's Portrait in the Context of the *Republic*	94
4.6	Conclusion	100

5 Diotima-Socrates: Mythical Thought in the Making — 104

5.1	Introduction: The Problem	104
5.2	The Elenchus of Agathon and the Question of Truth	108
5.3	The Role of Diotima	111
5.4	Eros-*Daimôn*	118
5.5	Diotima and the Art of Mythmaking Revisited: The Birth of Eros	121
5.6	Love: Relation or Substance?	130
5.7	Rhetoric and Dialectic	133
5.8	Criticism of Aristophanes and Agathon	135
5.9	The Curious Case of Procreation in the Beautiful	137
5.10	The Concluding Sections of the Lesser Mysteries	141
5.11	Preliminary Conclusion	145

6 The Greater Mysteries and the Structure of the *Symposium* So Far — 147

6.1	The Movement of Ascent: Structure	148
6.2	The Movement of Ascent and the Earlier Speeches	151
6.3	Immortality and God-Belovedness	158
6.4	Overall Conclusion	159
	6.4.1 "Platonic Love": The View So Far	159

7 Alcibiades and the Conclusion of the *Symposium*: The Test and Trial of Praise — 163

7.1	The Figure of Dionysus and the Face of Socrates	163
7.2	The Role of Alcibiades	165
7.3	The Test of Praise	168
7.4	The Trial of Praise	176
7.5	Eros, the Tyrant, and His Revelers	179
7.6	Identity and Diversity: The Uniqueness of Socrates	181

7.7	*Logoi* Opened Up: An Image for the *Symposium?*	183
7.8	The Concluding Scenes: Rest and the Self-Motion of Thought—"Socrates Standing Seeking"	184

8 Conclusion: Plato's Dialectic at Play — 188

8.1	Character, Voice, and Genre	188
8.2	Bakhtin and the Dialogical Character of Novelistic Discourse	197
8.3	The *Symposium* as the First "Novel" of Its Kind in History	200
8.4	Plato's Dialectic at Play: Art, Reason, and Understanding	203
8.5	Plato's Positive View of Art	215
8.6	Structure, Myth, and Argument	220
8.7	Soul-Body and Human Identity	224
8.8	"Platonic Love" and "Plato"	234

Select Bibliography — 241

Index — 255

Acknowledgments

We want to recognize the advice and friendship of Arthur Hilary Armstrong, who was our interlocutor when the first major ideas of this book were beginning to take shape. We also thank Ernie and Sue McCullough, without whose initiative and friendship this project would never have been possible.

Our very special thanks to Ken Dorter for taking the time to read the manuscript and for many invaluable suggestions, as also to Monique Dixsaut, Christopher Rowe, Yuri Corrigan, John Corrigan, Marina Glazov, Denis O'Brien, Carl Still, Daniel Regnier, and Stephen Blackwood for their encouragement, help, and support. We are very grateful to Sanford Thatcher together with the editors and readers for Penn State Press. Sandy's encouragement has made all the difference to us.

Finally, we dedicate this book to Louis Dupré and Lynn Freistadt, without whose spirit and industry, albeit in different fields of action, no university or academic enterprise would ever achieve that mixture of excellence and humanity we recognize in the real experience of the Liberal Arts.

Introduction

The *Symposium* is one of Plato's most accessible dialogues, an engrossing historical document as well as an entertaining literary masterpiece. Editions, translations, and commentaries abound. In the past decade alone a number of volumes have emerged in English, French, Italian, German, and other languages. Why then the need for another book?

This book addresses one of the central problems of the *Symposium* or of any major Platonic dialogue: the character of the connection between what are apparently nonphilosophical details, so strikingly embedded in the narrative, and the philosophical preoccupations of Plato's middle dialogues, most notably, the *Republic*. The Socrates of the *Republic*, for example, argues that the tragedian cannot be simultaneously a comic poet, while the Socrates of the *Symposium* argues with both a comic and a tragic poet (Aristophanes and Agathon) for the opposite view. Is this detail, among so many others, purely accidental? Much of contemporary scholarship has considered the question scarcely worth asking: such fleeting subtleties are too open to overelaborate or heavy-handed misreadings. Yet the puzzle of the relationship between the philosophical and the nonphilosophical in Plato remains a real question for any reader, inviting, yet frustrating, interpretation, not unlike Alcibiades' portrayal of a Silenus-Socrates in the concluding speech of the *Symposium*.

We take up a rather dangerous question here, namely, how to read a philosophical dialogue that, probably more than any other, is so disarming and ingenuous in its artful, literary qualities. No small issue is at stake. Is the artist who wrote the *Symposium* the same Plato whose Socrates banished artists from the *polis* in the *Republic?* Or, an even larger issue: does it make sense to bring together into one view, as it were, the nonphilosophical and philosophical pathways of Plato's work?

As our title indicates, in this book we argue for a new way of interpreting the *Symposium* and its various structures. In fact, we aim, among other things, to show that there is a strong, however playful, connection between all the speakers of the drinking party and what is perhaps the dialogue's central image: the metamorphosis of the apprentice, dedicated to love, as he or she moves ever up on Diotima's ladder of ascent to the beautiful itself. This connection, rich in its implications, only emerges fully, as we shall show, in the figure of the whole and cannot be grasped simply from the dialogue's surface or from one of its parts. Why then this artfulness, and how important is the structural organization of the *Symposium* that we propose here?

The dialogue's structure, hitherto for the most part unnoticed by investigators (so carefully is it concealed in the text), and the inherent literariness of this hidden structure reveal a Plato for whom the dialogical form was not merely ornamentation or philosophical methodology, but an integral part of both philosophical and artistic exploration. Plato's dialectic is not only argument; it is also play. This is why, we argue, Diotima's philosopher-Eros has inherited his artful craftiness from his divine father, Poros (Plenty, or Resource). If to play is a divine gift for Plato, then it becomes clear that, by ignoring this aspect of his writing, some contemporary scholarship has created a totalitarian, rather prohibitive Plato who can be attacked or deconstructed at will as the bulwark of unfashionable, institutional thinking or whose single-minded destructive and manipulative art can be contrasted unfavorably with that of the supposedly more authentic rebellious, anarchic martyr, Socrates.

We seek to show that the speakers in the *Symposium* are not merely inferior cartoon-figures surrounding the tour de force of Socrates-Diotima's view of love. There is, instead, a connection between the persona of each individual speaker and his (and in the case of Diotima, her) speech or view of the nature of love, and thus the ascent on the ladder of love is characterized by both the insights and the failures of each participant in the dialogue. In this light, the ladder of ascent is not only a philosophical or mystical vision, whose purpose is to instruct the unenlightened; it also operates in the narrative as a living structural axis that gives direction and energy to so many other seemingly accidental details that both precede and follow on Diotima's higher mysteries. In this sense, too, we argue, the dialogue has to be read as a whole, each part contributing something vital to the structure of the whole, in a pattern that goes beyond the speech of Socrates alone.

This analysis produces a rather new view of the *Symposium* and also permits us to demonstrate that the ascent to the beautiful, characteristic of the *Symposium,* provides a carefully articulated and subtle, positive theory of art, which was intended to be read as a companion piece to the examination of art in the context of the good, undertaken in the *Republic.* These two views of art and creativity, therefore, one so artfully concealed in the *Symposium* and the other explicitly argued by Socrates in the *Republic,* must surely be allowed to converse and contrast with each other rather than to constitute separate narrative fiefdoms. In other words, we propose a multidimensional

Introduction

and intertextual form of artistic thought in the dialogues, a complex form that undermines the current image of a linear Plato.

In turn, such an approach leads us to argue that if the *Symposium* is to be read as a companion piece to the *Republic* and, in particular, to Socrates' views and criticisms of art in that dialogue, then the extreme distrust of art commonly associated with Plato and deduced for the most part from the surface of only one of many dialogues is simply insufficient. Rather, the *Symposium* and *Republic* together constitute a necessarily broader tableau upon which at least two different directions of thought have to be pursued at the same time.

Why, then, is Plato's positive view of art presented in the *Symposium* in so covert and understated a way compared to the explicit critique of art in the *Republic?* This difficult question calls for a reading of Plato in a light that has not been characteristic of the majority of mainstream scholarship on the subject. We argue for a view of Plato as not merely a major philosophical thinker, but also a playful multidimensional writer who is saturated with all the subtleties of his highly cultivated Athens and yet, at the same time, so demonstrably capable of provoking self-critical trajectories of reflective possibility outside the boundaries of his own space and time.

In the first five chapters we develop the necessary background to the more detailed examination of the dialogue's structure as a whole. This complex design begins to emerge when a character is juxtaposed with his or her narrative or with those of others, and for this reason, our first speaker is not Phaedrus (who is often simply assumed to hold this position) but Apollodorus, the passionate disciple who has heard the tale from Aristodemus and checked it out with Socrates. The characters of the speakers are accidental neither to the voice, vision, or ideology that directs their lives, nor to the overall construction of the dialogue. This overall structure is presented fully in Chapters 6 and 7 (in connection to the *Symposium*) and the broader questions of the relationship between characterization, genre, and philosophy are examined in Chapter 8 in relation to the middle dialogues and especially the *Republic,* as well as to some contemporary concerns, notably in relation to our claim that, according to the major criteria worked out by the Russian theorist Mikhail Bakhtin, the *Symposium* is the first novel in history.

The precise design, then, is as follows:

In Chapter 1 we discuss the role of Apollodorus in the dialogue and show that his narrative, heard from Aristodemus, is not merely a story within a story, but rather a narrative, three times removed from so-called reality, albeit in somewhat tongue-in-cheek Platonic fashion. Apollodorus's acquired role as Socrates' disciple in this regard is highly significant, even if it has been overlooked by many earlier commentators. This frame of the dialogue and its potential relation to the *Republic* does not seem to have been noticed before.

The focus of Chapter 2 is the character of Aristodemus (and Socrates as initially presented by him) and his factual account of the events, to which he himself was an eyewitness. An examination of what appears to be straightforward unambiguous factuality, introduced by yet another disciple of Socrates (Aristodemus), shows that this particular level of discourse is not as straightforward as it may appear, but instead is destroyed, punctured, and transformed throughout by the thoughts, questions, and jests that it frames but cannot direct. For this reason, the seemingly accidental details of the mise-en-scène are so very hard to interpret: they appear at a level of narrative within which their significance can be neither fully understood nor determined. Nonetheless, this factual level of narrative implicitly contains them all.

In Chapters 3 and 4 we show, first, that if the orderly narrative frame of Aristodemus is insufficient and ultimately incapable of giving direction to the details it introduces, the subsequent narrative frame—the order and nature of the speeches—is as ambiguous and unclear as the structure and role of Apollodorus's and Aristodemus's prologues. Some of the more influential scholarly views about the early speeches are presented and evaluated in order to give context to the first five speeches and to the pronounced organizational and even "ascending" principle underlying their order. In opposition to some recent prominent views, however, we argue that each new speech does not so much "cap" the previous one as, instead, introduce an ever more complex, comprehensive, and potentially philosophical design that each speaker in turn fulfills and yet frustrates—fulfills, because of that individual's dedication and love, but frustrates, because of the weight of personal blindness, attachments, and narrow-mindedness. For this reason, the ascending order is hard to discern, for it is directed not only by the individuals' and genres' capacities, but also by their failures. From this perspective, above all, each of the speeches appears in an entirely new light. But perhaps the most striking questions at this narrative level concern Aristophanes' speech, and the level of inquiry that he both so brilliantly fulfills and yet also clearly betrays, and Agathon's masterful, inspired, but ultimately hollow speech. In the emerging examination of the relationship between the individual successes and failures of each speaker, the arguments of the *Republic* about mimetic art and the shortcomings of artistic vision return again not merely as a counterpoint, but also as an implicitly articulated and forcefully contrasting, philosophical challenge.

We examine in Chapter 5, first, the pivotal focus of Agathon's elenchus for the dialogue (also more comprehensively treated in Chapter 8) and, second, the new beginning involved in Socrates' introduction of a dialogical principle of inquiry as well as in the highly significant figure of Diotima. We argue for a more complex understanding of Diotima's position in the dialogue as well as of her teachings. Here, in the Socrates-Diotima conversation—framed, however, from many conversations—argument, myth, and structure come together in a rather unique form of dialectic, one in which Diotima's apparent capacity to "comment" on earlier proceedings (though she was not present) together with the hidden echoes of earlier speeches yields a dynamic interplay of ideas. The nature of these images or ideas as lenses through which to see beyond themselves—lenses to which both *mythos* and *logos* contribute—as well as the importance of *mythos* to dialectic, are examined in this context.

Chapter 6 contains an analysis of Diotima's higher mysteries and shows that here lies a major key to the structure of the *Symposium*, not as the center of a constructed discourse, but rather as a multidimensional energy focus for the pulsating design that informs so many of the narrative structures of the work. It is in this living relationship between multiple narrative designs in Socrates-Diotima's speech, in which different frames of reference momentarily coalesce, that Plato's positive theory of art first appears indirectly, a theory impossible to uncover if the narrative is viewed as a static structure or a preestablished hierarchy.

In Chapter 7 we explore yet another unstable, disruptive, and even violently intruding discourse: Alcibiades' divided praise and yet trial of a Socrates who is neither a Dionysus figure—contrary to what has so often been supposed—nor again an Apollo figure, but *Socrates*, a unique individual and yet at the same time an image, that is, not the solid paradigm whose figure determines the whole "get-together" or drinking party. In this perspective, Alcibiades' double-edged testimony bears witness to the radical freedom of dialectical thought, namely, its feature that it cannot compel agreement but must always stand open either to testing or to corruption. Alcibiades' love-hate relationship with Socrates is also colored by the language of praise and trial that poignantly evokes the broader context of the life and death of Socrates. Once again the relation between the individual character and the character of the vision that Alcibiades espouses is crucial to our investigation.

In Chapter 8 we take up the examination of the dialogue as a whole in relation both to broader issues of Plato's dialogues and to modern and contemporary concerns. Here we examine the genres of the narrative so far analyzed and argue for a broader principle of organization that can best explain the multiple narrative strategies of the *Symposium*. Here, too, we find confirmation of the general view held by Nietzsche that it was Plato who created the genre of the novel, but in our examination of the dialogical characteristics of this new genre we reject Nietzsche's insistence that Plato is governed by any procrustean or narrow-minded rationality and follow instead a dialogical polyphonic design, in part prompted by Bakhtin's development of the major criteria of novelistic discourse. On these strict Bakhtinian criteria, the *Symposium* is demonstrably the first novel in history.

In order to argue for this new understanding of the *Symposium*, we have had to revisit many common assumptions about the early speeches and have often disagreed with some of the most widely accepted scholarly interpretations. But one objective of the book is to show how many previous interpretations, though undoubtedly missing the mark, are nonetheless perfectly comprehensible in their own right from the perspective of the more complex design we have uncovered. The picture of the whole, as is clear from the preceding outline, emerges very gradually once some of the more habitual reactions to the dialogue's images are given a new focus: and the core of our argument begins to be articulated fully in Chapters 6, 7, and finally 8. The result is, first, a new interpretation of the *Symposium* as a whole as well as of each of its parts, speakers, and narrative layers and, second, a rather new view of the *Symposium* in relation to the other middle dialogues, especially the *Republic*.

Our general goal, however, is clear from the outset: we aim to bring to light the structural design that underlies the *Symposium* and, on this basis, we argue for a new way of understanding some major concerns of the middle and later dialogues. The result is a different reading of Plato that provides a new understanding of several important questions, such as the relationship between philosophy and art, soul-body and human identity, the nature of "Platonic love" and, finally, the unusual character of Plato's writing.

Apollodorus's Prologue

An Imitation of an Imitation

1.1 The Historical Frame

The *Symposium* casts us literally into the middle of things, for it starts with an answer to a question that is yet to be posed: "I think I am not unpracticed {*ameletêtos*} in what you ask about." So we seek the question and its context prompted by the answer. But the question turns out to be no simple affair, for its unfolding ultimately brings into play, and calls into question, some of the major issues of Platonic philosophy: the relation between "fact" and "fiction"; the problem of what is "true" in narrative, rhetoric, and philosophy; the nature of the good and the beautiful; the puzzle of the relation between soul, body, and love; the question of form and identity; and ultimately, the problem of the nature and scope of art. But we start at least in between an answer and its required question, even if in a sense we never get to the end of the question we are seeking.

Three curious features of the prologue are the anonymity of the person addressed; the placelessness of the conversation; and the timelessness, or timefulness, of the hidden dialogues nestled one within the other. The speaker, Apollodorus, addresses an unknown companion who is never named, or identified, in the course of the dialogue. The anonymous companion is perhaps you, me, Plato, or literally anyone who writes or reads the *Symposium*. It is fitting, then, that the space-time framework is also indeterminate or open ended; in the case of space, a journey from out of town into town, always in between, indeterminately ("we walked on together and discussed it"), always *in motion;* in the case of time, dialogues nestled within one another stretching back into the nostalgia of a time long past.[1]

Apart from the overt and yet hidden reality of a dialogue actually being written by Plato for his readers, there are at least three listeners listening to the same story told on at least three different occasions. The dialogue opens with Apollodorus telling the unknown companion what he had told Glaucon on a similar occasion in reply to his inquiry about the nature of the speeches to Eros.[2] Apollodorus is from out of town, a fact emphasized twice in the opening paragraph—both by Apollodorus himself and by Glaucon, who tries to catch up with him on the road and find out what he knows about the "get-together" of Agathon, Socrates, Alcibiades, and the others: "Hey there, you Phalerian . . . won't you wait?" (172a4–5).[3] The address is playful (*paízôn*), but emphatic (*Phalêreus . . . houtos*).[4] Apollodorus is from Phalerum on the coast east of the Piraeus, about two miles southwest of the city perimeter. In other words, Apollodorus is at one remove from inner circles of the city and, as we shortly discover, a recent adherent of Socrates and his circle. Glaucon, it turns out, had heard a garbled account of this meeting at third hand ("Someone else heard it from Phoenix, son of Philippus, and related it to me, and he said you knew too,

---

1. On the prologues and the overall "frame," see Bury 1932, xv–xxii; Rowe 1998, 3–5.

The *Parmenides* (126a–127b) also recounts a conversation that occurred in the distant past, and there too a detailed account of its transmission is provided (Friedländer 1969, 4), but the form of the prologue there is different. See Dover 1980, 8–9; and for the strong contrast with the *Theaetetus*, that is, between narrative in the *Symposium* (*diêgêsis* emphasized at 172b3–174a2) and dialogue form (emphasized at *Theaetetus* 143b–c), see Halperin 1992, 99.

2. In the *Republic*, Glaucon and Adeimantus, two of Plato's older brothers, are Socrates' interlocutors (together with Cephalus, Polemarchus, and Thrasymachus) and this may be the same Glaucon here. At *Symp.* 222b1, there is mention of another Glaucon, the father of Charmides and the maternal grandfather of both Plato and his brother Glaucon. Such details as this tend to suggest a connection, since typically the dialogues leave us to make our own connections, but the connection remains speculative.

3. As has long been noted by commentators, the word *symposium* does not occur within the dialogue, except indirectly, spoken by Alcibiades, who introduces the term *sympotês* (212e4, 213b7). *Synousia* (get-together), or *syndeipnon* (dinner party) are the words used. The reason is presumably that the dialogue considerably exceeds the limitations of a *symposium*. On the nature of a symposium, see Murray 1990. Aristotle (*Politics* 2.4.6.1262b13) gives the *Symposium* another designation (in the absence of a title?): *en tois erotikois logois* (cf. *Symp.* 172b3).

4. See Bury 1932, 2, at 172a, under (4); and for a possible play on *Phalêreus* and *phalaros* (bald), especially since Apollodorus is recognized from behind, see Bury 1932 again (1–2) and Rowe 1998, 128.

but he had nothing clear to say") and so wants to find out the story from Apollodorus, who is "just the right person" to relate the discussions of his friend (*hetairos*), Socrates. Apollodorus, then, is a companion of Socrates. "But first tell me," Glaucon continues, "were you present at this gathering yourself?" (172b).

Apollodorus's reply emphasizes both the apparent historical basis for his narrative and the secondhand character of his information as well as the gulf in time between the banquet meeting and the present occasion: the drinking party was long ago, when Glaucon and Apollodorus were "still children," and when Agathon won the prize with his first tragedy. Agathon has long since left Athens, and Apollodorus is only a recent associate of Socrates ("not yet three years"). So Glaucon naturally inquires if the source is Socrates himself: "Good heavens, no [*ou ma ton dia*],"[5] Apollodorus replies, clearly aghast at such a suggestion; but he goes on to clarify his source: "It was the same person who told Phoenix, a certain Aristodemus of Cydathenaeum, a little fellow, always barefoot. He had been at the gathering, and he was one of Socrates' most devoted lovers [*erastês*] at the time, I think.[6] But of course I later also asked Socrates about some of the things I heard from him, and he agreed it was as Aristodemus related it" (173a–b).

Thus, we arrive at the very nexus of the prologue's structure: the story's narrative is thrice removed from the event, but even in that state, its truthfulness is emphasized. What Apollodorus relates is not, as he puts it to Glaucon, what he saw, but what he heard from Aristodemus. And while Phoenix, who had heard the same tale, had nothing "clear" to relate, Apollodorus is very clear about most of the story and has even checked some of the details with Socrates (173b). The force of Apollodorus's "Good heavens, no," when Apollodorus is asked by Glaucon if Socrates were the source of his narrative, bears a comic, ironic undertone in the subsequent context, as we shall see, for Socrates is plainly not the sort of person given to the recounting of such narratives. But the narrative within a narrative within a narrative is as well grounded in historical "fact" as the situation will allow, although none of the actual speakers at the original meeting are directly present in our dialogue, just as our recitant was not directly present in theirs. A contemporary successful investigative reporter could claim little more, and probably a lot less.

---

5. For the emphasis, see below; at any rate this is probably the most frequent oath in the dialogues.

6. Aristodemus is a "lover," while Apollodorus is a "friend." This does not mean that Aristodemus is a sexual partner, but simply, perhaps, that his love for the beloved (a major theme of the dialogue) makes him closer to Socrates than is Apollodorus and places him at the party. But see also Brisson 1998, 183 n. 26, 17 n. 2. Cydathenaeum is the deme he comes from.

1.2 Apollodorus and Mimetic Narrative

From the outset, then, it is Apollodorus and Aristodemus, silent during the drinking party, who emerge as the keepers of the story, and it is emphasized on several occasions that the story of the *Symposium* has been preserved only because of their linked narrative. In this context, their characters are of crucial, if often overlooked, significance. We shall come later in the dialogue to appreciate the highly ambivalent connection between an individual person and his or her creative gift, which directs each narrative.[7] For the moment, it appears that neither Apollodorus nor Aristodemus possesses any outstanding talents. Indeed, they are only too aware of their own inferiority as compared to Socrates. They imitate or echo everything he does, but in this imitation lies the precise nature of their role in the dialogue's structure. Aristodemus goes barefoot, like Socrates and like Diotima's picture of Poverty later in the dialogue. Apollodorus betrays all the zeal of the even more recent convert, who lives by collecting every bit of Socratic data: "[I]t's not yet three years that I've been spending my time with Socrates and have made it my care [*epimeles*] each day to know what he says or does.... Before that I ran round this way and that and thought I was doing something when I was a more pitiable figure than anybody, no less than you are right now, thinking that one should do anything rather than seek wisdom [*philosophein*]" (172c–173a). Yet even in Apollodorus's unconsciously comic parody of philosophy (he's such a nosy parker!), the spatial journey from the outset also becomes a question of philosophy or the proper search for wisdom. Here in the *Symposium* the whole scene is part of a conversation that takes place somewhere indeterminately on the way up to the city. The verb *aniôn* (going up), used at 172a2, is the same verb as that used in the ladder of ascent in Socrates-Diotima's speech later (*epaniôn* [211b]).[8] So even the later philosophical notion of ascent is in some manner implicit in the physical movement that frames the dialogue and that will, of course, be centered on Agathon's house—as Socrates makes clear in his subsequent pun, the house of the "good": "[T]he good go of their own accord to the feasts of the good" (174b).[9]

One may ask the following question, however: does knowing everything that Socrates says or does free Apollodorus from the wretched condition he sententiously attributes to Glaucon or does this knowledge make him a

---

7. Cf. Chapter 4, passim.

8. Compare Sallis 1996, 17–22, on the first word of the *Republic: katebên*, "I went down" to the Piraeus, as signifying the philosopher's descent into the cave in *Rep.* 7 or the soul's descent into Hades in 10, and more generally still, on the playfulness of the dialogues and the importance of details.

9. On this "pun" and associated difficulties in context, see section 2.5, below.

well-meaning, but mannered and rather irritating imitator, who thinks he has grasped the truth once and for all? Both possibilities are clearly implicit in the subsequent conversation. As they walk on together, Apollodorus tells Glaucon how much philosophical discourse benefits and delights him, whereas he considers Glaucon clearly to be excluded from philosophical knowledge: "I get irritated myself and I pity you and your friends, because you think you're doing something when you're doing nothing. And perhaps from your point of view you think I am unfortunate, and I think what you think is true. However, I don't just think you are unfortunate, I really know you are [*eu oida*]" (173c–d). The claim to special knowledge (*eidenai, oida*), which may resemble the casual claim that he "knows" (*eidenai*) the story (172b5), but is really rather different, looks like a distortion of the Socratic spirit, something confirmed in Glaucon's reply: "You're always the same [*aei homoios ei*], Apollodorus; you're always speaking ill of yourself and everybody else, and you seem to me to think that simply everybody starting with yourself, is wretched except Socrates. And where you ever got the nickname 'soft' [*malakos*] I just don't know! For you're always like this [*aei toioutos ei*] when you talk, mad at yourself and everyone else except Socrates" (173d).[10] So in Apollodorus there is a recognizable *caricature* of Socrates' behavior, but a caricature different from that of Aristodemus. While Aristodemus is a happily established disciple, content to live as a reflection of Socrates, Apollodorus is oppressed by his lack of true philosophical insight compared to that of his master: everyone is imperfect for Apollodorus except Socrates. However, without these paradigmatic disciples (one content with his lot and the other irritated by the lack of perfection in himself and in others), the historical circumstances of the drinking party and the carefully assembled and verified details would never have been preserved. This is a significant emphasis of the elaborate prologue.

But the significance goes further still, for the contrast between Socrates and Apollodorus/Aristodemus goes beyond caricature. The assembling and careful recitation of the narrative does not require creativity, but rather the opposite: the simple recounting of events is opposed to what Socrates does as soon as he cites Homer. Socrates, we are told, "spoils the proverb by changing it" (174b). A striking resonance between the nature of the speaker and that of his narrative is thus further emphasized and a rather humorous philosophical note is introduced: as Apollodorus is to Aristodemus, and Aristodemus to Socrates, so is the tale of Apollodorus to the nature of the actual events recounted—*an imitation of an imitation.* In other words, the basic narrative structure of the *Symposium* is at least analogous

---

10. For the reading *malakos* versus *manikos*, see Chapter 1.4.

to that thirdhand imitation of reality examined in the *Republic*, namely, epic narrative and mimetic poetry in general. In the *Symposium*, this narrative force (while being gently mocked in the character of Apollodorus, who retells the events of the *Symposium* as a Homeric rhapsodist might recite poetry) is also presented as a necessary precondition for the preservation of the historical memory that makes the dialogue possible.[11] Without Apollodorus's single-minded dedication, no preservation of the past is possible.

This onion-skin form of dialogue, then, with its open-ended addressee and its claim to historical fact, caught, as it is, in between an answer and its complex question, a question already posed before the dialogue starts, but still to be posed in the frame of the dialogue—this very form brings into implicit play a much larger issue than that of historical fact; the narrative form itself implicitly introduces the question of a mimetic art and its relationship to truth, so forcefully scrutinized in the *Republic*.[12] At any rate, in the *Symposium* the question of a representation being thrice removed from its source is doubly emphasized in the prologue, once as a potentially successful representation in the persons of Aristodemus and Apollodorus, and another time as a somehow garbled account in the persons of Phoenix and another anonymous "someone" (172b). Yet one successful mimetic transmission reaches an anonymous addressee, that is, the reader, while the other unsuccessful representation is lost with another anonymous addressee who has nothing "clear" to say about it. Our attention therefore implicitly focuses on the character of the medium for successful mimetic transmission.

---

11. Halperin (1992, esp. 93–106) recognizes the representational strategy of the *Symposium* (with its emphasis on transmission and narrative structure) and sees this as manifesting the erotics of narrativity: "[T]o reveal narrative as both an expression and an object of desire.... By endlessly abolishing the distance it interposes and interposing the distance it abolishes, by making the past present without actually bringing it back, narrative at once satisfies and (re)generates desire: that is why we are both eager and sorry to come to the end of a good narrative" (108). Our own interpretation of the dialogue as a whole is very different from that of Halperin, but Halperin's view of the complexity of the frame and its narratives is, we believe, in essence correct. The frame is not incidental to the design of the whole.

12. *Republic* 2, 3, and 10. On this, see especially section 4.4.1, below. As Kosman (1992, 73–92) claims, books 3 and 10 appear to argue for two different kinds of *mimêsis* (in bk. 3 not for the view that art imitates nature, but that an author imitates his characters [Kosman 1992, 88] and in bk. 10, not so much perhaps that the craftsman imitates the bed, but rather that he imitates "the bedmaker, who in turn imitates God in his making of a bed" [88]). There is, he goes on to argue, "an interesting and revealing structural similarity" between the two views: "The issue of representation for Plato is not one of how the word embodies nature, but of how word and nature alike embody Being. The critique of *mimêsis* in book 10 is thus a critique of the very view of *mimêsis* which we are tempted to attribute to Plato, a view in which word is twice removed from Being and stands in need of mediation *through* nature, rather than itself a mode of mediation and representation on a par with nature" (90–91). If this structure in the *Symposium* is significant for the elucidation of this complex question (as it would appear to be), then it is surely noteworthy that the apparent imitative relation (*logos* [Apollodorus], *logos* [Aristodemus], *logos* [the *Symposium* event]) is actually a relation between three different *logoi*, and no one of them as such is privileged, as we shall see in different ways in Chapters 2, 3, 4, and following.

1.3 The Force of *Hybris*

Indeed, the information given by this prologue (and also by Aristodemus's prologue [174a ff.])—implicit and explicit—is still more finely nuanced on this and related issues. Aristodemus and Apollodorus are the preservers of a tradition. Is Socrates a keeper of this tradition? In some ways he appears antithetical to any notion of tradition or orderly transmission, which, of course, explains Apollodorus's emphatic denial that Socrates was the direct "source" of his narrative. That Socrates is a disruptor of traditional order, in some sense or another, crops up throughout the narrative: "You're outrageous [*hybristês*], Socrates" (175e)—this is Agathon's first response to Socrates' initial remarks on his arrival at the party. "Are you outrageous or not" (215b), demands Alcibiades much later at the beginning of his speech. *Hybristês*—outrageous, violent, lewd, wanton, lustful, or just plain sarcastic? Someone who treats others with contempt, ridicule, or violence.[13] This is a striking feature for the supposed hero of a piece. In Homer, the epithet characterizes the enemy and also divine, but monstrous, power.[14] *Symposium* 221e2–4 (Socrates' arguments, Alcibiades tells us, "are wrapped around on the outside with words and phrases like some outrageous satyr's skin") evokes the dialogue's well-known "Dionysiac" context, although Socrates' *hybris* is very different, as Alcibiades will show, from the usual *hybris* of satyrs (that is, sexual assault).[15] This *hybris* is not "polite" or the sort of characteristic contained easily within normal confines. Indeed, *hybris* designated a special offense in Attic law: anyone who struck, pushed, pulled, or restrained another person (and this could include a sexual element) could be liable for a prosecution on a charge of *hybris*.[16] So it does not fit at all with Erasmus's wish to include Socrates in the Litany of the Saints (*Sancte Socrate, ora pro nobis*)—or does it? Socrates' *hybris* displaces ordinary perceptions; like an irruption of the unexpected, it unsettles the comfortable course of normal life.

At any rate, the unrestrainable timbre of such a fellow is that he cannot tell a story without leaving his own mark. "So follow me then," says Socrates, a few sentences after we first meet him in Aristodemus's story, as he invites an uninvited Aristodemus to Agathon's party, "and we'll spoil [*diaphtheirômen*] the proverb by changing it." The joke or lighthearted irony does not remain on the level of the pure word-puzzle, but this becomes

---

13. See Liddell, Scott, and Jones 1940; Dover 1980, at 175e8.
14. Cf. *Odyssey* 3.205–7, 17.587–88; *Iliad* 11.695.
15. See generally Chapter 7.
16. Cf. Dover 1980, at 175e8; Rowe 1998 at 174b6, 131. On the whole of this section, see 2.5, below.

slightly grotesque when Socrates goes on to explain that Homer, by making Menelaus come to Agamemnon, had not simply corrupted the proverb, but "done outrage" to it (*hybrisai*): "Homer, in fact, is close not only to spoiling that proverb, but to doing outrage to it, for he makes Agamemnon an exceptionally good man of warfare, and Menelaus a *soft spearfighter* [*malthakon aichmêtên*], and when Agamemnon was offering sacrifice and making a feast, he made Menelaus go uninvited to the feast, a worse man going to the feast of the better" (174b–c). Since Socrates ironically compares Homer's conduct with his own (the charge of *hybris* and destructiveness occur in both cases), perhaps there is an implicit ambivalence toward Homer that we also find at times in the *Republic*. But even here Socrates changes the "text." Homer does not portray Menelaus as a "soft spearfighter"; Apollo attempts to bring Hector back into the battle by the taunt that he has shrunk before Menelaus, who used to be a "soft spearfighter."[17] The point, however, is (relatively) clear: unlike Apollodorus and Aristodemus, if Socrates spoils the proverb by his actions, Homer also apparently violates proverbial wisdom in his composition.[18] Were Socrates or Homer to be telling the story of the drinking party, the narrative would have had to assume a different form, different, that is, from Apollodorus's careful assembling of the reflections that still live in the memories of the participants, and this means that at least two notions of narrative, one imitative and one "outrageous," are already present in the prologue.

Moreover, Aristodemus's immediate reply to Socrates' treatment of Homer's *hybris* gently thematizes the disciple's intellectual and social dependence on Socrates and the relation of the "inferior" to the "better" person, which will become a major element in the later speeches (and their various treatments of the *erômenos* and the *erômenon*): "But perhaps I too will fail to fit your account but as in Homer's version, Socrates, I shall be an inferior [*phaulos*] going uninvited to the feast of a wise man [*sophos*]. So see what defense you're going to make for bringing me, because I won't admit I came uninvited, but I'll say it was you who invited me. 'As we two go together on the way (*Iliad* 10.224),' [Socrates] said: 'We'll think up what we'll say. But let's go.'"[19] And they actually do go "to the feasts of the good" in the house of Agathon and even Socrates must wash and wear sandals to approach the celebration in question (174a).[20] But Aristodemus, who would have been

---

17. *Iliad* 17.587–88, 2.108.

18. Cf. Dover's (1980, 82) assessment and contrast Rosen 1968, 27–28 and 1988, 106–7.

19. For this "misquotation," see Dover 1980, at 174d3; cf. *Protagoras* 348d, which quotes it correctly, and section 2.5, below.

20. "[B]oth things he rarely did" (*Symp*. 174a3). In Aristophanes' *Birds*, at 1554, Socrates is called *aloutos* (unwashed). But the detail in the *Symposium*, though surely significant, as we shall see (Chapter

invited had the gracious Agathon been able to find him, cannot go uninvited. Apollodorus the young Phalerian, of course, is at an even further distance both from Socrates and (socially) from the house of Agathon.

We can see, then, how in the context of the prologue not only two notions of narrative but also the temperaments of the narrators come into careful contrast. That is, the natures of Apollodorus and Aristodemus, besides being "inferior," are in some measure strongly contrasted with that of Socrates (and Homer). While we see Apollodorus retelling the story with the same dedication with which for so many centuries before him, the tales of Homer had been sung, we also know that Apollodorus only retells; he does not compose. Therein, like a singer who recounts what has been composed for him, he is a reciter of a potentially philosophical discourse. The narrative persists through time more strongly than the one who bears it, and the relative weakness of his imagination, if compared to the imaginative richness of the story, is proof that he shall keep it unchanged and as accurate as possible.

1.4 Malakos Versus Manikos: Soft or Mad?

In this light, it is possible to comment on the old argument concerning the epithet *malakos* (soft) versus *manikos* (mad) as applicable to Apollodorus. Since it is clear why Apollodorus is chosen to preserve a narrative the full richness of which he himself probably cannot comprehend, we can also see how the disputed reading *malakos*—"soft," "impressionable"—at 173d8 (Dover, Allen, and others) is preferable to the variant *manikos*, meaning "mad" (Bury, Robin, and so on):[21] "where you ever got the nickname 'soft' I just don't know! For you're always the same in conversation, mad at yourself and everyone else except Socrates." The argument for *manikos* is derived

---

6), does not mean that Socrates hardly ever washed at all; his morning wash at the end of the *Symposium* (223d) seems part of a routine (Rowe 1998, 130–31), a point emphasized after a night's drinking. It may mean little more than that he did not frequent the public baths (Brisson 1998, 184 n. 37) or pay much attention to "cosmetic" details for their own sake. In the *Phaedo,* Socrates bathes before drinking the hemlock (116a; on both the *Phaedo* and *Symposium* here, see section 8.7, below), but his unsandaled feet (cf. also *Symp.* 220b) "introduce" the first major philosophical theme of the dialogue—the strange connection between pleasure and pain in the cycle of opposites (60a ff.)—and the striking image that frames the rest of the conversation: he lowers his feet to the ground and sits thus firmly planted, as it were, for the rest of the "philosophical portion of the conversation" (*dielegeto* [61c10–d2]). The image speaks for itself.

21. More recently, in favor of *malakos*, see Rowe 1998, 130, at 173d7–8; Rowe thinks *manikos* makes no sense of what immediately follows. On the other side, Brisson (1998, 183–84 n. 34) thinks *manikos* is confirmed by what immediately follows (Apollodorus's use of the verb *mainesthai*). See also note 24, below.

from Apollodorus's subsequent reply: "My dear friend, is it really so obvious that in thinking like this both about myself and all of you, I've gone mad and lost my wits [*mainomai kai parapaiô*]?" But even if Apollodorus subsequently refers to his own "madness," *manikos* still does not fit the immediate context. Nor does Dover's suggestion that *malakos* suits Apollodorus—who upset everyone at Socrates' death by unrestrained howling (*Phaedo* 117d)[22]—sufficiently settle the argument, for it does not fully explain the adjective's descriptive function in the *Symposium*. We propose, then, that the softness of Apollodorus's narrative capacity is foregrounded in the *Symposium* because it is opposed to the *hybris* of Socrates and Homer. By making Apollodorus a "receptive" narrator, Plato also assures his readers that the story is least changed by the dialogue's first speaker: Apollodorus's nature is "soft" enough as not to leave its stamp on the narrative. In addition, this apparently incidental detail looks forward to the opposition between the hard (*sklêros*) and the soft (*malthakos*) that in different ways is such an important part of later speeches, for example, those of Agathon and Socrates-Diotima.[23]

This use of detail, anticipating subsequent images, is perhaps even evident in the contrast between Apollodorus and Aristodemus, one a frustrated and the other a contented disciple, a contrast foreshadowing, however faintly, lack and plenty in the character of Diotima's eros. We suggest, then, that not only do the various speeches in the *Symposium* comment on one another either directly or indirectly, but every part of the work can be seen as having something to say about every other part,[24] within the open-ended playfulness of the narratives. Yet how precisely this affects the reading of the *Symposium* is at this point in the dialogue far from clear.

But what is clear is that Aristodemus, however different from Apollodorus, possesses a similar nature as a narrator. The silence of Aristodemus at the party is surely significant. We know that he lies down beside Eryximachus, but there is no mention of his turn to speak. He is a speechless narrator whose presence is necessary for the preservation of the story. In fact, his silence (which is particularly felt because of the change of turns between

---

22. Dover 1980, 1979; cf. Friedländer 1969, 5.

23. Cf. 195d7 ff. (in Agathon's speech); 203c8 for *sklêros*, but not *malthakos* (in Socrates-Diotima's speech); for this, see Simmias's important observation, in principle developed by Socrates later, of the need for a provisional and risky, but aggressively rational and hard-minded, approach to life (*Phaedo* 85b10 ff.) by contrast with the mark of a "soft man" (*malthakos*) who does not make every effort to test (*elegkein*) what is said about the nature of things and who gives up before he has looked at them (*skopôn*) from every angle (*Phaedo* 85c4–6). It is possible to be a little "too receptive," just as is Apollodorus.

24. Cf. Rowe 1998, 8. On this feature of the dialogue, see sections 8.1–8.4, below.

Aristophanes and Eryximachus and then by Aristophanes' declaration that only Agathon and Socrates are left to give their eulogies)[25] is perhaps analogous to Apollodorus's inability to become a philosopher.[26]

Both Apollodorus and Aristodemus, then, are chosen for exactly the same quality: their complete, almost comic devotion to Socrates is a necessary precondition for the faithful transmission of narrative. Apollodorus is to tell us exactly what he heard and Aristodemus exactly what he saw. Faithful disciples, they will keep a relatively accurate story, unlike some friends of Glaucon who heard the story from Phoenix. It is significant how Apollodorus immediately realizes the inferior quality of this other storyteller who could not situate the story chronologically: "It seems he told you nothing clear at all" (172c). How true or accurate, then, is the story we hear from Apollodorus?

If we accept the conditions of the prologue and believe that Apollodorus is the actual narrator, we can reasonably ask the following two-part question: is the text of the *Symposium* a faithful historical representation of what happened at the party or at least what Aristodemus told to Apollodorus?[27] The immediate answer is *no*. As Apollodorus acknowledges, Aristodemus and he himself have forgotten some of the speeches entirely, and the ones they do remember they do not necessarily remember in their exact form.[28] By contrast, Apollodorus's own methodical reliance is more encouraging: "Well, [the speeches] were of this kind—or rather, I shall start from the beginning and try to tell it to you in the way Aristodemus did to me" (173e–174a). Thus, we can see that for Apollodorus it is easier to remember the story by heart and to be methodically true to the details by rote than to change anything in it. Apollodorus's penchant for saying, "He said that he said," at the most interesting parts of his narrative, is testimony that he never really moves inside the story, never grapples with it in his own imagination, but always remembers this drinking party as a narrative given by Aristodemus.[29]

Thus, with Apollodorus and Aristodemus, reality as audio-video reportage assumes its fundamental position; and a chronological, minute-by-minute account finds its way into the pages of the Platonic dialogue, making the dialogue so deceptively simple. We are thus led to believe that slowly, with each retelling, the insignificant details fade away and

---

25. *Symp.* 185c–e; 193e2–3.
26. Cf. *Symp.* 173c–e.
27. Cf. *Symp.* 173c 6–174a1; 174d5: *toiauta atta* (cf. *toioide tines* at 173e6). On the need for "clarity," see *Phaedo* 57b1, and *Symp.* 172b5–6.
28. *Symp.* 174d5, 178a1–4.
29. See, for example, the repetitious *ephê* (e.g., 175b4, c3, etc.). On this, see section 2.5, below.

get forgotten, and the story develops by its own rules, takes its own shape, and finds its own purpose in the soft hands of Aristodemus and Apollodorus. Moreover, the initial presentation of Apollodorus's narrative as an imitation of imitation and the negative context associated with the criticism of mimetic art in the *Republic* undergo an apparent transformation, for reality even in imitation continues to assert its own claims and to show an unexpected capacity for metamorphosis and complexity apparently unanticipated in the criticism of mimetic art in the *Republic*.

1.5 Anachronisms?

But it is also worth observing that the explicit issue of "truth" is conspicuously missing from the early part of the dialogue. The notion of truth, in fact, does not emerge as such at this level of narrative and is instead replaced by the description of the disciple's typical hunger for exactness or clarity of detail. What Apollodorus tells is what he had heard and verified, but the issue of truth still makes an implicit appearance and is called into question in the wake of the prologue by what appear to be three striking anachronisms later in the dialogue.

The problem is as follows. From the narrative framework of the prologue, we can date the original drinking party to 416, the date of Agathon's first victory at the Lenaea, when Socrates was in his early fifties and Alcibiades in his thirties. Pausanias subsequently, however, appears to refer to Ionia under barbarian rule, which must be after the King's Peace in 387. Aristophanes too appears to refer to the Spartan dispersion of the Mantineans in 385; and Phaedrus, even earlier, in his striking evocation of an army composed of lovers and their beloveds, may indeed refer to the "sacred band" of Thebes formed in or soon after 378. What are we to make of this?[30]

Whether these are genuine anachronisms or only the "appearance" of anachronism is a question that cannot be resolved by a modern reader and perhaps the same was true for the first readers in Plato's own day.[31] So the

---

30. Wilamowitz (1919, 1:369 n. 1, 2:176–78) argued against the generally accepted anachronism at 193a in Aristophanes' speech (the *dioikismos* of the Mantineans by the Arkadians) that this referred to events of 418, not 385. This view was defended by Mattingly (1958, 31–39), who suggested that Aristophanes himself might have served in the army in Arcadia in 418, which might provide an intriguing motive for mentioning the area. Dover opposes this interpretation in detail (1965, 2–20) and argues that the proverbial character of the simile "cuts . . . the ties which bind it to a particular historical event" (8) and that "Plato may be amusing himself by outdoing the comedian at the comedian's own game, inserting an allusion which is topical of the time of writing into a speech ostensibly delivered by Aristophanes thirty years earlier" (8–9). See also Bury 1932, lxvi ff. and Guthrie 1975, 365 n. 3.

31. One way of viewing this could be to suppose that while events referred to took place in 418, Plato's contemporary readers after 385 might have taken 193a to refer covertly to 385 (Rowe 1998, 159).

appearance of anachronism is sufficient to set up a gap between the supposed date of the drinking party and the actual date of the *Symposium*'s composition or, in other words, to foreground the dialogue's deceptive simplicity and to call the apparent solidity of the mimetic narrative structure into question.[32] Why should this be so? Undoubtedly there is here, in part, a movement of reversal, a rupture of the factual narrative that forces more fundamental questions to the surface: How are we to interpret the onion-skin layers of the dialogue that establish themselves in and through the mimetic level of the discourse? Is the apparently factual partly or completely fictional? How are fact and fiction related in the inquiry into the beautiful, the good, and the true?

Whatever the case, these questions emerge with much greater force, though always indirectly, later in the dialogue. The implicit subversion of the narrative structure compels us, as the dialogue progresses, to ask which is the most authoritative level of the dialogue and which the most authentic depiction of Socrates and the nature of philosophy. There is also a decidedly comic irony in hearing a story of such potential depth recounted by someone who wishes to mark only its most external, chronologically linear signs. No story, then, and least of all the *Symposium*, can be contained merely on the mimetic level (whose shortcomings are made equally clear in the *Symposium* and the *Republic*, but whose virtues are implicitly demonstrated in Apollodorus's care for every detail), since other voices, thoughts, and ideas caught in the narrative as if by reflection will continue to possess their own life, a life collected but not directed or challenged within the narrative of faithful disciples.

These possible anachronisms, then, which progressively call into question the deceptively simple answer-question structure of the prologue and the historical basis of an imitation of another imitation, also have a more obvious yet more subtle function: they call into play the most overt yet most hidden dialectic of the *Symposium*—that of the author, Plato—in such a manner that they permit us to date the *composition* of the *Symposium* itself to the period 384–79. Thus they implicitly bear fleeting witness, together with other

---

But the *appearance* of anachronism in three such instances is only intensified by such "literary" anachronisms as Diotima's refuting what Aristophanes says at the party (191a6, d5) *before* the party (205d10–e 8; cf. Dover 1965, 14). Whatever we are to make of Diotima's apparent "diachronisms" (her ability to comment on speeches she has never heard [and on this, see sections 8.1–8.4, below]), anachronism as an implicit gap between appearance and reality plays some role in the dialogue (see section 4.4.2, below).

32. On the date of composition and place in the order of Plato's dialogues, see Bury 1932, lxvii–lxviii; Brisson 1998, 13–15; and Rowe 1998, 11. Bury believes the *Phaedrus* to be earlier than the *Symposium* and prior to Xenophon's *Symposium* (on which, see also Guthrie 1975, 365 n. 3); Brisson and Rowe think the dialogue was composed before the *Phaedrus* in the second half of the 380s in the middle period of Plato's writing (along with the *Phaedo* and *Republic*).

instances, to the ever-vanishing "signature" of the author, which is erased—as it were—while it simultaneously establishes itself and vanishes before its presence is clearly registered. The vanishing author is replaced by a series of narrators, and a party from long ago begins to unfold before the reader's eyes.

For any reader of the text, the first speaker of the *Symposium,* then, is not Phaedrus, as is often for all practical purposes supposed—starting, for instance, with the practice of Ficino in his *Commentarium.*[33] Plato begins by creating the portraits of Apollodorus and Aristodemus together with their "speeches." The dialogue starts in a highly sophisticated fashion with an answer prompting an apparently simple question, framed within a series of dialogues and with an anonymous, open-ended addressee; at the same time we start from the depiction of the lowest level of creativity in its attempt to follow, register, and imitate chronological reality. Is it merely accidental that this audio-video narrative reportage is analogous to the view of art apparently criticized in the *Republic,* namely, that as an imitation of an imitation it stands thrice removed from truth? No accidental coincidence is impossible, of course, but the structure of the dialogue is almost too elaborate not to suggest some intentional cross-reference to the problem of mimetic narrative, several times removed from reality, in the *Republic.*

At any rate, in the prologue the notion of truth or of reality has not yet become an explicit issue or been unpacked as an issue for the question of the nature of narrative, for this can only come into focus on a very different textual level, whose presence is sensed but not accessible as yet when we have to be guided only by the voices of disciples.[34] Factual precision is not truth in any explicit or philosophical sense (though Apollodorus significantly characterizes, and thus foregrounds, his narrative *logoi* as "about philosophy" [173c2–5]). Neither of the two storytellers has the power to rearrange the story according to his own particular train of thought; the portraits of each reveal faces of individual types who lack the creative insight necessary for such work. So ostensibly the signature of the real author is erased, and we are led to believe that no rearrangement is effected by our first speakers and that there is no other purpose or goal than to tell a "clear" story of a memorable occasion.[35]

---

33. Ficino 1956, *Oratio Prima,* c. 1–2.
34. See sections 4.4.2 and 5.2, below.
35. Cf. Halperin 1992, 107. Halperin emphasizes the eager curiosity for gossip that reflects the operation of *erôs:* "To be sure, Apollodorus' interlocutors are not seekers after truth. They are wealthy businessmen (173c6), *hommes d'affaires,* and, if we are to believe Apollodorus, an admittedly hostile witness, they are motivated not by philosophical *erôs,* but by vulgar curiosity. Vulgar curiosity expresses the same desire to obtain and retain noteworthy speech, as the reverent attentiveness of Apollodorus. Gossip, then, is a low-level form of philosophical discourse, and philosophy, whatever else it may be, is at the very least, a high-class kind of gossip." Further on this, see Chapter 2, ad fin., and Chapter 4, passim.

Aristodemus's Prologue

The Destruction and Transformation of the Factual Frame of Reference

The deceptive simplicity of both Apollodorus's and Aristodemus's prologues creates a major problem for the reader. On the one hand, we want to enjoy the story simply for what it is: a story. On the other hand, the onion-skin layers of narration and the form of a dialogue suspended between an answer and a question, a question that just seems to grow more tricky, are at war with our impulse for simple enjoyment. How are we supposed to read a Platonic dialogue if every incidental detail is potentially significant? And where do we draw the line between legitimate interpretation and pure fancy? Here there are no simple answers, for these questions are the central issues of Plato's own thinking. All Plato's major dialogues, and especially the later *Sophist,* are dedicated in one way or another to this question: how in a world of deceptive simplicity, pervaded by dangerous, often fatal ambiguities, but with no privileged vantage point, can we tell the difference between the genuine and the counterfeit? So our impulse for a no-nonsense, just-get-on-with-the-story approach to the Platonic dialogue should be balanced by the realization that Plato's "philosophy" is not set out in textbook or treatise form. At the same time, while Plato succeeds in telling us many things in the dialogues, only the participants speak directly.[1]

So in this chapter we should decide what it is reasonable to suppose about the *Symposium,* on the basis of the two prologues themselves, with an eye ahead to the subsequent speeches. Since the prologues bear an unmistakable resonance with details in other earlier and contemporary dialogues, such as the *Protagoras, Phaedo,* and *Republic* (among others), we should also situate the *Symposium* in relation to some of the issues of these dialogues, so as to establish some basic context in which apparently incidental details may assume a more legitimate significance and, thus, guide our journey through the rest of the dialogue.

2.1 The Story

First, the story. Aristodemus meets Socrates bathed and wearing slippers, an unusual occurrence, and learns that he is going to a dinner party at Agathon's house on the evening after the public celebration of Agathon's theatrical triumph. Socrates had missed the public celebration because he was afraid of the crowd, or so he says. Socrates proposes that Aristodemus accompany him although he has not been invited. Under Socrates' playful wit, the proverb "to be beautiful when going to a beautiful man" undergoes several transformations: first, "the good go of their own accord to the feasts of the good," and then after an allusion to Homer, this now becomes "a worse man going to the feast of the better," which Aristodemus takes to fit his present situation. Socrates reassures Aristodemus and promises to vouch for him. On the way, however, Socrates is struck by a thought and falls behind, telling Aristodemus to go on without him. So Aristodemus finds himself in the embarrassing situation of arriving on his own, uninvited. Agathon, although disappointed not to see Socrates, makes Aristodemus welcome, sends a servant to look for Socrates, and bids Aristodemus recline beside Eryximachus. Aristodemus wants to let Socrates be, but Agathon is anxious to have him fetched in, when he hears that he is standing in a neighbor's porch and will not move. Agathon tells the servants to host the meal themselves as if they had invited Agathon and the others as their guests. In the middle of dinner Socrates arrives, and

---

1. Cf. the assessment of John Sallis (1996, 2) that Plato never says anything, an assessment that, although it sounds exactly right by contrast with those accounts that assume all sorts of things about "Plato," is not, in fact, really true. However, it is true that Plato cannot be cited or grasped. Cf. M. Dixsaut 1998, 127: "[I]l est impossible de citer Platon. Le citer, c'est citer Socrate ou Parménide, Protagoras ou Timée . . .—impossible donc de prélever un énoncé pour l'attribuer à l'insaisissable Platon."

Agathon asks him to lie down beside him so that he, Agathon, can profit from the wisdom that came to Socrates in the neighbor's porch. If only it were possible for wisdom to be transferred by mere proximity, Socrates replies, then he would be the one to profit.

They finish dinner, offer libations, sing a hymn, and then turn to the drinking; but Pausanias suggests that since they are all suffering from the effects of yesterday's celebration, the drinking should be voluntary and restrained. Eryximachus then proposes that they dismiss the flute girl, and following up a complaint by Phaedrus that Eros, god of love, is neglected, Eryximachus suggests further that each in turn from left to right deliver an encomium to Eros, starting with Phaedrus, since he lies "first" and is "the father of the discourse." Socrates strongly supports this suggestion on the basis that he claims to know nothing except matters of love. And so, each speaker taking his turn, the speeches begin: Phaedrus; Pausanias; Eryximachus, who exchanges position with Aristophanes because of the latter's fit of hiccups; Agathon; and finally Socrates, whose speech introduces Diotima. All these speeches are concluded or interrupted by the noisy entrance of Alcibiades and his speech dedicated to Socrates, after which the participants turn again to drink. Socrates, Aristophanes, and Agathon are the last party drinkers, and the dialogue is concluded with Socrates arguing that the same poet cannot write both tragedy and comedy. His last argumentative companions fall asleep and Socrates leaves to go about his daily business.

2.2 Sufficiency and Beauty: Emerging Criteria for Judgment

These are the bare bones of the story, but the text is so much more richly suggestive. How far should we press details in the prologues and early speeches? There are two extreme answers to this question, both of them in some measure attractive. Any detail of the prologue can become an inexhaustible source of readings and misreadings, and one inevitably tries to limit the growing world of suggestions and rebuttals. Socrates' allusion to Menelaus, for example, can serve the point in question as well as any other detail here. Dover, commenting on Socrates' presentation of Menelaus as a "soft spearfighter" (174c1), states with some reason that the juxtaposition of the Homeric text and Socrates' use or misuse of it is not a fruitful avenue of inquiry: "A Greek citing poetry seldom takes notice of the context in which the words were uttered, by whom, to whom, or (most important of all) for what purpose."[2] Guthrie adopts a similar view about the possibility of any

---

2. Dover 1980, 82.

deep significance in the early speeches and their order: "The speakers speak in their seating order, from left to right starting with Phaedrus, and some have seen deep significance in this order. I doubt if Plato was troubling himself much about it."[3] Rosen tends to go to the other extreme, if not on the order of the speeches, at least on the significance of Socrates' banter with Aristodemus about Menelaus and, thus, about the necessity of judging between the good and the inferior that the Homeric context intimates:

> The implied comparison between Menelaus and Aristodemus is the first instance in the *Symposium* of a frequent Platonic device: the use of quotation from, or allusion to, other works, especially poetry, in order to make an indirect point. The sentence which Socrates adopts is uttered in the *Iliad* by Diomedes, who volunteers to spy on the Trojan camp.... Among those who volunteer to accompany him, Diomedes selects "Odysseus the godlike."... There are three aspects to this Platonic joke. Socrates cannot wish unqualifiedly to compare himself to Diomedes and Aristodemus to the wily Odysseus, except perhaps to emphasize the martial character of his own role at the banquet. Still, as if in recompense for his previous harshness, Socrates gives Aristodemus a promotion from the comparison with the soft fighter, Menelaus. Finally, Socrates indicates that he and Aristodemus are about to enter the camp of the enemy.[4]

Such comparisons and speculations, however, open up the text for further questions, none of which can be authenticated by the text itself. And thus the problem of incidental details, which reverberate in the text without closure, remains open. Similarly, Dover's comments above are perhaps not entirely incorrect; yet given the characteristic indirectness of Plato's narrative, Rosen's somewhat tortuous interpretation cannot be dismissed altogether. Indeed, soon it will be suggested that a "contest" of some sort (dramatic or legal) is under way, and at 175e Agathon's language will become that of formal proceedings for deciding between the rival claims of two or more parties (*diadicasia*): "You and I will *adjudicate* our claims about wisdom a little later, using Dionysus as a judge." So too Socrates at 177d employs the language of judgment by jury at trial in his reply to Eryximachus: "No one will vote against you [*enantia psêphieitai*]." Surely there is an undercurrent of struggle, contest, trial in the language of the *Symposium*, an undercurrent that resituates the work in the context of the *Apology* and

---

3. Guthrie 1975, 367–68; cf. Wilamowitz 1920, 1:367.
4. Rosen 1968, 27–28; cf. 31.

Phaedo, but that may also be part of the quasi-serious/playful banter of the "erotic joust," as one recent commentator has put it.[5] Socrates himself immediately goes on to claim a knowledge of *erotika* in the context of other knowledgeable members of the party: "For I who claim to know nothing except the things of love would hardly say no, and neither would Agathon and Pausanias, nor indeed Aristophanes, since his whole occupation is with Dionysus and Aphrodite, nor anyone else among these people I see here. Yet it isn't fair to those of us who lie last; but if those ahead of us speak sufficiently and beautifully, it will be enough for us too" (177d–e). Socrates' claim is puzzling: why should he know nothing *except the things of love?* At this point of the dialogue, the reader has no idea why, but the simplest answer is twofold: Socrates has been taught "the things of love" by Diotima, and according to Diotima, as we shall soon see, it is characteristic for someone impelled by eros to be in search of what he does not have, that is, to know that he does not know.[6] Socrates' claim is a little tricky, then, and forces us to question it. So too is his remark about Aristophanes: amid the glittering throng of guests, we see only the "best people," except for the uninvited Aristodemus, a self-confessed "inferior," and here one can even meet with the brilliant poet whose "sole interest" is Dionysus and Aphrodite; these are, of course, gods of the pantheon. Socrates, however, *means* "wine and Aphrodite's things." A tradition of interpretation has seen this as a neutral remark or a harmless jest,[7] but it is a remark that casts a shadow and asks a question. Are the "best people" really superior beings? And in this context, Socrates' ironic "promotion" of Aristodemus from "Menelaus" to "Odysseus" in their conversation on the way to Agathon's house touches lightly on a *problem* broached in this prologue, as we shall see more clearly below: how do "inferior" people become "better"? Apparently, they become better by engaging in conversation with Socrates, and this may well be a dangerous business, as the Homeric comparison intimates.

So the chiastic balancing of Aristodemus's position by analogy with Menelaus, first, and then with Odysseus in Socrates' graceful, but ironic, manner of speaking and the signal that they are about to step onto risky ground for a contest of some sort seem to be justifiable inferences from what appears at first sight to be mere ironic playfulness. But the contest will be judged, according to Socrates' casual remark, not by any martial criteria (as Rosen implies), nor as an erotic joust simply, nor again by Dionysus, as many critics have suggested, but by an implied *standard* of sufficiency and

---

5. See Menissier 1996; also (for a very different view) Halperin, 1992, 93–129, esp. 124: "Plato... does not... directly represent the experience of *erôs.* Instead, he stages erotic *fictions.*"

6. On this, see Roochnik 1987, 117–30.

7. Cf. Rowe 1998, 136.

beauty: "if the earlier speakers speak *'hikanôs kai kalôs'* [with sufficiency and beauty], it will be enough for us" (177e). So there is method apparently even in the least and most playful of Socrates' statements, and the contextual and subtextual echoes suggesting competition and judgment, subtle as they are, are given a specific direction: toward sufficiency and beauty, criteria that will evidently need to be applied to the narrative of the speakers. What these criteria might involve remains an open question.

2.3 The Spatial Order?

This question of "sufficiency and beauty" is in fact of immediate significance, for Socrates beautifies himself in order to go to the beautiful, in the house of Agathon, and the notion of a transformative journey toward the beautiful or good (given initially in an ironic but still factual manner) is, of course, not without direct applicability to the subject matter of the dialogue. So where are we to set the limits that separate the futile from the fertile in the interpretation of yet another set of apparently incidental details?

What about the seating arrangements, for instance? Perhaps the description of the seating of the guests, like the order of the speeches, is simply what it is: a factual account of a seating arrangement.[8] We know that at a drinking party, the participants recline on couches, resting on their left elbows, eating and drinking with their right hands from low tables. The couches are broad enough to hold two or even three men lying obliquely, one below the other; the seat of honor is the farthest left-hand place on the couch, and the "lowest seat" is that farthest to the right and is commonly taken by the host. Presumably the couches are arranged in a semicircle so that the participants can see one another. The speakers deliver their speeches from left to right, beginning with Phaedrus. So there are, apparently, Phaedrus, Pausanias, Aristophanes, Eryximachus, Aristodemus, Socrates, Agathon, and later Alcibiades, who will sit between Socrates and Agathon.

But the details of the setting prove to be elusive: Phaedrus lies "first" (177d4) and Agathon "last" (175c7) until the arrival of Socrates, who then becomes the last. Normally, each couch holds two, but Agathon has a couch to himself at 175a, and three share the same couch at 213a.[9] And when Aristophanes has hiccups, it is mentioned that Eryximachus is lying "on the couch below him," that is, "below" as in relation to the "last" (*eschaton*), namely, Agathon or Socrates. But all this means that there are gaps in our knowledge of the seating arrangements: Are Phaedrus and Pausanias lying

---

8. Cf. Dover 1980, 11; Allen 1991, ad loc.
9. Cf. Bury 1932, 11; Dover 1980, 11.

together or are Pausanias and Aristophanes? Or is Aristophanes lying on his own? Or are there one or more couches between Phaedrus and Pausanias, as Aristodemus's account would seem to necessitate, since there were several speeches after that of Phaedrus that he did not remember very well (180c)?

So exactly how we are to envisage the spatial groupings is not entirely clear, while at the same time the general order is clear, and Plato draws attention to this order not only by the general setting, but also by three *displacements:* (1) that of Agathon by Socrates upon the latter's arrival, (2) that of Eryximachus by Aristophanes' hiccups, and (3) that of Agathon and Socrates by Alcibiades.[10] The last is particularly tricky. At 214b–c Eryximachus tells Alcibiades that "all the rest of us" have spoken, and so Alcibiades must give his speech and then prescribe that Socrates speak, and Socrates in turn must prescribe that the man on his right do so. But there is no one on Socrates' right, unless the seats are arranged in a circle or a rectangle.[11] But they seem not to be arranged in a circle or, at least, the order is not straightforwardly circular, which becomes clear after Alcibiades' speech (222e–223b), for when Agathon proposes that he lie beside Socrates (so that the new order will become Alcibiades, Socrates, Agathon) and Alcibiades counters with the proposal that Agathon sit down between them (that is, Alcibiades, Agathon, Socrates), Socrates insists that the *epi dexia* rule (that they proceed always to the right), proposed by Eryximachus at 214b–c, requires that Agathon sit on his right so that Socrates can then praise him. In other words, Socrates implies that there would be no one to his right, were Agathon or Alcibiades not to sit there. And this, in turn, seems to frustrate a straightforward circular or rectangular arrangement.

The upshot of this is that Plato (1) *draws attention* to the spatial ordering of the participants and yet (2) simultaneously leaves gaps in our information so that we are never able to visualize the ordering with *total* clarity. It seems hardly likely, given the complex structure of the prologues themselves, that this is oversight or accident. We can reasonably draw the following conclusion: the order of the speeches *is* going to be significant, since so much attention is drawn to it—even spatially. Yet at the same time, the spatial ordering is puzzling, for the gaps not only preclude total visual clarity but actually seem to question the ordering itself, compelling the reader as it were to observe both what is missing and what is not and therefore perhaps to find the question of order itself problematic, since it *cannot,* it appears, be solved on the purely visual level (we shall return to this point

---

10. Brisson (1998, 248) provides a spatial diagram, in which the seating order is visualized. Our thesis is perhaps not incompatible with this: the order can be visualized, but not *entirely.*

11. As Dover (1980, 11) suggests.

in Chapters 4, 6, and 8). Thus, we should note the following narrative character of Aristodemus's prologue: the many details intimated are not given any clear interpretive focus except in their reformulation, as it were, within the speeches themselves, while many of the apparently factual observations are actually out of focus and cannot be confirmed. The narrative, therefore, undermines what it intimates; it points toward and yet frustrates the expectation of complete factual or visual certainty.

2.4 Mimetic Versus Hubristic: The Destruction and Transformation of the Factual Narrative

So what is the principle of order within such a narrative? Let us go back to the beginning of the prologue itself. As we have seen, the notion of a mimetic art thrice removed from the "source" is framed so openly at the beginning of the dialogue that readers searching for more subtle clues have missed the larger stroke of the pen altogether. This mimetic frame remains integral to the subsequent textual strategy, for Aristodemus's narrative mixes together the three different perspectives: (1) that of Aristodemus in reported speech ("he, i.e., Aristodemus, said that . . ."); (2) that of Apollodorus, where Aristodemus simply gets missed out (e.g., 174a8; b3); and (3) reported direct speech, as if Socrates or any of the other participants were speaking directly. Yet it is clear in the larger context that this speech is still reported.[12] So the three levels of representation remain a basic part of the narrative structure, and the problem comes down to this: Is all art mimetic, or is there an art that can escape the apparent criticism presented in the *Republic*? Is this art perhaps exemplified in the *Symposium* itself, or even in Socrates' *hybris* with regard to established traditional patterns, a *hybris* so clearly emphasized in the *Symposium*? In other words, can the dialectical questioning, introduced by Socrates and nestled within the mimetic narrative, transform altogether the mimetic level of presentation?

Socrates' opening comments linking Homer and himself as spoilers of proverbial wisdom seem to call into question some of the negative assessments of Homer in the *Republic*. However, in the *Republic* the question of *hybris* goes beyond Homer and culminates in a psychological portrait of excessive political force, namely, the tyrant (bk. 9). What then is the difference between the philosophical *hybris* of Socrates and the nonphilosophical *hybris* that in the *Republic* results in tyranny?[13] Can philosophy overcome the apparent incompatibility between the "softness" necessary for faithful reception

---

12. Cf. Rowe 1998, 130; Halperin 1992, 97–98.
13. Cf. *Rep.* 573b–e.

and the violence or enthusiasm of creativity? And if so, what is the relation between the song of the muses (in the case of Homer and Socrates-Plato) and memorized repetitions without understanding (in the case of their various disciples)?[14] And even more important still, how do these compare with the relationship between the tyrant and the adoring crowd?

These questions are born out of the juxtaposition of these different dialogues and are foregrounded by Socrates' playful employment of the term *hybris* in his conversation with an adoring disciple. The awakened political echoes, however, cannot be evaluated without some clear sense of how we are to examine the growing questions of the text, that is, questions contained and implicit but not fully containable within the mimetic levels of the text. So the problem amounts to this: if mimetic art appears to represent an ordered story, but is unable to satisfy the questions it raises and does not carry in itself any deeper principle of order, are we to infer another narrative layer represented in the entry of Socrates himself and his relationship with other personages at the party? And if so, what does this second level have to say to the first?

We have already proposed that in the *Symposium* the playful twisting of the proverb at the outset of Aristodemus's story introduces us to the complex role of *hybris* in the dialogues and to the problem of intertextuality that indirectly juxtaposes, first, the *hybris* of mimetic epic poetry; second, that of the tyrant; and third, that of Socrates. At the same time, we should observe that just after *hybris* is ascribed to Homer and even to the journey of Socrates and Aristodemus we are introduced to yet another narrative informed by questions of friendship and even dialectic. *Dialegesthai* (to converse) first occurs, innocently enough, at 174d5: "It was with this sort of conversation, Aristodemus said, that they went on their way." Conversation, in the give and take of question and answer, is surely the beginning of philosophy for Plato. So the first moment of the inner tale of the *Symposium* juxtaposes conversation, or dialectic in movement, and other forms of narrative.

In fact, Aristodemus's prologue, as we have already partially observed, innocently undermines the mimetic frame of narrative from the very beginning. Instead of being shown the carefully preserved events of a glorious past, we are cast immediately into the *problems* of everyday life: that is, extraordinary and rather ordinary people, dinner invitations and the lack of them, and the endless play on words. But the prologue's capacity to undermine expectations does not stop there. Socrates' play on the proverb "to go beautiful to a beautiful man" is a conscious "destruction" (*diaphtheirômen*

---

14. Cf. *Ion* 533c ff.

[174b3]; cf. 174b6) of the original proverbial form, which might have been that "the good go of their own accord to the feasts of the inferior," but may well also have been "the good go . . . to the feasts of the good."[15] Homer, on Socrates' account, reverses the first form of the proverb by saying that the inferior go to the feasts of the better. And Socrates twists it yet again to say that the good go to the feasts of the good, with an implicit pun on Agathon's name. The commoner form of the proverb is rather like this last version of Socrates, so that editors have written *Agathôn* or *Agathonos,* "to Agathon's house," or even *Agathônôn,* "Agathon and people like him," instead of "good men's houses," on the understanding that the whole force of Socrates' change of the proverb (*metabalontes* [174b4]) is the pun on Agathon's name.[16] The pun is clearly intended, that is, "Agathon's" for "good men's," but the striking feature of this initial exchange is that the original form of the proverb is not present anywhere in the dialogue or that *it disappears already unsaid in the course of the conversation.* By contrast with the fundamental assumption of so-called mimetic poetry, there is in this narrative *no original material form* of the proverb. Even if it is to be recovered from the implied context of everyday speech, that initial form has already been punctured by an all-pervasive, destructive Homer, so that Homer and not the proverb is quoted by Socrates. What is left, then, in place of the unrecoverable original is the destruction and transformation of forms by language in conversation. The door leading back into some supposed foundational bedrock for "reality" or "language" is already closed, and we are literally compelled to look forward *into the conversation* between uneasy equals. In this sense, the movement into conversation emerges when the mimetic is punctured by the hubristic.

In this context, Socrates' play on the proverb "to go in beauty to a man of beauty" suggests another important question,[17] initially raised in the *Lysis* but unresolved there: whether friendship is a relation between the like and the unlike. In the *Lysis,* on the one hand, the like appears to be useless to the like (cf. 222b–c); on the other hand, what belongs to us (*to oikeion*) appears to be the object of love (*erôs*), friendship (*philia*), and desire (*epithymia*) (221e), and perhaps what belongs to us is the same as what is like (*to homoion*) (222b). So the *Lysis* ends in an impasse between apparently mutually contradictory positions. In the *Symposium,* this theme of likeness or unlikeness has already been broached even earlier, when Glaucon tells Apollodorus, "You are always the same [*homoios*]." Like what? "As you are

---

15. For the difficulties of this passage that were already felt in antiquity, see Renehan 1990, 120.
16. Renehen 1990, 121; cf. Rowe 1998, 131 at 174b3–c5.
17. As Friedländer (1969, 7–8) observes.

now" (*toioutos* [173d]). Apollodorus's eternal likeness to himself opposes him at the outset to the much more complex portrayal of a hubristic Socrates, who for all his destructiveness provokes a new narrative layer, that of conversation, even the continuing conversation of his own disciples long after his own death.

Even in these details, and without any definitive philosophical direction, the text already opens up into a meditation on how one participates in the beautiful, and it not only introduces the mimetic, hubristic, and dialogical levels of discourse but also points to one further crucial feature, that is, the necessity of departure from one's original state, the necessity of metamorphosis. While Aristodemus, like Apollodorus, remains cast in a certain mode, no matter what the occasion, Socrates is conspicuously at the outset *not like* his normal appearance. In pursuit of the beautiful to whose house he is on the way, Socrates is already transformed, not unlike the proverb in question. External appearance—both of one's own body and of one's belongings—would seem to be crucial to the preparation for dialogue, and here we perhaps begin to see that the goal of the inquiry (like the end of the journey) can transform the incidental, fleeting details of the approach and imbue them with new significance, namely, the significance of the preparation necessary for the approach to one's destination. Not only is becoming *unlike* oneself important for the progress of erotic passion (as we shall see later); the beautiful ordering of the body and one's possessions, in a way that is untypical of normal conduct, is the first "step" in Socrates' approach to the beautiful. The beginning of the account, then, emphasizes how important it is for the body to be included in the ascent: to be properly renewed and transformed. The second step is that of dialogue, "two going together"; and the third is Socrates' meditation: "focusing his attention upon himself" (*heautô pôs prosechonta ton noun*). Socrates is "left behind" (174d6); "he has withdrawn to the porch next door" (*anachôrêsas* [175a8]).

Furthermore, the aloneness of Socrates, by contrast with his capacity for conversation, will be stressed again by Alcibiades (220c–d), as will his capacity for long fits of abstraction or self-absorption. Yet in the present context this third step is not a "fit" of abstraction, or a manic enthusiasm, or mystical experience, but clearly a "concentrated intellectual scrutiny of a problem,"[18] a self-related mindfulness that does not stop him from giving instructions, as he does to Aristodemus ("When Aristodemus waited for him, he bid him go on ahead" [174d]). Socrates' capacity for concentration, unlike that of everyone else, is *thought* made manifest in him, and the focus of the dialogue, no longer contained by factual details,

---

18. Dover 1980, 173.

points toward a level of discourse on which ideas and not merely details can become manifest.

What, then, should we look to in the pattern emerging in the prologue so far? Evidently, we should seek to see, initially, the principal and most obvious details, even if their significance is unclear. Socrates is all dressed up, washed, and wearing slippers "to go beautiful to the beautiful" ("things he rarely did"), while Aristodemus, his faithful imitator, is not dressed up, feels inferior, and is embarrassed to go uninvited to the feast of a "wise" man. These oppositions are resolved in Socrates' rendition of Homer, that is, Socrates' version of Odysseus and Diomedes, of "two going together" in friendship and dialogue. Plato actually misquotes *Iliad* 10.224, which he quotes correctly at *Protagoras* 348d, substituting the words *pro hodou*, "on the way," from *Iliad* 4.382, for *pro ho tou enoêsen*, "one sees before the other": "As we two go together on our way, we'll think up what we'll say. But let's go" (174d2–3). If this is a deliberate misquotation,[19] then there is a strong double emphasis given by this quotation in its context in the *Symposium*: namely, that conversation is movement always "on the way," rather than an enshrined, frozen past.

So, this opening conversation of Aristodemus's prologue actually stands opposed, all unconsciously in the mouth of Aristodemus, to the basic assumptions of the mimetic narrative, for it suggests that all reality is plastic in a sense, that creativity of any sort destroys and transforms its supposed "original" material, and that the movement of creative thought cannot be contained in a clean, unambiguous factual picture of that material.[20] But the infinite plasticity of reality and language is not the only feature of this opening conversation, for the episode clearly poses a challenge: dialogue is a movement through destructions and transformations, between the gifted and the not so gifted, the invited and the uninvited, who together would find their way to the house of the "good" with a reasonable account to get themselves both admitted. But this in itself is not enough—we also need proper self-directed thought (in the figure of Socrates) as well as its absence (in the figure of Aristodemus) and, above all, a generous host, the good, to admit even the uninvited into the party of many voices at the house of the good.

There is much humor and irony here, but the upshot is that the principle of order has somehow to be sought, not in the "past," but in the "future," of Agathon's house. And what do we initially find there? A seating arrangement that cannot be satisfactorily visualized and a host who isn't a princi-

---

19. Dover 1980, 83.
20. For the development of this theme, see especially sections 8.1–8.4, below.

ple of order, because he hands this function over to his nameless and faceless slaves (175b–c)!²¹ But we certainly do meet a group of people who are no strangers to Plato's dialogues.

2.5 Sophistic Education in the Context of Other Dialogues: *Protagoras, Phaedo, Republic*

For all the images of jest, love, and friendship, which seem to pervade the prologues, what kind of people are these guests at Agathon's house into whose midst Socrates is about to enter? Here the details are supplied by a resonance that emerges not only between the first and second prologues, but also between the *Symposium* and other dialogues. Apart from the *Phaedo*,²² one further dialogue of particular importance in this context is the *Protagoras*. Since Gorgias is the teacher of Agathon and has an influence on the speeches of both Agathon and Pausanias,²³ and since the *Gorgias* examines critically the question of what sophistic education considers the greatest good and even suggests (however negatively) the possibility of a

---

21. See Chapter 4 (esp. section 4.6.2), for further significance of this detail. In light of Aristodemus's prologue, we learn often by what is not said some of the participants' characteristics: Agathon is one of the deeper drinkers and perhaps lacks self-control, by contrast at least with Aristodemus, Phaedrus, and apparently all the rest (except Aristophanes): "How is Agathon's strength for drinking? I've got no strength at all either, Agathon replied. Well, it seems that would be a godsend for us, he said—me and Aristodemus and these here—if you, the most capable drinkers, have now given up . . . I leave Socrates out of account; he's actually sufficient either way" (176b–c).

There are, as it were, two sides to Agathon, and this drinking intemperance is, so to speak, the shadow, unstated side. The other side befits, in an interesting way, Plato's outrageously open pun on his name, "good": overflowing generosity and complete freedom. When Aristodemus comes uninvited, Agathon is generous hospitality itself, and his reversal of the master-servant role is, in its way, a striking affirmation of the spontaneous liberality of his "goodness," even if it tacitly points to the *absence* of an authentic, or good, principle of order, as we have suggested: "You slaves, serve dinner to the rest of us. You always serve up whatever you want in any case, when someone isn't supervising you—which I've never yet done—so now assume that I've been invited by you to dinner, together with all these other guests, and tend to us so that we may praise you" (175b–c). Agathon's goodness permits liberality and offers a reversal of the normal social hierarchy (cf. Teuffel's assessment of "die Liberalität und Humanität des Agathon . . ." cited in Bury 1932; Hug 1884; and Rosen 1987). At the same time, as Rosen observes, he "contradicts his intendedly liberal appearance in emphasizing that such freedom is a novelty," and the grammatical difficulties in *epeidan . . . mê ephestêkê* (175b7) give a disjointedness to his speech that perhaps reflects his scarcely concealed agitation at the continued absence of Socrates, who was absent already at his triumph (cf. Bury 1932, 12; Rosen 1968, 27). This seems to be suggested also in the surrounding context. Agathon is insistent that Socrates be fetched, whereas Aristodemus persists in persuading Agathon to "let him be." Here the appearance of liberality in Agathon is belied by its persistent defense by Aristodemus to "let him be" (175a–c). So even the good casts a shadow, and yet its essence in some measure, if Plato's ironic pun is to be trusted, is graciousness, liberality, and magnanimity (cf. Plotinus, *Ennead* 5.5.[32].12.33–34).

22. On this, see Friedländer 1969, 5.
23. Cf. Allen 1991, 10.

positive rhetoric,[24] it also naturally forms a backdrop to the *Symposium*. But the connection with the *Protagoras* is more direct[25] and needs to be addressed while we are in the process of examining the apparently accidental, but potentially meaningful, structures of the narrative.

First, with the exception of Aristophanes, all the speakers of the *Symposium* appear in the *Protagoras*. On a visit to Protagoras at Callias's house, Socrates and Hippocrates find Eryximachus and Phaedrus listening to Hippias of Elis, a polymath, ready to answer any question, and a teacher of the "arts" (*technae* [*Protagoras* 318e]); Pausanias and Agathon are sitting with Prodicus of Ceos (*Protag.* 315c–d), best known, to Plato's readers at least— as Allen observes, "for his genius in distinguishing the meanings of words and determining the correctness of names."[26] He was also the author of an allegory in which Virtue and Vice present Hercules with a choice between opposing paths, upon which Hercules chooses the path of Virtue,[27] and in this capacity Prodicus is mentioned by Eryximachus (cf. 177b). The influence of Hippias is present "in the wide-ranging natural history of eros offered in the speech of Eryximachus"; that of Prodicus, together with that of Gorgias, are evident in the speeches of Pausanias and Agathon.[28] Rosen observes that "the *Protagoras* is a preparation for the *Symposium*: first the famous teachers are portrayed, then their students."[29] So if the *Protagoras* shows how the claim of the Sophists to teach virtue is founded on an ignorance of whether what they sell is good or bad, the *Symposium* may well show the actual effects of this teaching in the souls of their pupils.

Second, the rules for drinking parties, flute girls, and speeches set by Eryximachus in the *Symposium* are exactly anticipated by Socrates in the *Protagoras* (347c–348a),[30] but there is an even more concrete connection between the dialogues manifested in Socrates' first ironic exchange upon entering Agathon's house. Socrates, like the reader in the dialogue, enters "in the middle" of dinner (*mesoun deipnountas*) and Agathon immediately begs him to come over and recline beside him so that he can participate in the wisdom acquired by Socrates: "so that in touching you I'll profit from the wisdom [*tou sophou*; cf. 174c7] that came to you on the porch. For clearly you have found it and you have it in your possession; otherwise you

---

24. *Gorgias* 503a–504e.
25. Cf. Allen 1991, 9–10; Rosen 1968, 24–25.
26. *Prot.* 337a, 340a, 341a, 358a, d; cf. *Charmides* 163d; *Laches* 197A; *Euthydemus* 277e; *Meno* 75e; Allen 1991, 10 and n. 14.
27. Cf. Xen. *Men.* 2.1.21–45; Dover 1980, 88.
28. Allen 1991, 10.
29. Rosen 1968, 25.
30. *Laws* 736a ff., 640a ff., 666a–c.

wouldn't have left." Socrates' reply, "If wisdom [*sophia*] were the sort of thing that flowed from the fuller of us into the emptier" (175d), ironically thematizes one of the major theses of the *Protagoras*—there left unresolved and apparently supported by Socrates himself—namely, that morality is really just a question of a hedonistic calculus or a weighing in the balance of pleasure against pleasure, pain against pain, and pleasure against pain (cf. *Protagoras* 356b–c).[31] Such a view appears to make of morality a mere commodity that can be bought or sold in the market and conveyed in the simplest physical manner into the learner, comparable to the act of eating or drinking. It also appears to sit uncomfortably with Socrates' view, expressed earlier in the dialogue, giving rise to this calculus, that the necessities or commodities of soul are much more risky than the provisions of body. The passage in question from the *Protagoras* runs as follows:

> Indeed, the risk you run in purchasing knowledge is much greater than that in buying provisions. When you buy food and drink you can carry it away from the shop or warehouse in a receptacle, and before you receive it into your body by eating or drinking you can store it away at home and take the advice of an expert on what you should eat and drink . . . ; so there is not much risk in the actual purchase. But knowledge cannot be taken away in a vessel. *When you have paid for it you must receive it straight into the soul. You go away having learned it and are benefitted or harmed accordingly.* (Protag. 313a–314b; emphasis added)

The idea of a material exchange as the basis for excellence is also broached and rejected by Socrates in the *Phaedo*, by means of the image, first, of pleasure and pain being bound together (60b) and, later, by the argument that morality or *phronêsis* cannot be simply an exchange of emotions, but rather involves a *purgation* (67c–70a). Thus, Socrates' reply to Agathon in the *Symposium* assumes a different, ironic note: wisdom (*sophia*)—unfortunately—is not the sort of commodity that can be exchanged from one vessel to another just through touch: "It would be a good thing, Agathon, if wisdom [*sophia*] were the sort of thing that flowed from the fuller of us into the emptier if only we touch each other, as the water in cups flows through a thread of wool from the fuller into the emptier. If wisdom too is like that, I value lying down beside you very much indeed; for I think I'll be filled from you with wisdom of great beauty [*pollês kai kalês sophias plêrôthêsesthai*]. My own wisdom, I suppose, would be an inferior thing [*phaylê tis*], as ambiguous as

---

31. Cf. also *Phaedo* 60a ff.

a dream [*onar*], but yours is bright and promises much [*lampra kai pollên epidosin echousa*]" (175d–e).

The comic aspect of the gas tank approach to wisdom is finely balanced by the wish for our emptiness to be filled in this way. But *sophia* is not a physical element of exchange and cannot therefore be acquired by simple proximity or mechanical transfer. As Socrates takes his place at the banquet, the question emerges of precisely how wisdom is to be acquired and how the inferior can become better. Here the *Symposium* places itself in direct opposition to the notion of sophistic education as an exchange of commodities in the *Protagoras,* a notion accepted by the speakers who are common to both dialogues, but here rejected by Socrates.

The opposition of the *Symposium* to an acquired, "mechanistic" transmission of knowledge, a transmission thematized here by Socrates, does not concern the *Protagoras* only but also resonates with the *Republic*'s descriptions of tyranny. Indeed, several themes are to be discerned in the ironic language with which Socrates addresses Agathon in the preceding passage: a language of emptiness and filling is set side by side with the image of a life riddled with the ambiguity of a dream, and opposed to the bright clarity of the sun or the "good." All these images capture something of the light-and-shade motifs of the central books of the *Republic,* which are later taken up in the nightmarish depiction of a single worldview imposed upon a subservient world, namely, the description of the deviant tyrannical life in book 9, which "becomes in reality what it sometimes was in dream" (*onar* [574d, 576b]). Moreover, the notion of the transmission of knowledge from the fuller to the emptier also sums up the final arguments of book 9 of the *Republic* that contrast emptiness of body with emptiness of soul (585b) and conclude that what is filled with more real things and is itself more real, is more truly filled than that which is filled with things less real (585d).[32] In the *Republic,* the gas tank approach to information receives its most frightening visualization: the tyrannical life imposes the thought of one ruler upon everyone, fills its citizens to the brim only with those desires which belong to the hubristic ruler, and leaves them in a state of nightmare.

Can such a striking reflection of several of the major themes concerning the transmission of knowledge or excellence in the *Protagoras, Phaedo,* and *Republic* inscribed in Socrates' apparently casual remark be coincidental? Yes, it could well be. However, is the remark intended to draw the reader's attention to the central problem of knowledge and its transmission? These

---

32. On the major problems of these arguments, and particularly the question of any "gradational" account of "being," see Vlastos in Bambrough 1967, 1–19 for one view and Guthrie 1975, 493ff. for another side of the issue; and for the contrast between *hypar* and *onar,* see *Rep.* 520c6–7.

questions are too broad and complex to be answered simply in the affirmative and yet too important to be omitted altogether. One thing is clear: Socrates' rejection of a mechanistic approach to wisdom is, in this context, also a rejection of the tyranny of any superior political figure or dominant sophistic teacher and is thus an indication that Socrates' *hybris* employs a different style of communication.

Whatever the case, the problem of the transmission of *sophia* in the ordinary language context of the beautiful, the good, and the person of skill (the *sophos*) already emerges, and the means of transmission apparently accepted in the *Protagoras* are rejected at the outset. Yet how *are* art and wisdom really transmitted if not by means of some form of exchange, simple proximity, or imitation and reflection? And on what level of discourse are we to find the answer to this question? Finding a satisfactory answer to these problems constitutes a major part of the challenge of the *Symposium,* and as with previous questions, this one cannot be resolved on the factual or mimetic level, introduced by Aristodemus.

2.6 Between Religious Observance and the Cycle of Opposites

Several features of the immediate sequel are worth noting. First, Agathon's rejoinder (*hybristês ei* [175e8]) reminds us forcefully of the strong natural charisma embodied in Socrates as well as of the contest in which the speakers as human beings and not merely as narrators appear to be engaged. We are also reminded of the judge, Dionysus, whom, in the form of wine, Socrates will overcome (223b–d), insofar as Socrates is perfectly equal either to a soaking or to complete sobriety ("he's sufficient either way" [176c–d]): "You're outrageous, Socrates, Agathon replied. You and I will adjudicate our claims about wisdom a little later, using Dionysus as judge. But now please turn your attention to dinner right away" (175e). Socrates is therefore capable of rising above *the claim of opposites* (*hikanos gar kat' amphotera*) and even finally of vanquishing the wine god himself.[33] Moreover, this ability to rise above opposites is reflected in the narrative structure at this point, for the entire subsequent conversation is framed precisely within the double context of religious observance, on the one hand, and the exchange of opposites, on the other. First, there is religious observance, and this appears not without a touch of comedy at the end of the sentence: "After this, he said, when Socrates had lain down and he and the rest had dined, they poured libations and, after singing a hymn to the god and doing the other

---

33. This is Allen's (1991, 109) assessment, but he gives it far too much prominence.

usual things, turned to the drinking" (176a). The focus of this sentence, after the observance (*ta nomizomena*), is the comic gravitational pull toward drinking (*trepesthai pros ton poton*). There is then the mise-en-scène poised between the opposite pulls of pleasure and pain or pleasure and pleasure. Pausanias, sophist par excellence, poses the problem and the need for relief from extremes: "Well then, gentlemen . . . what's the easiest way for us to drink? I can tell you that I'm in a really bad state and I need a respite [*anapsychês tinos*];—I think most of you do too, because you were there yesterday—so consider what's the easiest way for us to go about drinking" (176a–b). Pausanias needs relief, just as Socrates needs relief or rest at the very end of the dialogue, at least in the words of Apollodorus-Aristodemus. In fact, the last word of the dialogue is "respite" or "rest" (*anapauesthai* [223d12]): "He went to the Lyceum and bathed, passed the rest of the day as he would any other, and after that he went home in the evening and *rested* [*anapauesthai*]" (223d). So the natural human need to rise above the claims of pain and pleasure and find relief is the motive cause of the drinking party—that is, the avoidance of surfeit or shame; and this accords with rather vague medical wisdom (176c–d), as provided to us by the good doctor, Eryximachus, and with the comic acquiescence of the doctor's lover, Phaedrus, with Eryximachus's medical advice ("Very well, I'm accustomed to listen to you, especially in whatever you say about medicine, and if they think about it properly, the rest will now listen too" [176d–e]). Here Eryximachus's wisdom proves to be lopsided (that is, caught in the exchange of opposites) for according to him in order to avoid *pain,* namely, a hangover, one should drink "only for pleasure" (*houtô pinontas pros hêdonên*) (176e6–7). Pleasure for pleasure, or pleasure in exchange for pain, is apparently the principle, (and one endorsed by medicine, for drinking further is simply unhealthy: "How drunkenness is hard on people"!) that propels the participants to find relief in further creativity, however halfhearted: "Hearing this, everyone agreed not to make the present get-together a drunken affair, but to drink only for pleasure" (176e). So after the vertical dimension evoked by the problem of *sophia* and the thematic relation of the worse to the better person, the rest of the story of the drinking party is framed between the context of religious observance and the horizontal dimension of an exchange of opposites. Such an exchange, one may suppose, remains part of the permanent framework of any *narrative* life (which is why Socrates may well appear to accept the hedonistic calculus in the *Protagoras*), but this movement from religious observance to medicinal relief is not the ultimate frame of the discourse, for the narrative is about to be transformed and balanced yet again by the exchange and clash of ideas. Thus, even before we hear the speeches of the guests, the figure of Socrates and the apparent self-direction of his thought have already been established as an important narrative level that directs and transfixes other textual layers, so powerful is his personality, "sufficient either way," and so enticing is his dedication to the thinking life.

2.7 "The Father of the Discourse"

The drinking rules proposed by Eryximachus, an echo of those proposed by Socrates in the *Protagoras* (and a foretaste of the Athenian Stranger's much longer discussion in the *Laws* of the "unnatural" quality both of *symposia* and of homosexuality),[34] afford a humorous portrait of medical pedantry. At the same time, Eryximachus seems to wish to generate a *consensus* among the drinkers and to follow out the wishes of each: "[T]his has been decided that each of us should drink only as much as he wants, nothing compulsory" (176e). This sense of liberality is also, perhaps, a reflection of another side of Eryximachus's nature: his implicit banishment of Dionysus and Marsyas, or of anything, in fact, that cannot fit into or be controlled by his scientific picture of the universe, since he wants to dispense with (*chairein ean*) the flute girl (176e), just as flute players and flute makers in the *Republic* are to be excluded from the *polis* (399d–e).[35] The instruments of Apollo, then, are to be preferred to those associated with Dionysus.[36] In the *Symposium*, however, one can only do this up to a point, for at the moment when a Dionysiac Alcibiades arrives, the assembled guests hear again "the voice of a flute girl" (212c).

But Eryximachus does not merely expel the flute girls; to secure order, he makes an important proposal, casting it in the form of a complaint by Phaedrus that Eryximachus requests the present company to remedy: Eryximachus proposes that each make an encomium to love. According to Phaedrus's complaint, no poet has ever offered an encomium to Eros, and nor has any Sophist, either. Friedländer remarks on the strangeness of this claim, in light of the fact that there are songs to love in both the *Antigone* and the *Hippolytus* as well as other evidence of the praise of love. Gould points out the relative truth of Phaedrus's claim beside the strong following of Aphrodite and the greater scope afforded Plato by the choice of Eros rather than of Aphrodite.[37] Perhaps the point may also be that this is a complaint *repeated* by Phaedrus: Euripides had already complained about this in his

---

34. See Price 1989, 229ff.; Allen 1991, 17–20.
35. Cf. *Laws* 812c–813a.
36. Cf. Allen 1991, 116 n. 171; see also Hadot 1995, 147ff.
37. Friedländer 1969, 9–10; Gould 1963, 24–25; Rowe 1998, 135; Brisson 1998, 187.

choric song to love, and Aristophanes later in the dialogue (189c) bemoans the lack of temples to the god. Indeed, Eryximachus has just introduced the whole question with a quotation from Euripides himself. Phaedrus may well be the ardent beginner in love matters, as it were, who follows or repeats the call of others, claiming it as his own.

There is, then, a certain irony in Phaedrus's being appointed "father of the discourse" (177d), since what we will see in his speech is a relatively undifferentiated universe in which all the crucial distinctions, to be introduced by later speakers, simply do not appear, and yet the impulse to appreciate the mystery of love in itself is also evident. In this sense, Phaedrus is innocent of subtlety and his speech remains at the level of relatively unselfconscious *mythos* or tale.[38] So perhaps it is not accidental that Plato represents Eryximachus as prefacing his remarks in the following way: "My discourse starts from [*hê . . . archê tou logou*] Euripides' Melanippe, for 'mine is not the tale' [*mythos*] but it belongs to Phaedrus here" (177a).

The *mythos* belongs to Phaedrus and, with tantalizing accidentality, Eryximachus employs Euripides' language from the lost play *Melanippe the Wise*, in which the heroine prefaces a didactic speech about the origin of the world with the words "mine is not the tale, but it is from my mother."[39] In the transposition that we find in the *Symposium*, the question of *whose* tale this really is implicitly emerges. In one way, this detail may make us think of Plato (and the altar to Eros created just at the entrance to the Academy), as Friedländer observes when her asks: "[W]hen we hear Phaedrus complaining . . . how can we think of anybody but Plato and the daring task he has set himself[?]"[40] In another way, however, as in the case of the narrative of Apollodorus, we are naturally led to question the *origin* of any tale or discourse, *mythos* or *logos*, that is apparently initiated by someone who is incapable of understanding, or developing, its fuller significance.

One further point about this is worth making: at 177a ("My discourse starts from Euripides' *Melanippe* for 'the tale is not mine' but it belongs to Phaedrus here") there is a casual, apparently insignificant switch from the female (Melanippe and her mother) to the male (Eryximachus and Phaedrus as the father), but the name, Melanippe, is *voiced* and this puts a woman at the origin of the dialogue, a woman who is immediately displaced. Further, the momentary presence of a woman at such a prominent place is perhaps insignificant, at least at this point of the dialogue, but it cannot be entirely accidental that Melanippe is a *mythical* paradigm of a wise woman who

---

38. For the distinction between unconscious, that is, "prephilosophical," and conscious myth, see Frutiger 1930; Elias 1984.

39. Euripides *Melanippe the Wise* frag. 484 (Nauck 1889); cf. Dover 1980, 87.

40. Friedländer 1969, 10.

mediates between the divine and the human, and whose semidivine offspring (at first unrealized by their human guardian) come to be acknowledged and nurtured by her human partner.[41] In a *mythical* way she looks forward to the figure of Diotima herself. As in the case of the proverb above, which Socrates "destroys and changes," the "source" of the myth is displaced, but voiced, and the erased voice anticipates the "source" of the story that Socrates has to tell about Diotima.[42]

Thus, Aristodemus's narrative, a relatively simple mimetic account that provides a second frame for the narrative as a whole, is saturated with minute yet highly charged details, which clash, erase, displace, and direct one another. Yet, if these details in the prologue are to be examined in the broader context of the *Symposium* as a whole and in relation to other earlier and contemporary dialogues, several major questions and issues require answers or pose interpretive puzzles later in the dialogue. Some of the implicit questions pertaining to the texture of the narrative are (1) how are the layers of the dialogue related to one another and which is the most authoritative? (2) Does there emerge a more positive rhetorical or philosophical art than the imitation of an imitation represented by Apollodorus? and (3) How is the inconclusiveness of the narrative mimetic level related to the rest of the *Symposium* as a whole?

In this chapter, we have sought for a way to determine which of the incidental details should be taken seriously and which should be overlooked. Our examination has demonstrated that neither this problem nor the preceding questions can be answered from the *Symposium*'s two prologues themselves, for the problem of interpretation is permeated with philosophical concerns that send us, in turn, to other levels of discourse and to other

---

41. According to the tale, Melanippe was impregnated by Poseidon, then blinded and imprisoned by her father; her two babies were exposed, but were found and brought to Metapontus, king of Icaria, who took them as his own and favored them over his own two children born subsequently. Metapontus's wife, out of jealousy, incited her own children to kill the two foundlings, but the foundlings—with the help of Poseidon—killed their rivals and Metapontus's wife committed suicide. At the urging of Poseidon, the sons rescued their mother, who subsequently married Metapontus (cf. Hyginus, *Fabulae* 186).

Now, the figure of Melanippe, of course, bears no *direct* resemblance to Diotima, yet the image of a wrong and violent way of divine love anticipates and contrasts with Diotima's "god does not have sexual intercourse with man" (*theos anthrôpô ou mignytai* [203a]).

42. If our interpretation is right, this an important, hitherto unobserved detail whose broader implications need to be examined in the context of the middle dialogues more generally. For something of this broader setting, see generally Tuana 1994; Ward 1996; and also sections 5.3 and 5.9 (together with notes), below. One further incidental detail: we have seen that Eryximachus and Phaedrus form a couple. Now at 177d, it seems, Agathon and Pausanias are also a couple; and this will be confirmed at 193b7 (Aristophanes tells Eryximachus not to poke fun at his picture of human beings in search of their other "halves" by thinking that he only means Pausanias and Agathon). Aristophanes is conspicuously on his own, but a master without peer on the subject of love.

dialogues. This manner of presenting details tells us something about Plato as a thinker and a writer: play and playfulness between many levels of signification is definitely not alien to his style and must be taken into account in order for one to grasp the very tenor of his philosophical thinking. This means that on the basis of our examination of the prologues, we can only conclude that there can be no part of the dialogue that is *simply* nonphilosophical, as Robin, Guthrie, and others have supposed,[43] and that at the same time no factual details constitute an end in themselves. By the very nature of Plato's thought, all those details are drawn into an open-ended interplay between the images and ideas of the text. Apparently elemental details point to their later philosophical development: even Socrates' way of going to the banquet in the house of Agathon foreshadows *per impossibile* the later ladder of ascent in Diotima's speech, yet this relationship appears to be just that—a shadow. This subtle interplay throughout means not that we experience a predetermined philosophical mystery play, but rather that each part of the dialogue in its own way comments upon the whole. But the means of articulating this understanding are at this point in the *Symposium* not yet at hand.

It is plausible to suggest, then, that the subsequent philosophical levels of discourse, in their relationship to these details charged with as yet undetermined significance, will provide a direction and focus that is lacking at the factual or purely literary level of narrative. It would also seem that since the seating arrangement is emphasized (but left unclear), the relationship between the order and the content of the speeches is going to be significant for the elucidation of the whole dialogue. In other words, since the problem of order cannot be resolved on the purely spatial or visual level, the early speeches must in some way be significantly ordered in relation to the whole, but these too cannot be elucidated unless we reconstruct the relationship not only between the speakers, but also between their "philosophical" and "nonphilosophical" preoccupations and their styles of living and loving. After examining the roles of Apollodorus and Aristodemus, we suspect that every figure in the *Symposium* makes a statement and yet casts a shadow. But if this is so, then in order to understand the structure of the *Symposium* it is necessary to suppose that each speech will also cast its own shadow and that the design of the dialogue will not emerge unless the reader is compelled to evaluate not only the order but also the relative truth of each speech, both in what is said and in what remains unsaid.

---

43. Robin 1992, xxxvi and 1964, 8; Guthrie 1975, 368ff.

The Order of the Speeches

Formulating the Problem

What do the early speeches contribute to our understanding of love and why should we see them as anything more than rhetorical exercises? There is considerable critical consensus that these speeches are an inferior backdrop to the Socrates-Diotima discourse, a collection of errors that Diotima aptly rectifies (198e–199a). Bury's formulation of this view, for instance, is hard to deny: "It thus seems clear that Plato intends us to regard all the first five speeches as on the same level, in so far as all alike possess the common defect of aiming at appearance only (*doxa*), not at reality (*alêtheia*), in virtue of which no one of them can claim to rank as a scientific contribution (*epistêmê*) to the discussion."[1] Such a view, however, tends to deemphasize Plato's close attention to the fine details of characterization, many examples of which we have already seen in the two prologues. The dialogue's popularity as a masterpiece owes much to the sheer delight the reader experiences when fine, apparently insignificant details of character become imbued with the ambiguity of satirical, yet sometimes poignant, life.

A bigger problem, however, presents itself when we try to assess the relationship between

---

1. Bury 1932, liii.

the speaker's personality and his vision of love, especially if he professes in some measure to be engaged in a "philosophical" or "technical" argument. But if a complex literary and philosophical design is enacted in these speeches, their relative banality and inability to reach the level of *epistêmê* do not constitute the only angle of inquiry from which the speeches and their order may be assessed, all the more so because it is ultimately unclear why Plato should spend his time imitating inferior minds just to provide a backdrop for Socrates. A more complex design, in fact, may well be enacted here, one that dramatizes the blindness and insight of a community whose best members were educated by Gorgias and Protagoras (as well as entertained by Aristophanes' *Clouds*) and that produced and fostered Socrates and then sentenced him to death. What this means, as we shall see, is that all the speeches, even the most rudimentary, are potentially philosophical, insofar as they require their hearers to assess the truth and consistency of the criteria expressed in them, however unconsciously, and simultaneously to see for themselves the speakers' insights and limitations. Since in Socrates' speech Diotima comments on and corrects all the important elements in the earlier speeches, this internal philosophical evaluation of the truth of the early speeches is an integral part of the dialogue, even if this cannot be a self-conscious activity in those speeches themselves. Do these speeches, then, reveal something of the many faces of that culture for whose ills Socrates prescribed philosophy? Let us, first, take a brief look at the meaning of the word *Eros* and the nature of a speech in praise of love in Plato's day and then go on to formulate the challenge one senses in the succession of these early speeches, a succession that seems at first glance to lack a clear organizing principle.

3.1 Eros

Erôs (in Homer and Hesiod, *eros*), *eran,* and poetic *erasthai* can denote any passionate desire for or joy in something (e.g., one's homeland [Aesch. *Ag.* 540]; children [Euripides *Ion* 67]; food and drink [Homer *Iliad* 1.469; Soph *Aj.* 693]), but usually means "love" in the sense of love for a particular individual (e.g., Sophocles *Trach.* 433), to fall in love with or to be in love with someone (*erasthênai*), a desire which often includes sexual passion (e.g., Euripides *Hipp.* 32; Homer *Iliad* 3.446). *Erôs* can also designate the god of love (Anacr. 65; Parm. 313; Eur. *Hipp.* 525) or the natural force of love itself, felt by the individual to be acting upon him or her with a superhuman power. In the tragedies, this power is often sung of as a hostile god who takes away our wits and drives us to injustice (qualities that Agathon rejects, for example, in his speech in the *Symposium*); and in the lyric poets,

Love is frequently called a madman, liar, tyrant, or deceiver,[2] something Plato is concerned to account for at *Republic* 573b–c, for instance, in his psychological portrait of tyrannical lust. Love's parents and his relationship to Aphrodite are uncertain. And the "Loves" are sometimes mentioned in the plural. So there is considerable range in the meaning of the verb and noun and a perhaps natural vagueness about the origin, parentage, and precise nature of the god.

Philia, another word for "love," denotes love or liking in a more general sense: it signifies affectionate regard or friendship[3] and may mean family affection (Xen. *Hier.* 3.7); it intimates friendship between states (Th. 5.5) or the regard of a dependent for a superior (Xen. *Anth.* 1.6.3) and may be opposed to *erôs* (Xen. *Symp.* 8.15) or include sexual desire. The question *phileis eme* (do you love me) can be used in a sexual (e.g., Xen. *Symp.* 9.6) or familial (e.g., Ar. *Clouds* 82) context.[4] Other words for love such as *agapê* and *agapân* have a similar range to that of *philia* and *philein*, but denote regard rather than affection,[5] though the two words are sometimes interchangeable and *agapân* may occasionally be used also of sexual love or of a caress,[6] so that we should beware of transposing the later Christian favoring of *agapê* and *agapân* to these words in classical times.[7] The distinction between *agapân* and *philein* can be seen at *Lysis* 215b, for example. How can a friend (*philos*) not be held dear (*agapêtheiê*)? Socrates asks (215a). If someone has no need of anything, he will not hold anything dear (*agapôê*). And the person who holds nothing dear (*agapôê*) will not love (*philoi*). Here *philein* appears to be a more intense and personal loving than the more general *agapân*, but there is nonetheless significant overlap between *erasthai*, *philein*, *agapân*, and even *epithymia* and *epithymein*, which denote desire in all its forms, but commonly sexual desire. Again, in the *Lysis* Plato underlines this close connection: "So what belongs to oneself, it seems, turns out to be the object of love [*erôs*], friendship [*philia*], and desire [*epithymia*]" (*Lysis* 221d). By contrast, words for sex or sexual intercourse have a different designation: sexual intercourse is called *ta aphrodisia*, "Aphrodite's things," and belongs to the province of the goddess, Aphrodite.[8]

So for Plato's purposes the choice of *Erôs* for praise has the advantages that the word (1) can designate the god or the superhuman force of love

---

2. Cf. Gould 1963, 24.
3. Liddell, Scott, and Jones 1940.
4. Dover 1980, 1–2.
5. Liddell, Scott, and Jones 1940.
6. Cf. Arist. *Clouds* frag. 76; Dover 1980, 2 n. 1.
7. Cf. Allen 1991, 95–98; Rist 1964.
8. Dover 1980, 2.

itself, (2) may signify the concrete experience of being in love with or falling in love with a particular individual while bearing a range of other cognate meanings, and (3) is distinguished from the common words for sex derived from the goddess, Aphrodite.

3.2 Encomium

A speech in praise of love is called interchangeably *encomium* and *epainos* (cf. 177b1, d2, e6). It involves "adorning the god" (177c7). Originally, *encomium* seems to have been a song of blessing and well-wishing addressed to an athletic victor, for example, by a festive crowd (*kômos*), but by the early fourth century it could take the form of a speech in praise of anyone or anything from Hercules to salt.[9] Later, explicit rules for the genre were formulated:[10] the speaker should praise, first, the subject's family, strength, beauty, and wealth, that is, qualities outside his own good character; second, his skill, honesty, courage and worthy pursuits, in other words, the "cardinal" virtues (not always the same ones) of the subject's character; third, his forebears; and finally his achievements (*Rhetorica ad Alexandrum* 35). In Agathon's speech, as in this later formulation of rules by the author of the *Rhetorica ad Alexandrum*, the cardinal virtues, for example, play a major role. Also later in Aristotle's *Rhetoric* we find a distinction between *epainos* and *encomium*, which seems to be foreshadowed in the *Symposium* by Agathon, who complains that all previous speakers have merely felicitated humankind for the goods given them by the god Love, whereas one should make proper *encomium* by praising him, first, for what he is and, then, for what he gives. Love's gifts and nature must be mutually unfolded in the proper form of praise. So the *epainos* or *encomium* is in process of developing proper rhetorical rules, and in the *Symposium* we can see a distinction between praise as merely touching on the external benefits of someone or some god and *encomium* as linking these benefits to the nature of the person or god praised.

3.3 The Problem of the Significance of the Early Speeches

Do, then, the early speeches that take up the task of providing *encomium* or praise to Eros give any sense of a developing order, and how could Phaedrus's

---

9. *Symp.* 177b; Gould 1963, 24; Dover 1980, 12; Ferrari (1992, 248) aptly implies that the praise of "salt" reminds us of the *bitter* in "bittersweet love."

10. Cf. Dover 1980, 12.

speech in particular provide us with anything remotely philosophical? Bury gives a history of four different interpretations of the order of the speeches, interpretations ultimately handicapped by either inconsistency or lack of forceful insight. First, according to Rötscher, they are arranged in order of ascending importance, from the slightest (*Phaedrus*) to the most impressive (Agathon). Unfortunately, however, Agathon's speech is not the most impressive. Second and third, according to Steinhart and Hug respectively, the speeches are arranged in pairs either in accordance with a logical principle, namely, the sphere of activity of Eros they concern (for example, the ethical [Phaedrus and Pausanias]; the physical [Eryximachus and Aristophanes]; the spiritual [Agathon and Socrates]) or an aesthetic principle (the second speech of each group is richer than the first, and so on).[11] This arrangement, however, looks somewhat artificial and does not tell us anything important about the nature of the speeches themselves or about the significant differences, for example, between Socrates and Agathon, despite the generic categorization of their speeches as "spiritual." Moreover, Bury, as we have seen, distinguishes the first five speeches from that of Socrates on the grounds that they are all on the same level: they all represent various phases of ungrounded opinion and of the "unphilosophic mind."[12] So too Robin (and Cornford): "Toute la première partie représente donc, sinon toujours le point de vue des Rhéteurs et des Sophistes, du moins un point de vue étranger à la philosophie."[13] In the same vein, Rosen regards the speeches as "rhetorical exercises rather than complex philosophical statements." And, of course, Guthrie goes much further, in commenting on the hiccups of Aristophanes and their effect upon the order of the speeches: "If Plato had simply wanted Eryximachus to speak first (according to those who believe in a "dialectical ascent" of the speeches) he could have altered the table-plan. Quite probably he wants to warn the reader that the order of speeches is not significant but accidental."[14] Nonetheless, as we saw earlier, given even the complexity of the two prologues, this influential view remains highly debatable.

By contrast, Dorter argues that each speech has to be measured by the adequacy of its conceptions of Eros and of goodness, which means that each speech corrects and transcends its predecessor's conception not of Eros, but of why Eros is good.[15] Dorter concludes his interpretation by arguing that

---

11. Cf. Rötscher, Steinhart, and Hug, in Bury 1932, liii–liv.
12. Bury 1932, lii ff.
13. Bury 1932, xxxvi.
14. Bury 1932, lii–lvii; Robin, in Vicaire 1992, xxxvi ff.; Cornford 1971, 121–22; Rosen 1968, xxxvi; Guthrie 1975, 382 n. 2.
15. Dorter 1969, 215–34; see also 1992, 253–69 (in which he corrects and develops his earlier article).

in Socrates' speech, "each of the previous portrayals of Eros is corrected (in ascending order of quality) and its kernel of truth incorporated into Socrates' position."[16] "The Ascent of Beauty" in Diotima's discourse is "the specifically original contribution of Socrates' speech, no longer a critique and development of the preceding speeches."[17] There is much to commend Dorter's view (especially insofar as he looks to address the question of order from inside the speeches themselves), but at the same time this approach may be a little too restrictive (in so far as each speech deals with more than the question why Eros is good). Later commentators such as R. E. Allen, L. Brisson, and C. J. Rowe take rather different approaches.[18] Allen avoids the issue of order altogether by commenting on the speeches in their context as preparing for Socrates' speech. Luc Brisson regroups the speeches into three sets of two: (1) Phaedrus and Agathon, for whom there is a single Love—oldest and youngest god, respectively; (2) Pausanias and Eryximachus, for whom there are two Loves, corresponding to the Heavenly and Vulgar Aphrodite; and (3) Aristophanes and Socrates, for whom Love is a god and a demon, respectively, who helps humankind, in different ways in both speeches, to realize the goal of its aspirations. The speeches of the first two sets are set against the background of traditional theology, transmitted by Hesiod and the poets in general, whereas the last set refers to less typical religious movements in ancient Greece: Orphism in Aristophanes' speech and the Mystery religions in Socrates' speech. Brisson tends to view the speeches as articulating "une typologie du comportement sexuel," each in rather different ways—male homosexual love in the first place, heterosexual love in the second, and female homosexual love in the third. This, as we shall see in Chapter 5, is highly problematic, but a more immediate concern is the following. Brisson, perhaps rightly, puts Socrates' speech together with the five earlier speeches, but his regrouping of the speeches, however suggestive, does not explain why they should be in the order they actually are or again why Socrates' speech should be so included. In fact, one might argue that Brisson's ordering obscures, rather than illuminates, the "order" as we find it in the *Symposium*.[19]

Finally, Rowe gives special attention to the literary quality of the *Symposium*, its "intertextuality" and "responsiveness," a feature of Plato's art that

---

16. Dorter 1969, 216.
17. Dorter 1969, 231–32.
18. Allen 1991; Brisson 1998; Rowe 1998.
19. Brisson 1998, 39–40, 48–49; for a rather different view, see Ferrari 1992, 250: "[T]he substantive view which distinguishes them is this: the speakers of the first group [Phaedrus, Pausanias, and Eryximachus] draw a fundamental distinction . . . between a good and a bad variety of love, while those of the second group do not [Aristophanes, Agathon, and Socrates]."

will concern us throughout the rest of this book. Rowe, not unlike Dorter in a sense, sees each successive speaker as "capping" the one before. Moreover, in his interpretation the first six speeches "represent a single whole" culminating first in Agathon's speech and then in Socrates' speech, which builds on "the ruins" of Agathon's. In contrast to Dorter, Rowe cautions against "supposing . . . there is . . . any gradually developing picture . . . with each speaker fitting new and better pieces to the jigsaw."[20] So what is the function of the first five speeches? For Rowe, each represents a *type* as well as an individual."[21] But why just *these* types? An examination of the speeches themselves provides the only real answer one can give to this question, but here again we are ultimately left with the old questions: Why do these types or individuals appear in just this order? Why should Agathon's speech, for instance, be the "culmination" of the first set of speeches? If Agathon's speech is a culmination, why should there not be a "gradually developing picture"? Is it only because Agathon is the victorious host or is there another design at work? And why should Socrates spend so much time "demolishing" Agathon's speech?

These are questions that in fact have an answer in the design of the whole dialogue, for no easy solutions will suffice here, all the more so because of the intensity and long history of the problem. The following chapter, therefore, will be dedicated to a careful analysis of the early speeches, and we shall argue not only that each speech reflects the character and situation of each individual speaker as well as a certain type or genre, but also that there is a distinct ordering pattern that only gradually emerges and that has much to do with the criticism of mimetic art in the *Republic*. This order is not a crescendo in the usual sense, preliminary to the "corrections" of Diotima. Rather, we shall argue that in these speeches Plato gives implicitly *at least* two sides of the "issue": the "private" face of each speaker and the generic character of the speech; but the implicit oppositions that emerge in each voice do form a definite design that culminates in Agathon's speech.

The beginning of a readjustment of former views about the order of the speeches starts for us with the figure of Phaedrus, whose exact role in the dialogue's structure has been somewhat misunderstood. He is not the weakest of the speakers for a very simple reason: in contrast to the speakers who follow on his encomium, Phaedrus does not *instruct,* but *wants to be instructed,* foreshadowing in this the position of Socrates, who asks to be instructed by Diotima. Phaedrus's teachers are, then, a reflection of an ascent on the ladder of knowledge open to every educated, intellectually

---

20. Rowe 1998, 8.
21. Rowe 1998, 9.

searching young man. Socrates, of course, will argue with the wisdom that has been taught in his cultivated world of Athens on the subject and with the instruction that the wisest and ablest of his city offer to the young. *Two ladders of ascent are thus present in the dialogue,* one that responds to Phaedrus's need for instruction and another that embodies Diotima's instruction to Socrates. The relationship between these two trajectories brings us very close to understanding the tenor of Plato's dialectic at play. It is unwise to summarize the conclusion prior to the analysis that will lead to it, but at least this much can be stated: when character type and speech are juxtaposed and set against the image of the lovers' ascent that transfixes the dialogue as a whole, what emerges is not at all a showcase of philosophically unsuccessful speeches or a catalog of inferior minds but much more a dialectic of strikingly complex structure, which simultaneously presents a series of *problematic images* and a comic-tragic document of the epoch preceding the trial and death of Socrates.

The panorama that emerges is also an artistic document that articulates its own artistic project, a project, in fact, that both completes and challenges the apparent criticism of art and its potential in the *Republic.* In that context, the order of the speeches is a part of the overall pattern, for once this order is seen with clarity, it helps to throw light on many Platonic questions, including the issue of imitative art, but for the reader to see this, the narrative requires a more active participation, that is, a reader who can bring together several layers of discourse, while examining carefully the details of each. In other words, the fundamental ordering pattern even for these early speeches cannot be seen properly until one comes to question the design of the whole dialogue itself (a questioning we shall undertake in a preliminary fashion in Chapter 5 and then more comprehensively in Chapters 6, 7, and 8). For long before we see Alcibiades' portrait of Socrates, with its intimation of an "inner world," we already sense this multilayered design in the order of the speeches themselves, but to open them up and see a pattern can be just as facile or as difficult as to open up "Socrates" himself.

From Character to Speech

The Early Speeches and Their Significance

4.1 Phaedrus: The Ardent Apprentice, but Confused Mythologue

The Phaedrus of the *Symposium* seems to be that same Phaedrus who accompanies Socrates out of town in the dialogue named after him: on the one hand, he is amenable to philosophical discussion and devoutly raises important problems; on the other, he lacks the ability for their thorough examination. He is a "shining," ardent beginner, and yet as a rhetorician, he is content to rest with appearances to the point of learning the apparently beautiful by heart. He is a "mythologue," accepting myth as the ultimate evidence of truth and occasionally twisting this to his own viewpoint, yet at the same time there is something engaging about him.[1] His speech is generally considered to be the worst of all the speeches. Some scholars have attempted to equate his description of Eros with mere sexual passion for boys.[2] That Phaedrus is a homosexual is clear, but this does not mean that his understanding of love is limited by sexual drive. His example of Alcestis speaks of love as related to nobility of spirit. Thus, his speech is not easy to encompass or pinpoint. In fact,

---

1. Cf. Robin 1992, xxxviii, in which the "composite portrait" of Phaedrus is excellent (xxxvi ff.).
2. Taylor 1960, 212–13.

Phaedrus reacts to many existing mythological accounts of love but is unable to give his speech a clear direction.

For Phaedrus, Eros is the oldest god[3] and "cause of the greatest goods for us." This goodness turns out to be "shame in shameful things and ambition in noble things," which is the foundation of all personal and public life: the doing of great and noble deeds (178d1–4). Love prevents us from acting shamefully, since we are afraid to be seen[4] doing so in the presence of the beloved, and inspires us to excellence (*entheon poiêseie pros aretên, hôste homoion einai tôi aristôi physei* [179a–b])[5] so that men and women are positively prepared to die on behalf of their beloveds. The gods prize the love of the beloved for the lover more than that of the lover for the beloved, apparently on the ground that the lover is more divine than the beloved, since he is inspired (*entheos* [180a–b]). What precisely this means is unclear (presumably that the beloved acts less selfishly and more self-dependently as uninspired), but the conclusion drawn from it is that the gods honored Achilles, who, contrary to the testimony of Aeschylus, was not the lover, but the beloved, of Patroclus, more than they honored Alcestis, who was the lover of Admetus.[6] So love is "the oldest, most honorable, and most authoritative [*kyriôtaton*] god with regard to the acquisition of excellence and happiness [*eis aretês kai eudaimonias ktêsin*] by human beings both living and dead" (180b).

Phaedrus's speech is unreflective in the sense that it presents an unselfconscious and unexamined view of life, accepting for the most part a mythical, traditional view. Yet precisely in this unconscious way it introduces casually some of the basic issues of the dialogue and also calls itself into question by its unreflective use of critical terms. People who intend "to live nobly" (*kalôs biôsesthai*) must be guided neither by kinship, nor by honors, nor by wealth, but only by love (178c–d). Phaedrus never explains what is involved in such a noble life, but it is clear from his examples that the romantic ideal of self-sacrifice and courage forms the criterion of what he considers good.[7] A lover, for example, would choose death many times rather than leave his station in battle (179a). Yet as Dorter observes, it is sometimes better to retreat, though undoubtedly not "beautiful," and Alcibiades later informs us how the courageous Socrates thought it better

---

3. Cf. 178b1–2: "among the oldest," yet see 180b7.
4. So apparently one can get away with anything if undetected, which is one of the major issues of the *Republic* (2.357a ff.: Glaucon's story about Gyges' ring; and then 362d ff., Adeimantus's even thornier problem: why one should be good at all?).
5. On shame and honor, two major principles of popular morality, see Dover 1974, 226–42.
6. Again, Alcestis seems to act not from love or passion so much as from fidelity—at least according to Euripides' version.
7. Dorter 1969, 216.

to retreat under certain conditions (220e8). So the inspiration that love gives to make anyone "like to the best nature" (*homoion . . . tôi aristôi physei* [179a–b]) is a noble ideal, even reminiscent of the Platonic *homoiôsis theô*, likeness to god, but in the present case it remains empty of reflective meaning. Consequently, in this casual way, Phaedrus's insistence on earnestness (*spoudê* [179d2]), excellence (*aretê* [179d2, 180a8, 180b7]), the esteem of the gods (179d1–3, 180a–b), self-sacrificial death (*apothnêskein* [179d6]; *hyperapothanein, epapothanein* [180a1]) and happiness (180b7–8) only serves to bring to light the implicit question of what these terms can really mean in face of the romantic catalog of beautiful deeds we are given.

This effect is felt more strongly in the concluding portions of the speech, first, in the uncritical catalog of beautiful deeds and, second, in the implicit confusion of, if not contradiction between, Phaedrus's observations about which is more virtuous, the lover or the beloved. The examples of Orpheus, Alcestis, and Achilles are presented as genuinely analogous, but they are not. Phaedrus thinks that Orpheus should have been willing to kill himself for Eurydice, as Alcestis was willing to do for Admetus, rather than going alive to the underworld. As Dorter observes, such self-sacrifice might well have been more "beautiful," but it would certainly not have been *better* or indeed more intelligent, since the two cases are not alike.[8] Alcestis knew that the gods would spare Admetus's life in exchange for hers, but Orpheus knew that he could only bring Eurydice back if he stayed alive. So the false analogy not only calls into question the casual presentation of appearance unreflectively presented in the speech, but also suggests that the speaker whose "evidence" comes from myth is susceptible of changing the myth to suit his own particular ends, a suggestion that innocently undermines the whole speech.

In this context, Phaedrus's closing contradiction is particularly revealing. On the one hand, only love can give sufficient excellence to the lover that he will be ready to die for his beloved. Yet, on the other hand, the gods honor more the beloved (the one who is younger and still beardless), who performs such a noble deed because he is apparently further removed from divine inspiration. And so Achilles, the beloved, is to be preferred to Alcestis, a lover. Just as the name Melanippe was voiced only to be immediately displaced, so Phaedrus makes of Alcestis an ideal to be displaced again by the male ideal, Achilles. At any rate, the upshot of Phaedrus's contradiction is not merely the displacement of the female by the male, but something more far-reaching still: if the beloved can die on behalf of the lover, removed from the inspiration of love, then the love of which Phaedrus speaks is not

---

8. Dorter 1969, 217.

the ultimate source of excellence. But this will disrupt the whole intention of making speeches in honor of love. So one is forced to the conclusion that whatever Phaedrus has in mind, love must have a wider meaning and sphere of action than he appears to allow for here. Indeed, further, just as the uncritical use of analogy tells us more about Phaedrus than it does about Eros, so too this apparent contradiction seems to show us the beardless face of Phaedrus himself rather than to reveal any real state of affairs about the relation between humanity and divinity, for Phaedrus is the beloved of Eryximachus and wants his position to appear as praiseworthy. And so his picture of love, in its ornamentation and confusions, is more a picture of himself than of the greatest, oldest, and most authoritative god, prompting us to ask what can be the most authoritative criterion—especially in the context of a mythological rhetoric that looks as though it has little else on which to ground itself than its own unconscious preferences.

Plato manages to present within the same space both the shining romantic idealist and the darker shadow cast unconsciously in his own idealist words. But this is where philosophy always starts: in the streets; in the gymnasium; in the uncritical, but experienced, assessment of Cephalus at the beginning of the *Republic* that justice or right is equated with telling the truth and paying back one's debts. Yes, but to whom and in what context? The unpacking of what is unthought in this assessment is the rest of the *Republic*. Phaedrus's speech has a similar, but even more emphatic, resonance in the *Symposium*. First, of all the eulogists, only two are absolutely devoted to their subject matter, the first and the last, Phaedrus and Socrates. Together they are the driving force for the honoring of love. Second, each point of Phaedrus's speech, unlike those of later speeches, will receive a thorough treatment from Socrates. We shall present Socrates' response in the same sequence as the main points present themselves in Phaedrus's speech:

1. A speech itself should be concerned not with mere appearance and ornament ("in ascribing the highest and most beautiful attributes to a thing whether it has them or not," 198d–e) but with the truth ("in my own way—though not in competition with your speeches" 199a–b). Socrates then asks Phaedrus's permission to go ahead on these terms. Phaedrus is of course the master of ceremonies, but he is also the "father" of the kind of discourse Socrates is rejecting.
2. The venerable old age of the god is "refuted" by the presentation of Love as *daimôn*.
3. Phaedrus's position that the lover or beloved will most of all be afraid to be caught in a shameful act in the presence of the other is implicitly

examined in Socrates' elenchus of Agathon. What will make Agathon more ashamed, Socrates asks, to be caught in inferior discourse before his friends or before the crowd applauding his play? Agathon replies that a few intelligent men are more formidable than many fools. Then Socrates starts to examine the comparative force of shame in the presence of the wise and of the many, when Phaedrus breaks in and demands in all simple-mindedness that no exterior matters should be discussed and that Agathon should proceed with his speech. Phaedrus's blindness is noteworthy, since the hidden questions in his own speech are under philosophical consideration in the light of what is to be Diotima's teaching that poetry is a higher kind of love.

4. Phaedrus's assumption that love inspires the highest excellence is under constant transformation in Socrates-Diotima's speech. As conceived on the birthday of Aphrodite, Eros always aspires to the beautiful and noble. As the lover takes each step in the ascent to the beautiful, he is filled with a new excellence until on the final step he will "beget, not images of excellence . . . but true excellence, because he touches the truth" (212a). Thus, Phaedrus's conception is given new insight. The excellence that Phaedrus thinks infuses the lover is bestowed in its real form only after a long and arduous path of seeking, learning, and begetting.

5. Phaedrus's view that only the influence of love can make the lover die for the beloved receives more extensive treatment from Diotima. Diotima explains that propagation is the love and desire for eternity and this instinct is strong even in animals so that even "the weakest of them are ready to stand up to their strongest in defense of their young and even die for them" (207b). Not only, then, is the lover prepared to die for his beloved and thus show his courage or excellence, but even the weakest of animals, is prepared under the instinct of love to die on behalf of their progeny, on behalf of their need to propagate and nurture in order to have a place in eternity.

6. The fates of Alcestis and Achilles follow from the preceding point. They did not die for Admetus and Patroclus, respectively, Diotima states, but for love of the immortal (208d–e). This development is foreshadowed in Phaedrus's speech by the contradiction we noted earlier, for if the beloved can die on behalf of the lover without the inspiration of love and this is more loved by the gods, then love, at least according to Phaedrus's presentation of it, cannot be the ultimate source of excellence and there must be a more comprehensive source, to include the love for eternal fame.

7. Finally, Phaedrus's claim that love is the source of happiness and excellence for both living and dead gets extended treatment in Diotima's

conception of love as a search for happiness and also presupposes the different sorts of immortality received by those devoted to love, such as Alcestis and Achilles. What is pleasing to the gods is also in question in Diotima's final words: "But in begetting true excellence and nurturing it, it is given to him to become dear to god, and if any other among men is immortal, he is too." (212a)

When viewed in this way, Phaedrus's speech can be seen to be far more significant than its poor press has been willing to allow. When A. E. Taylor says, "The triviality and vulgar morality of the discourse is in keeping with the character of the speaker . . . Phaedrus understands by Eros sexual passion and particular passion of this kind between two persons of the same sex," he is not being entirely fair.[9] Plato depicts Phaedrus's dedication as much as his weakness. True it is that his speech is unreflective, self-contradictory, and even perhaps self-serving. True it also is that it remains at the level of appearances, at a point where distinctions do not yet exist, and where evidence is, at best, traditional repetition or unconscious manipulation of myth for particular effect. Yet at the same time it is Phaedrus's sincere amazement at the power of love that leads Eryximachus to initiate the praise of love, and the figure of Phaedrus and his speech are thus unconsciously a driving force for the movement of this praise and the emerging critical evaluation that is evident in all the subsequent speeches. So the real importance of this speech is Phaedrus's genuine wonder at the effects of love. This gives birth to several crucial ideas, which however trivial or insignificant they might seem in situ, prove to be fruitful for the dialogue as a whole.

Phaedrus himself, however, remains incapable finally of seeing beyond his own desires or even of recognizing those ideas, when we encounter them in the playful dialogue between Agathon and Socrates, as in some measure his own (cf. 194d). Nonetheless, he symbolizes the beginning of the search itself. He is, then, a true apprentice, insofar as devotion to the study of love goes, but he has very little idea how to go about it. His companions at the party, however, are more than ready to remedy his ignorance.

4.2 Pausanias: The Sophistic Sociologue

There were several other speeches after that of Phaedrus that Aristodemus could not remember[10]—a point to which we will return, and then Pausanias speaks. If Phaedrus is a "mythologue," Pausanias is a "sociologue"

---

9. Taylor 1960, 212.
10. 180c1–3.

with all the sophistic passion for comparative culture, for presenting arguments on both sides of a question (*dissoi logoi*) and for balancing equally the portions of a paragraph by repetition of a word or rhyme in the style of Isocrates.[11] At the end of Pausanias's speech in a double play of words quite foreign to the tongue of Apollodorus (or Aristodemus for that matter), Plato himself seems to lampoon the "isological" rhetorical eloquence of Pausanias: "Pausanias paused, for the wise men teach me to say equal phrases in this way" (*Pausaniou de pausamenou, didaskousi gar me isa legein houtôsi hoi sophoi*) [185c5–6]). Here again is a hint of that vanishing signature of the author we encountered earlier. But why should Plato be playful in this way?

In Pausanias's speech, important new distinctions start to emerge: two loves, not one, and two Aphrodites, so that it is important to know which should be praised; the distinction between body and soul; the notion of law (*nomos*); the distinction between inferior types and the better; the idea that the soul is to be loved more than the body, since she is more steadfast and stable (*bebaios, monimos*); and the notion that excellence (*aretê*) involves becoming a better person in several different ways ("with respect to some kind of wisdom [*sophia*] or to any other part of excellence" [184c5–6]), but always subject to philosophical wisdom (cf. 184d1–2, 182c1, 183a1).[12] In fact, Pausanias presents what looks like a version of Socratic philosophy: love of the soul, apparent disdain of the body, and the criterion of philosophical excellence by which to determine what is right or wrong. Indeed, his fundamental thesis, that activities are neither good nor bad in themselves, but that they become "beautiful" if done "beautifully" and "properly" (*kalôs . . . kai orthôs* [180e–181a]), echoes Socrates' own words in the *Gorgias* 88c–d: "[A]ll qualities of soul in and by themselves are neither advantageous nor harmful, but become advantageous or harmful by the presence with them of wisdom [*phronesis*] or folly." Moreover, Socrates' speech in Xenophon's *Symposium* resembles that of Pausanias here. So Pausanias poses a special sort of problem: how do we tell the difference between two conditions or forms of thought that seem to resemble each other—Platonic and sophistic? Certainly, the spell of this speech is amply attested to by its apparent adoption

---

11. Phaedrus's style is also influenced by Isocrates or perhaps by Lysias (cf. the beginning of the *Phaedrus*). On Pausanias, see Robin 1992, xli–xlii. For the term "sociologue" see Menissier 1996; Lacan 1991, 70.

12. *Philosophias* at 183a1 is generally excised, e.g., by Bury, Robin, Dover, obelized by Burnet. Allen proposes to keep it but not on very good grounds: "the speakers are sometimes drunk not only on wine but on their own rhetoric" (123 n. 185). Here a conservative hand should be exercised since *philosophias* is read by all the major manuscripts and is "supported" by 184d1–2 and 182c1 not so much as a function of Pausanias's consistency but rather in terms of the consistent *presentation* of Pausanias's rhetoric.

as Platonic philosophy by later Platonists from Plutarch to Plotinus, by the favorable response of many modern critics, and by the initial reactions of many students in contemporary classes. Furthermore, Pausanias's case is not weak. He appears formidably well informed; he is not endorsing sexual license,[13] but a considered long-term, pragmatic, and even faithful view of relationships; in short, his case is serious and even reasonable in the circumstance, and presumably it would have been accepted as such by most Athenian males of his circle. So is there wisdom or lack of wisdom in Pausanias's own words so that we can test their coinage?

Pausanias's intention is to show that only the higher love for soul is supported by Athenian law and can justify a beloved's yielding his favors to a lover. This higher love for soul is a "Uranian" love, or more spiritual homosexual love, as opposed to the vulgar "Pandemic" and mostly heterosexual love for the body practiced by the "inferior" sort. If an action is beautiful only because of the way it is performed, then only the eros that turns us to loving "beautifully" will be worthy of praise. So the virtuous lover, inspired by the heavenly Aphrodite,

1. loves boys rather than women;
2. loves boys who show signs of more intelligence (according to Pausanias, this is to be measured by the emerging down on their chins {181d2–3});
3. loves soul rather than body (how, Pausanias does not specify, but the general criterion seems to be that if the boy is ugly, then the lover must love his soul; cf. 182d8);
4. has a love that must stand the test of time; and
5. has a love that must be a sharing of his whole life with his beloved.

This is the unwritten *law* that good men establish for themselves in their deeds (Pausanias shifts unconsciously from "beautiful" or "noble" to "good" at 181b7, 181e4). Pausanias then goes on to compare law and custom elsewhere in Greece and among the barbarians. He rejects the uncritical approval of the gratification of lovers as owing to "laziness of soul" and the uncritical rejection of it, together with philosophy and love of exercise, owing to vice, tyranny, and the cowardice of the ruled. Yet the law and custom in Athens seem to be ambivalent: on the one hand, the law favors the lover's doing shameful things in the name of love (slavish acts like sleeping on doorsteps, for instance), which if done for money or to obtain office would be condemned; on the other hand, society tries to

---

13. As Hamilton suggests (1951, 15). See, e.g., 181a ff.14. *Euthyphro* 10d.

prevent this gratification in practice. So Pausanias draws the conclusion that Athenian law is more discriminating in that it wants to test which sort of love, Uranian or Pandemic, is in question. For the authentic love, the unwritten laws of lover and beloved should be combined in order to observe all of Pausanias's conditions for authentic love listed above:

> "For when lover and beloved come together in the same place, each with a law, the one serving justly in doing any service at all for a beloved who has granted him favor; the other serving justly, on the other hand, in doing any service at all for one who makes him wise and good, the one able to contribute intelligence and the rest of excellence, the other needing to acquire them for his education and the rest of wisdom: only then, when these loves combine in the same place, does it turn out that it is beautiful for a beloved to grant favor to the lover, but elsewhere not at all." (184d–e)

So the "laws" of pederasty and philosophy must be combined, according to Pausanias. The sexual desire of an older, wiser, male lover should be gratified by his younger, male beloved only in exchange for wisdom, that is, a vertical (instead of the previous horizontal) exchange of opposites!

There is an earnestness and yet also a rhetorical playfulness running strongly through the preceding passage and the close of the speech. The idea that for the sake of education, one should be prepared "justly to do any service whatever" is repeated at 184d5–6 and 7 and then summed up at e4. To his credit, Pausanias is concerned to treat the problem of deception directly and to solve it through a certain "sensitivity" to context. Even if one is deceived in such love, there is no shame (e5). The reason is not clear at first. Pausanias states the general principle that in all other cases, whether one is deceived or not, it "brings shame" (e6) and then goes on, we expect, to illustrate this principle. If one grants favors to a lover because one supposes him wealthy, and then finds out he is not, this is no less shameful, Pausanias argues. Instead of an illustration, we get an applied development of the theme as Pausanias's thought runs on. Why is it shameful? Because such a man seems to reveal "his own face" (*to ge hautou*), in that he is prepared to do "any service at all" for money's sake (185a3–5), and this is definitely not a good thing (*kalon*). So there is a gap between the explicit criterion of justice, that is, wisdom, but without content, and the implicit criterion of injustice, that is, getting caught, or showing the wrong side of one's character too readily in public.

But Pausanias himself goes on to eliminate the gap in his rhetorically playful closing words. By the same argument, he says, even if someone grants favors to a lover in the anticipation of becoming better, and is deceived in this, the deceit is fair because "he too in his turn has shown his own character" (*to kath'auton*), in that he would be eager "to do everything for everyone" (*pan an panti*) to become better. So it is the right thing "in every way to grant every favor [*pan pantôs ge kalon*] for the sake of excellence" (185b1–5). The explicit criterion of justice, in other words, wisdom, comes to look somewhat like the implicit criterion of injustice: appearance. There is a right way and a wrong way to *show* one's own character, and the right way of showing is in the direction of excellence. This is not a simple black-and-white "presentation": on the one hand, the effective criterion of both correct and incorrect behavior looks like "appearance" or the proper showing of one's real intentions; on the other hand, even if "excellence" is empty of content, Pausanias still insists on "wisdom and the rest of excellence"; and this tends to pose the sort of dilemma to be found in the *Euthyphro:* is the "holy" holy because the gods love it or do the gods love it because it is the "holy"?[14] Which comes first: appearance/approval or excellence? One might suppose, on the principle of charity of interpretation, that Pausanias seriously means the latter: excellence. In fact, we should suppose this. But unfortunately, among other things, there is the insistent drum beating right through this section that becomes a playful tattoo in the closing lines (*dikaiôs hotioun an hypourgôn* [184d5–6, 7, e4; 185a3–5]; *pan an panti . . . pan pantôs* [185b3–4]), namely, the view that one should be prepared to do *anything* for such excellence. This view might withstand brief or dull-witted acquaintance; and it is surely also a basic force, often unacknowledged, in passionate intelligent love: people frequently are prepared to do *anything* for a beloved. But at the same time it can hardly be squared with any ordinary notion of morality, which is one of the reasons passionate love can have such unfortunate consequences.

Pausanias's speech, then, is surely one of the most powerful and yet most chilling examples of deconstructive drama ever presented, insofar as Plato, with no more than a murmur of additional comment ("the wise teach me to say equal phrases in this way" [185c4–5]) paints a picture of the sincerest sophistic rhetoric, apparently so close in thought and terminology to his own philosophy, which argues in the finest persuasive and pragmatic terms, but with mutually inconsistent theses and false statements, that it is *always right* for the student to grant his favors to the teacher (Pausanias) because the teacher knows best what is good for the student's authentic well-being (excellence of soul). And Pausanias accomplishes this *without ever being aware,* not simply that his argument is flawed, but that he could

---

14. *Euthyphro* 10d.

be effectively proposing mere sexual abandonment for what are apparently for him the highest moral reasons, but reasons that also cannot effectively be distinguished from pure selfishness.

Activities are neither good nor bad in themselves, Pausanias maintains (as does Socrates in the *Gorgias,* as we noted earlier). But one may think of significant counterexamples: killing, defrauding, robbing, raping. Everything, Pausanias maintains, depends on the way actions are performed; in other words, the means justify the ends. Yet for lover and beloved the end also justifies the means (anything is honorable if one does it to be improved spiritually). Again, laws are everywhere different, Pausanias holds, which would seem to deny any standard of goodness or beauty. Yet all laws are not equally good, he also maintains, which would suggest a standard outside of law.[15] And if the laws of lover and beloved are no more than a test (184a), an opportunity to test each other's worth, then they can apply their own laws; the universality of any regulatory notion of law or goodness is lost, so that the good becomes the law of selfishness, a self-contradictory notion insofar as the good is determined only by the individual's desire to excel in the context of socially acceptable values.[16]

So Pausanias's speech, in its powerful appearance of sophisticated self-awareness but innocent lack of self-conscious examination, is a chilling example of what *could be* absolute immorality disguised as the highest virtue, or again, of the apparently sincere innocence of the sexual predator who is always acting only for the good of the other, but who unfortunately cannot even be taken to task for any of his actions, because he is blithely unaware of the abysses hidden in them. But this is to imply a moral judgment that Plato never introduces, for in the *Symposium* Pausanias is another equally relevant view of reality: the powerful, even altruistic, but perhaps also self-serving, scholar and teacher who is genuinely, and therefore frighteningly, innocent of the deconstructive abysses in his own pronouncements. Pausanias unwittingly discloses much more about himself than about the heavenly qualities of the Love he praises.

A small detail may help to corroborate this reading. Pausanias distinguishes, as we have seen, between a homosexual Uranian Aphrodite and a heterosexual Pandemic Aphrodite. This distinction is not supported by our knowledge of actual contemporary practices. The title Urania was a mark of the oriental goddess and associated with cult prostitution. Pandemus, by contrast, "goddess of the whole people," "represents the highest political idea to which Aphrodite attained, notably at Athens, but also at Erythrae,

---

15. Dorter 1969, 218.
16. Cf. Dorter 1969, 217–19.

Thebes, Cos, and Megalopolis."[17] Might Plato have intended the reader to question the authenticity of Pausanias's distinction so as, also, to bring into question without any further comment Pausanias's very cleverness and his ability to transform details to adapt them to his own purpose, since casual disregard of reality, as of logic, betokens either a clever lack of intelligence or a typically serious, educated mind of the day, or again, at worst, ruthless, manipulative bloody-mindedness?

Among all these questions, Pausanias's speech does focus on the relationship between soul and body, and it is because of this that Pausanias's view looks so Platonic. Clearly, Pausanias introduces a binary opposition between soul and body that is too simplistic and constrained to account for the proper nature of eros in the human being. If body is to be despised, then there is something hypocritical in Pausanias's insistence that the beloved should physically satisfy the lover if the latter is moved by the highest virtues. Implicitly, therefore, Pausanias's speech intimates that simple sublimation and gratification of the sort he proposes (that is, the rejection of mere bodily passion and the gratification of bodily passion in the correct spiritual alignment) will be little more than self-deception. The needs of the body, no matter how mean or lowly, cannot be opposed or diverted. They must be acknowledged and understood.

So both Phaedrus and Pausanias unwittingly disclose more about themselves than they do about love. While Phaedrus relies on myth for his evidence, which he nonetheless uses to serve his own notions, and while he holds to the world of appearance, which is not without its own natural nobility, Pausanias distinguishes the soul, and its world of law, custom, and excellence, from the body and brute passion; but in the absence of any genuine criterion of goodness he fails, ever so naturally, to be aware of the pitfalls, in his own pragmatic argument, that could easily lead to selfish, sexual manipulation and control, ostensibly for the highest moral reasons.

4.3 Hiccups and Eryximachus, the Homogenic Doctor-Scientist

The episode of Aristophanes' hiccups that leads to Eryximachus's taking Aristophanes' place in the order of speeches is delightfully comic (Eryximachus means "hiccup fighter"). However, it not only draws attention to the fact that there are no lost speeches between Pausanias and Agathon and suggests that between these speeches there must be an ordering or organ-

---

17. *Oxford Classical Dictionary,* 2d ed., s.v. "Aphrodite."

izing principle;[18] it also reintroduces so casually one of the dialogue's most important themes: it introduces *disorder* into the proceedings. There is an ambiguity in the placement—Aristophanes' disorder should perhaps be earlier in the evolutionary scale of things than Eryximachus's precise passion for order and harmony. However, Eryximachus's universalist pretensions seem to prevent him from realizing that disorder and opposition can also be creative and that they are in fact fundamental erotic forces (as we shall see, forces dramatically enacted in Alcibiades' Dionysiac entry and his eulogy to a Dionysiac Socrates).

Eryximachus purports to speak with authority about the multiplicity of the sciences, yet everywhere he introduces the unity and forced harmony of his own preferences. Still, he extends and builds on the distinctions between two kinds of love used in Pausanias's speech, and he even introduces a noteworthy development into the discourse by proposing in effect a scientific vision of the universe and extending the scope of eros to "all beings," including animals and plants (a significant foreshadowing of Diotima's speech; 186a) and even "the communion between gods and humankind" (188b–c), but he nevertheless makes this universe principally in the likeness of the professional viewpoint of the doctor, Eryximachus. He even informs his audience proudly of this at the outset, and it is *natural* for him to be proud as a member of the guild of physicians (an Asclepiad): "I think I have seen from medicine, our art, how great and wonderful the god is and how he extends to everything both human and divine. I shall start from medicine in my speech so that we too may give honor to the art" (186a–b). In what follows he proceeds to apply his conclusions about medicine, constantly within the framework of an absolute division between the good and bad Loves—as in Pausanias's speech (186b–c; 187d–e), to all the sciences (*epistêmai* [186c6, 187c5, 188b5; cf. 186e1, 188d1; 176c7]): gymnastics, agriculture, music ("music, like medicine, puts agreement into . . . things" [187c]), astronomy, and divination (has to do with "nothing other than protection and care of Eros"). And he does this at the expense of Heraclitus, whom he, quite naturally perhaps, given his orderly character, seems to misunderstand (cf. 187a). This is not to suggest that the interpretation of Heraclitus's notoriously difficult fragments is either a simple matter or an issue that can be conclusively determined in the case of any fragment or set of fragments.[19] Nonetheless, Eryximachus's pedantic criticism of Heraclitus conceals a skillfully contrived joke: the orderly temperament of Eryximachus sees no need for any

---

18. Cf. Isenberg 1940, 60; Ferrari 1992, 250.
19. Compare, for example, Guthrie 1:1962, 403–92; Hussey 1972; Duckworth 1972, 22–59; Barnes 1982, 65–81.

disorderly complexity of the opposition that is apparently so necessary to the temperament of a Heraclitus.

Let us look briefly at his treatment of Heraclitus, for it illuminates the overall context of the speech. Eryximachus's capacity simultaneously for the illogical and the pedantic imposes itself on us from the beginning. In his account of medical art, he states initially that the medical expert as a master in "repletion and evacuation" (186c7–8) must instruct the medical practitioner to satisfy the healthy or good loves of the body and disregard sickly or bad ones,[20] as set out in Pausanias's argument about the case of the two Aphrodites (186c–d). Yet immediately after this, he concludes that the practitioner must be able "to make of the most hostile elements in the body friends and lovers of one another" (186d5–6). The apparent incompatibility between the two statements Eryximachus is plainly unaware of; nor in the string of examples of opposites he then produces does he consider whether the healthy and the sick are opposites in the same sense as the cold and the hot, the bitter and the sweet, the dry and the moist, and so on. Eryximachus plainly wants *his* single theory to cover all cases, to be comprehensive without any troubling instances that will not quite fit.

This is more obvious still in his attitude to music (which occupies a full Stephanus page of his speech: 187a–e).[21] Ironically, Eryximachus chooses musical notes, fast and slow etc., to illustrate his thesis that in order to produce harmony, the opposites must change their nature: "it is completely illogical to say that a harmony is at variance or made up from things still at variance" (187a)—as Heraclitus is cited as saying (187a5–7; D-K B 51). Eryximachus is not embarrassed in the least that musical notes in melody do not change their nature in the way in which contrary elements in the body will have to change theirs if healing is to occur. He is only aware of one kind of opposition: orderly scientific blending (cf. 188a5: *krasis . . . sôphrôn*). The dynamic tension of forces in opposition does not enter into his worldview because it is too violent, too disorderly. Dorter rightly observes that at 188d1–6 Eryximachus incidentally mentions four of the five "Socratic virtues": knowledge (*epistêmê*), piety, temperance, and justice; the fifth virtue, courage, is entirely left out. "Courage is one of Eryximachus's

---

20. Dorter 1969, 219: "Goodness and badness are, accordingly, understood as health and unhealthiness" (186b8–c4).

21. Rowe 1998, 147, notes that "the treatment of music actually takes up more space than the treatment of medicine," but the speech is still "framed" by medicine. This treatment of music, as Rowe suggests (150 to 186d2), may mean that "he is speaking with his eyes on Aristophanes, in whose place he is speaking." Yet it also surely suits (even a parody of) his "Pythagorean" profession that music should still be at its "core" (perhaps despite Eryximachus)!

'omissions'" (188e1).²² He is equally oblivious, it would seem, to the vertical opposition of repletion and evacuation of wisdom so casually mentioned by Socrates upon his arrival at the dinner party. His comprehensive scientific view is homeostatic, blind to any human transcendence or to any disorderly force from outside the desired equilibrium or indeed to anything really erotic. So when he says at 187c4–5 that music is "in the dimension of harmony and rhythm a science of erotica," one is surely justified in wondering what place "erotic things" have in this construction.

Perhaps Heraclitus meant, Eryximachus supposes, that attunement or harmony has come to be from "the high and the low that were formerly at variance, but that were then later brought into agreement by the art of music" (187a9–b2). With all the danger removed, Heraclitus becomes a fanciful, idealistic matchmaker uniting formerly disagreeable but now peacefully harmonized elements! At the same time, Eryximachus's recognition that there is a kind of connection running between all the sciences and exemplified particularly in the connection between music and medicine is a natural expression of his "Pythagorean" profession as well as a distant reflection (even a parody) of the importance that is, in some measure, accorded to the principles of music in the kinship of all the sciences (for example, in *Republic* 6.530d–531d).

Eryximachus himself, however, is almost entirely unaware of what he is doing and, like some ancient inferior Hegelian, is happy to conclude that medicine, gymnastics, agriculture, music, and communication theory are all busy introducing mutual love and unanimity. Over the course of the speech, love becomes not so much a guiding principle or deity as an effect that different sciences and arts produce (cf. 187c4–5, above), at which point Eryximachus, as if noticing that he has moved rather far from his original Hippocratic-Pausanian notion of two kinds of love, introduces the Uranian muse and Pandemic Polyhymnia (187e).²³ The former inspires good and orderly behavior, while the latter always creates debauchery, so abhorred by our doctor. He therefore eliminates any need for further harmonization between the two, thus dismissing so much of human experience and abandoning his own principle of including everything in perfect harmony.

Finally, Eryximachus professes his theory that is applicable to the natural processes (for example, the seasons). Higher love introduces temperate

---

22. Dorter 1969, 219. Perhaps, we might suggest, Eryximachus's world has such natural confidence that it does not need courage or really understand the need that other people have for courage.

23. Rowe (1998, 10) is almost certainly right when he argues that Eryximachus in introducing these two Muses is already looking at the two speakers who will come after him: Agathon for the "heavenly" Muse and Aristophanes for the "vulgar." Eryximachus's remarks, in fact, serve as an indirect, ironic foreground to the speeches of the two poets, as we shall see.

harmony between heat and cold, which when so blended become bearers of ripe fertility, whereas from lower, disorderly love arise frosts, sickness, and disturbances (188a–b). The similarity between Empedocles and this view has often been indicated, but the cosmic role of Love and Strife in Empedocles appears nowhere here, for Eryximachus refuses to regard them as opposites: there are healthy and sick states of love, the latter subordinated to the former more as higher and lower elements of the same nature than as genuine opposites. Indeed, Eryximachus does not mention Strife; and the lower love is "accompanied by outrage" (*ho meta tês hybrôs erôs* {188a7–8}), so presumably something of the disruptive quality (*hybristês*) of Socrates would have to be excluded from Eryximachus's wholly abstract, tidy, harmonized universe that contrasts powerfully with the passion for all forms of learning in Diotima-Socrates' ladder of ascent, especially since it manages to escape the abstraction of the single point of view (cf. 210d).[24]

To be fair to Eryximachus, his speech introduces new, important elements into the discussion: the extension of love's influence from the restricted homosexual sphere to all natural beings and to the intercourse between gods and men. This effectively brings a new vertical dimension into play, even if this is somewhat belied by the thrust toward bland homogeneity in Eryximachus's arguments. At the same time, there is the implicit emergence of a different standard of measurement than *epistêmê* or even eros. This development is implicit because Eryximachus, characteristically, as we now realize, juxtaposes two incompatible statements in his rather remarkable conclusion. First, he tells us that the art of divination has been appointed to oversee (*episkopein*) these loves and to heal them! In fact, the art of divination is "a craftsman of friendship between gods and men by knowing which love matters among men tend toward respect for the gods and piety" (188c6–d2). This first statement suggests a standard above eros and even above the science of divination as an *epistêmê* that is somehow able to judge the natural alignment and validity of piety. Whatever this standard is, it may or may not be subject to the approval of the gods. This much is unclear. But next Eryximachus says something very different: "So much and great is the power, or rather all power taken altogether that all eros [*ho hapas erôs*] has, but it is the eros perfected in good things with temperance and justice, both among us and among gods, that has the greatest power and provides all happiness to us and enables us to associate with one another and be friends, even with those who are stronger than us, gods" (188d4–e1).

---

24. On the implicit importance of this notion (together with *Republic* 9 on tyrannic *erôs*), see section 4.6 and Chapter 5 (on *Symp.* 205d2–3).

Let us pass over the apparent distinction between "all eros" and "the eros perfected in good things," and the natural puzzle that the second has more power than the first, which has "all power." How Eryximachean! But according to the second statement, there is a standard higher than both human and divine knowing that is the source of all happiness and friendship, divine and human. This is eros—in contradiction to what Eryximachus has just said. This is no small claim to be made in any context, but of course to readers of the *Euthyphro,* among other dialogues, it looks very Platonic too. How consistent it is, so to speak, that a transcendent dimension should implicitly emerge from two inconsistent statements in a speech full of inconsistencies and apparently dedicated in some unconsciously muddled fashion to the production of a bland homogeneous universe in which opposites as such do not even clash.

Eryximachus is so much the doctor that he sees the whole universe as ample ground for his profession. Most of us do this, of course, and from Plato's time to our own, it may well be argued, the situation has not improved—the explosion of research in modern times tends to mean that no one can genuinely hope to synthesize even a few branches of disparate sciences or perhaps even to keep abreast of accelerating developments in one field alone. So why should Eryximachus's case be "incorrect," if indeed it is? The answer points to the very character of Eryximachus, in whose face we can, so to speak, very easily recognize our own: his personal preoccupations naturally dictate his philosophical conclusions. He does not like debauchery, and the baser kind of love becomes for him a principle of disorder. But what if opposites bring development and growth? Eryximachus is not interested in this. He is quite comfortable as he is—sober, professional, well meaning, and pedantic. He cannot see that clash and opposition might be creative; his ideal is temperance, or tepidity, in which violent opposites lose their messy character by being blended. Most of all, Eryximachus can never allow disorder and debauchery to exist as necessary, even independent forces, not even when he speaks of a supposedly passionate, overwhelming Eros. So he protects his sober nature and, in his pomposity, even supposes that he has said virtually everything there is on the subject, so that Aristophanes can fill in the gaps (188e1–3). Naturally, he uses the medical verb *anaplêrôsai* (to fill up), and in the *Symposium* the reader is reminded of that hubristic Socrates (175e8) who wishes wisdom were the sort of commodity one could be filled with (*plêrôsêsesthai*) by mere proximity (175e3).

Strangely enough, Aristophanes *will* fill in the gaps, even by the force of his creative person. The strong and healthy but disorderly principle of hiccups and sneezes, together with disrespect and comedy (and ironically these are only things to be "left out" in the ordered proceeding of things for Eryximachus), will assume the upper hand, by their very presence, reconstructing the necessity of opposites and preparing us for the double nature of Diotima's Eros.

4.4 Aristophanes: The Poet as Educator

The deceptive simplicity of Plato's middle dialogues creates, as we have observed, a major problem for the reader: the infernal dyad of reading too much and too little in them. Among these uncertainties, Aristophanes' hiccups are, perhaps, the most well known example. As A. E. Taylor long ago observed: "The tone of this part of the dialogue is wholly playful and ... it would be a mistake to regard it as anything more than a delightful specimen of 'pantagruelism.' The numerous persons ... unhappily without anything of the pantagruelist in their own composition will continue, no doubt, to look for hidden meanings in this section of the *Symposium* as they looked for them in Rabelais, and with much the same kind of success."[25] However, those persons, "unhappily without anything of the pantagruelist" in their composition make for a rather large list starting from ancient times with the figure of Olympiodorus.[26]

This interest in the hiccups is not difficult to understand, for the presence of Aristophanes in the *Symposium* attracts the reader's imagination for many reasons. Here is the author of the *Clouds,* a man partially responsible—on Socrates' own account (*Apol.* 18c–d, 19c–d; cf. *Phaedo* 64b, 70b–c)—for the accusations which led to his death. So we expect to see some tension or rivalry between Socrates and Aristophanes. But Plato frustrates this expectation. Banter there is, but no tension or rivalry. Instead, Aristophanes' brilliant portrayal of the needy condition of human love or of what he himself calls "human nature and what has happened to it" (*tên anthrôpinên physin kai ta pathêmata autês* {189d5–6}) is so successful that at times in the history of interpretation, from the Renaissance to Freud and Jung, it has come to be synonymous with "Platonic love." In the sixteenth and seventeenth centuries Platonic love typically bore two faces, one the love of the heavenly ideal, the other the love between the separated halves of the androgyne. These two versions coexisted peacefully, though they are in fact mutually exclusive, insofar as each professes to identify a very different destination for human longing. So one cannot help wondering why, quite apart from any "playful pantagruelism," Plato offers no (overt) criticism of Aristophanes and why he writes

---

25. Taylor 1960, 216.
26. Bury 1932, xxiii.

a speech so powerful that it threatens to eclipse that of Socrates-Diotima for all audiences to come.

Let us briefly survey a range of assessments. For Guthrie, Aristophanes' speech is a "wild extravaganza . . . a skit on the erudition of the others, especially Eryximachus."[27] For Bury, "the great bulk of the discourse is . . . a caricature of the physiological opinions held and taught by the medical profession of the day."[28] Certainly, in the context of the earlier speeches, Aristophanes introduces something new. So for Taylor, "[t]here is real tenderness in Aristophanes' description of the love-lorn condition of the creature looking for its lost half, and a real appreciation of unselfish devotion to the comrade who is one's second self. Aristophanes shows more real feeling than any of the speakers who have been heard so far."[29] For Findlay, the speech "is in many ways merely comic, but it is also true to the phenomenology of sex."[30] According to Gould, the myth "must draw some of its vividness and power from the fact that it touches something we earnestly believe to be true."[31] Is it not curious that we should feel compelled to characterize as "true" a speech that is plainly *the* most fictional thus far? And yet perhaps we do feel compelled in some sense to make such an assessment.

Robin goes even somewhat beyond this, pointing to Plato's remarkable "impartiality" toward Aristophanes and finding in the experience of the lovers in search of each other the emergence "of a single soul in two people."[32] Allen goes so far as to emphasize that Aristophanes catches "the very nerve of Romantic Love."[33] But Dover comes closest to the view that this speech is the real achievement of the *Symposium:*

> Aristophanes, unlike all the other speakers . . . recognises that when you fall in love you see in another individual a special and peculiar "complement" to yourself; for you, union with that individual is an end, most certainly not a means, not a step towards some "higher" and more abstract plane, and very often you continue to love and desire that person even when much more powerful sensory or intellectual stimuli impinge upon you from

---

27. Guthrie 1975, 383–84.
28. Bury 1932, xxvi.
29. Taylor 1960, 219.
30. Findlay 1974, 197.
31. Gould 1963, 33. See also, more generally, Freud's use of Aristophanes' speech as the effective conclusion of or true criterion for understanding his radical revision of his instinct or drive theory (i.e., love and life as opposed to aggression and death) in his pivotal work *Beyond the Pleasure Principle* (Freud 1989, chap. 6, 69–71).
32. Robin 1992, lxiii.
33. Allen 1992, 24.

> alternative sources. Having composed for Aristophanes the only speech ... which strikes a modern reader as founded on observable realities, Plato later makes Diotima reject and condemn its central theme. (205d–e; cf. 212e)[34]

Now, we are not going to argue that Aristophanes' speech has been entirely misread. Instead, we shall argue that *too little* has been made of it. But prior to our examination of it, we should observe that Aristophanes teases Eryximachus and that his speech, while drawing a powerful picture of love, also contains a parody of current medical doctrines and allusions to the evolutionary theories of Empedocles (cf. 189e), as well as tongue-in-cheek references to "healing" the ancient wounds. Aristophanes' reply to Eryximachus, who sets himself up to become the "guardian" of the comedian's speech and even to stop him from being too comic, is a masterful shot: "I am not afraid that I should say what is funny [*geloia*] but rather what is ridiculous [*katagelasta*]" (189a–b); this reply can be construed to mean that "Aristophanes regards as *katagelasta* theories such as those of Eryximachus and his fellow-Asclepiads."[35]

4.4.1 Aristophanes' Speech and Socrates' Criticism of Mimetic Art in the *Republic*

But there is a good deal more to the speech than this, for Plato has woven several puzzles so artfully right onto its surface that they have gone entirely unnoticed. Whatever models from Hippocrates and Empedocles Plato might have used, he actually fashioned this speech primarily with his own thought in mind and while cognizant particularly of its shadow object, the mimetic art of the poets, because the major image of Aristophanes' speech *embodies* the kernel of Socrates' criticism of mimetic art in the *Republic,* and in this speech, again, Plato effectively signs his "name"—in his own inimitable, but indelible, way—against Aristophanes' conception of reality. But this is only one side of a much more complex picture, for at the same time as he portrays the extreme limitations of Aristophanes' thought, he contrives to present its remarkable power, a power that far outstrips the capacity of the individual sciences and points even through its limitations to the philosophical "muse" of dialectic. In the *Apology* we catch only indirect glimpses of Anytus, Meletus, and others. Here in the *Symposium,* we see vividly what Socrates was really up against in the brilliance of a much loved

---

34. Dover 1980, 113.
35. Bury 1932, xxxiii.

speaker (*Aristo-phanes,* literally "best-speaker"), in the unconscious limitations of ordinary speech and apparent political innocence, and ultimately in the indifference toward consequences and truth, which may make all the difference to whether one lives or dies. And all this in a brilliant comi-tragic tour de force!

Let us start with the casual banter between Eryximachus and Aristophanes before the speech begins, because this foregrounds several important notions. First, Aristophanes obliquely introduces one of the major questions of the dialogue, which is that order cannot be the abstract or bland regimen of an Eryximachus, for it requires and even desires the disruptive: "So I wonder if the orderly element of the body does not desire the sorts of noises and tickles a sneeze is" (189a3–5). Second, we are casually informed by Aristophanes himself that he speaks as a *comic poet*: he is not afraid to say something funny, "for this would be an advantage and home territory" for his muse (189b6–7). We are reminded that he continues to follow this comic muse later, as Dover has shown,[36] when Aristophanes gives his highest praise to male lovers for their courage and statesmanlike qualities, evidently in tongue-in-cheek fashion, for in the *Clouds* the political success of homosexuals is described in rather uncomplimentary terms and is the "knock-out blow of the Unjust Argument" (*Clouds* 1089–92).[37]

But, third, there is something more than just the comic muse involved, because of two details that call Aristophanes' task into question. Eryximachus, very much in character, tells Aristophanes: "Pay attention and speak as if you'll be called to account for it" (189b–c). The phrase "to give an account" (*didonai logon*) is used by Plato in regard to expounding the steps of a rational hypothesis or giving an explanation in dialectical conversation, on why one holds a particular view,[38] but it was also familiar to the Athenians because of its connection with the financial account that every magistrate had to render at the end of his year of office.[39] At any rate, Eryximachus's casual remark foregrounds the idea of *logos* or consistent rational practice and indirectly poses the question of whether Aristophanes will give a proper "account," that is, a consistently rational summation in and of his speech.

A second detail, too often overlooked but of crucial importance, radically extends Aristophanes' role: at the end of his introduction, Aristophanes says, "So I will try to describe to you his power, and you will be teachers [*didaskalikoi*] of others" (189d3–5). This is striking. Aristophanes attempts

36. Dover 1966, 45.
37. Cf. Guthrie 1975, 384.
38. Cf. *Protagoras* 336b9–c 1; *Republic* 531e4–5; 533b–c; 534b.
39. Dover 1980, 112. See also Lacan 1991, 157.

not to entertain or to amuse, but to give a *teaching*. So if Aristophanes' speech is to be in any sense *paideia* (cf. also 189d6–7: you must first *learn* [*mathein*] human nature and so on), then the role of poetry—dramatic and epic (rather than merely comic)—in education clearly forms an implicit backdrop to the speech. This, indeed, is a carefully balanced gesture. If Socrates, in the *Republic*, finds that poets cannot be trusted in matters of education, then Aristophanes' assumption of the role of teacher, dispersing knowledge, should be regarded as at least potentially significant. Furthermore, this sense that Aristophanes speaks for all poets is reinforced in the fairy tale beginning ("Once upon a time")—that is, Aristophanes' narrative is an etiological myth that casts him as a representative of the whole class of poetic mythmakers, whose role in education was so forcefully criticized by Socrates in the *Republic*. Indeed, the tale that follows has something in common not only with comedy but also with typical intellectual motifs in the fifth century, pre-Socratic and sophistic, as well as elements in tragedy (e.g., Aeschylus *Prometheus* 436 ff.; Moschion frag. 6), epic (Hesiod *Theog.* 570 ff.; *WD* 54 ff.), and fable (Aesop; cf. Callimachus frag. 192.15 ff.; cf. Plato *Phaedo* 60c).[40] Plato utters no direct word of comment; he simply shows that Aristophanes aims to train teachers, and this allows the details of the banter in situ to situate and pose of themselves the central question of the relation between poetry and responsible education.

With this in mind, let us give a brief overview of the speech. For Aristophanes, human beings have not perceived the power of love hitherto; otherwise they would have remedied this lack of proper piety. Love is the most philanthropic god, an ally and a doctor for the most pressing of all human ills, that is, for our fragmented nature. Original human nature was spherical and one of three different kinds (male, female, androgynous), according to whether each participated in sun, earth, or moon. This accounts for contemporary forms of sexual practice, namely, male homosexual, lesbian, and heterosexual. So strong and proud were these original spheres that they undertook to battle the gods, who were at a loss about what to do, since they did not want to lose their worship, but were unable to tolerate such outrageous behavior. After a lot of thought, Zeus finally came up with a plan to cut these monstrous spheres in half, as though slicing apples or eggs down the middle, thereby weakening them, but multiplying the worshipping population. Apollo (god of the navel stone) turned their heads and half necks around to the cut so that they could see it and thus be reminded to be more orderly, and he tied the skin together at the navel. The pathetic

---

40. See Dover 1980, ad loc. For a simultaneously male-female Eros-Phanes in Orphism and other parallels, see Rowe 1998, 154 at 189e3. Brisson is surprisingly reticent (1998, 40 n. 1, 47 n. 1).

sight of the halves separated from one another also prompted Zeus to rearrange their sexual organs in such a way that intercourse could take place between them and they could beget children or attain release. Love, then, is an inborn desire to find our other half and to unify our divided nature, a desire graphically manifested in sexual intercourse; yet the delight that lovers take in each other goes beyond the somewhat pathetic desire for sexual union, for the soul wants something else it cannot articulate, but only hints at: unity and wholeness instead of duality and fragmentation. Since we have been split apart by the god because of our former injustice, as the Arcadians were dispersed by the Spartans, we should take care that we do not get further split down the middle and go around hopping on one leg and in profile sawn in half through the nose. We should worship the gods and thereby be healed and restored to our ancient nature.

Aristophanes' speech is a comic fairy tale with much psychological plausibility to commend it. For the first time in the early speeches we are recalled to the reality of human longing (*pothoun* [191a6]), desire for kinship, wholeness, and intercourse (192b5–6, 192c1 ff., 192e1–9, 192e–193a) and the desperate need of human seeking (191d6–7). Love is an imperative need for the other as an end in itself, as Dover indicates, but this is still too simple. Aristophanes brings sexual intercourse into the foreground, but physical reintegration is pathetic beside the deeper longing of the soul: "No one would think this to be for the sake of sexual intercourse, that it is for the sake of this that the one so eagerly delights in being with the other; no, it's something else the soul of each clearly wishes for that it can't put into words, but divines what it wishes, and hints at it in riddles" (192c5–d1). This something that is yearned for, it turns out, is to be fused together bodily in life as in death, so that the deeper longing of the soul is for complete physical unity: "to become one from two" (192e9). But is this the only sort of unity the human being desires? Aristophanes hints at the importance of the *psyche* in sexual desire and in other forms of longing, but restricts that role to bodily coagulation as he depicts Hephaestus offering the pathetic lovers the true unity they desire.

On the one hand, then, Aristophanes goes far beyond the other speakers in capturing not only the fragmentation and genuine diversity of human experience, but also the longing for unity and wholeness at the root of desire. Without physical need, Eros remains abstract, universalized (as in the speeches of Pausanias and Eryximachus). On the other hand, he cannot articulate the spiritual significance of the longing for unity manifested, according to his own presentation, in the depths of physical need, because of the restrictive parameters of his own mimetic art, and this is to say that the central images of his speech are illogical to the point of self-contradiction. That is, piety and unity are supposedly the two major criteria of happiness for Aristophanes. If we are pious, we shall be restored to our original nature. But our original nature was violent and impious. Aristophanes implicitly broaches only one other possibility: when the original globular creatures were first divided, they begot and bore children "not in each other, but in the earth, like cicadas" (191c1–2), in other words, without thought, like irrational animals. So the development of intelligence that implicitly comes with need and vulnerability was not present at the beginning; the original globular creatures were violent, impious, and unintelligent, or they were content like animals and unintelligent; thus the conditions before and after division render piety meaningless. To restore such an ancient nature is not to fulfill human desire but to *contradict* it. Aristophanes' speech is therefore a gigantic contradiction, even to its own underlying spirit, a contradiction that may be appropriate to comedy, but perhaps not to art in general, and especially not to art as teaching or *paideia*.

The speech also presents an implicit contradiction even in its use of ordinary language, for "thought" in Aristophanes' presentation is really only the object of ridicule (190c1–3; and 6: "after thinking about it long and hard, Zeus . . ."); yet the ultimate criterion of human happiness at the end of the speech is not simply physical fusion but, on Aristophanes' own terms, some form of *discrimination,* namely, that the human being "hit upon some naturally congenial" beloved (*paidikôn tychein kata noun autôi pephykotôn* {193c7–8}). In ordinary speech, of course, to be *kata noun* is no more than this: "to be congenial," but it necessarily involves taste, preference, discrimination, and therefore some rudimentary notion of intelligence.[41] So it is noteworthy that Aristophanes himself cannot help introducing, in admittedly ordinary, unexamined language, both *psyche* and *nous* as important criteria for human compatibility and integrity and yet in the same breath he gives the upper hand to indiscriminate globular fusion alone.

Let us step back for a moment and compare some of the major items in Aristophanes' depiction and the major aspects of mimetic art that come under heavy criticism in the *Republic.* The speech itself is brilliant, and all the notions we shall itemize are humorous, but the speech is more brilliant still insofar as it bears within it, naturally and in seeming innocence, many other shadows (beyond its central illogicalities), especially the devaluation of both divine and human natures:

---

41. Compare Aristophanes *Knights* 549; *Peace* 940; cf. Sophocles *OC* 1768; Herodotus *History* 1.117, 7.104. See also Benardete 1993, 58–59, in the context of his broader interpretation of Aristophanes' speech and its defects (52–59).

1. In our primal state we were strong enough to fight the gods, but insufficiently intelligent or subtle. Aristophanes compares these original creatures to acrobats, which indicates well-developed bodies, but their behavior reveals no minds worth speaking of.
2. As in Aristophanes' *Birds*, Zeus's interest in humans is limited to the quantity of sacrifices and nonaggressive behavior.
3. The gods, themselves no intellectual or moral heavyweights, treat us like fruit or household objects.
4. In our present state we remain dumbfounded without any idea of what we really want and the only thing that maintains us in good behavior is the threat that we will end up being sliced in half.

Because Aristophanes' talent is so conspicuous, we may fail to appreciate that his conception of love commits us to a one-sided and illogical view of both divinity and humanity while simultaneously demanding *perfect ethical behavior*. It thus compels us to tacitly admit that existence has its focal point only in the physical and that the spiritual search, upon which ethical behavior is founded (since this requires self-organization, self-responsibility, and therefore *psyche* for Plato) has no immediacy. Was this not Socrates' implicit complaint in the *Apology*, namely, that Aristophanes' *Clouds* imitated everything about him except "a certain kind of wisdom" (20d), namely, his intelligence? Yet the force of Plato's presentation of Aristophanes here is precisely such that his ultimately cynical depiction of love restricts one's focus resolutely to the immediate experience of love, that is, *penia* without *poros*, for there is no way to change the ultimately hopeless nature of human beings and the selfish nature of the gods.

Here we come directly to the question of mimetic art. We leave aside for the moment the question of which is the object of poetry, reality or image, but come instead to another major focus of the arguments found in the *Republic*, so relevant in the context of Aristophanes' speech, namely, the question of what aspect of human nature poetry imitates, the best or the average. In *Republic* 10, Socrates argues explicitly that such poetry imitates for the most part only the inferior, for the intelligent and temperate disposition is not suitable for imitation (604e). Moreover, in *Republic* 10, behind the criticism of imitative poetry lies the phenomenon of the soul being pulled in two opposite directions simultaneously in the face of some misfortune (603c–d), and so Socrates poses the following question: should we clutch the hurt part to ourselves and weep or should we turn the soul as quickly as possible to healing and correcting the injury? In other words, are we to hug the body part and give way to emotion *or* to heal it and use our intelligence? The former tendency, Socrates concludes, "gives many opportunities for all sorts of imitations," while the latter is "neither easy to imitate nor easy to understand when imitated, especially for a nondescript crowd assembled in the theater, for the imitation for them is one of an alien experience" (604c–e). The problem with such imitation, Socrates goes on to argue in the *Republic,* is that it both reflects and addresses the weakest element in human beings and prevents the proper organization of the soul. As a result, the soul cannot tell the difference between things that appear superficially similar but differ greatly. In this, the imitative poet is "a maker of images very far removed from the truth" (605c3–4). But the worst of this situation is that it corrupts even the best people by eroding the ideal of self-restraint in private and collapsing all behavior into an indiscriminate physical release rendered all the more plausible because we gaze in the theater not on our own misfortune but on that of a fellow human being (605c–607d). To avoid the powerful charm of such poetry, we should act, Socrates concludes, like people who have fallen in love (*hoi pote tou erasthentes*) but realize their love is not beneficial: they force themselves *to stay away* from their beloveds (607e5–6) and are careful not to fall again "into the childish and popular love" (*eis ton paidikon te kai ton tôn pollôn erôta* {608a5}). In other words, it can surely not be accidental in this context that the headlong desire of the two material halves to be fused into a single globular being is the comic but *literal embodiment* of the mimetic art that Socrates criticizes in the *Republic.* Instead of hugging the hurt with unrestrained emotion, we should heal it through intelligence, that is, the body has to be *organized* by intelligence. By contrast, indiscriminate globular fusion not only annuls intelligence but also prevents any proper organic bodily articulation (such as Plato insists on in the *Phaedrus* {264c–d}). The reference to the appeal of mimetic art for the masses continues immediately after Aristophanes' speech in Agathon's exchange with Socrates: "Why, Socrates, . . . I hope you don't think me so full of theater so that I just don't know that to an intelligent person a few sensible people are more frightening than many fools" (194b). These words indicate again, from the mouth of the poet himself, the level of criticism to which Aristophanes' speech should be submitted. Meticulously, yet with such apparently innocent charm, Plato introduces all the major elements of Socrates' critique of such art, from which the speech is to be reexamined: Aristophanes declares himself a "teacher"; his speech ingeniously *imitate*s (cf. 190a4: *hôs . . . an tis eikaseien*) *human nature* or what is *most immediate and obvious* in human love affairs (the fact that no lover seems capable of staying away from his beloved); the gods are portrayed as self-seeking political manipulators, their lives prescribed totally by emotional longing; human beings are either ridiculous or tragically pathetic; and, finally, the speech is crowned by the debate between

Socrates and Agathon about *the nature of the audience which the poet addresses* and, thus, *the nature he is bound to imitate, address, and entertain* (193d–194e). At the same time as the precise context of the negative view of art in the *Republic* appears to be dramatized with all seeming innocence, the power and appeal of the very same art are exhibited. Indeed, Aristophanes is the only speaker so far who has addressed love's need and pain. This dynamic representation of the immediacy of love's need is rendered all the more plausible because of its virtual absence in the earlier speeches.

In this context, it is surely not accidental that the *first* occurrence of the word "true" in the narrative of the dinner party itself is Agathon's acknowledgment of what is, through Socrates' mouth, essentially the *Republic*'s account of the proper audience before which one ought to feel ashamed if one does something shameful (194a7–c10).[42] *Alêthê legeis*, of course, means little more than "you're right in what you say" (194c8), but in the context we have outlined of mimetic art and its literal embodiment, there is a careful irony in Agathon's unconscious acknowledgement of the "truth" of Socrates' own views in the *Republic*, views reintroduced in the *Symposium* immediately after Aristophanes' speech in the apparently casual exchange between Socrates and Agathon.[43]

Aristophanes' speech therefore is as close as one can get, without parody, to the paradigm of a poetry that Plato criticizes for its very hold over us, that is, a poetry:

42. A cautious reader would, of course, wish to check other (early and middle) dialogues (or perhaps *all* the dialogues) to determine whether we are justified in taking this detail seriously. We should then, of course, have to analyze by contrast the appearance and use of such important terms as *true, false,* and *clear* and cognates in all the dialogues, a task that would require an independent work (and not just a note) in order to capture the free incidentality of such a detail, to avoid mechanistic comparison, and to integrate our view in the broadest and yet most precise philological perspective possible. An obvious flaw to this approach, however, would lie in its tacit assumption that Plato might employ a similar pattern in cognate dialogues. Each dialogue has to be read upon its own terms, and yet intertextuality is clearly important. For a similar precise use of terms in *Republic* 6–7, see section 8.4, below. It is perhaps also worth noting that the issue of truth is broached in a similar oblique fashion in the *Gorgias*. Callicles "tells the truth" in saying Gorgias can answer any question (447d). And Gorgias himself introduces the question of truth, first innocently in reply to Socrates at 450e (where *alêthê legeis* means no more than *orthôs kai dikaiôs hypolambaneis* [though this is significant enough, one may argue (cf. 451a)]) and then explicitly at 452d–e by his claim that persuasion (and nothing else, not even truth; cf. 452d–453a) is "what is in truth the greatest good and cause of freedom . . . and of rule"! This leads directly to the questions of false and true belief (and *epistêmê*) (454d) and whether one can teach rhetoric without knowing the truth and without some real criterion of truth (459c ff.), ultimately without "living in company with truth (526c–d).

43. In Apollodorus's prologue, the context for understanding this, we might say, has already been subtly prepared. Apollodorus tells his anonymous interlocutor that if he supposes that he (Apollodorus) is unfortunate, what he supposes will be "true" (173d2), but Apollodorus doesn't just suppose the truth; he *knows* it. So in the only other occurrence of the word "true" prior to the conversation between Agathon and Socrates after Aristophanes' speech, the question of "truth" is indirectly and humorously evoked.

1. that purports to educate (cf. *Rep.* 606e ff.);
2. that takes hold of images or only a small part of the object, and that part an image (cf. 600c; 598b–c), or only the more facile and inferior part to imitate (cf. 604e), in the light of Aristophanes' claim to treat human nature and its condition as a whole;
3. that allows the emotions and appetites to rule "when they ought to be ruled" (606e), in light of Aristophanes' desire to make the emotional and physical side the ultimate determinants of human fate;
4. that depicts both mortals and immortals as devoid of moral excellence or intelligence.

Plato is therefore not impartial in the way that Robin (1992, in Vicaire) conceives him to be. Yet at the same time, the speech is intended to be attractive and to show the very appeal that the *Republic* considers dangerous because of its sheer power. The speech, indeed, has seduced many generations of readers of the *Symposium*, all the more because it embodies the nature of poetry in its opposition to the philosophical search for truth and shows in one way why philosophy has such a formidable opponent in art. Moreover, precisely because of this emotional appeal, the speech also cannot have its roots in poetry, even though it may well be reflected there. We shall return to this point immediately below. Suffice it to emphasize that Aristophanes' globular creatures, and their fight with Zeus, are the living incarnations of those aspects of mimetic art that are found to be inimical to philosophy in the *Republic*.

So which dialogue was composed first, the *Republic* or the *Symposium?* The evidence is inconclusive, but we *can* say that if Plato could embody in one single fundamental image the kernel of all that he found objectionable in mimetic poetry in the *Republic*, then it is plausible to suppose that in some fashion he must already have worked out in detail the substance of his critique before applying it in the *Symposium*. If this is so, then it is also plausible to regard the *Symposium* as a companion piece to the *Republic*, written either before, during, or even after the composition of the latter work, but more likely during its composition.

4.4.2 The Possibility of Anachronism and Plato's Vanishing Signature

Two auxiliary points. First, when human beings had first been sliced in two, they begat and bore children in the earth, not in each other, but "like cicadas" (*hosper hoi tettiges* [191c]). The cicada is the symbol of Athenian autochthony, and so fragmented human beings in their most destitute state connote "Athenians," which brings the human condition of these pathetic fragmented creatures closer to home for the participants at the drinking party.

Second, to be reduced to this state by the self-seeking political manipulation of the gods is analogous later (at 193a) to the dispersement of the Mantineans by the Spartans (*if* this is referred to by the words *kathaper Arkades hypo Lakedaimonion*) in 385 B.C., an anachronism if the events of the *Symposium* are to be dated before 399 B.C., the date of the death of Socrates.[44] Now, anachronisms in Plato's dialogues may serve many purposes, but this anachronism, if it is such, points not to Aristophanes, and the supposed date of the dinner-party, but to the date of composition (that is, post–385 B.C.) and therefore to the author himself, Plato. But why should Plato draw attention to himself in the middle of this speech with such an open yet vanishing signature? One logical reply might be that he wishes to lend his "signature" of approval to the consideration that there is a direct analogy to be drawn between what he considers the inappropriate use of images (viz., the acceptance of self-seeking manipulative gods as the ultimate truth of life) and real human political consequences. Aristophanes assumes at the outset that both divine and human powers are essentially self-seeking, but Socrates had argued powerfully in the *Republic* that the mutual reinforcement of such religious and political archetypes could only lead to the demoralization of the state and the dissolution of the individual. If this is so, then one may reasonably suppose that against the acceptance, without doubt or self-examination, of this apparent truth of life, Plato leaves his mark.

If this sounds outrageous, one might also argue there are other examples in which Plato points indirectly to himself in a similar fashion. To give but one example: Socrates' final words in the *Phaedo,* "we owe a cock to Asclepius," resist interpretation, but we cannot rule out the following one: Plato was sick the day of Socrates' death (a fact mentioned only in the *Phaedo*) and so Socrates' last thought (among other things) was typically of care for others, for Plato. Therefore, "*we* owe a cock . . . ," not "I." So Socrates hands on that healing care to his successor, Plato, and Plato's vanishing signature appears on the last page of the *Phaedo*.[45] At *Symposium* 193a, the anachronism (there are others of different varieties, as we have seen[46]), if it really is

---

44. On the question generally, see Chapter 1, notes 30–32.

45. We owe this suggestion to conversation with A. H. Armstrong. For other interpretations, see Rowe 1993, 295–96; Dixsaut 1991, 408 n. 382. Nietzsche's famous negative assessment about Socrates and other philosophical figures is simply wrong and too simplistic to be in any way right: "Everywhere . . . their mouths have uttered the same sound, a sound full of . . . weariness with life, full of opposition to life. Even Socrates said as he died: 'To live, that means to be a long time sick; I owe a cock to the saviour Asclepius'" (1956, 93).

46. See Chapter 1 (and notes 30–32).

an anachronism, can be understood in an analogous way. Plato is *not* impartial in the way that Robin (1992, in Vicaire) understands him to be, for he cannot help but sign his name against the injustice of an image which will turn out to have very real political consequences.

4.4.3 Aristophanes' Speech as a Parody of Philosophical Dialectic

However, the problem of interpretation involves more than a parody of mimetic art, for Aristophanes' tale includes not only the embodiment of Socrates' criticism of art so explicitly presented in the *Republic,* but also some fundamental ideas of what are often taken to be Plato's own philosophy. So if Plato "turns the tables" on Aristophanes, he also turns the tables on himself. And this means that having noted the implicit critique of mimetic art, we should also observe three further ideas that have escaped the attention of contemporary critics—recollection, division, and collection. The comic physical division of these original globular creatures and their longing to return to their original whole nature can also be read as a devastating parody and reversal of the division and collection of Platonic dialectic itself.[47] Zeus *cuts* the creatures into two from one (*temnein, diatemnein* [190d2, 6, 8]; *tmêgein* [191a6]; *tomê, tmêsis* [190e3, 4]), Apollo switches their heads and half necks so that they can see the cut, and thus be *reminded,* by their stomach wrinkles and navels, of "the ancient experience" (*mnêmeion . . . tou palaiou pathou* [191a4–5]). So, *"the form [to eidos] of man was whole"* (189e6). Consequently, Love for each other is inborn and is "a *gatherer [synagôgeus]* of their ancient nature, undertaking to make one from two and to heal human nature" (191d1–4). Let us compare this, however briefly, with some of the major marks of dialectic in the *Phaedrus* and *Republic.*

In the *Phaedrus,* recollection of the forms is made possible by means of the basic human ability to form general concepts as unities from many perceptions (249b–c) and also by means of the experience of love (249d ff.).[48] These concepts are "memorials" or means of remembrance (*hypomnêmata*), which enable the person who employs them "rightly," namely, the philosopher, to be "ever initiated into the perfect mysteries and he alone becomes really perfect" (249c6–8). But for most human beings, recollection of true reality by means of physical things is not easy and so whenever they are struck by some likeness, they are amazed "and do not understand their experience [*to pathos*] because they do not clearly per-

---

47. The idea is also suggested (quite prominently) in an important passage in the *Phaedo* (97a2–b3).
48. Only souls that have seen the true reality of the forms can be born as human beings (249b), which is because only human beings have the power to reason (for difficulties in the text, see Guthrie, 427 n. 1).

ceive it [*diaisthanesthai*]" (250a7–b1).⁴⁹ In Aristophanes' speech, the physical "cut" that divides original wholeness is intended by the gods to be "a memory . . . of the ancient experience" so that healing may lead to restoration (as is also the case in the *Phaedrus;* in the *Republic* the soul must turn to healing the wound [604c–d], which she achieves by reorienting herself in relation to the Good); and the noncognitive or precognitive experience of likeness leads to a sort of dim perception that there is more here than the soul, or body, can express (192c–d).

At *Phaedrus* 265c–e Socrates goes on to argue that *even in nonserious speeches and chance utterances* two forms (*eidos*) seem to be operative. The first is "to take a synoptic view and bring widely scattered things under one form so that one may make clear by definition whatever it is one wants to teach at the time," as in the case of love under discussion (265d; and Aristophanes' speech in the *Symposium* would be another instance of such a procedure). This is later called *synagôgê* (266b). Second, "to be able to cut it up again in accordance with forms [*kat' eidê*] at the natural joints, and not try to break up any part like a bad butcher"; just as the body, Socrates continues, is naturally divisible into two, right and left hand, so the discourses on love can be so divided (265e–266a). This is later called *diairesis* (266b). So dialectic is a collection and division of *forms* (277b–c), from many into one and one into many, and the division proceeds until we reach a form which can no longer be divided (*to atmêton* [277b7]).

Conspicuously in Aristophanes' speech, the *form* (*to eidos*) of man was whole (189e5–6),⁵⁰ and love acts as a *synagôgeus* from two into one in order to overcome the original division, whose cut remains a memory of our former condition. The Phaedrus's "cutting up parts like a bad butcher" in this context looks, we may reasonably suggest, like a typically Platonic cryptic reference to Aristophanes in the *Symposium*. One may also suggest that this division and collection reflect in a thoroughly distorted way the division of reality itself into multiplicity and the return to unity, and above all the division of thought and being in the *Republic*. If anything, in terms of the *Republic* (cf. 509d–510e), Aristophanes' division is an *eikastic* parody of dialectic, that is, a parody in some sense implicitly founded on images: *eikasía* is the word Aristophanes uses of his own tale (cf. *eikaseien* [190a]).

Why should Plato go to such trouble to inscribe in this speech a distorted parody of some of the apparent characteristic features of his own philosophy? There are several reasons for this complex composition, although a fuller treatment of the question will have to wait until we have looked at

---

49. Cf. 189a5: men don't seem to me to have *perceived* the power of Love.
50. Cf. *Ta genê* (189d7, 190a8–b1); *eidos* (189e3).

the dialogue as a whole (cf. Chapter 8). First, Plato presents a vivid and realistic impression of a genius whose limitations cannot cloud the brilliant, even visionary power of his art. Aristophanes' indifference to "truth" (as we saw earlier, the word has not yet cropped up in the narrative of the dinner party) bears implicit political consequences. But at the same time, Plato is much more than fair, since he gives Aristophanes a speech that contains real insight into the nature of need, lack, or "poverty" (by contrast with Agathon, who speaks only of Plenty). Aristophanes' lovers, locked in their embrace, only "divine" what they want and obscurely hint at something they cannot express which is clearly "beyond" the simpleminded material identity (*syntêxai kai symphysêsai*) that the stolid Hephaestus offers them, just as in *Republic* 6 every soul "divines" that the good is there (505d11–506a2) and this is the beginning of dialectic. The result of all this is far from the "straw man" that almost any other writer would inevitably have produced. Instead, we have a picture of a lively, brilliant, but cynical mind entirely indifferent to the consequences of its creations, a picture to give tragic color to the shadowy faces at Socrates' trial.

4.4.4 Aristophanes' Speech and Individual Identity

Yet Plato goes somewhat beyond a parody of dialectic to the deeper root of the problem, for in Aristophanes' speech the implicit puzzle about the relation of body and soul is also a puzzle about the nature of human identity itself. Each divided half in isolation is a broken tally[51] of itself, and it has to seek something so akin to itself in order to be itself that, without that something, it is merely pathetic (191d6–7, 192a5–6, b5–6). So each seeks what is "like" (*homoion*) to each, and what is like is plainly most akin (*syggenes, oikeios* [192b5, c1]) and best for each. This appears to be the view of pleasure expressed at the end of *Republic* 9—at least in some more complex sense. If the desires of lesser faculties follow intelligence, then these pleasures actually express their nature: they are "their own [*oikeia*], if that which is best for each may be said to be fully its own [*eiper to beltiston hekastô touto kai oikeiotaton*]" (586e1–2). So true identity, it would appear, on Aristophanes' terms should in some sense be integrative of soul and body and simultaneously intersubjective: they desire "to become in the same" (192d6–7), and Hephaestus will fuse and weld them "into the same" (*eis to auto* [192e1–2]).[52]

---

51. Cf. 193a7; 191d4 (*symbolon*); on which, see Dover 1980, ad loc.; Brisson 1998, 200 n. 242.
52. The "theme" has already been subtly introduced in Pausanias's speech: *eis to auto* (184d3–4); *eis tauton* (184e3).

But what is *to auto*, this "same"? Mere bodily unity? This is clearly what Aristophanes intends, but the notion of identity he finally proposes is something a little more profound than material or corporeal identity. Full human identity appears to involve both a horizontal and a vertical relation, and one which is grounded first and foremost in the divine-human relation: "for by becoming friends and reconciled to the god [*tô theôi*] we shall discover and meet with our own beloved, which few people do nowadays" (193b3–6).[53]

> 53. This sounds not unlike Socrates, in the *Alcibiades* I, for the theory of self-knowledge developed in that dialogue is more or less exactly what Aristophanes unconsciously here proposes. The authenticity of the *Alcibiades* I has been disputed. That the *Alcibiades* I was written by Plato himself seems to have been accepted by everyone until Schleiermacher (1973, 328–36), in the nineteenth century, who supposed that it was too "insignificant and poor" to be by Plato. For both sides of the issue, see Heidel 1976; Friedländer 1923; 1958; 1964, 348–49; 1969; Thesleff 1982, 214–17; Annas 1985, 111–38. As Annas rightly argues, none of the specific objections (against use of language, supposed anachronisms, etc.) nor the more weighty objections, (1) that the style and characterization are too weak (but surely Plato is permitted to have off days?), and (2) that the ideas in it cannot be ascribed consistently to Plato (surely not true) are conclusive. By contrast, the testimony of the ancient tradition seems strong. Aristotle does not cite it by name, but may well show knowledge of it (Annas 1985, 112 n. 5, 117 n. 23). Cicero cites its major themes (*Tusc. Disp.* 1.52, 5.70). Albinus made it the opening dialogue in a course on Plato's philosophy (*Eisagoge*). Plotinus echoes the work (*Enneads* 1.1.3.3, 4.4.43.20–21, 6.7.5.24). Some of the later Neoplatonists wrote commentaries on it (among them, Iamblichus, Proclus, Olympiodorus). On this, see Annas 1985, 112–15, and for the *Alcibiades* I in the later Platonist and Christian traditions, see Pépin 1971.
> In *Alcibiades* I the question of identity as such is first broached at 129b: "Come then, in what way can the same itself [auto tauto] be found? For thus we may perhaps find what we are ourselves" (*ti pot' esmen autoi*). At 130c, after defining the human being as his soul and apparently satisfying Alcibiades on this point, Socrates finds the definition fair, but limited (*metriôs*), and not strictly accurate (*mê akribôs*) without a clear grasp of *auto to auto* (it itself); for now, he goes on to say, "we have been considering, instead of the same, what each is itself" (130d). Here we appear to have a distinction between some ultimate principle of identity and individual identity, or perhaps, as Proclus sees it, between the intellectual soul and the individual soul considered as a homogeneous whole. Proclus is not altogether right, for he seems, at least in a fragment from the *Alcibiades* commentary of Olympiodorus, to make the *auto tauto* dependent on the priority of the individual itself: "the text says that if we are to ascertain what It-in-Itself is, we must also learn what is Each-in-Itself, since it is not enough simply to ascertain man, but we must know also what the individual itself is." But the sense of the text seems to be different, namely, that having ascertained roughly what the individual is ("in relation to us," as Aristotle might have put it) we still need to see what that individuality depends on, which will be the fundamental question of human identity. What the *auto tauto* appears to be is clarified by the eye analogy, and this is *not* simply the "intellectual soul," conceived as a part or even as one static faculty in the human being. The passage runs as follows:
>> "Then if an eye is to see itself, it must look to an eye, and at the region of the eye in which the excellence of an eye is found to occur; and this, I presume, is sight.—That is so—And if the soul too, my dear Alcibiades, is to know herself, she must surely look at a soul, and especially at that region of it in which occurs the excellence of a soul—wisdom, and to anything else to which this happens to be like—I agree, Socrates—And can we find any part of the soul that we can call more divine than this . . . ?—We cannot—Then this part of her resembles the god, and whoever looks at this, and comes to know all that is divine, will gain thereby the best knowledge of himself." (133b–c)

Aristophanes' speech, therefore, does far more than what has been recognized by both its supporters and its critics, for (1) it presents in its most striking image of fragmented globular natures seeking to be refused into each other the embodiment of the critique of mimetic art presented in the *Republic;* (2) it provides a comic reflection of Platonic dialectic, yet manages to avoid pure buffoonery (which Aristophanes himself wants expressly to avoid—189b5–8) and even catches, according to most contemporary critics, something "true" (though not strictly so) about the human condition though, as we have argued, this is only so to the degree that it manages to go beyond its initial image or hypothesis and the gigantic comic contradiction which it represents; and (3) it implicitly poses the problem of the meaning of human identity (which will become an issue later in the dialogue.[54]

In a very real way, Aristophanes' speech goes beyond that of Eryximachus. Whereas Eryximachus remains locked into the somewhat bland, regimented notion of order that he takes to be the indispensable hypothesis of his own science—medicine—and of all the sciences, Aristophanes unconsciously indicates a landscape and a principle outside the limitations of his own literary muse and, in his presentation of the driving force in human need, unwittingly uncovers the search for a wholeness that can transform the fragmented human condition. Many readers take Plato to task for putting rational science before art. And art certainly comes a long way down the list in the *Phaedrus.* But here in the *Symposium,* Plato presents a contrapuntal view to the predominant critique of art in the *Republic:* Aristophanes' defective art nonetheless bespeaks, far more than Eryximachus's science, the *Republic*'s philosophical muse of dialectic (*Rep.* 499c–d).

The *auto tauto* is clearly *intersubjective,* a place (*topos*) of shared souledness as in the most intimate *conversation;* it is that most divine wisdom in the soul in which divine and human friendship in some sense intersect (133b–c), by which "someone" (*tis;* i.e., not simply the soul herself) knows "all the divine" and "himself . . . above all," and furthermore, by which one knows each thing as a result (133c–135c), not only oneself, but even determinate practical knowledge that "our belongings are our belongings" (133d). All of which results in temperance and just action both for the city (134a ff.) and for oneself (134d ff.).

What is striking, then, at the end of Aristophanes' speech is that Plato implicitly puts a much deeper view about the nature of self-knowledge and identity casually (and in a garbled form) into the mouth of Aristophanes. Aristophanes' formulation is at variance with the contradiction which constitutes the rest of his speech. Nonetheless, even the sharp contrast serves to provoke the question how apparent *material* identity (being fused "into the same") can be related to what is here implicitly something even beyond *formal* identity, in so far as human intersubjective reintegration *presupposes* a new intimacy between god and man.

54. See sections 5.11.2 and 7.6, below.

4.4.5 Aristophanes' Hiccups Revisited

Take Aristophanes' hiccups, for instance, and the exchange of turns with Eryximachus. "Science," in Eryximachus's inimitable form, might, on most readings, be superior to "art," especially comedy. And so the doctor, hiccup fighter, expects Aristophanes merely to fill in some of the points he may have overlooked! But clearly, in the brilliant artist even disorder and lack of balance in the form of hiccups, not unlike the disruptive quality of Socrates' *hybris,* can go a lot further than pompous prescriptive science, though it stands somewhat further down the cognitive pecking line. So for Plato, in the *Symposium,* we suggest, philosophy has more in common with desirous art than it does with blinkered, comprehensive science.[55]

Why, then, should Plato have given such a powerful speech through the persona of Aristophanes? Perhaps it is a tribute to the comic genius itself; or a nostalgic farewell to Plato's own love of poetry; or a reminder of his own artistic nature as a poet, reflected even in Aristophanes and, through the dialectical prism of the *Symposium,* reflecting the philosophical poet at work in fashioning a new sort of dramatic philosophical art; or all of these. Whatever the case, in concealing the shades of his own face in the artistic power of the enemy, that is, Aristophanes, the author of the *Clouds,* Plato gave dramatic verisimilitude to his criticism of mimetic art and yet his most authentic tribute to the power of the art of Homer, Hesiod, and the dramatists. At the same time, by the very power of such art, he pointed to the other implicit pole of the dialectic, bastardized but still dimly reflected in that art, that is, to the unrevealed and ignored face of the philosophical muse herself.

4.5 Agathon: The Sophistic Theologue as the "Climax" of an Unselfcritical Tradition

Since it is the victory of Agathon that is being celebrated at the party, his speech, it might seem, should bear a special significance. However playful and ironic Socrates might be, Plato represents him as anxious about speaking after Agathon, and so the anticipation of Agathon's speech is heightened. To Eryximachus Socrates replies that the confidence Eryximachus feels is a result of his having already acquitted himself well: "but if you were where I now am, or rather perhaps where I will be once Agathon also speaks well, you'd be very afraid and exactly in the same position as I am now" (194a). Yet Agathon gives a speech that rather revealingly breaks the sense

---

55. For a development of this, see section 8.5, below.

of "crescendo" created by the earlier discourses and is also utterly mistaken about the nature of love, if we are to accept the logic of Socrates' criticism in the elenchus with Agathon immediately after Agathon finishes speaking (198c–199b).

Why, then, should this speech appear to be such an unexpected failure and what is the intention behind it? One possible answer might be that Agathon speaks as a tragic poet and so Plato continues his literary critique. This assumption might be corroborated by the fact that Aristophanes and Agathon, comic and tragic poets, speak in turn and by the further consideration that these are the only two at the end of the dialogue who continue the literary argument with Socrates (cf. 223d2–5). However, if Plato intends to show that Agathon's speech represents the tragic muse, then this representation is a failure not only on Agathon's part, but also on Plato's, for we are only too aware that Agathon's speech is far from the heights of tragedy and that it cannot therefore be emblematic of this genre. It would be illogical for Plato, after having created such a successful presentation of the poetic muse in Aristophanes' speech, to have intended Agathon's speech, in so many respects devoid of real content, to symbolize a further, perhaps even higher poetical vision. So what sort of vision is embodied in Agathon's eulogy?

4.5.1 Advance Over the Previous Speakers?

For Agathon, in a contrast with the earlier speeches, Love is the youngest, happiest, fairest, and best god: delicate, soft, supple, youth- and blossom-loving, full of the cardinal virtues, source of all creativity in the arts and nature, and cause of kingship, grace, and order. Unlike Aristophanes, who speaks in a lively, forthright way and on behalf of poetry as a genre as well as his own comic muse, Agathon mentions his own art only *en passant* in the course of his speech (196d6) and speaks in a highly stylized sophistic fashion, which is untranslatable at times (cf. espec. 196b7–9; 197d1 ff.), and which with its dense tapestry of balanced, interlacing words and phrases, particularly in the conclusion, is plainly effective for the audience.

At the same time, Agathon's speech—especially for the Greekless reader—may seem utterly removed from contemporary concerns, but it is in one way profoundly contemporary insofar as the usually unexamined proposition "God is love" trips so readily, and usually with far less linguistic talent than Agathon brings to it, off the tongues of so many contemporaries as an all too obvious truth destined to end conversation rather than open it up. Agathon to his credit at least attempts to think through the question for himself and to provide evidence for what he claims in each part of his speech.[56] In addition, he is remarkably open minded and openhanded. Very few people could so readily acknowledge their own stupidity as does Agathon in face of Socrates' subsequent questions: "Very likely I didn't know what I was talking about then, Socrates" (201b9). So what are we to make of *this* speech in relation both to the earlier speeches and to its own content?

Bury comments on the similarity between Phaedrus and Agathon in that both indulge in "mythological references."[57] But while myth is fact for Phaedrus, Agathon can disagree with the poets, if they go against common sense: Eros is young and associates with the young because "the ancient account is sound that 'like ever draws near to like'" (195b); however, Agathon does not agree with the out-of-date view that Eros is "older than Cronos and Japetus." Hesiod and Parmenides, "if they were telling the truth" were speaking about things that came about by Necessity, not by Love, for the excessive violence of that age is incompatible with Love's rule (195b–c). So Agathon, by contrast with Phaedrus, is prepared to interpret myth critically, if necessary, and to offer an implicitly philosophical reason for doing so.

Agathon, much more than Phaedrus, is also aware of myth as skill, or *techne,* in composition, for he praises Homer most of all as a master of description: "There is need of a poet to show a god's delicacy" (195d1–2). So Phaedrus's mythological position is assimilated in Agathon ("I agree with Phaedrus in many other things" [195b]) but has undergone some development into a critical, more rational and objective attitude. The great poets are still quoted, but as masters of expression rather than of content. At the same time, the improvement in analytical methodology does not safeguard the method in question, but rather exposes its shortcomings even further. Instead of a theological advancement, we encounter a striking demonstration of the potential anomalies of this attitude: superficial analogy and selective representation of evidence. To argue for Eros's beauty he indicates its delicacy, and to illustrate its delicacy he cites a passage from Homer about Atê, goddess of delusion: "hers are delicate feet; for not on the ground does she step, but she it is who walks upon the heads of men" (195d4–5; *Iliad* 19.92–93). But not only are the lines inappropriate, since they are part of Agamemnon's speech to Achilles condemning Atê; Agathon also leaves out the final words of the last sentence: Atê walks upon the heads of men, "harming men" (*Iliad* 19.94). As Dover remarks elsewhere, this sort of selective quotation is no more than normal Greek practice. However, this very practice, when employed in theological examination, leaves the narrative without any foundation and

---

56. E.g., 195a9–b1; 195d1; 195e1, e3–7; 196a2–4, 5–6; 196b7–9, etc.
57. Bury 1932, xxx.

many of its conclusions implicitly absurd. The introduction of the Atê analogy, for example, indicates that if Atê is like Eros, then Eros will often be the cause not only of good, but also of ugly things, which rather refutes Agathon's whole point.[58] In other words, Agathon's selective interpretation of myth is beginning to run away from him as he tries to fit it to his rhetorical procrustean purposes (heads "are after all not very soft anyway" [195d7]). Its real basis becomes Agathon's own preference for softness, delicate movement, beauty, youth.

Yet almost in the same breath, he seems to stumble on a much more profound thought, namely, that the delicacy of Love is revealed by his "moist nature," his capacity to dwell in the characters and souls of gods and men (195c1). Why should this be more profound? Because it seems to suggest that there is a qualitatively different principle at work here than the rough material principle conceived in the epics—if not a spiritual principle, then at least a rarer principle, such as Anaximenes' air, for instance. Indeed, the memorable description in the *Phaedrus* of the stream of beauty entering into the lover's eyes and moistening the wings of the soul, previously hard and dried up, has something in common with Agathon's thought here (cf. *Phaedrus* 251a–252c). However, Agathon proves himself incapable of developing any such point, for naturally his purpose is much simpler. Eros could not possibly dwell indiscriminately in every soul. Why not? Because he is rather like Agathon and Agathon would not like it. And so we are left with the rather comic picture of a very delicate mental image that causes cataclysmic benefits with its feet:

> But we ourselves shall also use the same evidence to show that Love is delicate but in the softest things he walks and dwells: he does not walk on earth, or on heads, which are not very soft anyway, but in the softest things he walks and dwells. For he establishes his dwelling in the characters and souls of gods and men, though not in every soul in turn, but from any soul he meets that is hard in character he withdraws, and in the soft soul there he dwells. So always touching with his feet and in every way the softest of softest things, he is necessarily most delicate. (195d7–e9)

While Agathon's speech, then, represents an advance over Phaedrus's mythological picture and demonstrates a new critical attitude to myth and to the technical language of proof and argument, it also barely conceals the

---

58. Cf. Dorter 1969, 225. See also Lacan 1991, 135ff.: "Agathon, le tragédien parle de l'amour d'une façon qui donne le sentiment qu'il bouffonne dans un discours macaronique"; and Benardete 1994, 58–65.

arbitrary playfulness of an imagination grounded in little else than ornamentation and its own preference. At the same time, there *is* talent here, but a talent in which charm, superficiality and potential profundity seem linked to one another like changing moods.

How, then, does Agathon differ from his lover, Pausanias, especially if both are indebted to the sophistic style of Gorgias? As in the preceding comparison with Phaedrus, there is certainly a continuity between the two speakers. Pausanias tells us at the beginning of his eulogy that he will first point out the Eros that should be praised and then worthily praise the god (180d). Agathon insists that there is "one right way for any praise on any subject, namely, to describe in speech the nature of the subject of the speech, and the nature of that of which he is the cause" (195a). So Agathon appears to be educated in similar rhetorical strategies, and yet he is more intellectually discriminating than Pausanias, especially since this procedure is subsequently approved by Socrates (199c). But Socrates is undoubtedly ironic ("I like that beginning very much"), and if good sense and Socrates' prominent judgment in the *Phaedrus* can be of any help to us, it is *least* likely that there is "one right way for any praise on any subject," for this is the mark of a purely abstract, technical education that remains outside the question of the truth of what it praises and the various audiences to be addressed in various ways.[59]

We can hardly look for the precision of mathematics in ethics, Aristotle will later insist (*Nicomachean Ethics* 1.3). And Socrates, in the *Phaedrus,* argues that if the function of speech is to lead souls by persuasion, then he who is to be an orator must know the different forms of soul, the various kinds of speech, and what sorts of people are influenced by which, and then be able to recognize the time, place, and character for address in real life (*Phaedrus* 271c–272b). There is, then, a very strong contrast between Agathon's single-mindedness of methodology and Socrates' awareness of the necessary flexibility and subtlety of the modes of persuasion. In sum, then, if Pausanias is a sophistic pedant, Agathon with a kind of artless innocence wants to mould discourse into a comforting abstract unity so that he can feel that all the angles have been covered (cf. "concerning the beauty of the god, then, this is sufficient, and many things still remain . . ." [196b]; "as far as possible, we must try to leave nothing out" [196d]).

Furthermore, Agathon's speech exhibits a much broader scope of reference than that of Pausanias and it also employs a more open and different kind of argumentative method. If Pausanias manipulates his illustrations and conclusions into apparent agreement and conceals paralogisms underneath a

---

59. Cf. *Phaedrus* 270c–272b.

well-structured speech, Agathon—while also prone to analogous failings—at least insists on emphasizing how he arrives at his conclusions as in some measure a direct consequence of what he takes to be the facts. So while Pausanias, however unconsciously, appears to reshape the truth (insofar as he may even be said to be aware of such a notion) to fit his own situation and his own ends, Agathon is plainly openhanded in a way that Pausanias is not, for Agathon has nothing to gain by the version of reality he presents and indeed seeks to present the truth in the way he sees it without any secret manipulation, being guided rather by his own attachment to the charm of an image, as in the case of Atê's delicate feet. Agathon's unconscious confidence in the comforting abstract unity of his abstractions, which permits him to view the whole genre of encomium in terms of a simple universal practice, is more a mark of his sophistic naïveté, and his privileged, cultivated upbringing, than of anything intentionally self-serving or sinister. Besides, he is at the peak of his profession and has been so long assured of his beauty, fortune, and success that such confidence is second nature (cf. 194b–c).

Agathon's position in relation to that of Eryximachus is less immediately apparent, but he effectively follows Eryximachus's lead in depicting Love as containing no inner contrariety. Eryximachus's disorderly Love he rejects in favor of Necessity ("the ancient things about the gods related by Hesiod and Parmenides . . . took place through Necessity and not through Eros" [195a]). So Eryximachus, while arguing for contrariety, in reality holds that inner conflict is not necessary for healthy human existence, but Agathon goes one step further and removes any doubleness from Love's character. Agathon's world, on this account, seems even more one sided than that of Eryximachus: a young, delicate, beautiful Love governs that world, attracting like to like. Moreover, the principle of like to like, so fundamental to Eryximachus's speech (cf. 187b13–14), is the principle behind the apparently more skillful argumentation leading to almost all of Agathon's major conclusions. For example, Love is young because he associates with youth and flees old age (195b–c); Love's gentleness is easy to prove because he dwells in gentle souls, but flees hard souls (195e); Love's gracefulness is proof of his well-proportioned and moist form, since lack of grace and Love are always at war with each other (196a); or again, beauty of color indicates Love's dwelling among flowers, for Love only takes up residence where there is a healthy bloom of body and soul.

Furthermore, both Eryximachus and Agathon list the "cardinal" virtues: Eryximachus includes knowledge, piety, temperance, and justice (188d1–6), but omits courage; Agathon treats the *aretê* of Eros in a separate portion of his speech and lists justice, temperance, courage, and wisdom as the immediate "goods" of Eros and initially omits piety. While he openly follows Eryximachus, in stating that he intends to show how love inspires poetry and all other crafts ("in order that I too in turn may honor our art, as Eryximachus honored his" [196d7–e1]), his notion of erotic *sophia* goes somewhat beyond Eryximachus's notion of *epistêmê*, for he extends the notion of poetry to include every form of inspired creative power, from poetry itself to the procreation and birth of all animals and the craftsmanship of the arts, archery, medicine, and prophecy (196e–197c). However, this emphasis on inspired creativity as *poiesis* in an extended sense (197a2) and the observation too that Eros aims at the beautiful (197c), although views that will later be endorsed by Diotima and that may therefore on those terms be regarded as expressing "right opinion" (202a9), remain otherwise undeveloped in Agathon's speech and subject to easy refutation. Why for instance should the wisdom of Eros inspire poetry among nonpoets, when such poetry is frequently bad and unwise?[60] And it is simply untrue either to say that "everyone willingly serves Eros in everything" when Eros most often seems to compel people to do what they least wish, or to see justice exclusively in terms of mutual consent, by arguing that "what a willing person agrees to with a willing person is just (196b–c), when justice is not a function *solely* of mutual consent. So both insight and lack of deeper foundation seem almost to occupy the same place, and yet Agathon is aware only of his own successful and charming rhetoric. Eryximachus's one-sided position that Love is of opposites, but of opposites transformed into harmony, and that Love has a comprehensive cosmic function, is further beautified and transformed by Agathon into the view that Love is made up of all the best things in the world. But like Agathon himself, it knows no *need*. Agathon is liberal in his account but, in the context of Aristophanes' speech, too liberal.

This, in turn, highlights Agathon's contrast with Aristophanes. If Aristophanes' literary muse is that of *Need,* Agathon's muse is very much that of *Plenty.* Both figures are contrasted as poets, comic and tragic, even if the emphasis is in each case different, as we observed earlier. But Agathon's muse is something less and yet more than tragic poetry, for in the peroration to his speech (197d1–e5), which reveals the sustained application of material units familiar in Greek lyric poetry, from ionic trimeter (197d3) to trochaic tetrameter (197d4), the combination of poetry and sophistic structure (Gorgianic) is striking.[61] So what we see in Agathon, by contrast with Aristophanes, is a kind of sophistic poetry turned to the questions of theology.

60. Dorter 1969, 225.
61. Cf. Dover 1980, 124.

4.5.2 Agathon as Theologue Without Need

So in many ways, some of the key positions of the earlier speeches are commented on and transformed in Agathon's speech, but with the personal and covertly emphasized weaknesses of the individual speakers omitted. Agathon himself has none of these "weaknesses." A child of Plenty, as it were, he touches and beautifies all the previous viewpoints with what he considers to be the most excellent philosophy, but what is really a kind of coincidence of opposites: clever appearance and empty abundance.

But there is something more than this. Once again there is a striking similarity between the characteristics of the speaker and his depiction of Eros (198d2). In Agathon's case, this relationship is not quite the same as that of Pausanias and Eryximachus, who pedantically make the world in their own image and likeness. Nor again does Agathon's manner of depicting Eros remind one directly of Aristophanes, whose drinking and eating habits, sarcasm, and a certain heaviness of nature are felt even in the images of his speech and certainly in the cynical, although profoundly poignant, picture he draws of humanity. If Aristophanes is a poet who is not "purified" by his craft, or even because of it, Agathon, who possesses beauty of manner, personal attractiveness, and kindness, puts into Love's character everything that is considered "good" by the tradition to which he belongs and of which he has had the personal fortune to be a darling. His speech, then, should be the crowning glory of a tradition manifested in the previous speeches, and Agathon does conclude—effectively, to judge by the audience's reaction—in the elegant, but artificial, language he has been taught. And yet the speech that should not have failed does somehow miss the mark. Part of the problem appears to be as follows: as objective as Agathon tries to be, the irony is that his Eros looks very much like himself—soft, delicate, effeminate, perfectly groomed, beautiful, giving, not really very thoughtful, and, of course, a darling of fortune. Just as the earlier speeches had been mostly self-praising, so Agathon, unknowingly, by summarizing the tradition and reinforcing all its conventional values, glorifies those values and, in doing so, glorifies, above all, himself.

In a nutshell, then, Agathon's speech provides a sophistic picture of theological superabundance (cf. "as far as possible one must leave nothing out"! [196d7–8]), an abundance that in ancient, as in modern times, often tends to mask a host of failings and to overlook entirely a good deal of human experience. Plato obliquely indicates the hidden contrast between theology and action with some deft comic touches at the end of the speech. The discourse on Love should, on its author's terms, bring only "peace" and "quiet" (197c5–6; cf. 195c6), but this little word from on high, so to speak, incites the crowd to unrestrained applause (*anathorybêsai tous parontas* [198a1–3]), "because he had done such credit to himself and to the god," just as the crowd, in the *Republic,* claps to excess whatever happens to please it (cf. *Rep.* 492b5–c2). Beautiful Agathon at the height of his fame and fortune—this, at any rate, is the way Aristophanes portrays him in the *Thesmophoriazusae* (and his compositions; *Thes.* 45, 48, 130–45, 148–67, 249–58, 191 ff.). A little later Socrates, in anticipation of his own speech, makes a pun on the names of Gorgias, the Sophist, and Medusa, the Gorgon. The speech, he says, reminded him of Gorgias, and toward the end of it, he started to get frightened that Agathon "would send up the head of Gorgias, formidable in speaking, . . . and turn me to dumb stone" (198c2–6). So Agathon's hyperbolic, sophistic theology, it would seem, has capacity for effects that are utterly at odds with its own apparent self-presentation: it will either incite excessive emotion or make any motion impossible, which at least on the surface of things would seem to imply that it is all emotional appeal, but an appeal that freezes the life out of Love itself.

In other words, Agathon, like many a contemporary street theologian, puts all his considerable talents into revivifying a tradition without rethinking it. He introduces the "correct" method and attempts to employ the "latest" in critical distance, that is, the appearance of objectivity in his method of presentation, but he only exposes the shallowness of his own position. This conclusion is also partly supported by the fact that Socrates later admits to having said the same things as Agathon, many years ago to Diotima. And, in part also, this helps to explain the failure of both Agathon's speech and that of the position of the young Socrates when he first met Diotima: the traditional view of Love they have inherited is like a tower that collapses just as it is completed. It means nothing that everybody believes Love to be a great god and the highest good. In conversation with Socrates, Diotima will refute this in a few sentences: "And what of this notion, I asked, to which everyone agrees that he is a great god? . . . I mean everybody in the world. At this she laughed and said, 'But how, Socrates, can those agree that he is a great god who say that he is no god at all?'" (202c).

But there is still something more than just sophistic poetry at stake in Agathon's speech. Plato loves reversals: Socrates turns the tables on Agathon immediately after his speech, and Alcibiades does the same to Socrates. Agathon's speech, some critics would hold, is an anticlimax after the brilliant heights of Aristophanes; and yet the speech is clearly in some sense a reversal of itself, that is, it is drawn so carefully as to be a sort of coincidence of opposites: empty superabundance, ornamented tradition. Then too, why should Socrates bring in the specter of the Gorgon's head, which, despite its play on the Gorgianic character of the speech, seems equally hyperbolic in the context of Agathon's good-natured but empty perfection?[62] Is this just part of Socrates' ironic banter? And is it possible that Plato intended Agathon's speech to be a climax of a very different sort from the climax he managed to create in Aristophanes' speech and that Agathon's speech, while being totally devoid of inner conflict, is paradoxically meant to be an *anti-climatic coincidence of opposites—superabundance and hollowness?*

4.5.3 The Shadow of the "Good": Agathon's Portrait in the Context of the *Republic*

Despite the apparent illogicality, this is precisely what Plato does, for in Agathon he presents a terrifyingly balanced portrait of stellar giftedness and potentially corruptible ignorance that in its very innocence threatens to strike "dumb" the one who can read its significance, or in other words, a portrait of the gifted youth in *Republic* 6, who despite his natural gifts, endowments, and upbringing will inevitably—except by divine intervention—be corrupted by sophistic education and the adulation of the mob, and thus, worse still, while capable of bringing the greatest good to civilization, is in danger because of his very talent—unlike so-called inferior natures—of bringing instead "the greatest evils upon cities and individuals" (495a–c).

Corruptio optimi pessima. The greater the talent for good, the worse the capacity for evil when corrupted. In the *Symposium* Plato catches Agathon *in motion,* as it were, somewhere in between those two extreme potentialities of his gifted nature. He is wealthy, superior, magnanimous, wise, noble, gracious, young, beautiful, courageous in front of the crowd, with qualities befitting a great man (*megaloprepeia* [cf. 194b2–c7, 198a2, 198d5; also 174c, 175e, 196a–b]): his eros possesses *eumatheia,* readiness for learning; his intelligence is capable of recognizing the truth—*immediately,* in face of Socrates' probing questions, and his openness is without any sense of grudge. Indeed, Agathon is the *first* person within the narrative of the *Symposium* to employ the word "true." Maybe we are not wise, Socrates says at 194c, but "if you met others who are wise, you'd perhaps feel shame before them, if you thought you were perhaps doing something 'shameful.' And Agathon replies, "[Y]ou speak the truth."

Insignificant in itself, this is not insignificant in the context of the dialogue as a whole. To utter the word "true" for the first time is also unconsciously to be able to recognize the force of a good argument. So there is

---

62. Stokes (1986, 114ff.) rightly attempts to think his way inside the *problematic* elenchus of Agathon (which is a pivot of the dialogue as a whole), but in his conclusions he cannot really get beyond this question (450: "Why use a sledgehammer to crush a butterfly?" But see Bernadete 1994, 60–61.

potential self-critical intelligence in Agathon. And more ironically still, there is nothing *agroikos* (of the country, boorish) in him, Socrates tells us in the same conversation (194c).[63] And yet at the same time this natural giftedness, which aspires to everything beautiful, is in the process of being trapped by an empty ornamental education and by its own perfect, easy nature, which does not know how to work out the hard depths of the facile insights it so easily receives, orders, and gilds. As Agathon speaks, whether we recognize this immediately or not, we see both these flickering images together in the gilded host at the height of his success; but also after the speech in Socrates' Gorgianic-Gorgonic pun we hear, as it were, the distant echo of the *Republic*'s multiformed, polykephalic beast (*Rep.* 588e–590b), lionlike and snakelike (cf. 590b), which in no way matches the golden appearance before us but, with the merest hint of something much more sinister, betokens the corruption of such natures in their most devolved forms—that is, for Plato, the democratic nature (as ruled by the mob) and the tyrannical nature. In *Republic* 8–9, tyrants are not made overnight. They live "in the same house" with others and also with the best of human beings, from whom they have, in a sense, emerged little by little over many years. So Plato's poignant portrait of Agathon embodies already in this most "perfect" form, that is, in Agathon himself, the most poignant of all human dilemmas, for it is a dramatization of the tragedy of great natural talent, caught between philosophical potential and the infinite corruptibility of a self that is exposed to facile education, adulation of the crowd, and self-congratulation. All reality casts a shadow, but the shadow of the good is darkest and has the most far-reaching consequences.

Plato's success in painting such a complex picture can perhaps be measured by the fact that no modern commentator has ever realized the force of Agathon's speech and portrait, which seems to indicate that Plato wanted to create a picture simultaneously most open and yet most hidden. But a brief comparison with some crucial passages in the *Republic* will serve less to render explicit what is clearly intended to be a living, ambiguous portrait than to show more poignantly the potential human drama of this gilded youth who is unconsciously suspended between superabundance and corruption.

At the beginning of *Republic* 7, Socrates searches for the philosophical soul. Such a soul, he agrees with Glaucon, must be quick to learn (*eumathês*), just like Agathon's eros, of good memory, in other words, able to retain what it learns, just like Agathon's reception of a tradition (cf. also 200a1–2); such a soul must be neither boorish nor graceless, but measured,

---

63. Cf. *Gorgias* 462e: Socrates fears it may be too boorish (*agroikoteron*) to tell the truth "on behalf of Gorgias."

gracious, just, gentle, capable of recognizing truth (486a–e), and akin to the cardinal virtues, exactly, in fact, like Agathon's eros. To sum up, no one can pursue philosophy properly "unless he by nature has a good memory, is a quick learner, is generous, gracious, and a friend of and akin to truth, justice, courage, and moderation" (*mnêmôn, eumathês, megaloprepês, eucharis, philos te kai syggenês aletheias, dikaiosynês, andreias, sôphrosynês* [487a]). When such people have reached maturity, Glaucon and Socrates agree, the city can be entrusted to them, but the real problem for Socrates, and Glaucon, is that experience seems to point in the opposite direction, since the majority of such people are vicious (490d), and so in examining how such a nature is corrupted Socrates draws the following preliminary conclusion:

> "[T]he philosophic nature as we defined it, provided it receive its proper instruction, will inevitably grow to reach every excellence, but if it is sown and grows in an unsuitable environment, it will develop in quite the opposite way unless some god come to its rescue. Or do you agree with the general opinion that certain young men are corrupted by sophists. . . . Whenever many of them are sitting together in assemblies, in courts, in camps, or in some other public gathering of the crowd, they object very noisily to some of the things said or done, and approve others, in both cases to excess, by shouting and clapping. . . . During such a scene, what heart do you think . . . the young man will have? What private training can hold out against this? (492a–9)[64]

So pessimistic is the picture and so strong the influence and sanctions of "educators and sophists" (492d5–6) that Socrates thinks that no such person will *ever* escape their influence except by divine aid.

The passage is so striking that it is worth citing here, since it betrays some of the pessimism and world-weary sadness that Plato must have felt in the presence of such young men as Agathon or perhaps even in his own presence: "There is not now, has not been in the past, nor ever will be in the future, a man of a character so unusual that he has been educated to virtue in spite of the education he received from the mob . . . if any character is saved and becomes what it should, in the present state of our societies, you would not be wrong to say that it has been saved by a god's intervention" (492e–493a). But Socrates' picture is even more resolutely pessimistic than this. If a youth who is by nature a philosopher, and possesses all the qualities stated above, his family and fellow citizens, as he grows up, will be all

---

64. Translation of the *Republic*, here and below, is from Grube 1974.

over him with requests and flattery, trying to secure for themselves the power they imagine will be his (494a–c). Socrates continues: "What do you think that such a youth will do under these circumstances, especially if he happens to live in a mighty city, is rich, of noble birth, tall, and beautiful? Will he not be filled with an impossible expectation that he will be capable of settling the affairs of both the Greeks and the barbarians? Will he not exalt himself to great heights, be full of self-importance and foolish pride?" (494c–d). This passage has been thought by many, including Plutarch, to describe Alcibiades exactly,[65] and so it does, though in describing the *type*, Plato also captures something of Agathon. In fact, we might well suggest that Alcibiades too, quite apart from his own distinctive role in the *Symposium*, is a continuing picture in motion of Agathon, in that the distant echo of the Gorgon's head becomes a little closer still in the conjunction of superior intellect, direct simplicity and vivacity, and yet obvious self-destructiveness that we see embodied in Alcibiades.

But Agathon with his own idiosyncracies, blinkers, and failings is also a different, powerful example of the *type,* and Socrates' next words in the *Republic* are even more applicable to him than to Alcibiades: "If someone then comes to a man in that condition and gently tells him the truth, that *there is no sense in him, but that he stands in need of it* [*nous ouk enestin autôi, deitai de*], but that it cannot be acquired *unless one works like a slave to attain it,* do you think it will be easy for him to listen in the midst of so many evils?" (494d). This is *exactly* what Socrates will do to Agathon, that is, tell him that there is no sense in him and that he and his Love *are in need of the truth* (cf. 199c–201c)! And Agathon *listens* to him, although perhaps we cannot imagine him being influenced somehow beyond the moment "because of his noble nature and its kinship with discourse," to the point at which he will be "led to philosophy," as Socrates envisages one possibility subsequently in the *Republic* (494d9–e2). Why not? Perhaps because of his character simply, but certainly because we cannot see such a child of Plenty *working like a slave* for anything. Indeed, need or poverty belong not to Agathon's muse; and even his gracious attitude to his own slaves (at 175b) is a strong indication that Agathon wants to trouble himself with service, or any such work, *least* of all. Indeed, in the *Republic*, it is characteristic of tyranny that the mind is enslaved to the passions to the extent that, for the appearance of boundless freedom, people have "slaves as their masters"! (*Rep.* 8.569b8–c4). Agathon's graciousness, then, in this respect, no matter how innocent in the *Symposium,* is decidedly double-edged in the broader context of the *Symposium* and *Republic*.[66]

---

65. See Adam 1965, vol. 2, ad loc., 25.
66. Compare also *Gorgias* 484b.

Next, Socrates takes up the other more likely possibility, that such a youth, overcome by the political intricacies that prevent his turning to philosophy, is undone even by his own good qualities and circumstances:

> "You see then . . . that we were right to say that the characteristics of the philosophic nature were, if the upbringing was bad, themselves somehow the cause of his falling away, as well as the so-called goods: wealth, and all those other advantages. . . . We say then that these are the many ways in which the best nature, rare enough in any case as we pointed out, is destroyed and corrupted with regard to the best of pursuits. It is among these men that we shall find those who bring the greatest evils upon cities and individuals, and also the greatest good, if the current takes them that way." (495a–b)

This notion that the gifted youth's best qualities, if not formed in the right soil, will cast a shadow proportionate to their power is part of the portrait of Agathon in the *Symposium*. His graciousness simultaneously betokens laziness and even the possibility of tyranny; his comprehensive ability to learn is also an ability that has already been corrupted by education and adulation with powerful effects; his superabundance of beauty, success, rhetorical style, and so on are also empty and needy; his capacity for insight remains undeveloped, unexamined; and even his ability to recognize the truth contrasts sharply with his self-satisfaction and his contentment to remain in an empty ornamented tradition if left to his own devices.

So what happens to such a character, according to the *Republic*? It becomes "twisted and altered [*strephesthai te kai alloiousthai*] like a foreign seed which if sown in alien ground is usually overcome and fades way. . . . so the philosophic nature fails to develop its full power, but falls out into a different character [*eis allotrion êthos ekpiptein*]" (497b). In other words, in the context of the overall thought of the *Republic*, if such a nature fails to discover and perform "its own task" (*to heautou*), it loses its kinship with its own best nature and ceases in a sense to belong to itself (that is, to be *oikeios*) and thus something foreign (*allotrios*) enters into it. In the context of books 8–9, this means that the tyrant emerges over several generations from an originally good and brilliant father; but in the tyrant all kinship is destroyed, for the tyrant is a parricide who *hates and flees old age* ("you are saying that the dictator is a parricide and a cruel nurse to old age" [569b–c]), ironically a distant image of one of Love's most striking features, according to Agathon. For the tyrant, as for Agathon, *erôs*—that fundamentally ambiguous force—must flee from old age.

Yet at the same time Agathon clearly understands the importance of kinship and comes close to a more sophisticated view of the "emptying" and "filling" associated with it by contrast with the mechanistic approach Socrates had earlier rejected: Love, Agathon says, "empties us of estrangement but fills us with kinship [*allotriotêtos men kenoi, oikeiotêtos de plêroi*], causing us to come together in all such gatherings as these"(197d1–3). This is by no means a negligible thought in itself; yet for Agathon it is hardly a thought at all, since not only is it not developed, but more fundamentally it appears in the Gorgianic character of his peroration merely as another ornament without any greater weight than any other well-turned phrase. By contrast, in the final arguments of the whole development of thought in *Republic* 2–9 (even if those arguments seem somewhat leaky, as they have done to generations of scholars)—this is a thought that receives some philosophical, analytic development:

> Are not hunger and thirst and the like a sort of emptiness of body—Quite so. And ignorance and lack of sense are an emptiness in the soul?—Of course. So the person who takes his share of food and the one who acquires wisdom would be filled?—Very much so. Which kinds of filling do you think have a greater share of reality, . . . bread, drink, meat . . . or . . . true opinion and knowledge and intelligence . . . ? So the kinds of filling concerned with the care of the body have less share in truth and reality than those concerned with the care of the soul?—Much less. If to be filled with things appropriate to our nature is pleasurable, that which is in fact more filled with real things will make one rejoice more really and more truly in true pleasure, while that which partakes of things less real will be less truly and lastingly filled. . . . Quite inevitable. . . . But . . . those desires of even the profit-loving and honor-loving parts, which follow knowledge . . . and pursue those pleasures which intelligence prescribes, will attain the truest pleasures possible for them, since they are following the truth. These pleasures are their own [*oikeias*], if that which is best for each thing may be said to be fully its own [*eiper to beltiston hekastô, touto kai oikeiotaton*].—Indeed, it is. If the whole soul follows the wisdom-loving part . . . , then each part will be able to fulfill its own task [*ta heautou prattein*]. . . . But when one of the other parts rules in the soul to any extent, it cannot find its own pleasure [*tên heautou hêdonên*] and it compels the other parts to pursue a pleasure that is foreign to them and not true [*allotrian kai mê alêthê hêdonên*].—That is so. (585b–587a)

So the optimistic picture of Love that is painted by Agathon casts a somewhat darker shadow, when compared to the thought of the *Republic,* for the kinship that Agathon so devoutly advocates is only a kinship of youth, which intimates the destruction of any natural sense of kinship based on family or heritage or moral and intellectual organization of the "parts" of the soul or body.

On the surface, this advocacy bespeaks graciousness, openhandedness, freedom, and community; but in the same space looms the shadow of laziness, inverted slavery, arbitrary unity according to one way of doing things, and exclusivity (hatred of "old age").[67] Agathon's speech and portrait, therefore, provide a "climax" of a rather unique sort, for Plato presents on a knife edge, as it were, a coincidence of opposites in motion, namely, a speech that will only be successful if it fails to be entirely successful and if in this failure it still possesses the power to be effective and gracious in its own way.

4.6 Conclusion

So the early speeches reveal *of themselves* a distinctive ordering pattern. For Phaedrus, Love is the oldest god, cause of the willingness of lover or beloved to die on the other's behalf. For Pausanias, Love is double, related to body and soul, but the only worthy love is in the service of excellence. For Eryximachus, Love is also double, but more comprehensive, for Love relates to the major natural forces in the universe and is examined in different ways by different sciences. Aristophanes, by contrast, sees love as the desire for wholeness, unity, and reintegration, caused by the fact that our natures are originally integrated. And Agathon finally sees love as the youngest god, a comprehensive power uniting everything in friendship and the source of different kinds of creativity throughout the universe. Phaedrus, Pausanias, Eryximachus, Aristophanes, and Agathon: orator, professor, medical doctor, comic poet, representative of the power of poetry as a genre, and the sophistic gilded youth—tragic theological poet.

What, then, have we discovered about the order of the speeches? We have established a pattern, and quite a remarkable pattern at that, one that concerns not only the speeches remembered by Aristodemus, but also the

---

67. This is pure appearance, we might argue, and yet appearance which faintly catches the internal rhymes and musical chimes of Socrates' own language about the forms. Compare Agathon: "Love neither does injustice to god or man nor suffers injustice from god or man" (196b) "good order of all gods and men, leader most beautiful and best whom every man must follow chanting beautifully" (197e). (Erôs oute adikei out' adikeitai, oute hypo theou oute theon, oute hyp' anthrôpou oute anthrôpon . . . sympantôn te theôn kai anthrôpôn kosmos, hêgemôn kallistos kai aristos, hou chrê hepesthei panta andra ephymnounta kalôs) with Socrates at *Republic* 500c or *Symposium* 211d ff.

speeches that he forgot. But a major key to this new pattern is this position of Phaedrus, and here we must carefully summarize our findings.

Since, as we know from Eryximachus, Phaedrus believes that the force of Love is unsung, his wonder provides the impulse for all the further speeches. Thus, Phaedrus wants further inquiry or instruction, and he is supported in this by Socrates, but of the speeches that follow that of Phaedrus at the party, there is a pronounced gap, namely, the forgotten speeches. Of these speeches, we know that only the last four before that of Socrates survived. In fact, by drawing attention to the lost speeches, the narrative of the *Symposium* emphasizes the actual sequence of the four speeches.[68] Moreover, the episode of Aristophanes' hiccups, by providing an interplay between the remaining speakers, removes any possible ambiguity about the sequence of the remembered speeches, and in this regard Aristodemus's account is clear: after the forgotten speeches, Pausanias is the first speaker. Upon the completion of his speech, Aristophanes has hiccups. So, instead of Aristophanes, the following speaker is the "hiccup fighter," Eryximachus, and only then Aristophanes and Agathon. Indeed, also, the speeches in their content plainly follow an ascending order, not so much in their relative quality or power, but rather in the expansion of the issues presented in response to Phaedrus's initial sense of wonder.

For Pausanias, Love is double, related to body and soul, and the only worthy love (presumably that of the soul) is in the service (presumably bodily and psychic) of excellence. For Eryximachus, Love is also double but more comprehensive, since Love is the force behind all the multiple impulses of culture, and this ever widening design is clearly present in the good doctor's speech even if Eryximachus himself fails to describe its diversity, and even if he applies his own slightly illogical, medical approach to the healing of all the major natural forces in the universe and in the different sciences. Aristophanes, in his speech, takes the position of teacher, and the content of his teaching, his "mathema," is a single myth, powerful enough to draw an unforgettable picture of Love as the desire for wholeness, unity, and reintegration, a desire caused by the fact that the natures of the lovers were originally united. Finally, Agathon, the poet-theologue, sees love not as need, but as a god whose character he, Agathon, tries to reassemble by applying the latest sophistic methodology of rhetorical inquiry and thereby transcending traditional mythological descriptions of Love. For Agathon draws a portrait of Love as the youngest god, a comprehensive power uniting everything in friendship and the source of different kinds of creativity throughout the universe.

68. On further aspects of the significance of the relationship between the gap and the speeches, see Chapter 6.

This is the order in a nutshell, but, of course, many other themes pervade the speeches. The speakers represent consecutively the worlds of traditional mythological, scholarly, technical, artistic, and theological narrative. Phaedrus, the ardent seeker of the noble, poses the issues that give energy to all the succeeding speeches but presents a world of appearances that are governed in part by mythological authority within which no formal differences yet appear. Pausanias, the sophistic sociologue, already starts to articulate a universe: body, soul, excellence, a universe of comparative anthropology ultimately determined by the strength or weakness of his own sophistic intelligence. Eryximachus, the doctor, tries to see the world as a whole, but only succeeds in making that world, more or less, in the image and likeness of his own profession, medicine. There is much comedy in this and even in Eryximachus's pomposity, but—in Platonic terms—he is plainly restricted by his science's limited hypothesis. In Aristophanes, we catch for the first time a real sense of the power of living poetry that aims to educate its audience; yet the force which makes his speech so attractive and so poignant is precisely its logical absurdity, that is, its wish to return to a supposedly primeval state of *tyrannical,* lawless globular stature, that is, to a state of thinking one can rule both gods and men (cf. *Republic* 9.573c). Yet in the hiccup episode, beside humor and playfulness, Plato plainly intends us to think about the greater importance of desire and even disorder, by contrast to the compact, hygenic, orderly world of Eryximachus. Aristophanes captures the force of need and shows this with all the formidable power of his talent, but he cannot develop it beyond the absurdity of his mythical and poetical paradigm. Plato, as we have earlier, presents simultaneously through this paradigm the very kernel of Socrates' criticism of mimetic art in the *Republic:* the globular structures of Aristophanes' speech, against the background of a mentally challenged and essentially greedy Zeus, are the literal embodiments of the criticism of *Republic* 2, 3, and 10 and an antithesis to Socrates' conclusion that mimetic poets cannot be the educators of the citizens of the *Republic.*[69] At the same time, Aristophanes represents, even in disorder, the ability to go beyond the limitations of a particular science, craft, or hypothesis and, because of the very force of desire, to uncover something quite transcendent of his starting point; and Plato possibly even weaves into his discourse a parody of dialectic: division and collection, absurdly comic, on the one hand, and yet a sort of superdivine, parodic dialectic, on the other. Art, even of the

---

69. For the chronology of the dialogues generally, see Brandwood 1990. On the basis of our examination we cannot deduce which of the dialogues was written first, but the relationship between the *Symposium* and the *Republic* does suggest that the dialogues were written in the same period.

absurd, illogical variety, somehow because of its reaching for Eros, has more power than blinkered science to reach beyond itself. Even such mimetic art catches a dim, but living, spark of the divine.

Finally, in Agathon's speech we have a tour de force of a different kind. It is an attempt at a theology in a new key, fueled by all the most developed patterns of rhetorical inquiry that were available in the cultivated world of Athens of the time. Such a theological undertaking, the articulation of an intuition of a god as yet unrevealed (according to Phaedrus's initial statement to Eryximachus), should be a climax to all the speeches, but instead it strikes an anticlimactic note. Agathon presents a picture of sophistic theological superabundance in which talent and emptiness seem to mirror each other in a coincidence of opposites. By contrast with Aristophanes, Agathon casually not only represents his own art, the tragic muse, but embodies something more: the golden youth of superior natural talent, birth, and ability, who is exposed to a sophistic education and the adulation of the crowd. Although we see only the successful youth before us, nonetheless, in his words, in the reaction of the guests, and in Socrates' comments, we catch a glimpse too of the many-headed beast of tyranny that may be part of his future, if his present course remains uncorrected. Tragic, powerful unforeseen consequences lie hidden in the most innocent gestures of the gifted golden youth. The good casts its shadow. Yet with Agathon the issue of truth as such is first broached, and this youth of ambiguous appearance is still quick to recognize truth, which remains an optimistic, if potentially tragic, sign in such a context. A further consequence to the speeches' order is this: every speaker not only contributes something new and important to the discussion of Love but also unwittingly calls into question his own and the others' contributions. In this sense, each is a *problematic image* of an individual face and also a type, apparently solid and self-complete in itself, but also empty and radically incomplete even in this early part of the drinking party. Illogicalities, contradictions, absences and so on, bespeak a field of hidden oppositions not yet aware of itself.

These are only some of the problems that the early speeches implicitly pose, but they at least indicate that for Plato there are in fact worlds of significance in even the simplest declarative utterance. In this sense, the early speeches represent the diverse fields of ordinary and technical languages, accepted uncritically as absolutes in themselves by their practitioners and by the crowd; but this is also where philosophy starts in a thoroughly critical fashion to call the unexamined into question[70]—that is, in ordinary and not so ordinary language.

---

70. Cf. *Phaedrus* 276e–278e. Dialectic *starts* with such speech.

Diotima-Socrates

Mythical Thought in the Making

5.1 Introduction: The Problem

Of all the speeches in the *Symposium,* that by Socrates is in some respects the most puzzling. First, Socrates proposes to tell "the truth" in his own manner, but immediately presents this truth in the form of a dialogue between himself and Diotima, a woman who appears to be just about as fictional as one can get. Second, we expect something more rigorous from Socrates, as in the elenchus of Agathon (199c–201c); instead we are given a myth arguably concocted for the occasion, in which gods or semidivine characters act in ways of which Socrates himself, in the *Republic,* might disapprove. Third, we have become accustomed in the early speeches to hidden contradictions, equivocations, and so on within the monologue form; yet is the Diotima-Socrates dialogue really more successful?

Dover, for one, thinks Socrates' speech is just as dishonest as the previous speeches: "Throughout this section (204c7–206a13) Plato uses the art of rhetoric more subtly than when he is caricaturing the verbal sophistries of others (e.g., 196c3–d4; *Euthyd.* 276a–b), but no more honestly."[1] Dover's view is extreme; but, we may ask,

---

1. Dover 1980, 145.

even if the illogicalities of the early speeches are more or less avoided, is Socrates' speech any more than the voice of a dogmatic lady simply telling us the "truth" as Socrates wishes us to see it? Finally, we start with the concrete position that love must be "of something"; yet this concreteness seems to have little to do with some of the most important themes in the rest of the speech, for example, the somewhat abstract search for happiness and immortality, and the apparently airy-fairy business of "the beautiful itself," as far removed from concrete fact or desperate need as one could imagine. Equally puzzling in this context is the fact that the character of this "Platonic love" is actually based on a fictional story in which Eros is born of divine Plenty and mortal Poverty and conceived on the birthday of Aphrodite in the garden of Zeus. So the character of love appears to depend on the philosophical and theological interpretations of a myth, and this creates a striking contrast to the well-known emphasis on the limitation of myths in *Republic* 2 and 3. What, then, is the difference between Homer's mythological stories and that of Diotima's narrative?

In other words, what are we to make of this speech that has inspired generations of Platonists, Christians, Arabs, and Jews to reverence, awe, and creativity? Was their awe ill founded? Or did they, like Plato apparently, want to avoid the potentially messy business of loving individuals for their own sake, thus leaving themselves free for the much more romantic flight above the moon to the source of beauty itself, so that instead of the place and facts of ordinary experience they substituted the other-world of Platonism? If so, the consequences are serious, for much of modernism and postmodernism must therefore find this speech virtually unreadable. What was acceptable for Gregory of Nyssa, Plotinus, Augustine, Nicholas of Cusa, and Ficino is probably unthinkable for people of more modest persuasions in the wake of Hume, Schopenhauer, Nietzsche, and Kafka.

The preceding problems are further compounded for the first- or second-time reader by the variety of interpretations of Platonic love that one encounters in modern and ancient critical assessments. For Vlastos, Dover, Nussbaum, Grube, and others, Platonic love flies in the face of ordinary experience, which is that we love individuals for themselves and not for abstract ideals or entities somehow beyond them.[2] Socrates' speech makes such love impersonal, if not incoherent. As Vlastos puts it: "This seems to me the cardinal flaw in Plato's theory. It does not provide for love of whole persons, but only for love of that abstract version of persons which consists of the complex of their best qualities. This is the reason why personal affection ranks so low

---

2. Vlastos 1981, 31; Dover 1980, 113; Grube 1964, 87–119; Nussbaum 1986, 178ff., 1990, 341ff.

in Plato's *scala amoris.*"³ In this context, Platonic love tends to belong to spiritual lovers who coo at each other and who are desperately trying to forget that they have urgent bodily needs or who have no bodily needs, urgent or otherwise. So the ascent to the beautiful also resembles a variant Freudian sublimation as the ego struggles to achieve release, or at least homeostasis or lack of conflict, between the blind instincts of the id and the social dictates of the superego.⁴ Or again, Platonic love is regarded as thinly disguised homosexuality insofar as Diotima argues "for what is essentially a male homosexual foundation for philosophical activity."⁵ To sum up, such love has typically been seen as impersonal, abstract, dishonest, spiritual love, Freudian sublimation, and homosexual.

From the other side of the spectrum a similar view is urged, that is, from the perspective of the Christian debate on *erôs* and *agapê*. Barth, Nygren, and others⁶ have argued that whereas in Christian love "the loving subject gives to the other, the object of love, that which it has," pagan eros is grounded not in self-denial nor in interest in the other, "but in a distinctly uncritical intensification and strengthening of natural self-assertion." Such love needs the other "because of its intrinsic value and in pursuance of an end."⁷ The two loves, Christian and pagan, are mutually incompatible (176), and thus *agapê* and *agapan* entirely supplant *erôs* and *eran* in New Testament usage, so that the Christian reader, according to Barth's interpretation, will not even be "reminded" of pagan love,⁸ which is essentially selfish or self-interested. Behind this interpretation, however, there is a yet deeper charge leveled against Platonism itself, namely, that the whole Platonic project consists precisely in what we might call "the flight of the alone to the alone," to use the oft-quoted words of Plotinus (*Ennead* 6.9.[9].11.51), or to the love of God or the One exclusively, and not in any meaningful sense to the real love of the other. Hannah Arendt, for instance, although sympathetic to Augustine in other ways, levels just this charge against Augustine and Platonism in general.⁹ To sum up, then, Platonic love on this account is selfish, "an uncritical augmentation of natural self-assertion," and certainly not "love of our neighbor." Furthermore, critics, who might not otherwise agree in much, at least agree in this, that Platonic love, as taught by Diotima, is not based

---

3. Vlastos 1981, 31; Dover 1980, 113; Grube 1935, 87–119; Nussbaum 1986 (refs. in Allen 1991).
4. Hamilton 1951, 13, 26; but see Price, in Gill 1990, 247–70.
5. Dover 1980, 137; Hamilton 1951, 12–13.
6. Barth 1962; Nygren 1953; but cf. Rist 1964, 79ff., 213–16.
7. Barth 1962, 173–76.
8. Cf. Allen 1991, 95–96.
9. Arendt 1996, 93–97.

on observable realities[10] or that once the "initiate" to the Greater Mysteries (*Symposium* 210a–212a) progresses from the soul to observances, laws, institutions, and so forth, on the second rung of the ladder of ascent, ordinary experience is left far behind, unconnected with the rest of an abstract ascent to the beautiful.[11]

What, then, are we to make of this variety of interpretation? The simplest answer is that all these views are demonstrably false, either because they ignore what Socrates expressly tells us he is going to do—that is, to define love, in its widest and yet most immediate application, and therefore not focus exclusively on one form of love that may or may not capture the essence of our ordinary experience of love—or because they restrict Platonic love to the apparently abstract doctrine of one speech alone and ignore the fact that Plato gives us two compelling portraits of what it means to love the individual for the individual's sake, first, in Aristophanes' speech and, then, even more powerfully and concretely, in Alcibiades' eulogy. We shall have to examine this further on its own merits.

But this "simplest" answer brings into play a further problem that we must introduce here: why is it that a speech that has helped to form an entire tradition in the Western world should prove so difficult to interpret and so susceptible to diverse interpretation? The great German Plato scholar Wilamowitz even went so far as to suppose that the teaching of Diotima does not represent Plato's own conviction, but is more in the order of a rhetorical exercise, as in the earlier speeches.[12] But while Diotima's teaching is rhetorical and even sophistic, a fact to which Socrates draws attention (208c1), this does not mean that rhetoric cannot be properly philosophical and capable of calling itself into question within the structure of the overall dialogue. For whatever else can be said about the speech, no one can accuse it of departing from or going against Socrates' deepest conviction that the proper function of philosophical reason is an ability to examine and test what is taught by another or what seems to be the strongest hypothesis and its consequences. In other words, the work of the philosopher is "either to learn how things are or to discover it oneself or if this is impossible, to take the best and *most hard-to-refute* human discourse, and riding on it as upon a raft dare to sail through the seas of life" (*Phaedo* 85c7–d2; cf. Simmias's reaction to Socrates' *deuteros plous* at 99c–100a). There is no good reason to doubt, therefore, that while Diotima's teaching could in some way represent the "cherished convictions" of Plato himself, this very

10. Cf. Dover 1980, 113, 138, 155.
11. Cf. Moravcsik 1971, 285–302.
12. Wilamowitz cited in Stenzel 1940, 5.

teaching also wants to be called into question, not least because the strangeness of Diotima's thought is emphasized throughout the speech. And this openness to question is reinforced by what both Socrates and Diotima have to say on this matter.

When Socrates first introduces his dialogue with Diotima, he says: "Now, I think I can most easily recount [*dielthein*] it as she used to do in examining [*anakrinousa*] me" (201e). Thus, close scrutiny or cross-examination, as of the credentials of a magistrate or the worth of slaves,[13] is the paradigm for understanding the nature of the speech. Socrates' close questioning of Diotima's answers is also Diotima's examination of Socrates. It is not surprising, then, that her teaching should raise even more questions in its course, as, for example, when she tells Socrates after he has agreed that he who loves beautiful things longs to possess them for himself, "But the *answer* still longs for the following *question:* what will he have who possesses beautiful things?" (204d). And when Socrates reaches the conclusion that people want to possess good things so that they will be happy, Diotima replies, "the answer seems to be final," but this answer, though final, is only the beginning of the major part of the dialogue itself (205a ff.). It is an answer that, "correct" as it may be, still has to be questioned and unpacked of its latent significance. Even more, then, the dialogue as a whole between Socrates and Diotima, insofar as it presents a *mystical* teaching of which Socrates himself is finally persuaded (212b), is not unlike a complex answer that calls into play an implicit set of questions in the reader. Any philosophical authentication and application of the Greater Mysteries, to give but one example, require a further evaluation with a reference point outside the speech itself. In other words, Socrates' speech is meant to be questioned, not least because the apparently airy-fairy business of "the beautiful itself" in the mouth of a barely fictional "Diotima" virtually compels us to question its authenticity.

5.2 The Elenchus of Agathon and the Question of Truth

Socrates' explicit emphasis on the need for truth rather than uncritical grandiloquence, and on authenticity rather than potentially conflicting appearance (198c–199b), introduces a new dimension into the dialogue: a critical standard, open in principle to everyone, by which one can evaluate the appropriateness of an encomium: "Consider then, Phaedrus, whether there is really any need for a speech of this kind, to hear the truth spoken about Eros in such words and arrangement of phrases as may happen to

---

13. Liddell, Scott, and Jones 1940, s.v. "anakrinein."

occur" (199b). As in the *Apology* (17a–18a), Socrates invites the audience to evaluate the claim to truth on its own merits (cf. 176b–c). And in the elenchus of Agathon he sets out a basis for such evaluation on which the teaching of Diotima and its consequences may be critically tested.

By contrast with the self-sufficient theological abstractions of Agathon and, in different ways, the abstractions of each of the earlier speakers, love is neither self-sufficient nor abstract. Instead, for Socrates, love is immediately "intentional." It is love of someone or something, yet what is involved in this need or lack is more difficult to unpack, for it will turn out to be grounded in all forms of the longing for a beloved, a longing that possesses elements of apparent selfishness or self-interest but that is also always other-directed. So the problem for Socrates, according to the method he takes over from Agathon, that is, to define love and then to show its works (201d–e), is *not* to describe a love of the individual for the individual's own sake or, on Barthian terms, an apparently unconditional love of neighbor, but rather to uncover the nature of Love as reflective of *more* than a single experience, that is, as manifested in the whole range of experience, without losing sight, on the one side, of its immediate physical concreteness and, on the other, of what appears to be involved in this deeply physical, but also spiritual, hunger for something in the other and yet beyond both the other and itself.

Love, then, must have a definite object: it must be "of" someone or something, and yet it also lacks what it desires, not in the sense that one cannot desire (*epithymein*) to have things one already has, like quickness or health, but that in having this desire one means, or wishes rationally (cf. *boulomai* [200d5]),[14] "things now present to be present also in the future" (200d5–6). Since Agathon has already stated that there is no love of the ugly (201a; cf. 197b), then if love is love of beauty, it must therefore lack beauty; and if good things are also beautiful, then love must also lack good things (201a–c).[15]

Part of the argument seems questionable and part overstated. Three immediate questions require some answer: Surely it is possible to love the ugly or to desire what is not really good for us? Then too, can it be the case that what lacks beauty has beauty "in no way" (*mêdamê* [201b])? Finally, is *good* really synonymous with *beautiful?* *Republic* 6 would seem, for instance, to hold a different view (the good and the beautiful are apparently differ-

---

14. Allen 1991, 56–57 and nn. 92–95.
15. For different views of this section, see Dover 1980, 131–36; Stokes 1986, 114–82 and 440–54; Rowe 1998, 168–73. Dover is unfairly critical throughout; Stokes attempts to get inside the problematics of the argument, though his conclusions are themselves problematic; and Rowe's judgment (particularly on Dover's criticisms) is very fair (see esp. 172). We leave particular consideration of Nussbaum 1986, 163–99, until Chapter 6, note 15, and Chapter 7, notes 7 and 20.

ent). We might reply to these questions in the following way. First, if we love the ugly, we do so under the guise of the beautiful, and so we do not love the ugly as such. We can desire as an apparent good what is not really good for us, and then the proper alignment of desire, rational wish of what is really good for us, and love of true beauty will be disrupted by love's pursuit of an unworthy object, as is envisaged in the *Phaedrus* and *Republic* (438a ff.) so that love can even be transformed into tyrannical lust (cf. *Republic* 9.573a–e). Socrates is not necessarily denying that love may be sometimes good and sometimes bad, depending on its object; he is concerned here rather with what he takes to be the natural tendency of all love, whether or not it aims at a real or an imaginary good. The ambiguity of love for good or ill is suggested in what appears to be a quotation from some unknown source at 205d: "Eros most great and crafty [*doleros*]." *Doleros* means both "crafty" and "treacherous."[16]

Second, to say that what lacks beauty has beauty *in no way* most naturally means in the context to be utterly deprived of beauty in those respects it lacks, in other words, that beautiful things may be present to it in the future. Strictly speaking, this is an overstatement, but given Socrates' clarification of his meaning (200b–d), it is reasonable to take it in this way. Finally, "good" and "beautiful" seem to be interchangeable, though they are treated separately (that is, with *kai* [beautiful and good]) and even appear to be distinguished (206e–207a). In fact, this speech may not let us decide conclusively one way or the other on this matter.[17] In which case it is more prudent not to assume that they are simply synonymous. And if this is one matter that cannot be decided within the *Symposium* itself, we may require the *Republic* to assist in providing a tentative judgment based on any evidence here.

Like the golden youth of *Republic* 6, Agathon is prepared to admit under the "gentle" force of questioning that "there is no sense in him and that he stands in need of it" (*Rep.* 494d), but Socrates will only "let him be" (201d) if he defers not to Socrates, but to the truth:

> And Agathon said, It looks, Socrates, as if I didn't know anything of what I said then. And yet you said it so beautifully, Agathon. But tell me one little thing more: don't you think good things are also beautiful? I do. So if Eros is lacking beautiful things, and good things are beautiful, he would also be lacking good things? I, he

---

16. Liddell, Scott, and Jones 1940, s.v. "doleros." Cf. *Phaedrus* 266a: *skaion tina erôta*. See also *Hippias Minor* 365c (of Odysseus). The two sides of Love, positive and negative, are thus implicit in Diotima's account. See Chapter 8, note 122, for a development of this idea.

17. But see section 6.2, ad fin., below. For a different view, see White 1989, 149–57.

said, cannot contradict you, Socrates. Let it be as you say. No, it's the truth, my beloved Agathon, you cannot contradict, since there is nothing hard about contradicting Socrates. (201c–d)

So the elenchus concludes in (1) a distinction between apparent beauty and real substance ("and yet you spoke so beautifully, Agathon"); (2) a movement through beauty to goodness as part of what it means to love "someone"; and (3) an explicit appeal to a standard beyond both Agathon and Socrates, to which both must be accountable. But above all, 4) the elenchus of Agathon renders explicit the previously implicit oppositions of speech in terms of the logical impossibility of self-contradiction (*antilegein* [201c7, 9]) and thus permits the question of the "truth" or "reality" of anything (the "what it is") to emerge with clarity.[18] At which point Socrates introduces his conversation with Diotima as a continuation of his present dialogue with Agathon, particularly because, as he puts it, he used to say to Diotima much the same sort of thing as Agathon had said to him and because of what traditional assumptions of repetitive commonplaces had taught them both, namely, that Eros was a great god of beautiful things.

5.3 The Role of Diotima

How are we to understand the introduction of Diotima and what weight should we give her role? Diotima is "a Mantinean woman ... wise in this and many other things" who once brought about a ten-year delay in the plague for the Athenians (when, where, and how we might know this are not mentioned) and who is knowledgeable in love matters (201d). In other words, despite the vague quasi-historical detail, Diotima appears to be a purely fictitious character made up for the occasion. The place-name Mantinea resembles *mantis* (seer), and so she is perhaps a prophetess, as well as a priestess or religious expert, and also an initiator into the mystery cults (cf. *Meno* 81a10), as will appear from her teaching. The name Diotima, meaning either "honored by Zeus" or "honoring Zeus," also looks fictitious, though it may have been a common name, however uncommon Diotima herself clearly is.[19] How curious, then, that the appeal to truth should result immediately in the purest fiction![20] But the situation is still more

---

18. For fuller development of the significance of this elenchus, see sections 8.4 and 8.8, below.
19. Bury 1932, 94; Dover 1980, 137; Rowe 1998, 173; Brisson 1998, 27–31.
20. Cf. Brisson 1998, 27–28 (the vocabulary and doctrine of 210a–212a involving the "doctrine of forms" is an "anachronism" [whose only equivalent is in the *Parmenides*] which leads us to doubt Diotima's historical reality about which we know "rien de précis").

problematic, since the reasons commonly advanced for the introduction of Diotima, however unobjectionable some of them might be in themselves, do not seem to touch on, much less capture, the heart of her role.

For example, on many current accounts,[21] Diotima serves one or more functions related to six different possibilities: (1) she permits Socrates to give a speech on Eros while preserving his mask of ironic ignorance; or (2) she explains his insistence that he knows only about love matters; or (3) she gives added importance to his account by suggesting that Eros is the subject of a mystery cult of which Diotima is a priestess; or (4) she represents "a masterstroke of delicate courtesy"[22] by means of which Socrates is enabled to correct Agathon without unduly criticizing him by relating the lesson he himself once learned; or again (5) in accordance with the narrative scheme of the dialogue, it would have been inappropriate for Socrates to offer an encomium to Eros that, when Alcibiades praises him, will turn out to fit Socrates himself;[23] or finally (6) the introduction of a woman as spokesperson for Plato "tends to allay our suspicion that cunning self-interest might be the mainspring of arguments for what is essentially a male homosexual foundation for philosophical activity.[24]

Of the preceding reasons, (1) and (2) are fair, but incidental—they tell us nothing about the function of *Diotima*—and (3) looks like an appeal to authority that is foreign to Plato's presentation of Socrates. The only trouble with (4) is that Socrates does not just criticize Agathon. The elenchus *demolishes* his speech, before gently reinstating something of Agathon's view later (204c). As for (5), it seems fair, but really incidental; and (6) is not simply foreign to Plato's thought if Dover means us to believe that Plato intends to deceive us for self-serving reasons; in fact, it makes no sense at all in the context of this speech, as we shall see below. In other words, Diotima's role is more powerful and important than these views seem capable of acknowledging.

Let us take up this difficult question from Socrates' point of view in the first place. By Socrates' recollection of a conversation that took place a long time ago, we are reminded of the beginning of the dialogue, when Apollodorus recollected the story told to him by Aristodemus. This technique

---

21. Among the many unconvincing reasons so often offered, Brisson (1998, 30–31) cites two: (1) that Plato was a "salon heterosexual" who wished to give greater dignity to heterosexual relations than "society" accorded them and (2) that Plato was openly homosexual and so described pregnancy "en termes de phantasmes homosexuals de procréation." Brisson's own account, following Halperin 1990, 113–51 nn, 190–211, is much more sensible (63–65). Our interpretation follows a different line from that of Brisson, Halperin, and others.

22. Cornford 1950, 71.

23. Allen 1991, 46.

24. Dover 1980, 137.

of a "story within a story" (or again, an answer that provokes further questions), thus recast here at this important point, signifies that the dialogue is making a fresh start. But the repetition of this stylistic device also, by contrast, points to the remarkable difference between Socrates' role and that of Apollodorus or Aristodemus. Socrates, above all, is not a simple reteller of experience, but an active participant in the drama he recollects.[25] Moreover, while he re-presents Diotima's teaching, Socrates adopts Agathon's method of stating, first, Love's nature and, then, Love's gifts, which reminds us that in *his* narrative (cf. 201d6) Socrates follows a certain pattern of thought that *orders* the sequence of recollection. In contrast to Apollodorus, Socrates does not succumb to the narrative, but has power over it. Thus, his own recollection is creative. But this only foregrounds the issue of *truth* in a more urgent way. Socrates has already said that he will tell the *truth, but in his own way,* in distinction from the early speeches (199a–b). What does this mean, and can veiled fiction be a substitute for truth?

In fact, the apparent evidence for Diotima's historical existence is so flimsy as to compel us to call it into question.[26] But what is important about her, we suggest, is precisely not her historical existence. She is presented as *an outsider* (like the male "outsiders" or "strangers" of Plato's later dialogues); that is, in the first instance, she speaks at a party at which she is *not present*. But she is also a foreigner to Athens although she saved the city in the past; and the fact that she is a prophetess-priestess and, therefore, relates a knowledge that is not her own only heightens her *image* as a nonparticipating participator, an image with just the right mixture of reality and mystery to make us realize that not her personality, but her teaching, is of ultimate importance.

But why, one asks, could not Socrates have conducted the examination himself? Why give the leading role to Diotima? An answer to these questions will shed new light on Socrates' unusual presentation "bathed and beslippered" (174a) at the beginning of the dialogue. Socrates' diligent care of his appearance at the outset of Aristodemus's narrative and his assumption of the role of apprentice to Diotima in his own discourse clearly intimate that *in relation to that truth that constitutes the core of Socrates' own*

---

25. On this, see Chapter 2, passim. Allen (1991, 89), like many other commentators, is puzzled by the absence of a doctrine of recollection in the *Symp.*: The *Meno*, the *Phaedo*, and the *Phaedrus* suppose that knowledge is recollection; but here . . . there is only reference to a guide (210 a)." This, however, misses the dramatically obvious point that Socrates-Diotima's speech is entirely a *recollection* (and of no single physical occasion as we shall see). Note the emphasis on attentive memory in the elenchus: 200a2–3, 201a2, 3. For the significance of this in context, see section 8.8 below.

26. Dover 1980, 10; Brisson 1998, 28, etc.; Lacan 1991, 144. ("N'est-ce pas dans la mesure où quelque chose, quand il s' agit du discours de l'amour, échappe au savoir du Socrate, que celui-ci s'efface, *se dioecise,* et fait à sa place parler une femme?—pourquoi pas, la femme qui est en lui" [Lacan 1991, 144]).

intelligence, even Socrates continues to be a pupil. Thus, the clause "so that I go beautiful to the beautiful" (174a), as part of Socrates' response to the first question asked of him in the *Symposium,* assumes a quite definite meaning in the light of his narrative approach to the beautiful. His unusual looks are not merely accidental, nor is his insistence that he possesses the truth about love matters. Rather, these foreshadow the extraordinary importance of the revelations brought to birth in him by Diotima.

Moreover, by making Diotima the source of his own speech, Socrates breaks the pattern established in the earlier speeches, the limitations of which are dictated by the shortcomings of their authors. All five previous speeches are caught in different cages of subjectivity. By adopting the dialectical method and giving his speech to Diotima, Socrates gives a new objectivity to his position. Thus, Diotima's leading role only intensifies the dramatic suggestion that Socrates' truth is not the child of his own preferences or limitations. She, of course, may dimly resemble the lady of Socrates' dream in the *Crito* or be a prototype of "lady philosophy" nine centuries later in Boethius's *Consolation of Philosophy;* but her dialogue with Socrates, just as Socrates' "imaginary" dialogue with the Laws in the *Crito,* opens up what is otherwise hidden to genuine scrutiny. The result is that the speech becomes something held in common—not at all a private view, but rather something to be examined and checked (however much we may find Agathon's and Socrates' responses to their respective interlocutors on occasion too acquiescent). In so far as this also takes Socrates out of the driving seat and makes him a *creative* participant, even if in the position of listener in dialogue with another (effectively symbolic of Diotima's apprentice ascending the ladder of Love in the Greater Mysteries [210a ff.]), creative recipience, symbolized primarily by the feminine and by a balance between the sexes as represented in the conversation between Diotima and Socrates, becomes the effective and yet surprising foundation for philosophical activity in this speech.

So we can now turn to the role of Diotima herself more properly. First and foremost, as a prophetess-priestess who bears a teaching that is not her own, she signifies the movement into the realm of the sacred; or to put this another way, she betokens the view that unguided discourse can only take us so far and that, in a matter so powerful as love, we cannot hope to look into its power and energy without a deeper reorientation of our original views, or at least without some new images by which to see, for this after all is a "*logos* pertaining to Love" (201d), not the claim that one has looked into everything and consequently knows "the truth."

Second, Diotima evidently represents in some measure that standard of truth beyond both Socrates and Agathon, yet open to all. While we in the contemporary world should be inclined to accord philosophical truth only the sanctity that we as human beings are willing to give it, Socrates was evidently of a different view, namely, the view that philosophical truth occurs in a much bigger amphitheater, where, in an important way, the philosopher is not even the principal actor in what is apparently his own play, but an active recipient.

Third, despite her powerful presence in this speech, and perhaps because of it, Diotima is meant to be an *image,* but not an image in the sense of a portrait from life, that is, of an actual physical or historical object. In other words, she is not, on the terms of Plato's critique of mimetic art, an imitation of an imitation, but more like a mental image, as we might say. Physical copies require distinct physical features; mental images certainly do not require features in the same way. The painting of a horse, for instance, has to be physically exact within the limitations and conventions of the particular genre. But "horsey" mental images are not similarly constrained; they may even have no individual physical horsey features. At any rate, this is one way of putting what Plato himself tried to get at in his criticism of art in *Republic* 2–3, and elsewhere. While the gods themselves would not use fictions or falsehoods (*to pseudos* means both "falsehood" and "fiction," just as does *mythos,* among other things), we may employ them, Socrates argues, in the absence of anything better and render them useful by making them as like the truth as we can (*Rep.* 2.382c–d). So we use the embroidery of the sky as "paradigms" from which "to grasp their truth" (530b), and when we cannot look directly at truth (as especially in the case of love!), just as we cannot look directly at the sunlight or living creatures after being released from the cave, then we have to employ "divine images" (*phantasmata*) in water and "shadows of beings" (*skias tôn ontôn*) in order to come, through the images, into the full power of dialectic and the vision of being (*Rep.* 7.532b–c). This use of images is in fact the journey of "dialectic," Socrates and Glaucon agree (532b4). It is precisely in this sense, we suggest, that Diotima is a dialectical image, not thrice removed from the original, but a paradigm herself through which one may see the truth she represents and of which she speaks. At any rate, if Diotima is an image in this sense, it is surely noteworthy that her image possesses no *physical features whatsoever.*

Finally, Diotima is a *woman,* the highest exemplar of *sophia* or wisdom in the dialogue. What we are to make of this is, of course, a difficult matter, but it should surely not be passed over without comment. Many of the early speakers have mentioned women, but generally the role of women or of heterosexual intercourse has been downplayed, the latter in Pausanias's speech, for example, and the former in that of Phaedrus, where the heroism of Alcestis is subordinated to that of Achilles. We might expect some treatment of the role of women by Eryximachus, since love on his account seems to be responsible for all growth in the cosmos, but for all intents and purposes women do not exist for the good doctor. And while Aristophanes emphasizes the importance of both homosexual and heterosexual love, the examples he chooses in illustrating the latter are not too promising: for men, adulterers, and for women, adulteresses (192d–e)![27] And no women—beyond Atê, Aphrodite, and Athena—make an appearance on the stage of Agathon's mind. So the introduction and prominence of Diotima is something of a *revelation* that cannot be overlooked. We might even say—to employ the terms of the *Symposium* itself in this "new beginning" that is Socrates' speech—that the original "mother of the tale," in the words of Euripides' *Melanippe* (" the tale is not mine; my mother taught me"), transposed into the fathership of Phaedrus at 177a, and thus displaced by Eryximachus and Phaedrus, is effectively reinstated in the figure of one who is a paradigm of wisdom and whose teaching comes from another.[28]

Whatever we are finally to make of this, in practical terms Socrates' speech is actually *framed* as a chiastic or cross-balancing relationship between its male and female figures: Diotima, a figure of divine "plenty" balances the feminine personification of "Poverty" in the myth she tells, just as the masculine "Plenty" is balanced by the relative "poverty" of Socrates.[29] And there are three further results of this that obviously have to be taken into account if we want to reach a reasonable assessment of this speech. First, this balance between male and female is cast into sharp relief, but this can easily go unnoticed because this framing is so open an effect on the very surface of the speech. Second, the philosophical ideal of shared dialogue is cast dramatically into a balance of conversation between the sexes in which the feminine remains the higher and *ideal* partner. So right from the beginning of the speech, there is put before us a striking example of purely intellectual friendship between a woman and a man. Third, the basic epistemological model for the content of Diotima's speech as a whole is sexual intercourse between man and woman, and then giving birth to, and rearing, the offspring. Here again it is the *woman* who primarily symbolizes all humanity in the full extent of this creative process, and this affects the language with which she characterizes love. The verbs *kyein, kyesthai* (be pregnant, conceive), for example, are used only of females, whereas, *tiktein, gennan, tokos,* and *gennêsis* can apply to both males and females, since they are used both of "begetting"

---

27. But on *hetairistrai*, see Rowe 1998, ad loc.
28. See Chapter 2. Cf. Halperin 1990, 149–51.
29. This chiastic relation is also reflected in the description of Love's generation and heritage (*Poros-Penia, Penia-Poros* [203a–c]).

and of "bearing" offspring.³⁰ Therefore, at each level of the thought—sexual intercourse, ordinary conversation or teaching, spiritual or intellectual intercourse—the very structure of the speech seems to propose a necessary balance between the male and the female and, more important still, a balance that *cannot even be conceived* without woman's capacity to symbolize, even in her special biological role, the higher intellectual and spiritual attributes of creative recipience. Dover's view of Diotima's role, then, can hardly be right. Diotima does not mask "what is essentially a male homosexual foundation for philosophical activity"—at least, not without any balancing note of all the striking qualities of Diotima's role in Socrates' speech. The opposite is true. Diotima's role and the new set of images and linguistic terms introduced in her speech reorient and expand in the most fundamental manner the previously unquestioned homosexual framework of the earlier speeches.

If we now put together these two sides of the picture, that is, from the viewpoints of Socrates and Diotima, we may ask how, if truth is the result of dialectical questioning, the method of question and answer affects a pupil. It clearly does not "fill" him with knowledge and wisdom, as Socrates had playfully indicated to Agathon at the beginning of the party (175d), if by "filling" one means some form of mechanical transfer. How, then, do wisdom and knowledge enter the soul? Agathon seems to be unable to go beyond the notion of education-by-touch: Love's feet "touch" the softest things (195e–196a); all whom Love touches become poets, even if they were unmusical before (196e). A highly unlikely hypothesis! So ingrained is Agathon's cultural inheritance that wisdom can be merely transferred or taken away and that the role of education is only to "put in" rather than "draw out" or engender and bring to birth. But for Socrates here, as in the *Protagoras,* the acquisition of wisdom is a messier, more far reaching business.³¹ Wisdom does not flow from the fuller to the emptier. We are reminded of other dialogues, earlier and later than the *Symposium,* in which knowledge comes either as a recollection of the soul, as in the *Meno,* or as the child of the soul's birth pangs, as in the *Theaetetus.*³² In the *Symposium* and the *Gorgias,*³³ we are like leaky vessels: knowledge is constantly flowing out of us by forgetfulness so that we are forced to fill the soul up again just to maintain some sort of equilibrium (207e ff.). However, the image of birth, so central to the teaching of Diotima, implies that knowledge and wisdom come as a new self-realization brought about by the search for yet

---

30. Cf. Dover 1980, 137.
31. *Protagoras* 313a–314c.
32. *Theaetetus* 148e–151d, 160e–161a.

another kind of beauty, a search dictated by the pregnancy of soul and the desire to beget in the beautiful. Thus, Diotima points to a search that is simultaneously directed inward and outward. It is a way of living by *transformation* rather than by being filled with something that is useful and ultimately consumable or absorbable. In this sense, Diotima represents the living reality of dialogue itself, whether she is fictional or not, namely, that the other dialectical pole be really *other,* and not one's own voice or wishes masked as otherness, so that one can be genuinely changed by the experience of encounter and come to give birth to a reality that is not digestible, but that can be *tested.* At root, this is the function Diotima assumes, together with Socrates, in this speech.[34]

5.4 Eros-*Daimôn*

Diotima now takes up the conversation. If Eros is neither beautiful nor good, this does not mean that he is ugly or bad—"Quiet, don't blaspheme [*ouk euphêmêseis*]," she said (201e)—but only that he is between wisdom and ignorance, like right opinion (cf. *Republic* 477a–478e; *Meno* 97a ff.).[35] So

---

33. *Gorgias* 493a ff.

34. The broader implications of Diotima's femininity, in the context of the middle dialogues, in particular, go beyond the scope of the present treatment. On the question of Plato's "feminism" generally, and in relation to the *Republic,* in particular, see Vlastos 1994, 11–23, Annas 1996, 3–12, Levin 1996, 13–30, and in relation to the *Symposium,* Bowery 1996, 175–94, Irigaray 1994, 181–96, Nye 1994, 197–216 (in Tuana 1994; Ward 1996). For generally unfavorable views of Plato in this regard, see du Bois 1994, 139–56; Nye 1994, 197–216; Tuana and Cowling, 1994, 243–65; and for more positive assessment (that Plato also challenges male paradigms of rationality and subverts gender identities in a "curiously gendered discourse on epistemology" thus providing a "critique whose resolution he cannot provide"), see Brown 1994, 157–80 (157–58). The view of Tuana and Cowling (1994, 243–65) (presented as chiastic dialogue) that the Platonic conception of rationality at least in relation to the cave may be represented, even in part, as the appropriation (cf. du Bois above) or exclusion of the feminine, as masculine compulsion primarily, or as providing a model of disembodied knowledge is belied, in the first instance, by *Republic* 7.540c (Socrates and Glaucon have been speaking throughout books 5–7 not just of *tous archontas,* male rulers, but *tas archousas,* female rulers, in the second instance, by 7.536d–e (no free person should learn anything by compulsion like a slave, Socrates argues) and in the third instance by the fact that the model throughout books 6–9 is plainly an *embodied* model for understanding soul-body (cf.7.535a ff., 9.591b–e). The further view that this conception privileges vision over touch (soul over body) may be tangentially true of *Republic* 6–7 but not of the *Symposium* where "touching upon the truth" (212a5) is the final step of Diotima's greater mysteries. The view of Diotima's role presented above is more in tune with Brown's assessment but at the same time suggests a way of going beyond it or, at least, of not resolving it.

35. See also 202a5 ff.: "Don't you know . . . that having right opinions, even without being able to give an account of them [*logon dounai*], is neither a question of knowing . . . nor ignorance . . . right opinion is presumably something like this, in between wisdom and ignorance?" Although the views of the early speakers are, as we have argued, where philosophy starts, none of their speeches really rises to the level of *orthê doxa,* as Eryximachus's "warning" to Aristophanes (on which, see Chapter 3) that he

Love cannot be a great god (as all the previous speakers had supposed). Instead, if all gods are happy and beautiful, and happiness means possession of what is good and beautiful,[36] and if Love lacks and desires these things so that he cannot be immortal or again simply mortal, then Love must be intermediate between the immortal and the mortal and "a great *daimôn*" with the power of acting (*dynamis;* in the *Republic* this power can be directed in different ways to different objects; cf. 477b5, 8; c1–478b) as the communicating link between gods and men (a theme in the speeches of both Eryximachus and Agathon). Love "fills in between so that the all is bound together with itself [*symplêroi hôste to pan auto hautôi syndedesthai*]" (202e), and through this medium all priestly and nonpriestly arts move, including prophecy and enchantment. "God does not mingle [*mignytai*] with man, but all intercourse [*homilia*] and converse [*dialektos*] between gods and men, waking and sleeping, are through this medium" (203a2–4). So Love unites opposites, without their having to be tamed in the process, as Eryximachus had supposed, and the unity of heaven and earth through love is more than the unity of divided blobs rediscovering their original globular nature, as Aristophanes had represented it. In this context, *ou mignytai* also means "does not have sexual intercourse with," that is, god does not have sex with man. The idea that the all is bound together with itself is, of course, reminiscent of Heraclitus's "being at variance with itself is drawn together with itself" from Eryximachus's speech (187a) as also of Aristophanes' desire for wholeness, "to join and be fused" with the beloved (192e ff.).[37] So the earlier speeches are already under implicit consideration and the myth of Aristophanes figures prominently here insofar as the questions of what constitutes the whole and what consequently is the true object of our desire are being reconsidered on the grander scale.

What is a *daimôn,* or spirit? The word is used in poetry as a synonym of *theos* (god), but it also designates supernatural beings below the level of gods such as the spirits of the "golden race" who roam the earth as beneficent

---

might have "to give an account" gently thematizes. Love here in Diotima's account is in between wisdom and ignorance, just like the philosopher (cf. 203d–e; 204b) and so the province of "true belief" which is able to give an account of itself is that of *such* (but perhaps not all) philosophy. We shall suggest (in Chapter 7) that Socrates' speech is also on this level of "justified true belief." The position of the *Meno* (97a–99a) is similar to that proposed by Diotima here but, in our view, neither passage commits Plato to the view that *orthê doxa* plus a *logos* is *simply* equivalent to *epistêmê* (in the strict sense on which, again, see Chapter 7). *Orthê doxa* plus a *logos* might be a sign of *epistêmê* or *noêsis* (after the fact, as it were), but surely scientific understanding is not *reached* by having a correct opinion and then justifying it. Here we surely refer to a different sort of *grasp* or *understanding,* in light of which justification (*logos*) may *then* be *scientific.*

36. *Symp.* 204a1–2, c3–5.
37. Compare also *Gorgias* 507e–508a.

guardians in Hesiod (*WD* 122); in the *Apology* Socrates treats *daimones* as "either gods or children of gods" (27b–e),[38] and there is also his "spiritual voice" (*to daimonion*), which tells him what not to do (40a–b). The English *demon* is a term of opprobrium derived from the Christian rejection of polytheism.[39] So a *daimôn* is a supernatural or spiritual being either good or bad (a guardian "angel" or a "demon"), but not a literary fiction or a simple personification, as Allen seems to take it[40] (at least at this stage of the speech, before the myth of Love's birth).

In the *daimôn*-Love, the horizontal and vertical dimensions interact: human love of someone or something and human need of what is lacking, on the one hand; and communication of every sort between the human and the divine, on the other. At least, at this point of the speech, the analysis of what is involved in desiring what one lacks has led to the conclusion that while Love is always concrete, that is, "of" someone or something, it possesses a spiritual nature with much broader implications that go beyond the confines of the individual experience. There is, then, a natural ambiguity in Plato's language between *Love itself* and the *person loving,* an ambiguity felt, for instance, already at 201b1–5: "Now, it is agreed that one loves what one lacks and does not have? Yes, he said. Then Love lacks and does not have beauty?" So we shall have to take up the question how precisely to understand this in due course.

But for the moment let us draw attention to one point that Diotima makes. The clause "god does not mingle with man" must include the meaning "god does not have sexual intercourse with man" (203a: *ou mignutai;* cf. 207b: *symmigênai*), as the ancient myths had it. So what is the relation between gods and humankind? *Daimôn*-Love is the medium and he "fills in, or up, between" (*symplêroi*). We recognize the filling metaphor, as in the case of *sophia* earlier (175d–e), but we are none the wiser for it. Is Love the "glue" that holds "the all" together? The glue metaphor, it would seem, would be out of place, because in Diotima's account the difficulty we experience is precisely that we cannot envisage in material terms what she is talking about, which suggests the strong possibility that we are meant to *think* the relationship Love constitutes rather than to translate it into equivalent physical images.

So what is the filling function of Love? Apparently, this is pure communication on a two-way basis, a channel of motion (cf. *chôrei*), part of whose essential nature seems to be some sort of genuine *two-way* friendship

---

38. Dover 1980, 140.
39. Cf. Allen 1991, 48.
40. Allen 1991, ix.

between gods and men (as opposed to the common scholarly view, for example, that in Plato's thought we love the gods, but the gods do not love us back), if *homilia* and *dialektos,* friendly association and conversation, mean anything at all. On this account, at any rate, Love cannot be a physical substance evidently;[41] but neither can it be an accident in the sense of a quality, quantity, or simple relation that depends for its existence entirely on the individual subject, *for there is something in Love that goes beyond this.* So Love must be a spiritual relation or substance (whatever this might mean) linking the individual subject through the world of sacred arts to the gods and yet at the same time permitting direct two-way conversation between the two. It seems a reasonable inference at this point that while we could hardly suppose divine "love" to be like human "love," since Eros is a spirit and not a god, nonetheless friendship and love in some sense must also mark the gods' relation to humankind.[42] On the basis of just a few pages of conversation, therefore, a new theology is suggested, so close to traditional accounts in some ways and yet with a new emphasis on the dialogical relationship of Love between the divine and human worlds. This may help to explain for a modern reader the peculiar enthusiasm of all later antiquity for the story that is to follow.

5.5 Diotima and the Art of Mythmaking Revisited: The Birth of Eros

It is significant, indeed (and this certainly requires a reexamination of Aristophanes' way of treating "desire"), that in order to explain love's capacity for constant need, on the one hand, and for the creation of "wholeness," on the other, Diotima, like Aristophanes, tells a "myth." Her setting is even less "historical" than that of Aristophanes, for although Zeus and Aphrodite are mentioned in the story, the main characters, Poros, the son of Mêtis ("Resourcefulness," or "Plenty," son of wisdom), and Penia (Poverty) seem to be more or less explicitly allegorical, in the sense that they provoke *hyponoia* (underthought, undermeaning), which is Plato's word for what we might call "allegory" in the *Republic* (cf. 2.378d). To personify forces as deities is a common Greek form of characterization (compare, for instance, Agathon's "father of Delicacy, etc.," 197d6–7), and so we need not suppose that Plato takes over an already existing story, though *penia* is personified by Aristophanes in his *Ploutos; poros* ("way" or "trace" in the void) is personified in a cosmogony by Alcman (frag. 5.2.ii.19 Page);

---

41. See section 4.6, below.
42. Cf. Rist 1964, 7ff.

and Mêtis in Hesiod is the first wife of Zeus (*Theog.* 886) and mother of Athena (frag. 343).[43]

The famous story is deceptively simple. On the birthday of Aphrodite, the gods feasted, and Poverty came begging. Plenty got drunk on nectar, for wine did not yet exist, and weighed down with drink, slept it off in the garden of Zeus. Poverty, because of her resourcelessness (*aporia*), plotted (*epibouleusa*) to have a child with "Resource," or Plenty, and lay down with him and conceived Eros, who is therefore a follower of Aphrodite, since he is begotten on her birthday, and a lover of beauty because Aphrodite is beautiful. But because of his parentage, his fortune (*toiautêi tychei*) is to be the child of opposites. On his mother's side, he is not delicate and beautiful (as Agathon's attempt to sum up a traditional understanding has it: *hoion hoi polloi oiontai* [203c]), but poor, rough, hard, homeless, and barefoot, living a vagrant's existence. And on his father's side, because of resourcefulness, he plots for beautiful and good things (*epiboulos*); he is courageous, eager, intense, a clever hunter, desirous of wisdom and truth, clever at enchantment, a sorcerer, a sophist, and a philosopher. The mixture of both parental lines gives him the strangest existence (perhaps a sort of heightened psychological portrait of the state of being in love). He is by nature neither immortal nor mortal: "but sometimes on the same day he flourishes and lives, when he has the resources, and sometimes he dies, and comes back to life again, because of his father's nature; but what is provided is always flowing away so that *Love* is neither at a loss nor ever rich" (203e). So Eros is a lover of wisdom, a philosopher, unlike the gods, who do not desire what they already have, and also unlike self-sufficient ignorant human beings, who cannot desire what they do not know they lack. In fact, Eros is not the beloved—which can indeed be perfect, as Agathon, and Socrates, had previously supposed—but the lover: "You thought, to judge from what you say, that Love is the beloved, not the loving. That is why, I think, Love seemed all-beautiful to you. And in fact what is beloved is really beautiful, charming, perfect, and most blessed; but loving has quite a different character [*idea*] of the kind I have described" (204b–c). How are we to take this story? And this prompts the bigger question: what role does myth play in Plato's thought? Friedländer and others hold the reasonable view that the story helps to make concrete the previous "conceptual clarification of the nature of love"[44] This is true, but the concentration is less embodiment than it is *idea,* since the sparse physical images—garden, barefoot, sleeping in doorways or out under the stars—apply to human experience but

---

43. Dover 1980, 141–42.
44. Friedländer 1969, 25; Allen 1991, 49.

actually describe an archetypal experience or spiritual reality: the *idea* of desiring and searching; that is, loving. So how should we understand *mythos* in this context?[45]

The word *mythos* itself can mean "story," "fiction," "tale," "lie," "fable," "narrative," "account," "hypothesis," and so on. Its very range of meaning indicates the impossibility of pigeonholing it. *Mythos* is not simply "story"; nor is *logos* simply "rational discourse," as if parts of the dialogues could be classified under either heading. Indeed, if Diotima is an image in the sense we suggested earlier rather than a historical person, then the whole of Socrates' speech is framed as a *mythos* (and not just this story, but the entire *Symposium* as well). The Poverty-Plenty story is simply an intensification of that mythical narrative. So a *mythos* can be a form of *logos,* and vice versa. In fact, in the whole of this section only the word *logos* is used, and Diotima herself employs no term (*mythos* or *logos*) to characterize the story she tells, one that is simply continuous with the rest of the conversation.

But in what sense can we speak about "truth" or "Logos" in the context of a story that represents gods in ways of which Socrates apparently disapproved in the *Republic?* In the *Phaedrus, Cratylus,* and *Republic,* allegory appears to be rejected, on the basis of etymology or dubious overt morality (*Crat.* 407a; *Rep.* 378d), as is also the rationalization of mythology (*Phaedr.* 229c ff.). So how does Socrates' speech in the *Symposium* avoid the twin horns of this dilemma, namely, allegory or the rationalization of mythology, and how does the myth of the birth of Eros avoid Socrates' criticism of Homeric or Hesiodic myths in the *Republic?*

What Socrates appears to find objectionable in the *Republic* are stories that present a bad image of the gods—gods committing injustices or atrocities and thus undermining or limiting our concept of the divine by making it reflect the behavior of unjust mortal rulers. Even if some of the details in these stories are true, Socrates argues, they should not necessarily be narrated to everyone, especially children, for this will lead to corruption. If such stories are to be related at all, they should only be told to specially prepared audiences (*Rep.* 377b ff.). Allegory and rationalization, therefore, should not detract from more serious pursuits (as, for example, Socrates' study of his own soul in the *Phaedrus*) or simply confuse the young, who "cannot distinguish what is allegorical from what is not" (378d7–8). But this does not mean that myths cannot have any deeper sense (*hyponoia*) to them. And Socrates, whose inner life, Plato stresses, is particularly fertile and part of whose preoccupation lies with meaning in poetry (cf. *Phaedo*

---

45. For an account of the history of the interpretation of *mythos* in Plato scholarship, see section 8.6, below.

61b), himself frequently searches out the inner meaning in the words of the poets.[46] On the whole, Socrates tends to reflect with pleasure on those myths whose exegesis opens up rather than closes other avenues of discourse, that is, myths that serve as pathways into broader and more fertile conversations through questioning.

In the *Gorgias,* for instance, before recounting his eschatological myth, which is in its essence a *logos* in the form of a *mythos,* Socrates tells Callicles: "Listen to a very fine story [*logos*], which you, I think, will consider myth [*mythos*], but I an actual account [*logos*]" (523a). So while *mythos* can mean "myth," "fiction," even "lie" (otherwise, *to pseudos*), it also seems capable of generating "true account," or of opening up into a "rational discourse." Certainly myth or allegory expresses "truth" in its own particular way when, as we argued earlier, the more the image is foregrounded, the more we are conscious not merely of the image itself, but also of the possibility of other inquiries, made available through (rather than restricted by) the image. The image, then, must be a lens by which one can see that of which it is the image.

In the *Republic,* such use of images is already the journey of dialectic (532b–c), but this is also characteristic of earlier dialogues, of the great myth in the *Gorgias* (cf. 524d; 527a ff.), as also of the final myth in the *Phaedo* (114d). Stripped to its essentials as a lens with which to see beyond itself and open up into other nonreductive philosophical and theological discourses, fiction can express the truth much more readily than can the relatively mindless repetition of basic narrative. The conclusion to the *Gorgias* myth makes this clear. Socrates tells Callicles that for his part he is convinced "by these accounts" (*logoi*) and seeks because of them to show his "judge" "the healthiest possible state of soul" (526d). He then concludes:

> Perhaps, however, you think this is an old wife's *tale* [*mythos . . . hôsper graos*] and you despise it, and there would be no wonder in your despising it, if in our searching we could find anywhere something better and truer than this, but as it is you see that you three, who are the wisest of the Greeks in our day, you and Polus and Gorgias, cannot prove that we ought to live any other life than this, which is also evidently of advantage in the other world. But amid all these *arguments* [*logoi*], while the rest are refuted, one argument alone stands unshaken, that we should beware more of doing than suffering injustice and that above all a man should study not to seem but to be good, whether in private or in public life. (527a–b)

---

46. *Apol.* 22b–c; *Ion* 533d–534e; *Prot.* 342a–347a; cf. Rist 1964, 8–9.

So it is reasonable to suppose that myth can be a fundamental part of dialectic when it does not debase its subject, and that the whole of Socrates' speech is properly "mythical" or "fictional" in the sense that it presents a narrative account, which is not an imitation of a physical image, but a "phantasm" or "paradigm" by means of which to get beyond the image to the essential idea of the account.

For these reasons, the gods do not need myths, but we do, especially in cases in which we have to see *through* the present and take account of events in the long-distant past: "because we don't know the truth of what happened in antiquity, we make the lie [*to pseudos*] as close as possible to the true, and so make it useful" (*Rep.* 2.382d1–3). So the myth of the birth of Love is exactly a case in point. Why does Diotima tell a story? Because nobody was there to witness the event and therefore the fiction must be made as an imaginative image of the genesis of those forces that generate love. Such myth therefore *requires hyponoia*—underthinking or deeper meaning—if it is to be successful.[47]

Does this story, then, give a bad image of the nature of the gods or limit their nature through the image? The only details that might do so are the drunkenness of Plenty, if one lives in a temperance colony, or the sex between Poverty and Plenty, if celibacy is one's only or supreme value. But these details stand in the background to something more fundamental at work here. The difficulty is not to press the images too far, but at least we can say straightforwardly that the story turns on the procreation and birth of two children: (1) Aphrodite, implicitly the daughter here of Zeus and Dione, as opposed to "the motherless daughter of Ouranos" in Pausanias's speech (that is, the goddess born from the severed genitals of Cronos [180d6]) and (2) Eros, child of Poverty and Plenty. So the divine feast celebrates, again implicitly, a *divine paradigm* of expansion—of procreation and birth. The feast plainly signifies an abundance that reaches out, within its own nature (that is, Poros stays in the garden of Zeus) beyond itself (namely, Poros finds a "way"). Poverty habitually begs at such feasts, and the tradition of interpretation in antiquity that was born in reaction to the *Symposium* found little that was derogatory in these images of the gods. Quite to the contrary, as later Platonists were to say, the good is in some sense self-expansive and self-giving, even if in this case it has to get a little divinely drunk to be so! There is, at any rate, a habitual place for the profane within the sacred, if Poverty symbolizes the profane and the garden of Zeus the sacred.

---

47. Just as the "myth" of the *Symposium* as a whole itself necessarily provokes such *hyponoia*. We should note that Socrates and Diotima treat the narrative (203b1: *deêgêsthai*) of the birth of Love, as well as "Aristophanes' speech" as *logos* throughout (205d9–10; 201d1, 6, e6, 7). The word *mythos* is never mentioned.

But what about Plenty? Does he have to get drunk to father an illegitimate, demonic child? Does his drunkenness on nectar signify a forgetfulness so that his high morality will not be tainted? And as for Poverty, is she the initiator of such a union? She uses her brain to get what she wants, but he presumably is insensible—is this not a fair reading?

An initial answer about Plenty's behavior can only be in the negative in the story's context, at least, for if the gods are wise and thus they have no need to seek for wisdom, then they cannot be prone to forgetfulness, insensibility, or the need to deliberate in the way that human beings are so prone. Poverty and Eros have to deliberate (*epiboulos*). In traditional mythology, mythological creatures do of course deliberate, and we remember that Zeus's somewhat dull-witted plotting was a conspicuously humorous feature of Aristophanes' speech: "Zeus and the other gods took counsel [*ebouleuonte*] about what they ought to do, and were at a loss [*êporoun*]" (190c). In other words, Zeus and other gods were somewhat dimmer in Aristophanes' speech than Poverty is for Diotima. "After thinking about it very hard indeed [*mogis . . . ennoêsas*], Zeus said . . ." (190c). But here the contrast between the two accounts could not be greater. The divine in Diotima's discourse does not deliberate or work laboriously to a conclusion. Clearly, Plenty's sleep betokens something like pure divine superabundance, as expressive of both its inner festive nature and its consequences; and this divine superabundance provides the occasion of generation for a different sort of reality, if Poverty is not divine in the same sense.

But who is Poverty? She is evidently a primordial, material principle of desire, as indicated by the fact that wine did not exist. Her primordiality is not unlike the "space" or "receptacle" of the *Timaeus,* but this should not be pressed any further for the obvious reason that it lies far outside the immediate scope of the *Symposium.* The child, Eros, at any rate, has a double nature: on his father's side, but also by virtue of his mother, he is a more philosophical, heavenly being, whereas on his mother's side, but again also by virtue of his father, he is a much more earthbound spirit, in whose devolved states will be manifested the demon lust of tyranny, as in *Republic* 9: "the next stage is that those in whose soul the tyrant Love dwells and directs everything, go in for feasts, revelries, banquets, mistresses, and all that sort of thing" (573d2–5). Alcibiades will be a sophisticated and urbane example of someone apparently on the path to such self-realization. The images of Poverty and her child Eros are reflected in Alcibiades' portrayal, supplying not a mythological but a psychological insight on this occasion.

At whatever level of discourse, however, the key to Love's nature is the constant renewal of his being as a conjunction of opposites. On the horizontal level, and from the perspective of his mother's nature, Love is only loss or serial succession. On the vertical level, however, as a conjunction of two inheritances, there is renewal and rebirth. Thus, in the character of Love we see indeed that like is attracted to like, but we also become aware that the rule of like to like should only be taken in conjunction with the law of the unity of opposites (unlike the views of Eryximachus and Agathon, or Aristophanes' "whole"). If we forget about the necessity of opposites, we shall never go in search of wisdom, for we shall become single natured as the gods and ignorant humankind are single natured. Seekers after wisdom, therefore, should resemble Love's character and be constantly hungry. Homeostasis and perfect equilibrium are characteristics of ignorance or death, not of maturity or perfection. This is particularly important if we remember that all the previous speakers, with the exception of Phaedrus, are perfectly satisfied with their positions. Agathon is not even aware of what such a hungry, needy search might be.

Whatever the particular details, then, the myth of Poverty and Plenty in its context presents in its essentials the following important features.

1. A triple male/female paradigm for what is to be, in the subsequent parts of the speech, the fundamental epistemological model of procreation and birth, which expands and transforms the models of the previous speeches:
    a) the silent or implicit divine, hypercosmic (that is, beyond the cosmos) paradigm of Zeus, Dione, and Aphrodite;
    b) the explicit cosmic (or even precosmic, if the nonexistence of wine represents a stage before the formation of the cosmos) paradigm of Plenty, Poverty, and Eros; and in the broader context
    c) a paradigm of philosophical friendship in Diotima and Socrates, whose offspring will have to be *judged.*
2. The notion that divine superabundance reaches out entirely within its own nature (in other words, within the garden of Zeus) beyond itself, to give of itself to those who can claim its care, namely, beggars such as Poverty. So if divine love, as the beloved, *is* beautiful and delicate, as Diotima is now prepared to allow, given the total change in perspective from that of Agathon's speech (cf. 204c), we might say that a kind of divine self-forgetfulness, not in any way deliberative, but still appropriate to its own proper nature, occasions the generation of Love in the cosmos, which is the love human beings experience in loving one another and things. So to love that which is best in another and thereby to know oneself is in some measure also to experience divine love, which also appears to be the view of *Alcibiades* 1.[48]

---

48. At least on the evidence of *Alcibiades* 1.133c8–17 that is preserved in Eusebius and Stobaeus.

3. Since Love is a conjunction of opposites, his nature is susceptible to a wider range of expression, not initially understood because of Love's needy particularized focus, which traverses the entire field of experience from the most earthly to the most spiritual; but the key to his nature is its constant rebirth and transformation in its vertical focus, constant loss and serial succession in its horizontal focus. So the principle of like to like has to be taken in conjunction with the law of the unity of opposites, so that the single-natured appearance of self-satisfied perfection, so characteristic of ignorance, can be avoided.

These features are too important to suppress, since they provide a divine mythical paradigm, as it were, for understanding some of the major issues in the subsequent presentation, and they suggest lines of interpretation and forms of supplementary evidence that are rarely mentioned in commentaries on the *Symposium*. For example, the fact that there is no paradigm of homosexual love, equivalent to the triple paradigm outlined above, is no conclusive evidence for or against the view that Platonic love is essentially homosexual, but one cannot and should not claim at the same time that the "love with which the dialogue is concerned, and which is accepted as a matter of course by all the speakers, including Socrates, is homosexual love" and that this "alone is capable of satisfying a man's highest and noblest aspirations" without at least mentioning that the picture is really a good deal more complex than this.[49]

Equally significant is that some of these theological and cosmological considerations can only be appreciated if the images of the myth are called into question. We may, of course, consider it too naive today to ask questions of these mythological details; but if myths for Plato are complex images that bear the sign of "image" more explicitly than "argument" in their very presentation, and if they are therefore to be broken up so that one can see through them, then myth in this developed dialogical sense is a kind of *idea* that compels us to fill it with thought, but not to translate it or reduce it to a propositional calculus. In such myths we are surely looking at the pure play of ideas, and ideas that are actually questioning us. The general silence of much contemporary scholarship or the purely scholarly, archeological inventories, one finds, for instance, even in careful treatments of myth[50] relegate ideas found in myth, either explicitly or in practice, to mere objects, partly rational or completely irrational, but certainly arcane. Yet for all their supposed textual naïveté (and predilection

---

49. Hamilton 1951, 12.
50. Frutiger 1930, 240 (and especially in relation to the two "myths": Aristophanes' speech and the birth of Eros).

for "logical realism"), some Neoplatonist attempts to *think* these myths *as myths* for themselves may well be preferable to some modern scholarship which holds to the rather pedestrian and too restrictive principle that only "arguments" make the hard core of real philosophy.[51]

Indeed, too, the myth of the birth of Eros tells us something valuable about Plato's "theology" and "cosmology," which the Neoplatonists, on occasion with considerable insight, transformed into some of their basic principles. We recognize echoes of Diotima's myth in so much of what later became traditional inquiry and interpretation, specifically the idea that the "good," for example, is essentially self-giving (*bonum diffusivum sui*) and that all divine principles are creative in the sense that while they remain what they are, they also give of themselves to something else. These are fundamental principles for later Neoplatonism, as is the view that "Poverty" is a primordial material principle representing lack or need in body, soul, and the cosmos.[52] These principles do not represent a crazy mystical impulse to find meaning where there is none; nor are they simply a misguided allegorization of one myth or one part of an argument: rather, they may be an attempt to put together creatively things that are separate, as Plotinus, for instance, puts it,[53] and to think through the dialogues as problems or puzzles for thought as a whole (and not just thought as arguments). Some

---

51. This is not to downplay the necessary force of philosophical argumentation as such, but rather to suggest, as M. Frede has also done, that a too restrictive view of arguments is incapable of doing justice to the richer *philosophical* nature of the dialogue form itself. An examination of didactic, elenchic, gymnastic forms of dialectic, etc., together with various modern tendencies to "overdetermine" the Platonic dialogue, as well as the consideration that we need to take into account Plato's "particular conception of reason and rationality," leads Frede to conclude with good reason that "the dialogues are not philosophical treatises in disguise. . . . It would seem rather that the very dialogue form and the dramatic setting. . . . Are due to philosophical, rather than superficial literary or expository considerations. The dialogues are supposed to teach us a philosophical lesson. But they are not pieces of didactic dialectic with Plato appearing in the guise of the questioner. A good part of their lesson does not consist in what gets said or argued, but in what they show" (Frede 1992, 219). In this work, Frede concentrates upon arguments and so his conclusion too is necessarily restricted. But it is nonetheless illuminating. What is still at issue, however, as also for Neoplatonic attempts to think myths, arguments, etc., in their own way (different, *toto coelo* though they be from anything in modern scholarship), is precisely "the particular conception of reason and rationality" (219) the potential problems of which, one may argue, become clearer in Frede's concluding sentence: ." . . and the best part perhaps consists in the fact that they make us think about the arguments they present. *For nothing but our own thought gains us knowledge*" (219; emphasis added). One well understands what Frede means, but one may equally doubt if Plato would have agreed. Philosophical dialectic should be open, one might argue, not only to its own future as conversation, but especially to that dimension towards which Socrates remains an apprentice. See further section 8.6, below.

52. See Plotinus *Ennead* 3.5.(50) generally.

53. "But myths, if they are really going to be myths, must separate in time the things of which they tell, and set apart from each other many realities which are together . . . the myths, when they have taught us as well as they can, allow the man who has understood them to put together again that which they have separated" (*Ennead* 3.5.[50].9.24–29; trans. A. H. Armstrong).

of the best Neoplatonic attempts go beyond the letter of the text in ways that the Socrates of Aristodemus's prologue would surely have approved of, for they implicitly recognize that a dialogue is a transformative interplay of ideas rather than the atomization of discrete units of information. To give but one example, Pseudo-Dionysius implicitly links Agathon's speech and the birth of Eros in a strikingly novel theological way: the divine thearchy—by which he means the "trinity—he writes, without departing from its own essential nature, nonetheless, because of its ecstatic *Eros,* already reaches out to include and embrace the whole universe and is "enchanted" (*thelgetai*) by the "beloveds" it finds in the universe.[54] The *Eros* of Socrates-Diotima's speech has undergone considerable amplification by the time of Ps. Dionysius to become *ekstatikos,*[55] but the idea represented through Poros in the myth is still recognizable; and the verb *thelgein* (to enchant, charm, or bewitch) is taken from the closing phrase of the most theologically superabundant speech, namely, that of Agathon: Love "enchanting the mind of all gods and human beings" (197e4–5), and applied daringly to the Christian dialogical "first family." Some Thomists do not care to have anything but an inscrutable, impassible deity, and good philologists naturally want to keep everything in their respective textual places. But Ps. Dionysius, we suggest, thinks more like Plato, for all his differences, and transforms what is for him a very well known *topos* into a strikingly provocative *idea*.

To put this in simple and naive form, we might say that Diotima's myth has left its imprint on much significant thinking in many different traditions, thinking that has held to the philosophical view that the "divine" world is not a world of unconnected units or logical cyphers, but more a feast or *synousia,* that is, a being together, which involves the give-and-take of conversation and of friendship, so as to include human beings, and the physical cosmos as a whole, *dialogically*.[56]

5.6 Love: Relation or Substance?

Before we move on to the rest of the speech, let us take a brief look at another controversy, the view that Love is a relation, not a substance. Against this

---

54. "[W]e must dare to say even this on behalf of the truth that the cause of all things himself, by his beautiful and good love for all things, through an overflowing of loving goodness, becomes outside of himself (*exô heautou*) by his providential care for all beings and is, as it were, enchanted (*thelgetai*) by goodness, affection, and love, and is led down from his place above all ... to dwell in all things in accordance with his ecstatic, superessential power which does not depart from itself" (*Divine Names* 4.13, in *Patrologia Graeca* 3.712a–b).

55. See Corrigan 1995, 36–37.

56. On this theme, see especially Sallis 1996, 143–53.

view Cornford and Robin, like Plotinus, seem to hold the position that Eros is a substance in its own right, an *ousia*.[57] For Cornford, Eros is a single force of psychical energy that can be directed upward or downward, but that operates at a deeper level than the tripartite psychology of *Republic* 4. This energy is identified with the soul as a self-moving motion (as Plato argues in the *Phaedrus*): "It is the energy of life itself, the moving force of the soul; and the soul was defined by Plato precisely as the one thing that has the power of self-motion."[58] Dante, however, had already suggested in the *Vita nuova* that Love "is only an accident occurring in a substance,"[59] and following this interpretation, Allen has more recently argued that Love is a relative term "taken distributively," and not a Platonic "absolute" term:

> Because desire is a relative, desire is not a substance, as Plotinus had it, nor a force nor a fund of energy, as Cornford had it, nor the soul, as Robin had it; these are metaphors that merely obscure. The ascent to Beauty is, and is explicitly said to be (210a), that of the lover. If we choose to describe this as the ascent of Eros, we do so by virtue of the logical import of a literary fiction, namely, Diotima's personification of Eros; Eros is the lover qua lover, the lover just insofar as he loves. The lover insofar as he loves is neither a motion nor a force nor a fund of energy; and since he is not, qua lover, immortal, neither is he his soul.[60]

Rightly, it would seem, Allen wants to avoid hypostasizing eros, that is, to avoid turning it into some superhuman thing somehow responsible for the passion of love but not really connected with individual human loves and experiences. Moreover, he clearly wants to avoid two consequences, making

---

57. Plotinus is a curious case here, for he held the view that Eros is a substance (*ousia*) sprung from the soul's (or heavenly Aphrodite's) aspiration toward Intellect (*nous*), but he is also a being in its own right which is the cause of the affection of love in the human soul, and so the lower (or pandemic) Aphrodite who is "not only soul or simply soul . . . produced Love in this universe, who himself, too, immediately takes charge of marriages and, in so far as he, too, possesses the desire for what is above, in the same degree moves the souls of the young, and turns the soul with which he is ranked to higher things, in so far as it, too, is naturally able to come to remembrance of them" (3.5.[50].3.30–36; cf. 9.24–57). In other words, Plotinus invokes Pausanias's speech to interpret that of Socrates, apparently without any critical awareness that Pausanias does not speak directly for Plato! Following this and subsequent more complicated Neoplatonic interpretation, Ficino (through the mouth of Tommaso Benci "a diligent imitator of Socrates") effectively does the same thing (Ficino 1956, *Oratio Sexta, caput V*). But for a different view of the rather more complex issue still of Neoplatonic interpretation of Plato (a task beyond the scope of the present work), see section 6.4.1, below.
58. Cornford 1952, 70–79; cf. Robin, *Phèdre*, 1933 (1994), cxxxviii–ix.
59. Dante Alighieri 1995, 25.
60. Allen 1991, 95; cf. ix.

personifications into substances in their own right and identifying Love with soul, motion, force, or a substantial fund of energy (with Plotinus, Cornford, Robin, and so on).[61] Since the soul is immortal and Eros is not, then Eros cannot be identical with soul.

> It may be said that Plato treats Eros as the domain of a relation, taken distributively. The personification of Eros in the speech of Diotima is merely a literary device: Eros is the lover qua lover, each lover just insofar as he loves. It will be evident that the lover qua lover cannot be identified with the lover considered apart from that relation. If the soul is immortal, as Socrates argues in the *Phaedo,* then, given Diotima's claim that the lover qua lover lacks immortality and desires to possess it, this must imply that Eros is not Psyche and it is a root of error to confound them.[62]

Now, the personification is, indeed, a literary device, but Diotima does not tell Socrates that *Eros* is a relative term (*pros ti*) or, *per impossibile,* that Eros is a relation as a category inherent in primary substance (as in Aristotle's *Categories*). She tells him that he is a great spirit, and both Socrates and Diotima seem to believe in the real existence of spirits. Certainly, too, it is the lover qua lover Diotima is interested in, or rather the *loving,* and this is definitely relational, but in the *idea* or image she describes, the power of the spirit *is* that power by which each lover loves. For Diotima the existence of this power does not annihilate individual lovers but at its best *augments* them (cf. 210d7), and we are certainly justified in thinking that in the Greater Mysteries the lover is "strengthened and increased" because this too reflects the nature of the *daimôn*-Love.

Furthermore, Love is not a motion, like any other motion such as movement in place or change, but that in which other things move; and if Love is said to be a power, then why is it not also a force or a fund of relational energy? The two ideas are cognate with that of power. So there is no reason to dismiss Cornford's view out of hand. The fact is that while Love is certainly relational (to the point that it can make sense or nonsense of life), it is nowhere called either a relative term taken distributively or a substance. So the dilemma Allen poses is not one that arises directly from the text.

What, then, about the soul? If love is a spiritual being, then it is part of the content of soul, just as human souls or other animal souls are also part of that content. *Daimones* have souls, but their range is much wider than

---

61. Allen 1991, 95.
62. Allen 1991, ix.

that of human souls, as is conspicuously the case for Love. Thus, Love does not have to be identical with soul to have its own soul, unless all souls are one, but that is certainly a later problem and in any case one that does not crop up here. Indeed, too, in the subsequent argumentation it is going to be a debatable point whether soul is immortal, simply so and without any complications, as it were. Even in the *Phaedo,* where one might think it does not suit the argument very well, the soul is capable of a death in its own way (69c; 81b–e), just as Eros is susceptible of its own peculiar form of death here in the *Symposium* (203e3). So the immortality argument is not entirely persuasive. Eros is not identical with soul absolutely, but that does not prevent him having, or perhaps being, his soul.

Finally, there is the problem with substance. Allen seems to take substance univocally to signify a physical thing, such as in two senses of Aristotle's primary substance, that is, matter and the compound, or perhaps (since Aristotle says on several occasions that primary substance is soul, and even intellect) to signify a concrete, real *agent*.[63] But Diotima understands Eros to be a real agent even before she personifies him as the child of Poverty and Plenty. Now, of course, Plato uses the term *ousia* much more variously, and especially in the *Timaeus,* where he distinguishes different sorts of *ousia* that go into the making of the World Soul.[64] The soul is a complex organic reality in which there are many different kinds of *ousia* as well as many different kinds of soul. But if Plato can use the words *ousia* and *psyche* in this way, and if Diotima believes that Eros is a real existent, as she plainly does, then why cannot Eros be a substance? The Eros and Psyche of Apuleius's tale, no matter how inventive or illuminating they may be in their own right, do not limit (as Allen appears to imply) the interpretation of this much earlier tale.[65] So the interpretations of Plotinus, Cornford, Robin, and others should not at all be excluded, at least on account of these particular objections.

5.7 Rhetoric and Dialectic

Socrates is apparently convinced by Diotima's narrative, but not without irony: "Very well then, stranger; you speak beautifully" (204c). The repetition of the words uttered to Agathon not so long before (*kalôs legois;* cf. 201b–c) intimate Socrates' recognition that Diotima speaks rhetorically. Both sophists and philosophers, to the extent that there is a distinction between the two, which is often hard to discern, as in the *Sophist* or in the

---

63. Cf. *Metaph.* 1035b14–16; 1043a35–36.
64. *Timaeus* 35a.
65. As in Allen 1991, ix, cited above.

picture of Love's nature in the *Symposium*, employ rhetoric. The trick is, perhaps, to tell the difference between good and bad rhetoric (cf. *Gorgias* 563a; *Phaedrus* 261a ff.).[66] The right use of rhetoric, with truth and justice in mind, can save "body and soul," in Plato's estimation (*Gorgias* 511c–d; 527c). Nonetheless, Socrates acknowledges Diotima's rhetorical flight and continues, "but what use is Love to mankind?" Here we also recall Agathon's method and Socrates' promise to retain it; and the ease with which the latter applies this method shows that the appropriate method can simultaneously order the discussion and be born in it. Like Love, it should not only be correctly applied, but on occasion reborn anew.

When Diotima restates the question "Why is Eros of beautiful things?" in more concrete form as "Why does he who loves love beautiful things?" Socrates replies that it is to have them for himself. But the answer calls for another question: "What will there be to him who has beautiful things?" Socrates is unable to answer, but when he is asked to replace the beautiful with the good and answer the same question, he immediately replies that the lover of the good wants to make the good his own and thereby acquire happiness (204e–205a). The language of acquisition (*ktêsis* or *einai* + dative) runs right through this part of the speech and is perfectly appropriate;[67] love, just like much of human identity in body and soul in the subsequent argumentation, remains self-interested even in its focus on the other, and this is undoubtedly part of the irony of the situation since, by means of all the various forms of love, organisms strive to preserve themselves when there is no real self to preserve in the first place, that is, no "self" beyond a constantly fluctuating material and formal identity.[68] At this point in the dialogue, "the answer appears to have reached a goal." The lover really wants to be happy (cf. *bouletai . . . boulomenos . . . boulesis* {205a]). But the answer still needs to be unpacked further into a definition that marks the "common" feature (205a6–8) in human love. Just as there are many forms of creative production (*poiêsis*), but we limit the name of poetry (*poiêsis*) to one of them, so there are many forms of love, from moneymaking to athletics and philosophy, but we limit the term to romantic love. Love, however, is "every desire for good things and to be happy" (205d). Again the "answer" or conclusion needs to be unpacked or called into question. Even the best rhetoric is in need of dialectic or of well-meaning, but critical, conversation.

---

66. See Thompson 1979, 325–38; Dover 1980, 145. Because of elements suggesting sophistic rhetoric (208 c 1), among other things, and Socrates' "reaction" at 212b2 (*pepeismai:* "I am persuaded") Wilamowitz (1920, 2:170) thought that Diotima's views do not receive full assent from Socrates. But "persuasion" is an appropriate reaction to philosophical rhetoric of this kind (see sections 8.1–8.5, below).

67. For a different view, see Dover 1980, 134 at 200a6, 139 at 202c11, 144, ad fin.

68. Cf. *Symp.* 207d–208b.

5.8 Criticism of Aristophanes and Agathon

At this point, Diotima-Socrates comments on two crucial features in the speeches of Aristophanes and Agathon. First, she reveals love in its widest but also most immediate sense as longing for good, our ultimate goal and yet our everyday ethical principle, somehow omitted by Aristophanes in his "teaching" on piety and reverence toward the gods. So Aristophanes' position is criticized on two accounts—that as a definition it is not sufficiently comprehensive and that as a teaching about human nature it is conspicuously forgetful of our love for goodness: "a certain story [*logos*] is told, she said, that those who love are seeking the half of themselves. But my account [*logos*] says that love is of neither half nor whole unless it turns out actually, my friend, to be good" (205d–e). Diotima even parodies Aristophanes' "cuttings" and indirectly Agathon's notion of good: "people are willing to cut off even their own hands and feet if they think these possessions of theirs are bad. For they each refuse, I think, to cleave [*aspazontai*] even to what is their own [*to heautôn*], unless one calls what is good kindred and one's own, and what is bad alien [*to men agathon oikeion . . . kai heautou, to de kakon allotrion*]" (205e).[69] Goodness is more important than apparent integrity. Instead of "hugging" the hurt limb, we should heal it (*Rep.* 10.604a–d). Or like people who fall in love, but realize their love is not good, we should force ourselves to stay away from what only *appears* to be ours (607e). So people will even destroy themselves in order to achieve what they believe to be good, which is just about the opposite of Agathon's notion of goodness. For Agathon, love "empties us of alienation, but fills us with kinship (*allotriotêtos men kenoi, oikeiotêtos de plêroi* [197d1])," but what Agathon means by kinship is the good only of what is akin to himself, which may well turn out to be a form of pure self-interest. The apparently self-interested happiness Diotima speaks of is not that of one's own making, yet there is naturally a certain self-interested quality to it. Dover seems to miss the greater subtlety of Diotima's position when he states: "There are particular senses in which we wish to 'have' or 'possess' persons with whom we are 'in love' or objects or situations which we strongly desire, but in a general sense it is absurd to say that we wish to treat as items at our disposal those whom we love."[70] The language of acquisition is not that of using disposable items

---

69. Cf. *Republic* 607e5–6 cited in its wider context in section 4.4.1, above. Clearly, at 205e, Diotima "tells" the reader precisely how to read Aristophanes' speech as a deconstructive critique of mimetic art.

70. Dover (1980, 144) reads the whole of this speech as though it were a sham dialogue intended to deceive, by masking its counterfeit quality, but both Diotima and Socrates in different ways draw attention to the fictional and rhetorical quality of the dialogue, and in this way prick the illusion of reality, but this does not trivialize the form. On this further, see sections 8.1–8.4, below.

for our own preferences, because the good that Diotima describes, while naturally self-related, since it is the object of every desire and longing, is genuinely other-focused, that is, the object of love and rational wish does not reflect only our own inclinations.

One may also note that Diotima does not criticize Aristophanes' myth as a depiction of people in love with each other. She conspicuously omits discussion of such love because she expressly wishes to arrive at a definition of love as a "whole." For Diotima, the object of our desire, while immediate, is bigger than ourselves, and to become "whole," we have to long for something that will increase our nature. Aristophanes' account of desire for the whole is horizontal and planispheric, despite the fact that the vertical dimension should logically be a more integral part of his vision, since the search for wholeness and unity is also the longing to be restored to the divine world in friendship. We argued earlier that it is not so much Eros that Aristophanes describes as Love's mother, Penia, Poverty. Aristophanes gives us an account of how Need, rather than Love, appears. Moreover, we can apply the vision of Aristophanes to that of Diotima if we imagine her Eros striving after what is good and beautiful with the same desperate hunger as Aristophanes' lovers experience in searching for each other. Conversely, Agathon's speech describes Plenty, rather than Eros, and is in need both of Aristophanes' vision and of Diotima's new notion of the good if it is to capture the tumultuous, comprehensive force of love.

So Diotima does not simply tell us the immediate truth of the human condition, for at the outset her focus is that of the "*in between*" the human and the divine worlds. In other words, she wants us to see something we do not know by process of the dialectical questioning of something we do comprehend only too well. In this context, Vlastos's evaluation of "Platonic love" is surely off the mark. Vlastos argues that Diotima's failure "to say or to suggest anything of the kind [of love between two human beings] is no accidental oversight, but is an integral feature of the structure of Plato's theory."[71] "Whose theory"? one might ask. The difficulty of attributing *anything* to Plato is obvious,[72] but the problem of identifying Plato's view with one speech or part of a speech more obvious still. On Vlastos's interpretation, (1) the individual is loved only as being "good" or insofar as one loves an idea in him and (2) "the high climactic moment of fulfillment—the peak achievement for which all lesser loves are to be 'used as steps'—is the one farthest removed from affection for a concrete human being."[73] However,

---

71. Vlastos 1973, 31.
72. See, e.g., Frede 1992, 201–20.
73. Vlastos 1981, 32.

Diotima is not a marriage counselor, but a priestess and teacher who speaks of love as a universal experience shared both by those connected through the ties of love to other human beings and by those who are not. It was a role chosen by Aristophanes to enable him to give an account of love between two human beings and to remind us indirectly of the intellectual and spiritual forgetfulness therein involved. Diotima shows us that we must not stop there, but continue that search; she does not advise dropping our partners on the spot. Her teaching is intended to go beyond the focus of our immediate experience, for had she concentrated on that focus exclusively she would have become either an "imitator" explaining something that we could already see for ourselves, especially after Aristophanes' teaching, or a boring moralist. Diotima shows us instead *what we do not know* or *cannot immediately see.* But *how* we are to understand Diotima's teaching is left ambiguous or open ended. In insisting that Diotima reduce her focus to the immediate psychological level, Vlastos misrepresents the subtlety of the dialogue form, which permits speeches to speak to, and for, each other. Diotima outlines the journey, but she does not moralistically prescribe it in detail. Her account of love is a path of constant discovery, and in this we see how the philosophical muse (cf. *Republic* 499c–d; 548b–c) differs from the traditional literary goddess.[74]

5.9 The Curious Case of Procreation in the Beautiful

Diotima now draws out a further conclusion that has been implicit in the previous argument. If human beings love the good and want it to belong to them, then presumably they must want it to be theirs forever (*aei* [206a]). This agreement seems to follow naturally from Socrates' previous conclusion with Agathon that love involves wishing things present to remain present *in future* (200d). In the subsequent argument dealing with various kinds of "deathlessness," this is more or less all that is meant by "forever," in other words, for the conceivable future. And it is left open, at least in this portion of the argument, whether or not this will include genuine immortality. In the early part of Diotima's speech, the conclusion has been prepared by two admissions, at 205a "that everyone wishes to possess good things for themselves *forever,*" and at 205b, why it is that we do not say that "everyone loves . . . and *always.*"

What is the work of Eros that we see in those who pursue it? Socrates is at a loss and the strangeness of what Diotima has to say is emphasized

---

74. For development of this theme, see 8.4, below.

(206b). This work is *tokos en kalôi,* "begetting or bearing children [*tokos*] in beauty both in body and soul." All human beings are pregnant, according to Diotima, and when they reach a proper age, they desire to beget. Thus casually the fundamental Neoplatonic principle of creativity is born! "When anything . . . comes to perfection we see that it produces, and does not endure to remain by itself, but makes something else" (Plotinus *Ennead* 5.4.2.26–28). They shy away from ugliness and seek to beget in beauty. Diotima continues to expound an extraordinary teaching:

> The intercourse of man and woman is a begetting,[75] and this is a divine thing, and pregnancy [*kyêsis*] and procreation [*gennêsis*] are an immortal element in the mortal living creature. It is impossible for birth to take place in what is discordant. But ugliness is in discord with all that is divine, and beauty concordant. So the Goddess of Beauty [*Kallonê*] is Moira and Eilithyia at the birth. That is why, when what is pregnant [*to kyoun*] draws near to the beautiful, it becomes tender [*hileôn*] and melts with gladness [*euphrainomenon diacheitai*], and begets [*tiktei*] and procreates [*gennai*]; but when it draws near to the ugly it shrivels [*syspeiratai*] in sullen grief and turns away and goes slack [*aneilletai*] and does not beget, but carries with difficulty the conception within it. Whence it is that one who is pregnant and already swollen [*spargônti*] is vehemently excited [*ptoiêsis*] over the beautiful because it releases its possessor from great pangs [*ôdis*]. (206c5–e1)

What is remarkable about this passage is that while it makes sexual eros the paradigm, on the material level, for understanding the work of Love and, as Dover observes,[76] of the individual's desire to secure immortality

---

75. Bury with other editors wants to excise this clause as a meaningless intrusion, but most modern editors rightly retain it (Vicaire 1992; Rowe 1998).

76. Dover 1980, 146. See also du Bois 1994, 139–56, on the problem of the Platonic appropriation of the figure of pregnancy in relation both to the *Symposium* and the subsequent history of thought. du Bois makes the powerful argument that the imagery of the *agalmata* inside Socrates in Alcibiades' speech echoes the pregnancy motif in Diotima's speech and thus reappropriates the vocabulary of female reproductive powers in the service of a reinscription of the feminine within the metaphorical network of male philosophical power (as in Foucault's figure of mastery), thus establishing "a space for a new inscription, the metonymic placing of the female in relation to her superior and inferior. This occurs in the text of Aristotle and defines her place for centuries" (155). Here du Bois is implicitly reworking Lacan's notion of splitting (Lacan 1991, 144: *Spaltung*), as a "lack" at the heart of desire and transference, and the "doubling" of two "signifying chains" that constitute the subject (Lacan, 201), namely, "the dialectical definition of love," as developed by Diotima, that meets and envelops the "metonymic function in desire" (Lacan, 155). The metonymic is reinscribed by Plato within the metaphorical supremacy of dialectical power (du Bois 1994, 155). du Bois (cf. also Irigaray 1994, 181–96, Nye 1994,

(immediately following, Diotima draws the conclusion that in procreation Eros is love of immortality), nonetheless the passage itself does not present a consistent or even any possible physical image, but rather thematizes the *image* of sexual desire and arousal in vivid physical language that does not describe any actual physical encounter. Pregnancy does not come before intercourse, and, generally, pregnant women may melt with gladness in the presence of the beautiful, but this is incidental to the birth process, which is not normally a delightful experience. So too most hospitals are ugly, but even so they rarely cause pregnant women to "shrivel" and "go slack"; nor does strong excitement over the beautiful generally release swollen patients from their birth pangs. Finally, men, strictly speaking, have no place in this picture, since only women can be pregnant. In short, the image is sufficiently absurd that it is reasonable to believe that Plato, despite the strange views of his day and the lack of microscopes, was aware of this, even if most readers of the *Symposium* appear not to be.

Strange as it may seem, the image nonetheless catches something of the essence of sexual arousal or aversion by rendering such desire *psychic*, so that the apparent encounters, impossible in the physical world, can apply to the actual experience of both men and women only on the psychic level, where both can be pregnant and where intercourse and birth are also open to both. So, Diotima creates a new goddess, Kallonê, to preside over such birth;[77] and the vivid sexual language is inclusive of both sexes: "shrivels" (*syspeiratai*), "goes slack" (*aneilletai*), and "swollen" (*spargônti*) describe the reactions of both male and female genitals to sexual stimulus or revulsion, as Dover notes,[78] while also according to him, "melts" (*diacheitai*) is more appropriate to the female. "Pangs" (*ôdines*) usually refer to labor pains, but it can also mean pain or the tension created in either sex by sexual stimulation.

So why should Plato go to such lengths to undercut or undo the very paradigm of sexual *erôs*, "the intercourse of man and woman," that Diotima appears to have adopted? The reasons we suggest are these. Diotima is discussing pregnancy in both body and soul. Her focus is therefore on both. But clearly what she describes is not physical intercourse, but rather the

---

181–96, Nye 1994, 197–216) has a real point. On the lines of our interpretation, by contrast, the emphasis is less upon the appropriation of the feminine or the subordination of the metonymic function of desire as upon the problematization of the complex image itself and upon the deceptive ambivalence of gendered discourse. Other interpretations, both compatible and incompatible with du Bois's views, are also possible and may, together with these views, open new ways of thinking about Plato's problematic use of this and other images.

77. *Symp.* 206d2.
78. Dover 1980, 147.

"divine element" in intercourse, which is why the goddess Kallonê is introduced, to mark the sacred birth. So instead of imitating the physical image, Diotima presents a fictional image through which the vividness of physical desire can be intensified as a psychological experience open to all humanity. This is not to leave sexual intercourse behind, but rather to show in a dialectical way the augmented landscape of its *idea*. Socrates presents an even more striking image in the *Phaedrus* of the growth or swelling of the soul's wings after long aridity, and the image, though again physically impossible, is more highly erotic than any straightforward description of body parts could ever be:

> But when one who is fresh from the mystery (and vision of truth) . . . beholds a godlike face or bodily form that truly expresses beauty, first there come upon him a shuddering and a measure of that awe which the vision inspired, and then reverence as of the sight of a god, and but for fear of being thought a very madman he would offer sacrifice to his beloved, as to a holy image of deity. Next, with the passing of the shudder, a strange sweating and fever seizes him. For by reason of the stream of beauty entering in through his eyes there comes a warmth, whereby his soul's plumage is fostered, and with that warmth the roots of the wings are melted, which for long had been so hardened and closed up that nothing could grown; then as the nourishment is poured in, the stump of the wing swells and hastens to grow from the root over the whole substance of the soul. . . . Meanwhile she throbs with ferment in every part, and even as a teething child feels an aching and pain in its gums when a tooth has just come through, so does the soul of him who is beginning to grow his wings feel a ferment and painful irritation. (*Phaedrus* 251a–c)[79]

Few could more vividly describe, in this passage and the rest of the *Phaedrus* myth, the immediacy of sexual desire, the desperate need of sexual release just for its own sake, and yet at the same time the experience of being so deeply in love with one individual that the rest of the earth, and heaven too, is nothing beside this one individual. Dover remarks a propos of *Symposium* 206b–207a: "Since on most occasions people have sexual intercourse for its own sake and not as a means to procreation (indeed, they usually hope, and try to ensure, that procreation will not result), the argument requires the assumption that humans, like animals (207a5–c1), are

---

79. The translation is by R. Hackforth (1952).

impelled by forces of which they are not aware."[80] Neither Socrates nor Diotima may have been aware of the intricacies of birth control, but Socrates and Plato were surely aware that people do many things just apparently for their own sake and that they are thereby driven by forces they do not even suspect exist. Most of human life, Plato apparently believed, is like this, individuals being impelled by a blind herd instinct. The problem, for Socrates and Plato, was to become aware of such forces, to organize those forces within one's power and to respect those that are not. "The unexamined life is not worth living" may not be our favourite maxim on a Friday evening, but there is enough truth in it for other days of the week. Plato appears to have been convinced, for better or worse, that there is something sacred, in fact, even divine, in the experience of love, as in sexual intercourse, and he saw this as being intimately connected with what he knew of human biology and reproduction. In this he was apparently of the view that the significance of the body only emerges in the landscape of the soul, that is, we only see sexual arousal for what it is in the context of the soul. So Diotima's physically impossible description of sexual eros seems to open up the universal landscape of soul in which the apparently serial succession of physical time can be manifested as a vertical longing for different sorts of psychic time or immortality. And she concludes this particular conversation (which is actually patched together, so we discover at 207a5–6, from different conversations)[81] by implicitly distinguishing the beautiful and the good. We do not love the beautiful for its own sake as we love the good, she says, but we love it because of our desire to procreate and beget children in the beautiful (206e2–5). It would appear therefore that even happiness (which appeared to be a final "answer" at 205a) and the beautiful are not the ultimate goals of all human longing, though the *Symposium* does not develop this line of thought any further (except indirectly).[82]

5.10 The Concluding Sections of the Lesser Mysteries

In the concluding sections of what turn out to be the preparatory stages of initiation into a mystery religion, such as the Eleusinian Mysteries (209e–210a), Diotima argues that the immortality sought in love is (1) the physical immortality of the perpetuation of the species (for example, in the animal world the search to live forever takes the form of "always leaving

---

80. Dover 1980, 146–47.
81. The conversation represented, therefore, was (significantly) never a *single* physical event. See also Chapter 1, notes 30–32 and Chapter 2, section 2.5.
82. But see below on the Greater Mysteries, in Chapter 6.

behind a different new thing in place of the old" [207d3–4]) and (2) the psychic immortality involved in the begetting of the soul's children—the virtues, poetry, laws, and so on—and here lasting fame is the ultimate goal. So curious are these sections that they have been thought to show that Plato did not believe in the immortality of the soul when he wrote them and that they contain nothing of the characteristic Platonic theory of the soul-body relation.[83] Indeed, as we shall argue, the interpretation of love given by Diotima at this stage does not represent the full range of Plato's thought.

When Diotima discusses the "strange" state that all animals are thrown into when they want to procreate, she observes how they are ready to die on behalf of their young, even the weakest of them being ready to fight against the strongest. The repetition of the verb *hyperapothnêskein* (207b4) reminds us of Phaedrus's speech (179b4–5), but the thought goes somewhat beyond Phaedrus's point that lovers alone, whether men or women, are willing to die on each other's behalf. Later, however, Diotima criticizes Phaedrus's view when she says that human beings will do anything for fame and glory, and that neither Alcestis nor Achilles would have died for Admetus and Patroclus if they had not thought the fame of their virtue would be immortal (208d). The idea that Plato applauds such a view and holds it to be superior to that of Phaedrus has not delighted critics. But Plato does not applaud this view, because the whole of this section presents an *incomplete* picture of biological and psychological life that yet requires a deeper philosophical point of view beyond itself. In the text this is casually indicated by Socrates' remark that Diotima replies like a professional Sophist (*hoi teleoi sophistai* [208c1]). He refers apparently to the phrase "know it well" (*eu isthi*), which may well have been characteristically sophistic (cf. *Euthyd.* 274a; *Hippias Major* 287c), but is also quite common. So it is not unreasonable to think that the remark about professional sophistry also signals the immediate context in which the timocratic ideal—the love of honor—is presented as the highest value. And this is surely not Plato's own view. But it may be as far as "mortal nature" can go on its own.

We should note too that Diotima does not deny that human beings are also prepared to die on behalf of their young, simply for love's sake, but, unlike other animals, they do so on the basis of reasoning (207b7; 208d1); she thinks, however, that there is something more complex in most human motivation, and there can be no question but that Plato himself believed fame and honor to be powerful motivating forces, even more powerful in most cases than other forms of love, and certainly more grotesque. We

---

83. Hackforth 1950, 43–45; Morrison 1964, 42–55; but see O'Brien, in Gerber 1984, 185–206; Rowe 1998, 185.

surely cannot suppose, for instance, that Socrates himself would not have found such an exclusive reason for dying grotesque.[84] In a shame or guilt culture, however, these are the primary accepted values.

The case of body and soul in the context of identity makes this general point even clearer. Diotima presents a bundle theory of identity for both body and soul that anticipates the view of the Scottish philosopher David Hume (1711–76).[85] Each living creature is called the same (*to auto*), in the conventional sense that someone is said to be the same from youth to old age, but the reality is that "he never has the same things in himself," since he is always becoming new while all the features of his body are perishing (207d–e). And the same is true, Diotima continues, not only of the body but also of the soul (character, habits, opinions, desires, pleasures, pains, fears are never the same) and even of the sciences ("still more absurd . . ." [207e5]): "we are never the same not even with respect to the sciences" (208a).

Is this extraordinary theory really Platonic? Yes, for it can also be found in earlier and later dialogues, the *Gorgias* and *Theaetetus*, for instance.[86] The point surely is that this theory does not give the complete picture of Plato's own view, but it *does* demolish Pausanias's apparently Platonic view of the soul-body relation, a view shared by Eryximachus in his presentation of the sciences. What is the difference between Pausanias/Eryximachus and Diotima on this crucial question? The difference is that for Pausanias and Eryximachus, the soul is its own standard of truth insofar as the virtues or the sciences, in each case, determine right thought and action. A natural consequence of this self-dependence is that truth comes to reflect the preference of each speaker instead of being genuinely open to all. For Diotima, by contrast, the soul is not primarily self-determining, which is not to deny that the soul is a necessary principle of self-organization but rather to acknowledge that there must be a perspective beyond the individual soul, indeed beyond the soul itself, if we are to explain the soul's capacity, however flawed, to recognize the truth, even against our own preferences, and to share that knowledge, which is not the intellectual property of "my" soul

---

84. The *Crito*, for example, provides a practical case in point, that is, a detailed examination of why Socrates should remain in prison and drink the hemlock. It thus presents a rich dialectical picture, i.e., an internal dialogue opened up for Crito's scrutiny, which explores the range of Socrates' self-examination of all the issues at stake, from 1) the nature of the jury one needs to impress, 2) the principles at stake, 3) the general and particular case at hand, and 4) the consequences of his refusing to flee Athens. All of these elements together constitute this moral decision-making and Socrates' approach is forthrightly practical and comprehensive, but glory and the timocratic ideal are not the determining features of his action.

85. For skepticism about the real Platonic character of the passage, see Crombie 1962, 363. Cf. Price 1989, 21–25.

86. *Theaetetus* 157b–c; *Gorgias* 493a ff.

or "your" soul, with others. In this context, it makes sense to say that the soul is not immortal in its own right *tout court,* but since Diotima does not make this explicit claim here, we shall take up this question in relation to other dialogues in Chapter 8.

At any rate, Diotima proposes the view that the principle of identity is not to be found in either the body or the soul except by the convention of recognizing sameness in what is extreme Heraclitean flux or by the desperate venture of maintaining the fictional appearance of a quantitative self by lifelong education. There is much irony in this view; but it is certainly directed against Pausanias's and Eryximachus's self-satisfied and self-sufficient views of the soul, the virtues, and sciences. The consequences are far reaching, for much of what we take to be essential to human life, including material and formal identity, turns out on this account to be adventitious: that is, the virtues and the sciences turn out to be largely a matter of conventional association, or a failure to examine what is really happening, or even the desperate attempt to hide the awful truth from ourselves by education! This, however, is neither Plato's nor Diotima's last word on the subject.

Two final points on these Lesser Mysteries. First, the children of the soul are the virtues ("practical wisdom and the rest of virtue"). Apparently, all the poets procreate these and also those craftsmen who are said to be "inventors." So art is, or should be, inventive; that is, art should involve the discovery of something beyond itself. But the highest virtues are concerned with the regulation of cities (209a). Are we to be reminded that in the *Republic* the interests of the *polis* should dictate the kind of poetry that is to be allowed? Hesiod, Homer, and "their children" are praised, but more modestly than the immortal children of Lycurgus and Solon, the laws, which are praised together with their noble deeds. Again, we may compare *Republic* 10.599b–c: "if he [the poet] truly had knowledge of the things he imitates, he would much rather devote himself to actions than to the initiation of them, and . . . would try to leave behind many fine deeds as memorials of himself." Or 600a–b: "is Homer himself, while alive, said to have been, in his private life, a leader in the education of some people who loved him for his company and left to posterity a Homeric way of life . . . as Pythagoras was himself particularly loved for this . . . ?" In other words, Diotima's presentation touches in its own way on some of the fundamental themes of the criticism of mimetic art in the *Republic,* but still suggests a more positive, heuristic function for poetry (on this, see below, Chapters 6 and 8).

Second, Plato's silence about the physical side of homosexuality is conspicuous (209b–c), although the divine element in heterosexual love has been prominently stated. The youth who is pregnant of soul is said to be "divine" (*theios*), which is a preferable reading to "unmarried" (*êtheos*), accepted by Burnet and Dover, in the light of 206c6 (and c3–7 generally) and *Meno* 99c–d, as well as because of the intimate "divine" connection between Eros and the lover in the *Symposium*. He "welcomes" (*aspazetai*) beautiful bodies, and if he meets a noble soul, he "welcomes" the combination (*to synamphoteron*), but this is a prelude to conversation and education (209b7–c2). Yet he does "touch" the beloved and beget more beautiful and more immortal children than the human sort (209c2–7). Or rather he "touches" the beautiful (*tou kalou*) and is in close company with it or with him (*homilôn autôi*). The Greek is ambiguous, perhaps naturally, since the beauty manifest in his friend is a "divine" one. But the emphasis of the passage, far from being sexual, is rather on the greater commonality such friendship brings: "he remembers what has been begotten in common"; this stable friendship (*bebaia philia*) shows "a far greater communion" (*koinônia*) than that of the sharing of children, since "they have shared in common" (*kekoinônêketes*) more beautiful and more immortal children (290c). If we put this together with Diotima's subsequent use of the verb *paiderastein,* in the phrase "ascending through the right love of boys" (211b5–6), we might reasonably suppose that while there is a continuity here with the sexual themes of Pausanias and Phaedrus, sexualized pederasty is not directly envisaged, especially in light of Alcibiades' testimony later (218a–219e). So the question of homosexual love in the *Symposium* is finely nuanced: Diotima does not ignore one of the most evident contexts of her time nor does she reject such obvious human experience as friendship between persons of the same sex; but she avoids direct sexualized pederasty and puts the focus instead on "the far greater communion" involved in sharing an immortal discourse.[87]

5.11 Preliminary Conclusion

To give the final portion of Socrates-Diotima's speech the importance it deserves, it is necessary and more useful to treat it as a whole in a separate chapter of its own. What we can say about Socrates' speech so far, however, is this. The absence of apparently key Platonic "doctrines," such as the "doctrine" of recollection, from the *Symposium* has troubled commentators, but this is actually because of a failure to see what is staring us in the face. Through Aristodemus and Apollodorus, we find ourselves, uninvited, in the house of Agathon. Our host is all-seeming perfection and, in Socrates' pun, the "good." As soon as this apparent good, however, admits that he is

---

87. Cf. *Republic* 3.403a–c; *Laws* 8.838e, 836c–e, 841d.

not the real good, that is, that the "truth" is something to which both he and Socrates have to be accountable, the house of Agathon disappears for the first time in these speeches and we find ourselves literally inside a *recollection,* and one that makes little pretence of being directly historical or factual. In fact, neither the frame of the conversation nor its argument and myth are mimetic (in the sense criticized in the *Republic*); instead, they are prismatic ideas that talk to each other and to earlier elements in the dialogue. The speech is, therefore, a recollection of the interplay of ideas in a conversation that is placeless and that occurred at no *one* time, and that is conducted with a woman from outside who has no physical characteristics. The force of this speech is to open up the closed, self-contained worlds of the earlier speakers into playful dialogue. This involves not only criticism of those positions, and even comment upon the mimetic narrative itself,[88] but also considerable broadening and deepening of perspective so as to include them, as we shall see immediately in the following chapter.

---

88. Cf. Diotima's comments at 208a3–b3 upon *meletan,* "going over" or "conning" material; Apollodorus's first words at 172a1 are that he is not without "conning" practice. This is the only way the mortal can be "preserved" (*sôzetai*), Diotima states (208a8), just as the myth of Er is "preserved" in the *Republic* (*sôzetai*) or one "etymology" of *sôma* in the *Cratylus* is that it is "preserved." For the notion of *meletê* as representing "an instance of the procreative impulse" (in Diotima's speech)" which achieves a certain stability and permanence in the boundless sea of becoming by replacing what is lost with a new version of itself," see Halperin 1992, 103.

The Greater Mysteries and the Structure of the *Symposium* So Far

"Into these love matters, Socrates, perhaps even you may be initiated; but I do not know whether you can be initiated into the final revelations [*ta telea kai epoptika*] for the sake of which these actually exist if one approaches correctly."[1] These words have been thought to imply a Platonic criticism of Socrates' limitations, in other words, that the final mysteries represent Plato's own vision as opposed to that of the historical "Socrates."[2] Yet they can be explained perfectly well within the dialogue. The young Socrates, on his own admission, is in need of learning and is constantly surprised at the extraordinary quality of Diotima's teaching to this point. He comes to Diotima in the first place because he is unable to explain what he sees by following customary patterns of thought, such patterns as are illustrated by all the previous speakers and especially Agathon. Diotima's Lesser Mysteries have taught him the right method of investigation, these being dialectic and the law of the necessity of opposites in the creation of a whole, together with the attraction of like to like. Finally, therefore,

---

1. There is no object of the verb "approaches" and so one might naturally supply *tauta*, "these things," i.e., referring to *ta telea kai epoptika*, but in the context it is perhaps better to emphasize the simple active movement (the proper approach) rather than supply the object.

2. Cornford 1950, 75; against, Taylor 1960, 229 n. 1.

like an honest teacher, she admits that these are insufficient and only constitute an avenue to the final revelations, which go far beyond the analysis of language, experience, and behavior that has formed the basis of both Socrates' elenchus of Agathon and Diotima's more extraordinary conclusions thus far. It is not enough to retrieve the everyday thought and knowledge that is constantly disappearing into the past; one has instead to search for and be faithful to that highest beauty of which every other beauty partakes. And this, Diotima believes, is the most important part of one's knowledge. So the man who starts out on the inquiry insisting that love must be "of" someone or something might well have difficulty following the final secrets of this mystery cult. This is not simply dramatic verisimilitude or mock modesty. Everyone needs a guide, from the prisoner in the cave (*Rep.* 7) to Socrates himself (*Phaedo* 99c).[3] And, indeed, these Greater Mysteries are no simple matter. In Bury's words, here "we find the passion of the intellect passing into a still higher feeling of the kind described by the Psalmist as 'thirst for God.'"[4] By contrast, Dover notes, "Having parted company with love, Platonic eros now takes wing."[5]

6.1 The Movement of Ascent: Structure

Diotima presents the apprenticeship of the lover in the following ascending order:

1. *From the love of a single body to that of many bodies.* First, he must be in love with the beauty of one particular body and beget beautiful discourse there, and then he should recognize the kinship of beauty "upon" all bodies and by pursuing the beautiful as it attaches to form (*ep' eidei*) come to the realization that all bodily beauty is one and the same, thereby becoming a lover of all beautiful bodies and relaxing the intensity of his focus on one (210a7–b6).
2. *From bodily beauty to the beauty of souls and laws.* His second step (we take *meta de tauta,* [after this], at 210b6, which is repeated at regular intervals, to be the dividing mark, a division supported by Diotima's later summary [211c–d]) is to set a higher value upon the beauty of souls, even where the "bloom" of soul is slight, and there in loving and caring, to beget and seek[6] those discourses that will make the young

---

3. *Phaedo* 99b–c: *ê mathein . . . ê heurein.*
4. Bury 1932, xlix.
5. Dover 1980, 155.
6. This is to include *kai zētein* (210c2), bracketed or excised by Ast ([1835] 1956), Vicaire (1992), and Brisson (1998, 214 n. 466), but rightly included by Rowe (1998).

better in order that he might be compelled to contemplate the kinship of beauty in laws and practices so as to see bodily beauty of little account by contrast (210b6–c6). It might seem that this section should be subdivided: (1) from body to soul and (2) from soul to laws, but the text indicates otherwise. Diotima unites the notion of caring for the soul with care for the beauty of laws by putting the latter into a subordinate final clause (210c3–4), and the beauty of the laws she opposes not to the beauty of soul but to that of body (210c5–6).

3. *Love of the whole of wisdom.* The third step (the same division occurs: *meta de ta epitêdeumata* [after practices; 210c6]) is the movement to all the branches of science, by loving which he must (1) avoid slavery to the beauty of one single thing and (2) in being turned in contemplation to this great ocean of the beautiful he may beget beautiful "discourses and thoughts in ungrudging love of wisdom" (210c6–d6).

4. *From all studies to a single study.* The fourth step, stylistically marked off by *heôs an entautha* (until to this point; 210d6) signifies a movement from many different knowledges to a certain *single* knowledge (*tis epistêmê mia*), which is the knowledge of the beauty yet untold (210d6–8).[7]

5. *The self-disclosure of the beautiful itself.* The fifth step (and here Diotima demands Socrates' special attention) is the "sudden" sight (*exaiphnês katopsetai*) of the beautiful itself, the goal of all earlier labors and cause of all beauties, but not to be ranged with them,[8] unalloyed, pure, unmixed (211e), pure self-identity (and, as *monoeides,* in some sense presumably a cause of unity and uniqueness in others).[9] This he will see reflexively "with that by which it is visible"[10] and will beget, "not images of virtue, because he does not touch an image (*ouk eidôlou ephaptomenos*), but true virtue, because he touches the truth (*tou alêthous ephaptomenos*). . . . And in begetting true excellence and nurturing it, it is given to him to become dear to god [*theophilês*], and if any other among men is immortal, he is too" (210e4–212a7).

---

7. In the revelation of the beautiful, the quantitative and qualitive multiplicities of earlier stages are transformed more intimately into a unified multiplicity which desires its unity in something beyond itself. Cf. Dixsaut 1998, 150–53. The "pédagogie d'erôs" is "l'ordre même de la dialectique de l'un et du multiple" (151).

8. Cf. Ebert 1974, 143–46. *To kalon,* like *to agathon,* is an *Ausschlussbegriff*; i.e., it excludes alignment with classes or genera.

9. The *Symposium* will not answer the implicit "question" of unity it poses (and one has to wait for the *Parmenides* for a "treatment" of form, and of unity and multiplicity, posed here), but it will suggest an answer to the problem of identity or uniqueness (see Chapter 7, esp. sections 7.6, and 8.7).

10. As the eye of the soul sees the good and becomes good-formed (*agathoeides*) in *Republic* 7. Cf. Robin 1992, xciv.

This five-stage subdivision is confirmed by Diotima's own summary at 211b7–d1:[11]

> For this is the right way to proceed in matters of love, or to be led by another, beginning from these beautiful things here to go ever upward for the sake of that, the beautiful, as though using the steps of a ladder, (1) from one to two and from two to all beautiful bodies, (2) and from beautiful bodies to beautiful practices, (3) and from practices to beautiful studies (*mathêmata*), (4) and from studies to end up in that study (*mathêma*) that is the study of nothing other than that, the beautiful itself (5) in order that one might know in the end by itself what it is to be beautiful.

Diotima insists (1) that we have to start from physical objects, and from one particular body, but (2) that we have to go beyond this to escape the restrictive focus of only one point of view and get some sense of what is universally true or beautiful; yet (3) even scientific knowledge is insufficient unless it is brought into a single vision that (4) is ordered and occasioned by something quite transcendent, the beautiful itself. She also insists (5) that at every step there are practical consequences, fellowship, and the making of discourses, but (6) only at the highest step are these consequences realities, not images. Clearly too each step is not meant to be arrested development, but a flowing motion of ascent.[12]

The apparent abstractness of this ascent is mitigated by the fact that the ascent refashions and transforms the positions of the earlier speakers, though this has escaped attention entirely and so only its subliminal force is felt. Since this transformation is not at all obvious and since it would be inappropriate to press details beyond a certain point, we should outline the connections with each of the early speeches. These connections should not be understood in a mechanical way either as a form of subordinationism or

---

11. Plochmann in Anton and Kustas 1971, 339, itemizes nine stages, and in n. 42, indicates seven steps in 211b–c, but his views bear no relation whatsoever to the text, nor does he attempt to make a correlation. Just as in the case of the ordering of the speeches, scholars presumably feel that it is "bad form" either to impose any order from outside (and on this account they are right) or to draw attention to any internal order which may mar the reader's open-ended reading of the text. But Diotima *draws attention* to the order by providing this recapitulation. So the absence of any direct comment is perhaps understandable, but not warranted by the text. Brisson, for instance, has very little comment on this section (1998, 71, 214–15 nn) and at 210a–211b only notes the change from *epistêmae* to *mathêmata*, but the single *epistêmê-mathêma*, is surely significant too (see section 8.4, below). Cf. Robin 1992, xciii–xciv, and Brisson, 71, for 4 steps (which omit the all-important dialogical, but transcendent, fifth).

12. Cf. the contrast between *ephexês*, *orthôs*, and *exaiphnês* (Brisson 1998, 215 nn. 473–74); Dixsaut 1998, 153: "Le déroulement continu et ordonné trouve sa raison d'être dans son interruption."

even as filling in the pieces of a jigsaw from a privileged vantage point,[13] for there are pressing philosophical reasons for this structure, but these will not be entirely apparent until we have looked at the whole dialogue and had a chance to take a broader view still of its design (in Chapter 8).

6.2 The Movement of Ascent and the Earlier Speeches

1. On the face of things, there is little similarity between Phaedrus's position and the first rung of this ladder that presents the development of love for one particular body into a love for bodily beauty as a whole. There have been attempts, though not in this context, to view Phaedrus's speech as a description of "low" passion for boys,[14] but this is clearly an oversimplification. Phaedrus's speech evidently has two main purposes: it must possess enough energy to propel the reader to further interest in the study of love and it must be a first step in this study. So his eulogy evinces sincere wonder at the effects of love, love being understood (and taken for granted) as a physical passion uniting lover and beloved. Phaedrus's role, then, is that of the apprentice so interested in the question of love that it is because of him that all the eulogies take place. Like the apprentice on the first rung, he understands love as a physical passion for one particular person and both here and in the *Phaedrus* he is keen "to generate noble discourses" (cf. *Symp.* 210a7–8). Yet the extended content of this first step, physical beauty as such, does not particularly interest him and is, in fact, absent from his speech. This is the precise point at which the lost speeches play a role.

If we recall, Aristodemus could not remember several speeches after Phaedrus and before Pausanias, and when Pausanias announces his distinction between love of the soul and love of the body, this comes as an entirely new notion. Now Aristodemus's and Apollodorus's forgetfulness can easily be understood if we consider, especially given Apollodorus's own physical condition, that love of physical beauty is hardly their principal interest if they spend most of their time in the company of Socrates! It is with a certain humorous, dramatic, and psychological plausibility, therefore, that after Phaedrus's speech, which remains so much at the level of mere appearance, the other forgotten speeches (in other words, bodies) act as the missing link between the positions of Phaedrus and Pausanias in the movement of ascent.

But granted that we might start with one instance, it seems somewhat indiscriminate, even nonsensical, to strive to become a lover of *all* beautiful bodies. Does this step make any sense beyond the rather mechanical

---

13. Rowe 1998, 8.
14. Findlay 1974, 145; Taylor 1960, 212.

movement from Phaedrus through a series of forgotten speeches? Is Diotima even advocating promiscuity? The answer must, on balance, be negative. Diotima envisages a movement toward *discrimination,* not a bland homogeneity, and so the beauty that is one and the same must nonetheless also be diverse.[15] In this, Diotima advocates *recognition* (*katanoêsai* [210a8]), active pursuit of formal beauty (b2), and *thought* (c2–7). But how far does this represent actual human experience? Certainly, it is not representative of *some* human experience: lovers tend to take a dim view of their beloveds' wanting to examine the whole field of physical beauty! Yet sexual jealousy is possible precisely because another's beauty is preferable or at least akin to the beauty one might hope to have oneself. So, one might argue, the view that all bodily beauty is alike is rather risky insofar as it tends to fly in the face of the normal wish to possess the other for oneself. But such possession is perhaps even riskier, since in this focus love tends to turn into physical obsession. So if one is forced to admit that all physical beauty is related in a positive way, as Diotima envisages, one is presumably prepared to see that love in any deeper, more permanent sense must be based on something other than physical beauty alone, and this predicament or puzzle is certainly part of our experience. What can be indiscriminate in our experience, then, has to become discriminate if we are ever to begin to understand the power of love over, in, and through us.

2. The second speech, that of Pausanias, corresponds directly, at least on the level of its intention, with the development that transforms the lover on the second rung. Pausanias intends to show that only the love for soul, which is a higher "heavenly" love, permits the beloved to gratify the lover; but as we have seen, since there is no criterion genuinely beyond the soul to determine right action, Pausanias's notion of soul is really and only *his own soul,* that is, his own preferences. He talks like a sociological Sophist of practices and laws, but the society of souls to which he appears to appeal masks the idiosyncracy of his own interpretation; and so despite his best intentions, he

---

15. Martha Nussbaum's (1986, 180ff.) interpretation, however appealing in other ways, follows Vlastos's critique of the supposed Platonic view of individuality and therefore sees in this ascent a homogeneity or "qualitative indifference" which leads to a radical choice between the contemplative life and the ordinary experiential viewpoint: ."... this body of this wonderful beloved person is *exactly* the same in quality as that person's mind and inner life ... what would it be like to see in the mind and soul of Socrates nothing else but (a smaller amount of) the quality that one can also see in a good system of laws, so that the choice between conversing with Socrates and administering those laws was, in the same way, a matter of qualitative indifference. . . . At each stage, then, the teacher persuades the pupil to abandon his or her cherished human belief in irreplaceability in the service of his inner need for health." The ascent to the *unique* revelation of the beautiful, from out of the quandary of the constant need to replace every item of psycho-physical existence, is surely *not* a question of quantitative exchange ("a smaller amount of the quality") or qualitative indifference, since discrimination, recognition and thought (210 a–c) are here empowered and augmented, not eliminated or rejected.

effectively sets himself up as a sexual predator on what appear to be the highest moral grounds. While Pausanias may appear to rise "a little above" the "extremely low level" of Phaedrus,[16] then, Pausanias defeats the advance represented by the distinction between body and soul and the emphasis on the primacy of soul and unconsciously betrays the shadow of his own face. The unconsciously manipulative self or "soul" whose sole criterion of excellence is its own judgment, or lack of it, is a far more sinister and dangerous presence than its predecessor, Phaedrus, and yet it represents a distinctly psychic and social achievement that points at the same time necessarily beyond the limitations of its individual and typological preferences.

This contrast between the second step and its deconstruction in Pausanias shows more clearly why this step, though hardly part of what we think of immediately as love, is in its own way psychologically appropriate and does negate the physical side of love. To love another for the other's sake is not simply to love that person's character, personality, and so on in themselves, but to "care" for them (210c1) and to wish to create something for them which will "make them better" (2c1–2). But as soon as one wants to foster the best condition of soul, Diotima indicates, one is compelled to live in a community of souls and to "see" (*idein*) the kinship which unites everything (c4–5). The beauty of body pales by comparison with that of the beauty of such community. We should also note that Diotima does not talk of the landscape of soul in abstraction from concrete circumstance. This is a journey of recognition and transformation which is part of the experience of loving other people, but which also has to be ordered or directed.

3. The third speech is that of Eryximachus, the man of science, who attempts to account for the many sciences in the light of Love. The person who proceeds correctly on this level, according to Diotima, must be able to escape slavery to a single instance and, "turned to the multitudinous sea of the beautiful," must bring forth noble discourses "in ungrudging philosophy" (210c7–d6). Despite, or because of his pretensions, Eryximachus fails on both these accounts. His obsessive sense of order eliminates the passion necessary for really inventive scientific work; and he makes all the other sciences in the image of his own profession and preference—medicine. Neither is he capable of philosophical thinking, as his propensity for hidden contradiction attests.

But does he not simply represent the human condition, pretending a universality it cannot deliver because of the "tragic flaw" of his being a limited individual with potentially fatal blinkers? Yes, indeed, and to this extent the gap between the third rung and Eryximachus is as important for

---

16. As Findlay 1974, 145, puts it (unfairly, in our view—see Chapter 3).

our understanding as the third rung itself. If Diotima's project at this level seems unrealistic, we should at least remind ourselves that our universities are founded on something of this model to the extent that we hold it crucial that all forms of scientific and artistic endeavour worthy of the name should constitute the field of human concern, that such concern should include the study of much more than just humanity, and for its own sake,[17] and that, despite the practical impossibility of mastering more than one discipline, or even a part thereof, in an expanding information culture, it remains the mark of an educated person that she be able to tell the genuine from the counterfeit when she meets it and reach out beyond her own preferences to discover the truth, with the assistance of a community to remedy her blind spots. So it is perhaps not surprising that Diotima points to the need for *ungrudging* philosophical creativity at this level: surely any authentic science that tests the boundaries of more prosaic thinking is liable to be destroyed by jealousy and rigid typology.

Something of this model is perhaps what Plato had in mind both here in the *Symposium* and in the *Republic*, where Socrates argues that the sciences serve as assistants to turn the eye of the soul around so that she can contemplate reality (7.533c–d; 518b–d) and discern in the practice of the sciences their kinship (*syggeneia*) and commonality (*koinônia* [531c9–d4]).[18]

4. Aristophanes' speech and the fourth rung of the movement of ascent seem furthest removed from each other, at first glance. Diotima says: "until, having . . . grown and waxed strong, he beholds a certain single knowledge" (210d); "one comes in the end to that study [*mathêma*], which is the study of none other than that, the beautiful itself" (211c). On the surface, there is simply no similarity; and this apparent incommensurability has been the cause, to a great extent, of the reluctance of much scholarship to find any principle of organization at work in these speeches and in the dialogue as a whole. But again the truth is that despite the striking gap, there is also a strong and close correlation between the two, a correlation that, in each case, turns on the single *mathêma*.

According to his *mathêma*, Aristophanes considers himself a "teacher" representative of his art, through which he provides a study of human nature (*dei . . . prôton hymas mathein tên anthrôpinên physin* [189d5]). According to Diotima's fourth step, a single *epistêmê* or *mathêma* should emerge about the beautiful, as yet unrevealed. The juxtaposition of these two positions brings us back to Socrates' criticism of art in the *Republic*, with one notable exception. In Diotima's fourth step, we discover not where art fails

---

17. Cf. Aristotle *Nicomachean Ethics* 6.7.
18. On this, see section 8.4, below.

(as it does in Aristophanes' speech, according to Socrates' criticism in the *Republic*), but rather where its potential lies, according to Diotima's scale of love, if its individual blinkers are removed. The implicit argument here is so important that one should examine it more thoroughly, step by step.

Indeed, Aristophanes' gods and globular beings embody Socrates' criticism of literature: the gods are a dim-witted, self-serving bunch, and the globs are an absurd, mimetic parody of human nature. Moreover, in the *Republic*, poets are criticized particularly for their lack of *epistêmê* (e.g., 599b). And of course Aristophanes' "study" is not a *mathêma* of the beautiful, that is, invisible beauty, but of physical beauty. So the gap between Aristophanes and the fourth rung points directly to the *Republic*'s literary critique. When Diotima speaks subsequently of the vision of the beautiful itself that causes the apprentice to give birth to truth, since he "touches" the true and not an image (*ephaptomenôi*), we also recognize the literary terms of this criticism: "imitative art is far removed from *the true* and that is why, so it *seems*, it can fashion everything, because it *touches* only a small part of each thing, and this an *image*" (598b).

Yet it is also true that Aristophanes' art is double edged. On the one hand, it is single minded in its pursuit of an image and of physical beauty; on the other hand, it captures something that is not present in its basic image of physical globular wholes hopelessly fragmented: a spiritual longing for unity and wholeness; and it attempts in its own inimitable way to see human nature as a whole and to restore it to god. Aristophanes' fragmented lovers can only "divine" (*manteuetai*) the integral unity they "wish" (*bouletai*) in their desire (192d1–2), but they cannot grasp or express it. In exactly the same way in *Republic* 6–7, there is one ultimate study (*mathêma*), that of the good (504e–505b) (which also implicitly includes the beautiful; 505b2–3). Every soul pursues this, Socrates argues, and does everything for its sake "divining that it is something [*apomanteuomenê ti einai*], but is at a loss [*aporousa*] and cannot adequately grasp what it is" (505d11–e2; cf. 506a6). The eye of the soul has to be turned round to this study explicitly to produce philosophical thought, dialectic, for by this organ alone is the truth perceived, and it is more worth saving than a thousand eyes (527b–e; 522a–b; 526a–b; 526e). In this *mathêma* is "the end of the journey" (532e3; cf. *Symp.* 211c6–7); the power of dialectic will only "appear to one who has experience" of the sciences (533a8–10; c6–d4), and it involves bringing all the studies (*mathêmata*) taught indiscriminately in one's youth together in order to give a synoptic view (*synopsis*) of their kinship with one another and with the nature of reality (537c1–3), for "the one who sees things as a whole [*synoptikos*] is a dialectician" (537c7). This is precisely what is involved on the fourth rung of ascent in the *Symposium*: "from studies to end up in that study," the study of the beautiful (211c6–d1). And even Aristophanes' pathetic lovers in their need "divine that it is something," the source of wholeness and unity. Where science has not taken Aristophanes, need, lack of resource, and desire have been able to, and for Socrates in the *Republic* this *mathêma* is the only one really needful (504e–505b).

So Aristophanes catches something of the passionate longing for unity in the search for the beautiful but imprisons it in the parodic image of halves in search of their original whole natures, which were so monstrous, impious, and vicious in the first place that Zeus had to perform a bastard kind of division upon them so that Love could later act as the "collector" of their separate halves! Aristophanes thus presents a bastardized form of Platonic dialectic, but dialectic nonetheless, whose object is wholeness, the return to original unity, and friendship with god. His "halves" want *to grow* into wholes so that they can regain their original *strength* (cf. 190b5: *rômê*). The apprentice on the fourth rung must *grow* and *be strengthened* to see this single study (210d6–7: *rôstheis kai auxêtheis*). This verbal echo is significant, since it catches the double-edged quality of phenomenal existence—in this case, either monstrosity or integral wholeness. To be capable of integrity is to be open to something true and bigger than one's own preference; to be purely self-directed is the beginning of monstrosity. To be open to that which is bigger than and beyond oneself is also the difference yet correlation between the two capacities, and this is the measure not only of Plato's criticism but also of his admiration for the potential in art, as well as his recognition that great art does not need to be slavishly mimetic at all. Great art, like dialectic or the philosophical muse (*Rep.* 499d3–4), is the *mathêma*, the experiential learning or study of that hidden beauty that reveals itself to the person prepared for and needful of it.

In the *Republic*, the synoptic vision of dialectic is clearly not intended to be bland universalism or a kind of quantitative polymathy. Yet it still seems an impossible, if noble ideal, requiring a lifetime's education and practice for the rightly gifted man or woman. If the capacity for synoptic vision is not simply the preserve of the philosopher-king but implicit in any really creative art, science, image, or thought that reveals something true about our world (or even just a distant and distorted image of the true), then the gap and correlation between Aristophanes and the fourth rung in the *Symposium* add an important dimension to our understanding of this ideal.

More important still, this gap, yet correspondence between the fourth step and Aristophanes' speech permits us to see, in its very fracture, the possibility of a positive theory of art—a study of the beautiful as yet unrevealed. In the spirit of Diotima's insistence that the apprentice search for the beautiful unceasingly, being always in need of that which he or she grasps but loses, the silhouette of a positive art appears, however, momentarily, when the complexity of the whole dialogue's structure in motion is approached with attention and care. For this reason, Plato's broader theory of art can only be grasped indirectly,[19] and this means that reading the *Republic* as the only focus of his criticism is surely an error.

5. Agathon criticizes all previous speakers for one particular fault. They were all unable to portray the nature of Eros. He will show who the god really is (195a). But the portrait Agathon draws, as he himself is soon to discover, does not fit the character of Love. Later, Diotima will discuss this with Socrates: "What you thought love to be is not surprising. You supposed, if I take what you said as evidence, that the beloved and not the loving was love. That is why, I think, Eros seemed completely beautiful to you. In fact, it is the beloved that is really beautiful . . . and blessed; but loving has this other character" (204b8–c6). Now in the Greater Mysteries the highest beauty is the goal of our entire search and our ultimate beloved; and so Agathon does portray that beauty, at least on Diotima's (unconscious) testimony, but again reveals so much of his own ambiguous face in the process (cf. 198a2–3): the golden youth whose Gorgianic head threatens to make Socrates as dumb as stone. *Corruptio optimi pessima.* So Agathon, the beloved, like his Eros, represents that last step on the ascent of love, but in his own flawed way, for he will never see true beauty face-to-face until he learns the nature of needy desire or faces the necessity of going outside himself and recognizing that his nature is not whole or self-sufficient. Without need, he will see only his own image.

Agathon, the beloved beautiful itself, is also in Socrates' pun the "Good" (*Agathôn: agathôn,* 174b4). It is surely a testimony of Plato's genius that he can employ a pun so openly, yet let it live so freely. For of course "the beautiful itself" is the highest "form" in the *Symposium,* except that behind the beautiful, as it were, lingers the shadow of the "good." After the implicit distinction between the good and the beautiful in Diotima-Socrates' earlier conversation,[20] the good is never mentioned again, except that since Agathon's speech represents the shadow of the fifth step on the ladder of love, the "good" remains the shadow or silent counterpart behind or together with the revelation of the Beautiful. If we put the *Symposium* in the context of *Republic* 6–7, we may say that Plato simply leaves the afterimage of the good in the *Symposium!* So the "good" is "present" (1) by means of a pun, (2) in the course of Diotima's argument and (3) by virtue of its afterimage or shadow.

19. On this, see section 8.5, below.
20. See Chapter 3, and compare White 1989, 149–57.

We *expect* the "good," but the really significant feature for the *Symposium* is finally its "absence" (as we shall also see in Chapter 8).[21]

6.3 Immortality and God-Belovedness

So for Diotima it is only from the perspective of that which we can prepare for, but cannot compel, that immortality and god-belovedness become living *possibilities* for the *human being:* "in begetting true virtue and nurturing it, it is given to him to become dear to god, and to him, if to any human being, to be immortal" (212a5–6). Why possibilities? Because immortality and god-belovedness are *gifts.* We should not listen to those who tell us only to think mortal thoughts, but should strive to think immortal things, Aristotle tells us in the *Nicomachean Ethics* 10.7, following Plato in the *Timaeus* (90b–c); finally, however, one cannot make oneself immortal or beloved by anyone. To be beloved is a gift from the other. So the language of acquisition that has run right through Diotima-Socrates' conversation, *ktêsis, genesthai* or *einai + dative,* finally turns out at the end of the ascent to the beautiful to be the language of gift (212a–b): there is no better helper than Love in the acquisition of this goal for human nature (212b). We saw in the Poverty-Plenty story how the superabundance of divine life does not depart from its own territory in the generation of Love and yet reaches out to make that birth possible. In a similar fashion the beautiful does not come to us, but we have to approach it, like Poverty. Yet it gives us a different nature, and if friendship (*philia*), company (*homilia*), and conversation (*dialektos*) between gods and human beings mean anything in Diotima's earlier account, then god-belovedness means to love and to be loved by god.

One of the major long-standing puzzles about the *Symposium* is that Diotima apparently has nothing to say about the immortality of the *soul,* a theme that figures prominently in other "middle" dialogues, the *Phaedo, Republic,* and *Phaedrus.* So perhaps the *Symposium* should predate these dialogues and be assigned to a period before Plato became committed to the idea of the immortal soul?[22] or when he was for a time skeptical about the issue?[23] Or is it rather that the *Symposium* represents a different perspective? The last view is surely to be preferred, since the gift of immortality Diotima speaks of at 212a is a gift to a "human being," that is, to an *embodied*

---

21. Cf. also section 2.5, ad fin., above, and section 8.8, below.
22. Morrison 1964, 42–46.
23. Hackforth 1950, 43–45; and for the dating problem in addition, Dover 1965, 2–9, versus Mattingly 1958, 31–39, and Morrison 1964. Cf. Chapter 1, notes 30–32.

being, not to the soul as such.[24] This positive evaluation of the soul-body relation is an important feature of all the "middle" dialogues, which has been unfortunately overlooked or at least significantly underestimated by generations of critics. But, again, we will not be able to chart out the fuller implications of this view until we have looked at the *Symposium* as a whole.[25]

6.4 Overall Conclusion

Socrates' speech, then, overthrows, comments on, and reshapes every major point in the earlier self-possessed speeches, but the "form" of this reshaping, so to speak, is not imposed from outside, but rather emerges out of the "nature" of the various speeches themselves, just as Diotima seeks to discover the need for vertical movement to the mystic beautiful in the natural range of desire experienced, so she holds, by all living creatures. So the correlation and yet gap between the early speeches and the rungs of Diotima's ladder are not the product of an arbitrary forcing together of things that do not meet but, first, the emergence of form and order in life and, second, the recognition that archetype and image go together, just as in the psychological and sociological phenomenology of archetypes outlined in the *Republic* archetypes and derivatives are still akin to one another and in fact live "in the same house."

This device of light and shade also serves another useful purpose, for it makes concrete what may appear abstract and shows that the ideal is accessible not only to the philosopher-kings but to anyone on any moving rung of the ladder of ascent. Art, for instance, in its most authentic form is inseparable from a form of dialectic; and the whole of Socrates' speech is a kind of mythical narrative in the form of a dialogue; but instead of imitating the physical image, it turns the fictional narrative of Diotima into a prismatic idea from which to grasp what Socrates holds to be the essential features of the truth and the self-disclosure of the beautiful. Such philosophical art can give an account of itself, is not unduly limited by a particular scientific "hypothesis," and leads up to a conclusion beyond its starting point. In these ways, it is a powerful example of Platonic dialectic.

6.4.1 "Platonic Love": The View So Far

But how can we know that the apprentice beholds the beautiful? How do we distinguish this Socratic individual from the pleasant, charming, talented,

---

24. O'Brien 1984, 198–205; Luce 1952, 137–41; Rowe 1998, 184–85. See also *Symp.* 208b4: *athanaton de allei* (sc., *athanasias metechei*).

25. See section 8.7, below.

self-possessed Agathon? The "sudden" revelation of the beautiful may be the most essential precondition of an authentically human life, as both Socrates and Diotima evidently believed, but it also looks, to the casual observer, like airy-fairy fiction or the ultimate stage of self-delusion. And Plato knew this too, which is why he immediately makes it vanish into thin air in the "sudden" revelation of a very physical Alcibiades (cf. 212c6: *exaiphnês*). But we do know and might want to test some features of this Socratic individual. We know he is always in need, even at the "top" of the ladder when he is least limited by subjectivity or partiality. And we know he always needs to be re-created. If he feels completely free of any desire, then he is not a true lover or philosopher or poet, but either like Agathon or identical with the beautiful itself, yet the latter is not possible for mortals, because when one reaches maturity at any "stage" one needs to procreate in the company of one's beloved, and in the beautiful, and thus nurture the community of one's love. Each "step," then, is intersubjective, yet vertical and self-expanding; it involves (1) love of someone or something; (2) an expanding landscape so that one's own determination of reality is not all that exists; (3) perhaps, and preferably, a guide; (4) the revelation of the beautiful by and through itself, to the degree on the lower steps that one recognizes or finds beauty beyond oneself; (5) the generation of a community of dialogue (even on the lowest step); and (6) like the unshackled prisoner vested with the political and moral responsibility of returning to the cave to free his or her fellow human beings, the moral responsibility to care for that community and to make the young better. One might well conclude, then, that in principle one should be able to *test* such a vision.

Furthermore, to the degree that "Platonic love" is represented by the whole of the *Symposium* up to this point, such love is plainly not impersonal or abstract (and we shall see additional reason in Alcibiades' speech to draw this conclusion), for it is directly personal and intersubjective and has practical, testable consequences, and while it does involve an expanding view of the universe, this is not at all the reflection only of one's own preference or of some abstract projection, since the "spiritual" world it inhabits is the highly concrete world of other selves, laws, practices, and sciences. For similar reasons such love cannot fairly be accounted "dishonest, spiritual" affection in denial of bodily passion, in the first place because bodily passion is the acknowledged necessary basis of progress in "love matters" and Diotima even thinks there is something "divine" in it. At the same time, what seems to link lovers most is the deeper spiritual bond based partly in the psychophysical necessity that they cannot simply freeze-frame human love as complete or self-sufficient in any moment, but are forced among other things to live in constant motion and talk to each other in helpful, even noble ways. There is nothing dishonest or abstract in the realization that if lovers are in some sense to share a soul, they should be concerned about the soul's well-being and the quality of her language, if only to avoid deadly boredom and eventual disillusionment. Nor again does this love resemble "Freudian sublimation" in any simple-minded sense, because, first, instinct and desire are not, in Diotima's account, blind;[26] second, neither the superego nor the ego is the ultimate mouthpiece of "morality" (authentic or conventional) on the terms of the *Symposium* so far; and, third, homeostasis, or freedom from tension and disruption, which may be thought to be one goal of Freudian psychotherapy among others, is explicitly *not* the character of such Eros. Moreover, the highest expression of such love is not sexualized pederasty, for in the first case there is no divine or cosmic paradigm for this and, in the second, Alcibiades' testimony to Socrates' *sôphrosynê* or self-restraint by its very language is a rejection of Pausanias's view that the lover should be "gratified" sexually for the sake of virtue and educational improvement.[27] Similarly, the "Christian" charge that this pagan love is inherently selfish and grounded "in a distinctly uncritical intensification and strengthening of natural self-assertion"[28] might characterize Aristophanes' original globular natures, but it has nothing whatever to do with Diotima's movement of ascent, which is inherently *dialogical* and the very opposite of uncritical *self*-assertion.

Finally, while Diotima's Eros *is* relational, there is no reason to suppose that he is a "relation taken distributively" or that he cannot be a "substance" as long as we do not project the meaning of terms employed in late antiquity or the Renaissance (Ficino) back onto the middle period of Plato's

26. For a useful analysis of Freudian and Neo-Freudian thought in relation to Diotima-Socrates' speech, see Lear 1998, 123–66, especially with regard to the following conclusions about positing forces for organization and disorganization in Freudian drive theory: "Yet there remains a question why these phenomena [e.g., forms of destructiveness] need to be linked by a fundamental principle like the death drive. . . . [T]here is the ironic possibility that positing a *fundamental* force for disorganization might have a disorganizing effect on psychoanalytic theory. Any attempt at theorizing will be an effort to carve up psychological reality at the joints. The death drive brings together destructiveness and the limits of analysis into a basic unity. Might we thereby be blinding ourselves to more natural unities? So, for example, suppose we simply took the *limits of analysis* as a category, and made no presumption as to whether what lay beyond the bounds was destructive or constructive. Then we would include in that category not only the unanalyzable destructiveness of the negative therapeutic reaction but also the creative genius which Freud acknowledged lay beyond the bounds of psychoanalytic understanding. In that case, the fundamental category might be the *sublime*. . . . And in place of the opposition of eros versus the death drive, we might have instead the opposition of *the sublime versus the mundane* [or, in Lear's terms, an opposition framed by the categories of Diotima-Socrates' speech]. The limits of analysis would then, plausibly enough, coincide with the limits of human understanding" (146). See also the *differences* between psychoanalytic and the Socratic approaches to the "human-erotic," 165–66.

27. Socrates perhaps expresses the "view" of the *Symposium* at *Rep.* 402d–403c.

28. Barth 1962, 174.

writing career.[29] Even Plotinus's interpretation, in particular, that Eros is a substance that has sprung from soul's longing for Intellect, and that this longing in soul has two principal manifestations, first, as a heavenly "Aphrodite" in its higher relation to Intellect and, second, as a lower "Aphrodite" caring for marriages and for the souls of the young and so on[30]—this interpretation still looks a little wild, but perhaps not entirely crazy *if* (1) "the beloved" (on Diotima's account) is beyond soul[31] and yet is also different from the Good (given the Middle Platonic identification of Plato's "World of Forms"—with Aristotle's Intellect, Plotinus naturally ranges "Love as the beloved" with Intellect), and (2) if "loving" is regarded as having two phases, one corresponding to the more mundane concerns of the Lesser Mysteries (bodily and psychic reproduction) and the other corresponding to the enlarged spiritual focus of the Greater Mysteries (the production of "true things," not "images," and immortality in the full sense). Whatever the case, Plotinus's interpretation is still superior to many modern accounts in at least one feature, namely, in that he evidently holds the view that "Platonic love" is not to be restricted to Socrates' speech alone, but that even Pausanias's or Eryximachus's view (which we know indirectly that Plotinus himself rejected[32] is in some dialectical relation with Socrates' speech, just as Eryximachus can "address" "Aristophanes" and "Agathon" via Pausanias's conception of the two "loves" before they speak, as it were, and must therefore be taken seriously, even if it needs to be transformed. This is not crazy, but already somewhat sophisticated.[33]

But while Socrates' speech is magnificent, and while it "recollects" both itself and all the previous speeches in a complex structure of address, contrast, destruction, dialogue, and yet also ascent, the speech is still *not* self-sufficient, for it raises far more questions than it has answered: the questions of immortality, the soul-body relation, human identity, and the relation of art and philosophy, to mention but a few. It also, of course, raises the mysterious issue of the relation of Socrates to his or (through Diotima) her own speech, as also to the vision to which he already aspires and of which he is "persuaded."[34] Furthermore, how does this "positive" picture fit with that other "destructive" picture of the "Dionysian" bully who "forces" others to agree with him, an object of considerable hatred for generations of critics from Thrasymachus to Karl Popper? These are questions we shall take up in our two final chapters.

29. Allen 1991, ix.
30. *Ennead* 3.5.3–4.
31. Cf. *Symp.* 204c3–6.
32. See Porphyry *Life of Plotinus,* chap. 15, lines 8–12.
33. For a development of this view in relation to the *Symposium,* see sections 8.1–8.4, below.
34. *Symp.* 212b1–3.

Alcibiades and the Conclusion of the *Symposium*

The Test and Trial of Praise

7.1 The Figure of Dionysus and the Face of Socrates

The figure of Dionysus looms large in the *Symposium* and finally, in Alcibiades' eulogy, comes to touch the equally mysterious face of Socrates. The *Symposium,* of course, honors Agathon's prize for tragedy at the god's festival. So it is natural for Agathon to claim Dionysus as judge in his wisdom contest with Socrates: "You're outrageous, Socrates.... You and I will adjudicate our claims about wisdom a little later, using Dionysus as judge" (175e). But the full power of the outrageous god has to be restricted, it appears: Pausanias is still the worse for yesterday's drinking and so the doctor Eryximachus (and therefore from the camp of Apollo, god of medicine) gives the party a brief lecture on the evils of drink and proposes limited drinking, "as much as each wants, nothing compulsory" (though Socrates is equal to anything, he admits), as well as the banishment of the flute, a Dionysian instrument, and the girl to play it, "who may play to herself or to the women within" (176c).[1] The flute girl also signifies, then, the presence of Dionysus.[2]

---

1. Cf. Rowe 1998, 135 at 176e, and 203 on 212c7–d 1; Anderson 1993, 11–13.
2. Allen 1991, 116 n. 171.

But though banished, the god is still represented, as it were, in the two poets, Aristophanes and Agathon; in Aristophanes' disordered eating and drinking, epitomized in his hiccups (the irruption of disorder); and also in Diotima's portrait of Eros, who by dying and coming back to life on the same day is not unlike Dionysus, the god who dies and is reborn. If Socrates is not unlike the Eros of his own speech, then perhaps he too resembles Dionysus.[3]

Enter Alcibiades, very drunk, roaring like a bull (*boôntos* [212d]), supported by the flute girl, and crowned with ivy and violets, like the very incarnation of Dionysus himself. The transcendent pierces human life with the suddenness of revelation and it can take many forms: in the Greater Mysteries, the apprentice "will *suddenly* [*exaiphnês*] see a beauty wondrous in nature" (210e4); a "*sudden*" (*exaiphnês*) loud knocking on the courtyard door, "as of revelers," precedes the entry of Alcibiades (212c6–7); and when Alcibiades at last notices Socrates, this comes upon him with revelatory force, with Socrates "*suddenly* appearing" where he least expects him to be (213c1–2); and finally the orderly proceedings are disrupted forever after Alcibiades' speech when "*suddenly,* a mob of revelers come to the doors" (223b2–3). So, like the highest beauty, Alcibiades, Socrates, and the last group of revelers burst onto the scene with the force of a revelation that cannot be compelled or managed. And since Alcibiades compares Socrates to satyrs and Sileni, who formed the entourage of Dionysus, as well as to the flute player Marsyas, who was flayed alive by Apollo for his hubris in competing with him, and since Alcibiades goes on to award the judgment of Dionysus to Socrates rather than to Agathon, then it might seem that Socrates is a "creature of Dionysus"[4] or that through Alcibiades in his likening Marsyas to Socrates "Plato is speaking here for himself."[5]

This, however, would be a major mistake, since the figure of Socrates is much more subtle than a pastiche of Dionysiac elements or a simple reflection even of his own Eros. Yet the Socrates of the *Symposium* is problematic for, as Pierre Hadot has argued, if Socrates acts as a mediator between the ideal norms and human reality, we should expect to see in him "a harmonious figure, combining divine and human characteristics in delicate nuances,"[6] yet there is nothing further from the truth: the figure of

---

3. See particularly Hadot's great essay on the "figure of Socrates," 1995, 147–78, which is full of provocative thinking on Socrates, Kierkegaard, and Nietzsche; also Anderson 1993, Mitchell 1993, 185ff., and Bonelli 1991, 79ff.; compare Nussbaum 1986, and Allen 1991, 99–102. Wilson Nightingale 1995, 119–32, is excellent. See also Lacan 1991, 163–213.
4. Anderson 1993, 14.
5. Friedländer 1969, 31.
6. Hadot 1995, 147.

Socrates is ambiguous, troubling, and strangely disconcerting;[7] he is outrageous and ugly, like the Sileni, a dissimulator who pretends to be completely ordinary and superficial, yet is not, and someone who lives with perplexity and doubt. He appears to want seduction, but ends up seducing, according to Alcibiades' testimony. So in Alcibiades' speech, and in the concluding scenes of the *Symposium,* we are compelled to contemplate the enigmatic figure of Socrates himself and to test the "truth" of Socrates' teaching on love as well as of Alcibiades' testimony, whose "truth" Socrates is invited to refute on every point, but conspicuously does not. Fascination with a specific individual—the outrageous Socrates—not only opens the pages of the *Symposium;* the dialogue's final movement returns to this issue in a somewhat different key. Why, then, should this individual face, albeit of Socrates, but individual nonetheless, remain important even after Diotima's teaching? An answer to this question, as well as some elucidation of Alcibiades' compulsion to tell the truth about Socrates, will help us to bring a still clearer focus to questions of the dialogue's structure and its thematic consistency.

7.2 The Role of Alcibiades

What, then, is the role of Alcibiades and what is the force of his speech? The humor surrounding his entry is some of the most delightful in Plato, and the power and intellect of Alcibiades himself are striking. As Dover remarks, "[D]espite his drunkenness Alcibiades proves to be prodigiously articulate."[8] Alcibiades emphasizes from the outset that though drunk, he still knows he speaks the truth (213a), and Plato holds back the moment of his recognizing Socrates: Alcibiades is untying the fillets on his head to put them on Agathon's head so that he does not immediately see Socrates—with the result that we catch the force doubly intensified, of Alcibiades'

---

7. See Martha Nussbaum's (1986, 184) treatment of this important feature. Our interpretation, though perhaps not entirely incompatible with hers, is at variance, however, with her thesis (based on Vlastos 1973) that while Socrates and Diotima describe one kind of love, Plato, as author, has described two kinds, the love of unique individuals described by Aristophanes and evinced by Alcibiades, and the love of Beauty, between which there is a tragic and irreconcilable choice. Her view of Socrates in particular (and of Alcibiades in this relation) is, in our view, simply mistaken: "Socrates is put before us as an example of a man in the process of making himself self-sufficient" (though a part of her view is not so misguided: "." . . put before us, in our still unregenerate state, as a troublesome question mark and a challenge" (184)). For criticism of Nussbaum's view of Alcibiades as possessing a "lover's knowledge of the particular other, gained through an intimacy both bodily and intellectual, . . . a unique and uniquely valuable *kind* of practical understanding" (1986, 190), see Wilson Nightingale 1995, 121, and also note 20, below.
8. Dover 1980, 10.

jealous passion for Socrates through his own startled eyes: "Lying in ambush for me again, suddenly appearing as you used to where I least expected you to be. And why have you come now? And again, why are you lying here, and not beside Aristophanes or somebody else who is funny and wants to be? Instead, you have found a way to lie next to the most beautiful person in the room" (213b9–c5).

Unlike Apollodorus, whose devotion to Socrates is much more straightforward (he makes it his business each day to know what he says or does [173a]), Alcibiades' passion is double edged; he tries to avoid Socrates, and his love is tinged with hate, even violence (as Socrates, perhaps primarily in jest, makes clear in his reply [213d]). He is drawn to Socrates not because of but despite himself (*odi et amo*—a familiar love-theme in the Roman poets). At least, the tension or ambiguity in this complex feeling cannot be resolved on Alcibiades' part: "Why, it's impossible to reconcile you and me, said Alcibiades" (213d), so that on the one hand he wants to take it out on Socrates ("But I'll get my revenge on you for this another time") while on the other he wants to praise and love him ("give me back some of those ribbons, so that I may crown this fellow's head too, this wonderful head" [213d–c]).

So if we take these opening salvos seriously, the role of Alcibiades is complex, indeed. His role is, first, to dissolve the mood of mystical sublimity at the end of Socrates' speech with a striking piece of dramatic realism; second, to contrast the airy-fairy, but orderly, spiritual ascent to the beautiful with the physical disorderly Alcibiades, or to contrast apparent fiction with apparent fact; third, to turn the tables on Socrates in a humorous way and to cast the spotlight of intense scrutiny on Socrates' himself—Alcibiades will exact his penalty (213d8) by *praising* Socrates, a point he is strikingly, if humorously, aware of himself *before* he starts his eulogy ("shall I punish the man and exact a penalty from him in front of you?" [214e2–3])—and, perhaps most important, finally, to present *a complex picture of the double-edged nature of passionate love* for an individual who does not simply appeal to the lover's soul (a condition envisaged and discussed abstractly in many of the *Symposium*'s speeches), but who starts an inner war, a divisive, heartrending tension whose authenticity is only too evident. Socrates, the beloved, is drawn for all to see, his character as enigmatic as so many themes in the dialogue. Why do we find this emphasis on the peculiarities of his nature?

In the early speeches we have seen the correlation between the limitations of each speaker's character and the influence of these limitations on the nature of the speakers' creative ability and vision. We have also noted that Socrates' transposition of his own speech into a dialogue with Diotima, in which he represents himself as a pupil, breaks this previous correlational pattern between the limitations of character and the ensuing creative vision and transposes it into a new relation, that of one between vision and character. The flow of influence switches and its direction changes drastically, for it is no longer character that influences vision, but vision that can also have a more profound influence on character. Indeed, this switch in the direction of influence is emphasized at the culmination of Diotima's teaching when the highest creative vision emerges uncompelled of its own accord; there the disclosure of the highest beauty is capable of changing in the most radical manner the nature and limitations of the artist's character, even to the radical point of conferring immortality on his/her mortal nature.

When Diotima draws her picture of Eros, we know only too well that the sturdy child of Poverty and Plenty, ever hungry in his hunt for the beautiful and in his pursuit of philosophy, reminds one of Socrates, but we have good reasons for believing that this correlation does not originate with Socrates. Socrates, we are led to believe, looks like Diotima's Eros not because it is ultimately he (and not his perhaps fictional Diotima) who tells the tale, but rather because of his lifelong dedication to *erotica*. In other words, it is Socrates' love for philosophy that makes him more and more like the *daimôn* Eros. Until Alcibiades' speech, we are prepared to accept this premise and the powerful flow of the narrative, but we do so with caution, knowing only too well that we have perhaps succumbed to the power of a fiction created by a tricky Socrates. Alcibiades' speech, with its portrait of Socrates, disrupts this caution by the very poignancy of Alcibides' love-revulsion. As we listen to his praise, we sense that Alcibiades would have loved most of all to denigrate Socrates, to prove him a liar, and to do away with his world altogether. But in spite of himself, he testifies, and the historical authenticity of his picture is so vivid that we accept its vibrant power.

Socrates, we hear from the grudging Alcibiades, is a follower of a vision that he seeks and serves daily. His loyalty to philosophy, which makes him so much like Diotima's picture of Eros, is not a rhetorical trick, but a reality, whose veracity is established from a most reluctant source. For Alcibiades, as a lover, has chosen a path opposed to that of Socrates. If Socrates' appeal is that of a man, always in transformation in front of a truth he finds, yet misses, and seeks again, his appeal is also that of loyalty to the life of thought. Alcibiades in his own life, or so he tells us, has no allegiance to such a lifestyle; in fact, he actively shuns it, but in spite of himself, he cannot flee Socrates altogether.

Alcibiades' proposal to praise Socrates, then, turns the tables on Socrates in a very precise way, that is, insofar as Socrates is now placed in the role of visionary model and teacher to Alcibiades' pursuit of wisdom and love, a pursuit that Alcibiades has rejected while knowing its power and while being deeply drawn to Socrates' manner of conduct, conversation, and thought. Plainly, then, Alcibiades' role is not just to *test* the coinage of Socrates' vision but to show on the basis of his own reluctant admission (surely, impeccable credentials) how real is this change brought about by the search for the "beautiful" and how it has made Socrates appear, and really be, so different from any other human being.

In other words, if Alcibiades is to speak the truth, as he will so often proclaim he does, then we should be able to *test* the authenticity of Socrates' search for the beautiful by looking to the effects of this search in Socrates' own character and establishing thereby that the vision is not simply a static reality but a dynamic source of transformation. Dover sees such a view as Plato's weakness: "Plato was inclined to believe, contrary to ordinary experience, that there is a correlation between the truth of a belief and its effect upon the conduct of the believer."[9] But to us it seems reasonable to suppose that the effects of people's real interests do betray themselves consciously or unconsciously over sufficient periods of time in their ordinary conduct. In Euripides' *Bacchae,* for instance, Pentheus's prurient interest in sexuality, as opposed to his professed motives, is chillingly displayed in his effeminate concern for how he looks in the dress that Dionysus has given him as a disguise, so that he can spy on the Maenads. It is surely no more unreasonable that we become in some measure what we think than that we become what we eat. At any rate, we can only test a theory by its behavior in practice. However, if Alcibiades is genuinely to exact his penalty and turn the tables on Socrates, the test of authenticity will also be to put Socrates on *trial,* but in a complex, dramatic, and poignant fashion. As we shall see, this is precisely what does happen in the course of Alcibiades' speech.

7.3 The Test of Praise

In these opening scenes, the shadow of love violence, love avoidance, and love hatred is simply part of the general humorous banter. Although he is "led in by his retinue" and asks for permission to join the company, Alcibiades soon takes over the proceedings; he has a wine cooler filled to the brim, he drinks it down, and then he orders a second for Socrates, who will never get drunk, he proudly announces, no matter how much one bids him drink (213e–214a). Alcibiades' subsequent exchange with Eryximachus is a delight in itself. Eryximachus, of course, complains about this turn in the

9. Dover 1980, 159.

proceedings. Are they not going to say or sing something rather than just "drink up like thirsty people"? (214a–b). The talented Alcibiades combats temperate prose with ironic poetry:

> "Eryximachus, best son of a best and most temperate father, hello. And hello to you too, said Eryximachus. But what are we to do? Whatever you tell us to do. For we must obey you: 'for a doctor is a man worth many others in exchange.'[10] So make the prescriptions you wish." (214b)

The humorous combat between, yet combination of, Eryximachus and Alcibiades[11] becomes the occasion for Alcibiades' eulogy of Socrates. It is Alcibiades' suggestion to praise Socrates, a suggestion that arises out of his rejection of Socrates' previous charge that Alcibiades is jealous and envious and will even use force to get his way with Socrates. Alcibiades claims that it is the other way round: Socrates cannot keep his hands off Alcibiades if he praises anyone other than Socrates himself. We are forced to ask if there is any truth in this picture of a grudging, jealous Socrates, but immediately the other, tender side of Alcibiades' mercurial, and presumably alcoholic, disposition presents itself. Socrates is taken aback by his charge, and Alcibiades immediately intervenes: "don't add another word, because I could not praise one other person with you present" (214d).

If Socrates and his *Eros* are a difficult conjunction of opposites, Alcibiades represents an even more difficult conjunction as he switches from ironic poetry, to accusation, to tenderness, and then even to the humorous menace ("Shall I punish the man . . . ?" 214e) of the brilliant individual divided from himself in some manner beyond his own control. But the double-edged nature of Alcibiades' eulogy (in his own terms, praise and punishment; in those of Socrates, "to praise me in order to make fun of me [*epi ta geloiotera*]") introduces with a sure touch a tragic picture of a man who plainly knows Socratic method and philosophy and yet in some strange but all too understandable measure remains untouched by it. In other words, Alcibiades unwittingly presents a self-portrait, that is, a portrait of Socrates' most brilliant student, who will, in time to come, be the ruin of Athens and who, together with Charmides, Critias, and others, became an unfortunate example of what the charge of corrupting the youth appeared to be founded on.[12]

---

10. *Iliad* 11.514.
11. I.e., between the "representatives" of Apollo and Dionysus.
12. On Alcibiades' profanation of the mysteries and the mutilation of the herms, see Rowe 1998, 206; Brisson 1998, 32–34. Lacan's extended commentary on the *Symposium* (1991, 11–213) comes into the special focus of the psychoanalytic notion of transference in his treatment of Alcibiades and Socrates

The notion of "truth" in the dialogue has hitherto only emerged in the conversation of Socrates and Agathon—that other golden youth whose speech also happens to flank that of Socrates. "Truth," however, is where Alcibiades *starts*. To Socrates' question, Will Alcibiades praise him to make him look ridiculous? Alcibiades knowingly replies: "I'll tell the truth. Just see if you permit it." For once Socrates is humorously upstaged: "Why certainly if it's the truth, I give my permission; in fact, I insist upon it." "I can hardly wait to start, said Alcibiades." But Alcibiades is an acute student and he puts further conditions to Socrates, a fact that reveals the following: not only the truth, but question, answer, and refutation are to be part of his eulogy, on the understanding that Socrates exercises the principle of charity of judgment, given Alcibiades' inebriated condition: "But you must do this: if I say anything untrue, interrupt me right in the middle, if you like, and say that I am lying about it; for I won't willingly [*hekôn*] say anything false. If, however, in recollecting [*anamimnêskomenos*], I say one thing here and another there, don't be surprised; it is no easy thing for someone in my condition to count the qualities of your extraordinary character [*atopia*] fluently [*euporôs*] and in good order [*ephexês*]" (214e9–215a3). From the buzzword "recollecting," to the Socratic paradox "no one errs willingly or wittingly [*hekôn*]," Alcibiades plainly knows his Socrates, and since he proposes subsequently to praise Socrates "by means of images" (*di' eikonôn*) on

---

(163–213) and of the broader triad composed of Agathon, Alcibiades, and Socrates (cf. 160). For Lacan, if we understand him correctly, Alcibiades is "le démon de Socrate" in the sense that Alcibiades gives "a true representation, without knowing it, of what Socratic *askesis* implies" (193), not in the later Christianizing gloss of the relation between knower and known and of the ascension "to the known in the knower by knowing" (194) but instead in the sense that "les choses vont de l' inconscient vers le sujet qui se constitue dans sa dépendance, et remontent jusqu' à cet object noyau que nous appelons ici *agalma*. Tel est la structure qui règle la danse entre Alcibiade et Socrate" (194). Love or desire is founded on a lack or delusion (*leurre*) and is, in a sense, narcissistic, one's own ego made real on the imaginary or symbolic levels. The psychoanalytic transference between Alcibiades and Socrates is, then, a "reciprocal delusion": "Alcibiade montre la présence de l' amour, mais ne la montre qu' en tant que Socrate, qui sait, peut s'y tromper, et ne l' accompagne qu' en s'y trompant. Le leurre est réciproque. Il est aussi vrai pour Socrate si c'est un leurre et s'il est vrai qu'il se leurre, qu'il est vrai pour Alcibiade qu'il est pris dans le leurre" (194). This narcissistic dance of reciprocal delusion should also be seen more broadly in the light of Lacan's prelinguistic/post-Saussurian linguistic development model (by contrast with the—arguably—biological model of Freud) on three levels, (1) the real, (2) the imaginary, and (3) the symbolic, according to which the formation of subjectivity in relation to the "Other" occurs by a kind of splitting, first, in the recognition or misrecognition of the self's image and, then, in the misrecognition of the real in the constructions of language. Julia Kristeva's recasting of Lacan's model into (1) the *chora*, (2) the splitting/abject or mirror stage, and (3) the fetishism of language makes it look a lot more Platonic and also brings out more of the horror or terror (which Lacan also recognizes here of Alcibiades-Socrates) if the deceptive, double-edged, narcissistic character of this self-confessed love also bears its deeper and fated political, as well as personal, consequences (Lacan 1991, 194–213; see Kristeva 1984, 1983). See also Benardete 1994, 92–95.

the understanding that "the image will be for the truth, not laughter" (*hê eikôn tou alêthous heneka, ou tou geloiou* [215a4–7]), Alcibiades also proves to have an up-to-date understanding of Socrates' preoccupation with images in the *Phaedo* and the *Republic,* wherein the image is not necessarily an imitation thrice removed from reality, but a path that permits the philosopher to proceed dialectically to a deeper appreciation of reality (cf. *Phaedo* 99d–100a; *Republic* 6–7), as we saw in Chapters 3, 4, and 5.[13] Here, then, is someone who really knows Socrates and who seems to have shown us his special credentials for knowing the "truth" about Socrates.

What is this "truth" in Alcibiades' words? It is Socrates' "extraordinary character," his *atopia,* or "placelessness," that seems to disarm Alcibiades the most? Socrates' geography, so to speak, is not of this world. We recall the placelessness of the setting for the narrative of the *Symposium:* somewhere indeterminate between the Piraeus and the city, but somewhere always in motion. We recall too the placelessness of the conversations between Diotima and Socrates, and the constant motion of the apprentice on the ladder of love. So Socrates' placelessness is somehow connected with the very fabric of the dialogue itself, and we naturally wonder what inner landscape will be uncovered by Alcibiades in singling out this unique character of Socrates that does not quite fit any conventional setting. Alcibiades has the credentials to be a positive witness on Socrates' behalf and we shall take up this positive side of his speech first. But a positive witness in favor of what?

Clearly, in his testimony, Alcibiades wants to show that Socrates' hypnotic effect on others and, most of all, on Alcibiades himself is not the result of clever rhetorical tricks or of a happy gift of physical charisma, occasioned by a rich assortment of testosterone in Socrates' physiological makeup. Socrates' appeal is his inner world, but how can one draw a portrait whose reality cannot be represented by what is easily visible, but rather can only be signified by what is difficult to discern? Alcibiades chooses to begin with a simile, or rather two similes.

First, Alcibiades compares Socrates to wooden Sileni (similar to our Russian dolls-within-dolls, but that held within them little figures of the gods) that Athenians could buy in the market. Second, he compares Socrates to the satyr Marsyas, because Socrates has the power of entrancing people with his discourses, even though he requires no additional instrument to do so. These two images appear again and again in Alcibiades' speech, for they sum up the incongruity of his own experience of Socrates, that is, the strange disparity between Socrates' external appearance and the wondrous power of his personality and words.

13. But compare Dover 1980, 164.

Yet the images, of course, do not fit. The Sileni represent the negation of culture and civilization and the license of human sexual instincts. Marsyas is more representative of the hubris of Aristophanes' monstrous globs than he is of the hubris attributed by Alcibiades, and Agathon, to Socrates in the *Symposium*. Alcibiades wants to capture the "out of place," semidivine, untameable character of Socrates, and so he employs these images, but he is also aware of their deficiency. Socrates is like a Silenus, but "if you open him up" you see something divine within him. Marsyas charms his listeners by the beauty of his flute playing and his enchanting melodies. Socrates speaks plainly: he employs no melody, poetry, or rhetoric, yet his effect is even stronger than that of Marsyas (215a–216b). This disparity between external appearance and internal reality is also a function of Socrates' playfulness, which ultimately remains a mystery to Alcibiades, and in order to capture it, Alcibiades returns to the reality of the external Socrates, a reality that he can verbally control and denigrate, but finds himself instantly divided between external characteristics, so easy to dismiss and parody, and inner qualities, impossible to grasp in an adequate manner.

Thus, Socrates, according to Alcibiades, is always erotically disposed to beautiful men and invariably makes himself out to be ignorant, but this is not, he also claims, the true Socrates: on the one hand, "he is ironic and spends his whole life playing with people" (216e4–5); but when "he is in earnest and opened up," one finds those divine images within him (216e–217a). Thus, the pretence that angers and disturbs Alcibiades turns out, in the would-be seduction scene, not to be a pretence at all, and this is an even greater affront to the vanity and beauty of Alcibiades (218d–219e). The apparent *vertical* exchange of wisdom for sex is nothing more than a bad market-exchange of gold for bronze (as in the case of Glaucus in *Iliad* 6.236):[14] "But please, dear friend, give it more thought in case you're wrong about me and I'm nothing" (219a1–2). So while Socrates pretends to be interested in beautiful men, but does not really care if someone is beautiful (216d), and thinks "all these possessions"—fortune, wealth, beauty—are of little value (by contrast with the language of acquisition, which turns out finally to be a question of being *given* the greatest "possessions" by the gods, in Diotima's speech), the reality is that in Socrates both external appearance and inner reality are subordinated to the "vision of the mind" (*tês dianoias opsis*). "Give it more thought," Socrates tells his would-be lover, Alcibiades: *ameinon skopei,* that is, "look better." And this sight is what distinguishes Socrates primarily. On campaign, Alcibiades tells us later, Socrates began to think something over and "stood from dawn on the

---

14. See Chapter 5, on Pausanias's similar vertical exchange.

same spot *looking* [*skopôn*]" (220c4) and when the solution did not come to him he did not leave but "*stood seeking*" (*heistêkei zêtôn* [220c5]). This picture of Socrates, charged with inner energy, yet physically at rest, comes almost as a disappointing denouement amid the many riches of Marsyas's music, Alcibiades' good looks, and passions aplenty.

Thus, with all the Dionysiac characteristics initially attributed to Socrates, we might wonder if Socrates' prolonged intellectual ecstasies and transports bear a similar mark, just like the magical power of Socrates or his Marsyan music, which, according to Alcibiades, "alone causes possession and shows those who need the gods and rites of initiation because they are divine things" (215c).[15] Yet the Dionysiac images, as much as they capture something of the uncontrollable mystery of Socrates himself, conspicuously miss the mark, something that Alcibiades' language nonetheless itself shows us. The inner Socrates, pregnant in soul, "teems with temperance," and even when he stands still, there is motion, the motion not of Bacchic transport, but of *seeking* and *looking*.[16] As in the early instance on the way to Agathon's house, Socrates is not transported or possessed by thought so much as he is himself a mindful agent in search of something "wise" whose mindfulness does not preclude awareness of other events.

By contrast with the picture of Socrates in thought, Alcibiades' activity has an obsessive driven quality to it,[17] which results in further enslavement to Socrates, who "escapes" him in the only way, Alcibiades thought, "he could be caught," that is, by his beauty and sexual charm (cf. 219e). So the Dionysiac images and context implicitly unweave themselves in Alcibiades' genuine wish to present the truth of his experience. True, there is something Dionysiac in Socrates, or rather in the environment around him, but he is neither Silenus nor Marsyas, but Socrates; and despite the pathetic reality of the love Alcibiades so vividly portrays, Socrates escapes him. Plato is the master of such dialectical transition of an image into its opposite, for in the *Republic* he already, as it were, invents Hegel's phenomenology: "excessive action in one direction usually sets up a reaction in the opposite direction. This happens in weather, plants, bodies, and not least in politics . . . for too much freedom, both in the individual and in the city, is likely to change into nothing else but too much slavery" (*Rep.* 563e9–564a4). Alcibiades' freedom, talent, and brilliance taken to excess lead to his enslavement, his swift transitions from affront to praise, and the drunken darkness he inhabits. Yet even the dark

---

15. Cf. Hadot 1995, 169; Anderson 1993, 7–15.
16. *Symp.* 220c2–4, 7; d4–5; 174d5–8; 175a8; b1–2; c8–d3.
17. Cf. 215d8, e5; 216a4–5, 6, 8, c5; 217e6–7; 222b7.

Dionysian images with which he clothes Socrates cannot occlude entirely the clear-sighted features of the original.

Before looking at the negative side of Alcibiades' eulogy, let us first sum up some of these more or less positive aspects, quite apart from the function of Alcibiades' entry itself, which acts as a pivotal, defamiliarizing reversal in the structure of the dialogue, as we argued earlier.[18] Alcibiades' eulogy presents a firsthand account of Socrates to his own face, triply authenticated in that (1) he claims to put truth first and has Socrates at hand to refute him on any point; (2) he is drunk, and beyond caring what anyone thinks of him (217e3–4: "wine with or without slaves is truthful";[19] Alcibiades was to be prosecuted in 415 B.C. for mocking the Eleusinian Mysteries while drunk, on the evidence of slaves and metics [cf. Thucydides 6.28.1]); and (3) his love of Socrates is strongly tinged with resentment and hatred, and he is thus almost beyond caring what even Socrates thinks of him. We are therefore able to *test* the "truth" of the mystical ascent to the beautiful of Diotima's speech in the transformation effected by this search in Socrates himself, and on the basis of an eyewitness who knows enough about Socrates' methods and criticism of mimetic art to insist that any real portrait of a person must depict what is "inside him." The beauty hidden inside Socrates is of much higher stature than any apparent physical beauty, and the beauty of his words surpasses by far the eloquence of the best orators, but to grasp these qualities is not an easy enterprise.

Alcibiades' eulogy also implicitly sets up a dialogue with other elements in the *Symposium*. In a contrast with Aristophanes' sliced halves in search of each other, Alcibiades seems to insist that human beings need to be "opened up" so that we can see the rather different reality we are dealing with when we talk about the need for restoration, healing, and integrity. At any rate, Alcibiades' graphic image casts new light upon what we might mean by uncovering the landscape of soul: we look into the soul not so much to find the "self" as to find "divinities."[20] Again, we recall Phaedrus's view that the

---

18. See also sections 8.4 and 8.8, below.

19. Cf. Allen 1991, 163 n. 262, Waterfield 1994, ad loc., Rösler in Murray and Tecusan 1995, 106–12, and Rowe 1998, 208–9.

20. Martha Nussbaum (1986, 192) gives special emphasis to the "puzzle: why Alcibiades should persistently speak of his soul, his inner life, as something of flesh and blood like the visible body" and she concludes (poignantly) that without a "metaphysical view of the person . . . what he knows is that this inner part of him is responding like a thing of flesh. He says he feels like a sufferer from snakebite, only he has been bitten by something more painful. . . . I've been bitten and wounded in the heart, or soul, or whatever one should call it, by the philosophical speeches of Socrates" (217e–218a). She goes on to develop this into a broader, anti-Platonic theory about the vulnerability of body: "Whatever is flesh or fleshlike is vulnerable . . . Alcibiades, without a philosophical view of mind, gives an extraordinary defence of 'physicalism' for the soul of lovers:

lover or beloved would be especially ashamed if caught doing wrong in front of a beloved partner. For Phaedrus, this pain of shamefulness was evidence that both lover and beloved try to behave nobly always (178c–e). In corroboration of this, Alcibiades proclaims that only Socrates can make him feel shame. But somehow his shame before Socrates is not sufficient to make him change his life. Instead, he tries to avoid Socrates, so that he can go on living as he pleases. The explanation for this failure is poignantly missing in the *Symposium,* but it is implicitly there in the gaps between speeches, as it were. In the light of Diotima's teaching, the love for one person, even if that person is Socrates, is not sufficient for virtue. Apparently, only the love of, and faithfulness to, the highest beauty can assist in such an endeavor. In this context too, Socrates' rejection of Alcibiades' advances, though not of friendship or of human warmth between them, is Plato's answer to Pausanias. And Plato seems to have been aware in composing Alcibiades' speech that this rejection was fraught with potentially fatal and very real consequences in and through the person of Alcibiades.

This sense of covert desperation colors the reader's reaction to Alcibiades' speech, even if Alcibiades does exactly what we are so much in need of at this point in the *Symposium*. Indeed, in his eulogy, the reality of the beautiful itself of Diotima's teaching, which seemed the most removed from ordinary experience, is corroborated in the actual person of Socrates, and the figure of Eros too is evoked, both with apparent innocence and subtle complexity, in some of Alcibiades' anecdotal information: Socrates is normally

---

   All and only body is vulnerable to happenings in the world.
   I am inwardly bitten, pierced.
   Therefore this whatever-you-call-it is bodily (or very like body).

It is an argument that appeals to subjective experience, indeed to subjective suffering, to deny a 'Platonic' view of the soul as a thing that is at one and the same time the seat of personality and immortal/invulnerable. The seat of my personality just got bitten by those speeches, so I know it is not 'pure,' 'unaffected,' 'unmoved'" (192). One may well reply that it is surely of some importance that it is *Plato* who writes this dialogue, and not someone familiar with contemporary mind-body preoccupations. Alcibiades is not the Form of the Beautiful, any more than is Socrates, and so neither of them can remain totally pure, unaffected, unmoved, since they are plainly not the perfect item. Alcibiades is aware of the Socratic view of the "soul"; how could he not be? And how could he not be torn between that view (subtle as it is) and so-called ordinary experience, which also had held that the seat of vulnerability was the heart or the soul or whatever one chose to call it. Plato was surely aware that life or soul was what one risked on the battlefield or in love (cf. Homer *Odyssey* 1.4–5; *Iliad* 9.401–9; Archilochus frag. 84 Edmonds [A. is unsouled (*apsychos*) by love]; cf. Theognis, 910). This is not an argument for physicalism or against "Plato," but a deep apprehension, yet one divided against itself, that it is still the soul or the heart or the center of the human being that is the root or terminus of all deepest feelings. This is *my* experience, psychic, cardiac, or whatever one wants to call it. There *is* a tragic tension between this apprehension and the divinities that Alcibiades seems to uncover in Socrates with the very same passionate conviction.

barefoot, covered by a coarse coat that barely protects him from the winter cold; he is tough and virtuous, placeless (*atopos*) like Eros, that is, in between everything, clearly not god, yet not simply man, but he knows that he is not wise and therefore he is dissatisfied, always searching. Does he die and come back to life again on the same day? Coming back to life is easy for a *daimôn,* but not for a human being. Socrates unfortunately is only *like* his Eros, just as the Dionysian images do not quite capture him. Rather, Dionysian elements point more and more in the direction of Alcibiades, who in his frustration and anger is much closer to outrageous madness than the thoughtful picture of Socrates that he draws. Thus, in Alcibiades' speech, as nowhere else after the *Phaedo,* we have a sense of Socrates endangered, a Socrates who is unfortunately the cause of a madness that he invites, ironically it seems, by his very stillness. Socrates the beloved, praised by an inebriated and garlanded Alcibiades, stands here in the presence of death. We shall come back to this tragic foreshadowing below.

7.4 The Trial of Praise

Alcibiades' mercurial transitions from praise to opprobrium, from love to hate, seem to capture exactly the divided psychological character of a certain alcoholic behavior. From one perspective, Socrates might seem like the ideal lover of Socrates' own speech, but for Alcibiades' unrequited passion, this is far from true. Alcibiades' story is so deeply affected by the real pain and shame he feels in Socrates' presence that this alone would preclude any romantic or sentimental coloring of Socrates' portrait. But there is something more negative and tragic still in Alcibiades' speech that threatens to disrupt any harmonious, romantic combination of Diotima's Eros and the person of Socrates, and this is summed up in the element of *trial* that pervades Alcibiades' divided mentality.

In the silence at the end of the *Symposium,* as all fall asleep except Socrates, the poet C. F. Meyer imagined the presence of the flute melody of death: "Still! Des Todes Sclummerflöten klingen!" (Silence! The sleepy flutes of death are sounding!).[21] These flutes are already present in Alcibiades' eulogy, first, in the *divided compulsive forces* set up in Alcibiades *by Socrates himself:* "And still even now, I *know well in myself* that if *I were willing* to give ear *I wouldn't be able to hold out* against him; *I would suffer* the same things. For *he compels* me to agree that though I am myself much in need, *I neglect myself* and *do* the business of Athenians. So *I stop my ears by force* as if

---

21. Cf. Hadot 1995, 166, 177.

I were running away from Sirens, so that I shall not grow old sitting there beside him" (216a). The contrasts between active agency and passivity, compulsion and active flight, the demands of self-knowledge and of politics, paint a vivid picture of a self divided against its better self and also against Socrates and thus compelled to put distance between the conflicting demands of philosophy and politics. But the growing conflict in Alcibiades' soul between philosophy and politics is again prey to the same divided compulsive forces that, on Alcibiades' own account, lead him to realize that he would be glad to see Socrates dead:

> Before him alone I feel ashamed. For *I am conscious* that *I cannot contradict* him and say it is not necessary *to do what he tells me to do,* but when I leave him, I am *worsted* by the honors that comes from the multitude. So I *desert* him and *flee,* and when I see him *I am ashamed by what I have agreed with him.* I'd often happily see him *not existing among humankind,* but *I know well* that if this happened, I'd be much more distressed; so I don't know what to do with this man. (216b1–c3)

The "flutes of death," therefore, are very much present in Alcibiades' love-hate passion, divided so compulsively against itself; and the wish for Socrates' death of which he is so honestly, but as yet innocently, ashamed arises out of the conflict between philosophy and politics (an ominous sign in itself) occasioned in his talented, self-aware soul *by Socrates.* In other words, there is a strong rational pattern in Alcibiades' presentation and it is this: the very qualities for which he seeks to praise Socrates are those hated compulsive forces he wants dead. Alcibiades' praise is therefore both the test and the trial of Socrates.

How does this work out in the concrete details of the rest of Alcibiades' speech? Alcibiades turns the tables on Socrates by promising simply to tell the truth, that is, to use Socrates' own criterion, if necessary, against himself. Yet what seems initially to be a perfectly clever, humorous stratagem turns out in what follows to be somewhat obsessive, even for someone as drunk as Alcibiades. He wants to tell the truth, certainly; but he also wants to beat Socrates over the head with it! "Truth," "refutation," "witness," "evidence" become the nails he hammers at every opportunity[22] until these terms become interwoven with the legal language of "charge," "penalty," "caution," "blame," "hubris," "arrogance"[23] and Alcibiades in humorous

---

22. 214e6 ff., 215a, 215b6–7, 216a, 217b1–3, 217e4, 218d8, 218e6, 219c1–2, 220a5–6, 220e4.
23. 213d–e; 214e; 217e5; 219c5–6; 221e3–4; 222a8, b6–7.

self-deprecation addresses the assembled guests openly as "judges" of Socrates' arrogance (*hybris, hyperêphania*)[24] in refusing his sexual advances:

> And not even in this either, Socrates, will you say I am lying. But when I'd done this, this man was so superior and contemptuous to my youthful bloom that he ridiculed [*kategelasten*] and outrageously insulted [*hybrisen*] it; and it was just in that regard that I thought I was really something, O gentlemen of the jury [*andres dikastai*], for you are judges [*dikastai*] of the arrogance [*hyperêphania*] of Socrates, for know well, by gods and by goddesses, when I arose after having slept with Socrates, it was nothing more out of the ordinary than if I'd slept with my father or elder brother. (219c2–d2)

Here the trial and death of Socrates are already represented in the petulant, divisive force of Alcibiades' praise: the test of Socrates' virtue is to prove fatal, to be put on trial for the corruption of the young, and the evidence, as Alcibiades keeps on insisting, is himself and people like him, who show that they did not believe in the gods of the city by profaning the mysteries and mutilating the herms and who bore testimony to the "corruptive" power of Socrates by proving themselves to be the ruin of Athens. Into the heart of this "satiric, Silenic" mask (222d3–4), then, Plato has woven a tragedy: the tragedy of the shadow inescapably cast by the "good." And this theme of test and trial proves to be no minor key in this instance, for Alcibiades himself, with innocent mockery but ignorant tragic menace, makes it the substance of his entire address in his closing remarks:

> This, gentlemen, is my praise of Socrates: and again I've mixed in with it the faults I find [*memphomai*] in him, and told you of his outrageous insult [*hybrisen*] to me. But it's not just me he has done this to, but also Charmides . . . and Euthydemus . . . and a great many others, whom this man deceives as a lover [*exapatôn*] and ends up himself as beloved instead of lover. I warn you too, Agathon, not to be deceived [*exapatasthai*] by him, but learn from our own experiences and watch out [*eylabêthênai*], instead of, as the proverb has it, learning like a foolish child by suffering. (222a7–b8)

After the tender words of devotion to Socrates immediately preceding this passage, it is natural that Alcibiades should temper love's tenderness

---

24. Dover 1980, 169 and Rowe 1998, 209, both on 217e4, take a positive view of this, Brisson 1998, 219 n. 549, a negative view.

with a little mock outrage. Yet at the same time, his praise is literally swallowed up in these closing words by the charge of *hybris* and deceit and the warning that Socrates is a social (if not quite yet a political) menace. The final proverb (changed very much in the Socratic fashion; cf. 174 ff.) from Homer and Hesiod, with the meaning "think before you act," is Plato's final ironic comment on the tragic plight of a man who thinks he has the whole situation taped down, but in fact does not even know what he is doing.[25]

7.5 Eros, the Tyrant, and His Revelers

Alcibiades' speech, so comic, so humorous, is in fact also the tragic climax of the *Symposium*. Socrates is flanked by three devoted admirers, each of whom exhibits passionate attachment, proportionate to his temperament or character: Apollodorus, who is always searching out and repeating what Socrates has said and despising every one else; Aristodemus, who imitates Socrates' physical mannerisms; and the larger-than-life Alcibiades, who wants to escape him, but cannot, and who damns him by loving him. None of them captures the essence of Socrates, but they are powerful examples of the love of the individual for the individual's sake that powerfully miss the mark, and with fatal consequences in Alcibiades' case. But Apollodorus's slavish devotion, while responsible for the faithful repetition of thought, is equally the death of philosophy. Socrates' own death is therefore flanked by at least several other forms of death: the death of living thought in the type of Apollodorus or Aristodemus and the ruin of self and political life in the fluctuating opposites of Alcibiades' obsession.

However, Socrates' own speech is also flanked by those of two golden sons of Athens, Agathon and Alcibiades, a flanking physically represented in the seating arrangements.[26] Although Alcibiades has taken his place between Agathon and Socrates, Socrates now proposes that he sit between the other two so that he, Socrates, can praise Agathon. This unlikely attempt to mediate between those two incarnations of tragic opposites at different levels of degradation, Agathon at the height of his brilliant success and Alcibiades already on the path to destruction, is destined not to be—at the very point Agathon gets up to sit next to Socrates (223a–b): "suddenly, a mob of revelers came to the doors, and when they found them open because someone was leaving, they came straight in to us and lay down, and everything was full of uproar, and no longer in any order they

---

25. Again, for a development of these concluding lines, see sections 8.4 and 8.8, below.
26. And also foreshadowed in the opening lines of the dialogue at 172b1–2: "because I wanted to find out about the get-together of Agathon, Socrates, and Alcibiades."

were compelled to drink a lot of wine" (223b). As we suggested earlier, the irruption of the transcendent ("suddenly") comes in different ways, ways that nonetheless all look alike. As the night draws on, and as more wine is drunk, things begin to resemble one another, even though they may be very different. Here is the final manifestation of the Dionysian element: the loss of all order (*kosmos*), and there is much humor in it, of course. But the echo of the *Republic* is at this point very strong and, in the light of our entire argument so far, this cannot be accidental.

Revelers appear in the *Republic* only at two crucial spots, book 6 and books 8–9. In the first instance, in the discussion of the philosophical nature that fails to develop its proper potential and is altered into a different character, that is, an alien nature, Socrates argues that the house of philosophy stands empty until people from outside force their way in, occupy the house, and consequently justify by their behavior most people's rejection of philosophy: "Think this also, then, namely that the intolerance of the many toward philosophy is caused by those *outsiders* [*exôthen*] who come to philosophy, where they do not belong, like *a band of revelers.* They are continually abusing each other [*loidoroumenous*] and being quarrelsome; *they invariably make their speeches about men,* which is least suited to philosophy" (*Rep.* 500b1–6). This first wave of revelers, then, is like the band that comes in with Alcibiades from out of doors. Furthermore, Alcibiades' speech is conspicuously ad hominem (cf. above: "they invariably make their speeches about men . . .") and humorously abusive, which, in terms of this detail at least in the *Republic,* is not properly philosophical at all.

The second wave of revelers occurs during Socrates' penetrating discussion of the origin and nature of the tyrant. The tyrant and his "fellow revelers" are like parasites on his father's estate (568e) and this parasitism leads ultimately to parricide. The tyrant wants everything to belong to him alone, and he consequently hates old age (569b–c). Then, in book 9, Socrates describes the first stage of the tyrannical nature: this occurs when his nature or pursuits make him drunk (*methystikos*),[27] lustful (*erôtikes*), and melancholic (*melancholikos*); and the following stage is where the tyrant Eros dwells in the soul and directs everything, and the young man pursues "feasts, revelries, banquets, prostitutes, etc." (573c7–d5). This second wave of revelers, then, is like that second wave in the *Symposium* that utterly disrupts the proceedings and brings compulsion to bear on all. We recall Eryximachus's proposal that each should drink as much as he wishes, and *nothing should be compulsory* (176e). Here at the end of the *Symposium,* behind the ordinary scenes of merriment and good humor, there is the introduction of

---

27. Cf. *Rep.* 403e.

universal compulsion and the disappearance of good order, for most, if not all, of those present. In this gradual denouement of a complex of themes which has been intensifying gradually in the dialogue, but that finds conspicuously brilliant expression in the speeches of Aristophanes, Agathon, and Alcibiades, we find, as in a subtle musical variation, the emergence of hidden patterns: Alcibiades' tender love for Socrates has already more than a hint of the tyrannical love of the *Republic,* and this in turn reflects that brilliant conjunction of opposites we saw in Agathon's speech. Agathon and Alcibiades, on either side of Socrates, are among the most striking last images of the *Symposium.* Is it accidental that only these two want to make legal trial of Socrates and that only these call him "hubristic"? *Corruptiones optimorum pessimae.* Alcibiades' language is vivid, clever, and devoid of artifice, but this does not mean that Plato speaks necessarily with and through him. Socrates is not Marsyas, as the *Republic* also makes very clear: "will you admit flute makers and flute players into the city? . . . The lyre and the cithara then are left to you as useful in the city . . . and the pipes for herdsmen in the country. . . . We are certainly not doing anything new, my friend, . . . in prefering Apollo and his instruments to Marsyas and his" (*Rep.* 3.399d–e). The image is for the sake of the truth, not to poke fun, Alcibiades had announced at the outset, and so it has proved to be; but the image hypothesis still limits the vision of the speaker, Alcibiades, even if it does not limit the "wonderful head" of the one praised.

7.6 Identity and Diversity: The Uniqueness of Socrates

Yet nothing is ever quite so simple, for in two major respects Alcibiades' speech goes far beyond almost anything in the previous speeches. In the climactic concluding paragraphs, he vividly draws a portrait of Socrates' strangeness (*atopia*), his "placelessness," and then the equally remarkable character of his "words." In the first case, he unconsciously provides an implicit answer to the problem of "human" identity, which is of such emotional importance in Aristophanes' speech[28] and of such puzzling character in Diotima's account. If we are but physical and mental bundles of constant contiguity and psychological association,[29] then what makes us individuals? No answer had been forthcoming in Socrates' speech, but just the hint of one emerges in Alcibiades' tribute to Socrates. The most remarkable

---

28. A "theme" already touched on in Pausanias' speech (185a3–4, b1–2; see Chapter 4) and the figure of Apollodorus (173 d 4, 8–9; see Chapters 1 and 2).
29. Cf. *Symp.* 207c ff. (and see Chapter 5).

thing about Socrates, he tells us, is that he is like no other human being, past or present (*to de mêdeni anthrôpôn homoion einai* [221c4–6). One can find comparisons for others, but not for Socrates, "unless perhaps one were to compare him to those I mention . . . Silenes and satyrs" (221d4–5). Alcibiades is touchingly aware that his own image does not really fit, but it is the best he can do.

But why should this be an "answer" to the problem of identity? Clearly, it is not an answer as such, but in a context in which speeches can address one another and even speak, as it were, on one another's behalf, an answer suggests itself. Most people's identity is minimal, perhaps predominantly a question of the bodily, psychological, social, and political associations that make up the largely unexamined husks of our existences. Identity in any meaningful sense, for Socrates and Plato, starts with self-examination and the development of a reflective subjectivity that can organize itself psychologically and physically. Yet even here there is much that remains unexamined, received from others, even slavish, since the problem of self-development is also the problem of escaping the tyranny of self: the prisoner freed from the cave in the *Republic* has to enter a world where things are least dependent on his or her preferences and then, following the vision of the Good, must reenter the cave to continue that self-release by helping to free his or her fellow human beings.[30] Two crucial points in this image are the following: (1) for Plato, the transforming vision of the Good over prolonged education and practice is the major precondition for an intelligent orientation to the world; and (2) this orientation to the world necessarily involves care for others. The good gives of itself (or, on Socrates' terms in the *Republic*, the would-be philosopher-king must even on occasion be compelled to go back into the cave!). The consequences for human identity in the *Symposium* become somewhat clearer. Socrates' genuine lifelong pursuit of the beautiful (and not merely of his own preferences projected onto some abstract ideal) has transformed him into the unique human individual Alcibiades loves. "Sameness" is a function, in part, of bodily or psychological continuity, but "uniqueness," the quality of being like nobody else, is a gift of the beautiful itself, reflected in every aspect of a person's existence.

If this is a reasonable reading of Alcibiades' simple observation, these further consequences are noteworthy. First, the self-identity of the "form" (*auto kath'auto*) is in itself the source of genuine diversity and uniqueness even if its more distant reflections possess a "sameness" like that of bodily parts, customs, or other things. Yet even in these instances, Diotima has

---

30. *Rep.* 7.514a–520d.

intimated, there is reflected a great ocean of beauty that is the "same" everywhere. So diversity and unity are to a lesser degree reflected in bodily beauty. Second, identity in the sense of uniqueness, while a property of psychosomatic existence, is not guaranteed by that existence or by any individual subjectivity. Rather, the identity seems to be a consequence of the search for divine beauty in the dialectical form of creative intersubjectivity, whose effects are therefore not only to be cared for but also tested. At least this reflects Diotima's account of the matter. An important corollary of this view would appear to be that while the "ascent" must go beyond the body after its initial step, care for the body as an effect of this ascent is an essential part of the dialectic of love.[31]

7.7 *Logoi* Opened Up: An Image for the *Symposium?*

Alcibiades' closing comments on the extraordinary character of Socrates' *logoi* (words, arguments, discourses) also go beyond anything in the previous speeches for two reasons: they provide an apt image for the structure of the *Symposium* itself and they suggest the *extent* of the change brought about in Socrates by his lifelong pursuit of the beautiful. The *Symposium* starts with an answer in search of a question, and the opening up of that question unpacks the different layers of narrative nestled one within the other. Alcibiades' image for Socrates' arguments develops and reinforces the necessity to open up discourse further, for Socrates' arguments are "most like Sileni that have been opened up" (221d8–e1). From the outside they look at first "like the hide of an outrageous satyr," for of course Socrates' examples are mundane; he talks about donkeys, smiths, and cobblers and "always appears to be saying the same things in the same ways" (221e5–6). But the reality is different: "when they are opened up and *one comes to be inside of them,*" one finds that they are the only arguments with any sense, and that they contain so many divine statue-images (*agalmata*)[32] of virtue that they turn out to have universal relevance for anyone who intends to be noble and good "to consider" (*skopein* [222a]). To consider or to look at (*skopein*) is what Socrates does, according to Alcibiades, in the motionless movement of his thought (*heistêkei skopôn . . . zêtôn* [220c4–5]). But the opening up of the arguments from the inside involves a major change: what appear on the surface to be the most mundane examples turn out to contain sacred images and to be both *unique* and yet *universal*.

---

31. Cf. section 8.7, below.
32. For *agalma,* see especially Lacan 1991, 163–78.

Alcibiades' comment on Socrates' arguments is also a comment on the dialogue form itself, as well as on the nature of "form" for Plato: the self-identity of form, it would seem, is not remote or abstract or merely "conceptual," since such self-identity is measured both by comprehensive universal meaning and by uniqueness. This is probably too much to read into Alcibiades' innocent comments, of course; yet these comments capture something of what Plato thought about form, as well as what he thought about Socrates.

7.8 The Concluding Scenes: Rest and the Self-Motion of Thought—"Socrates Standing Seeking"

With the entry of the second group of revelers and the ensuing disorder, Alcibiades disappears from the *Symposium*. Eryximachus, Phaedrus, and some others are mentioned as leaving, but Aristodemus falls asleep and sleeps for some time "because the nights were long." But when he wakes up at dawn with the crowing of the cocks (cf. *Phaedo* 118a 7–8), only Agathon, Aristophanes, and Socrates are still awake and drinking from a large bowl in clockwise fashion (*epi dexia* [223c5]). Eryximachus has left, but his order still prevails!

The compulsion to drink a lot of wine (*anangkazesthai* [223b6]) ultimately yields, despite the pomposity of the good doctor, to the order of his patron god (Apollo) and to a different sort of compulsion (223d2, 6), that of Socrates, "compelling" Agathon and Aristophanes "to agree that the same man knows how to compose comedy and tragedy and that he who is a tragic poet by craft is also a comic poet" (d3–6). Aristodemus was too drowsy to remember the other arguments, but he does remember the "main point"—the conclusion. The *Symposium* ends, as it began, in an answer or conclusion, to which the question has been lost and must somehow be reconstructed. There are many possible explanations for this (and we shall examine this question in the context of Plato's theory of art in Chapter 8), just as Socrates' final words in the *Phaedo*, "Crito, we owe a cock to Asclepius; pay it up and don't forget" (118a7–8), as we have argued, naturally bear different interpretations.[33] And since Plato leaves the matter open ended, more than one possibility should perhaps be adopted simultaneously. Nonetheless, there is a simple, elegant metadramatic possibility that should not be excluded from any shopping list. In the *Phaedo*, it is mentioned that Plato is sick and absent from the conversation in prison. The impenetrable "a cock for Asclepius" is therefore, on one level at least, Plato's

---

33. See, e.g., Rowe 1993, 295–96; Dixsaut 1991, 408–9.

own vanishing signature, for among other possibilities we cannot exclude that Socrates' last explicit thought was for his absent pupil, whom he had known virtually from birth and who, he might have thought, was his most talented friend. In the *Symposium,* conversely, we have seen the importance of art for Plato not only (negatively and by contrast) in Aristophanes' and Agathon's speeches, but also in those of Socrates and Alcibiades.

The argument with Aristophanes and Agathon, which Aristodemus forgets, is also Socrates' argument against his own negative criticism of art in the *Republic,* and, thus, evidence of Plato's open argument with himself. In *Republic* 3, Socrates claims that imitative poets cannot cross, or extend, the boundaries of their talents: "The same people cannot practice well at once, the two forms of imitation that appear most nearly akin, as the writing of tragedy and comedy" (395a). In Diotima's speech we have learned that humans beings can be changed by the visions they pursue, and the search for the highest beauty transforms the seeker and permits him to step beyond the boundaries of a single science or craft. Alcibiades' depiction of Socrates presents a portrait in motion of a man transformed by an apparently motionless thought. Socrates' argument with the poets leaves us guessing that, perhaps, the same apparently motionless search can transform the work of what are otherwise only imitative poets and permit them to extend or open up the boundaries of their art.

Indeed, in the Silenic play of Alcibiades' speech, as elsewhere in the dialogue, we have watched the tableau of comedy and tragedy unfold together; and, in fact, the whole of the *Symposium* bears this double mark. Again, therefore, this answer without a question—which naturally forces us to go beyond the framework of this dialogue in order to determine what Socrates-Plato may think and say elsewhere—is Plato's own vanishing signature, pointing implicitly to the possibility of a higher philosophical but literary muse that we surely experience in its most brilliant expression as the *Symposium* itself, that is, as a work which weaves together different narrative forms, from dialectic to imitative narrative (as we shall explore further in Chapter 8), and yet *in the light of the whole* is never simply imitative itself (even on the basic level of Apollodorus-Aristodemus), but acts as a prismatic lens ultimately through which to see the various refractions of the beautiful. Other explanations are possible and probable, as invariably seems to be the case in the *Symposium,* since we only have the answer, not the question and process.[34]

So the two poets, comic and tragic, are being compelled to agree, but they are not following very well and are drowsy, and first Aristophanes falls asleep, then, with daybreak, Agathon, and only Socrates is left. Is Socrates

---

34. See further section 8.5, below.

the sole self-sufficient, absolutely independent one who can thus overcome the god of wine? Not quite; after putting them to sleep, he gets up and goes off. The participle *katakoimisanta*, (putting them to sleep) is literally what he has done, but it also bears an appropriate undertone of care for the two poets, as a mother might put her children to sleep (223d9; cf. *Laws* 790d).[35] Nor is he alone, for he cannot shake his shadow, Aristodemus, who "as usual followed him." Socrates can overcome the god of wine, but he is not self-sufficient in the sense that he is devoid of care for others, even down to the semiautomatic details of ensuring that they are comfortable, and neither is he self-sufficient in the sense that *he can ever escape his shadow!*[36]

Socrates then goes to the sanctuary of Apollo Lykaios, with its accompanying gymnasium, and baths, as well he might after a night on the town with Dionysus and company. This remains in striking contrast to his apparently more normal, unwashed state (cf. Aristophanes *Clouds,* 835–37), but he washes before death (*Phaedo* 115a)[37] and so why not too in the celebration of the "whole tragicomedy of life"?[38] Socrates then spends the rest of the day as he would any other, under the watchful eye of Aristodemus. He has passed through the dominions of *both* Dionysus and Apollo, and he remains *Socrates.* Aristodemus, of course, knows everything Socrates does, and we cannot help wishing he would give us a bit more detail, which makes us just like Aristodemus, but with that added prurient modern interest in all the details of the lives of the "rich and famous," as it were. After reading the *Symposium,* too, we know that this is the least important question of all: what the great master actually does. So Socrates' day concluded; and he went home in the evening and "rested" (*anapauesthai*). With Aristodemus now on his own, as it were, we are back again in the video reportage of serial succession, that is, the exchange of opposites: action then rest. But perhaps having read the whole dialogue, we cannot help recalling Aristodemus's own experience of Socrates' "restful" halts and Alcibiades' subsequent testimony. "He sometimes just stops and stands wherever he happens to be . . . don't move him, but let him be" (175b1–3), Aristodemus tells Agathon. Socrates' stops are full of the motion of thought. On campaign he stands still all night long, just as if he were resting, but Alcibiades tells us: "he stood there looking . . . seeking" (220c). The final word "rested" means exactly what it says, of course; but if we want to learn more about Socrates, then we have to read the dialogue again, forward and backward simultaneously, as any second or more thoughtful reading must

---

35. Cf. Bonelli 1991, 154.
36. Cf. *Theaetetus* 176a6!
37. Cf. Robin 1992, civ–v and n. 1.
38. For this phrase, see *Philebus* 50b.

always proceed. And if so, that final "rest" is the end of Socrates, the historical figure, for this dialogue, and our attention naturally turns back to the striking vertical image of Alcibiades' speech: "he stood there seeking." If Plato started to write the *Phaedrus* immediately after the *Symposium,* he could not have had a more vivid image than the self-moving thought of Socrates at rest to provoke its major themes: love, self-knowledge, the divine feast (by contrast with its human counterpart—the *Symposium*), and the problem of the apparent self-motion of soul's own life.

Conclusion

Plato's Dialectic at Play

As almost all observers would agree, the *Symposium* is a "literary masterpiece." Yet this claim tells us virtually nothing about its real significance—which is more than just being "a literary masterpiece"—and it implies that the dialogue bears limited philosophical significance or represents a break from the hard rational business of some of the other "middle" dialogues. The *Symposium* is a preeminently philosophical work, but one that is cast in the mold of an enigma or question and, above all, in a form entirely new to the development of human thought. Let us examine each of these claims in turn, starting with the problem of the *Symposium* as an aporetic dialogue in a new form.

8.1 Character, Voice, and Genre

As we have seen, the *Symposium* calls itself into existence literally by calling itself into question, for it starts with an answer to a question already posed and, therefore, its very first words require the voice of the other as the dialogical key to understanding the discourse. Mutual reflexivity of discourse as dependent on the question of the other is, therefore, part of the very frame of the work itself. Furthermore, each speech, from the basic narrative of Apollodorus-Aristodemus to the apparently most "fictional" dialogue of Socrates with Diotima, which culminates in the ascent beyond all recognizable "fact," both calls itself into question and is called into question by the speeches of the others. The sheer physical force of Alcibiades' entry, for instance, is in violent revelatory contrast to the "mystery" revelations of Diotima. And even at the end of the dialogue the same theme of dependence on the voice or question of the others reoccurs in Socrates' compelling the two poets, Aristophanes and Agathon, to the conclusion, or answer, that the same person can write comedy and tragedy, a conclusion whose question, premises, and preliminary arguments have been lost by the lateness of the hour and Aristodemus's sleepiness. Again, in a different vein, in the closing systole and diastole of Socrates' daily life—in which we know Apollodorus has an all-consuming interest—the dialogue is literally forced back on itself to ask again about the reality of Socrates' inner life, since the serial succession between opposites, which constitutes the flow of daily life, does not capture the significance of the inner world of Socrates' attention to himself, manifested in some manner in his dialogue with Diotima. So dependence on the voice of the other, that is, on a dialogue already initiated, into the middle of which we suddenly awaken, is fundamental to the very framework of the *Symposium*. To be in search of the question of the other is therefore a leitmotif fundamental to understanding the dialogue as a whole.

Who or what is "the other"? The *Symposium* is evidently a drama of many voices and many different characters, so vividly drawn as to be observable from many different angles. In a sense, each new voice adds another angle to all the voices of the drama. Yet, equally important, the *Symposium* is a drama of many different *genres,* each free and playful in its own way, and yet all of them brought together into what is essentially a new artistic and philosophical form, that is, an experimental form of dialogues and characters nestling within one another, and not only this, but addressing, commenting, criticizing, reshaping, testing, and trying each other. So the "other" is not only the many voices and characters, but the different genres which help to frame the work.[1]

What are these genres? There are at least seven generic layers within the dialogue. First, there is the audio-video reportage of Apollodorus-Aristodemus, which is framed as an imitation of an imitation, that is, a more or less exact replication of an event long past, at which neither the teller, Apollodorus, nor the immediate listener were present. There is, then, an "epic distance" between the events recounted and the present conversation and, at the same time, an immediate closeness for the reader, who enters the dialogue in the middle of a conversation already initiated and, as in every

---

1. On the question of Plato's incorporation of specific genres of poetry and rhetoric into his dialogues, see Wilson Nightingale 1995; also more generally Nancy 1982; and on argument and the dialogue form, see Frede 1992.

human life, is forced to discover a context for the flow of events from the past through the present and into the future. This basic generic layer, although framed within the closeness of immediate dialogue, is representative of the kind of mimetic art that is criticized in the *Republic*.[2] It purports faithfully to reproduce an actual event but at third hand. As in the case of epic, the tale is more or less frozen in an absolute past and the telling requires no creativity beyond the use of memory itself. So in this first genre, which remains essential to the survival of the tale and thus to the very fabric of the *Symposium,* Apollodorus supplies a first example of how a so-called factual truth should be reported: he must not change anything (unlike the apparently "hubristic" Homer and Socrates); he must be utterly devoted to his subject matter; and he must pay particular attention to the chronology of events (a point emphasized by Apollodorus's contempt for another narrator, Phoenix, who had nothing "clear" to tell). In this genre, however, the question of "truth" does not even appear. Mimetic art of this epic, mnemonic kind is concerned only with a slavish, chronological "clarity."[3]

The second generic layer undermines the first and is more closely related to the immediacy of the dialogue into which the reader is first introduced. This is the conversation between Socrates and Aristodemus on the way to Agathon's house that casts the reader not into events of epic distance but rather into the problems of everyday life, that of ordinary and not so ordinary people; dinner invitations and the lack of them; the eternal flow, as it were, of the play on words; and so on. This conversation suggests, by contrast with the first narrative genre, that all reality is infinitely plastic—that creativity of any sort destroys and transforms its supposed original material so that one cannot get behind the transformations to get a clear, unambiguous picture of that original material. The "original material" in this case is, of course, folklore or the proverb that Socrates claims that both he and epic have corrupted and transformed to fit the changing circumstances of a changing world, both the epic world itself and the ordinary world of "inferior" people, one of whom Aristodemus takes himself to be. It is not accidental, surely, that in the mutations of the proverb, the original form *never clearly appears.*[4] We can only *conjecture* that Socrates' version of the proverb "good men go to good men's feasts of their own accord" is perhaps closer to the original than Homer's version, "good men go to inferior men's feasts of their own accord"; but the "original" is already lost in the conversation. There is, therefore, in this generic layer no original version or historical

---

2. Cf. Chapter 1; *Symp.* 172a–174a.
3. On the question of truth, see Chapters 3–5, and also below in this section.
4. See generally Chapter 2, esp. section 2.5. *Symp.* 174a 3–d4.

bedrock, but only infinite plasticity, from folklore through epic into the endless voice of the other that is present in all human conversation. The irony of this genre is that from the very beginning of the epic-mimetic accounts of Apollodorus-Aristodemus, the fundamental assumptions of the mimetic narrative are *contradicted* by the dialogical form, without the narrators ever being aware of the contradiction. This dialogue, then, moves away from the supposedly frozen epic or folkloric past into the present and future of everyday life as it attempts "to find a way": "As we two go together farther on our way, we'll think out what we'll say. So let's go" (174d2–3). Even in this present conversation, the voice of the other, that is, Homer (*Iliad* 10.224), sounds clearly like that of an absent participator; and in this context, it is reasonable to suppose that just as the present conversation is a destruction and transformation of the voices of the past, so too were Homer's words a transformation of folklore and historical elements, whose forms are but the dimmest shadows of an irretrievable past.[5]

So this second generic layer, although borne innocently and unsuspectingly by the first, is actually opposed to it. But the infinite plasticity of reality is not its only feature, for it bears its generic label precisely in itself: dialogue is a movement through destructions and transformations between the gifted and not so gifted, the invited and the uninvited, who together might find their way to the house of the "good" with a reasonable account to get themselves both admitted. But life is never quite that simple, for it is not just creative movement that is important but proper self-directed thought (in the figure of Socrates "standing seeking"), that is, rest or motionless movement, and, just as important, a generous host. Dialogue is not just the measure of the participants or the quantity of their words; it depends much more on the "substance" of their thought and the generosity of the good. And, in fact, the generosity of the good is *the* most important feature, since Socrates and Aristodemus conspicuously fail to devise what they are going to say, and "the little nugget of wisdom" Socrates is supposed to have come across in his meditation in the porch of a neighboring house becomes a theme that reoccurs in various permutations throughout the rest of the dialogue and that, apart from the indirect manifestations of his own speech, remains unsaid—somewhat like the folkloric proverb that furnished the original material for the whole occasion. So the endless play of words and the plasticity of reality have this serious function: the destruction by transformation of the word serves to introduce the reader, by means of the movement of dialogue and the disruption of movement that is thought, into the party of many voices at the house of the good, on which

5. *Symp.* 174b3–d4.

mnemonic imitation, the vanishing landscape of folklore, and the many speech genres all depend.

There are at least five other genres in the *Symposium* as a whole. There are the "interludes" themselves so carefully crafted as to contrast, even destroy, entire moods, as well as to foreground elements and absences in the speeches themselves. There are the formal, rhetorical speeches that contain elements of myth, drama, lyric poetry, and fable, and that represent certain generic faces, but that also catch something of the individualities that are irreducible to mere typology. Each speech provides a different vision of reality that interacts with all the other visions, and that all together furnish a somewhat fragmented view of a principle that is both older and younger than anything else, namely, the god Eros (the "logic" of which Plato will later develop in the *Parmenides*).[6]

The notion of truth as such has not yet emerged. It first occurs, informally, in Socrates' discussion with Agathon about the nature of the audience before which one ought to feel shame and then, formally, in the elenchus of Agathon.[7] And with the emergence of this crucial notion, self-questioning as an explicitly philosophical feature of discourse becomes for the first time a real problem: which genre is fundamental and most authoritative? The imitation thrice removed from reality that makes the *Symposium* possible, or the plasticity of reality that is characteristic of transformative dialogue, or each of the early speeches with its own irreducible vision, or even perhaps the interludes "in between" where we can sometimes catch the speakers off their guard in the flow of things? Or is the most authoritative and most truthful to be found in the fifth genre, Socrates' speech, which marks a new beginning[8] and which casts monological encomium into dialogical form, wherein the author freely adopts the role of disciple and recipient in relation to a higher, sacred, feminine teacher?[9] Certainly, the dialectical form is more authoritative than the earlier speeches, for not only does it open itself out for closer scrutiny but it also includes all the earlier speeches within it as transformed stepping stones in upward movement toward the beautiful.[10] But the precise version of truth is not what we might expect, for it is the truth of a complex psychic image, illuminated by both argument and myth,[11] which stands in

---

6. In this way the early speeches themselves seem to look forward already to the treatment in the *Parmenides* of the one and the many (*Parm.* 152a–155e, 140e–141e). A treatment of this much larger issue is beyond the scope of the present work.

7. *Symp.* 194a1–c8, 200b8, 201c6–9.

8. See Chapter 5, passim.

9. See section 5.3, above.

10. See Chapter 6, passim.

11. See sections 5.3, 5.10, above, and 8.6, below.

strong contrast to the apparently "factual" reportage of Apollodorus and Aristodemus as well as to the historical-legal "truth" of Alcibiades that is to follow and that constitutes a sixth genre. The Socrates-Diotima dialectic, more than any other genre in the *Symposium*, calls itself into question precisely by its very form, for its truth is not that of fact or of corroboration by testimony but of what appears to be least factual; and if important elements in the earlier speeches are "corrected" or "focused" in a new way in the ladder of ascent, as indeed they are, this is also because those speeches have more in them than they are themselves conscious of, so that they can and do speak to one another as well as find a new integrated focus in a dialectic that *factually* has nothing to do with them (for the dialectic took place before they came into existence). Yet the dialectic can address them beforehand, as it were, not only because of its own "fictional" power but because such speeches say more than they actually mean, as we shall see in more detail below (section 8.4). In other words, the Socrates-Diotima dialectic is not a procrustean reduction of heterodoxy into monochromatic hierarchical Platonic orthodoxy, but the free play of the reflection of others' voices, of ideas, in dialectical transformation; and this is also a recognition that others' voices are not closed compartments of hermetic meaning, but naturally have more in them than they mean and look to the fictional "future" for the unfolding of their potentiality rather than to the absolute past of epic "fact."

But this dialectic too is not a finished business, for it remains radically incomplete without those voices that give it context and which address it with new meanings even when *they cannot hear it*. Such—above all—is Alcibiades' legal-historical role and speech, which can never hear the Socrates-Diotima dialectic and pricks into nothingness the sublime ascent, as if it had never been, yet also corroborates the real transforming power of what had looked to be least true or factual (the vision of the beautiful in Socrates) and, furthermore, adds and develops elements in Socrates' speech that are plainly left open ended and unfinished.[12] No matter how important Socrates' speech may be, it is still only a part of the *Symposium* itself, one genre among many, which continues to need the contrast and corroboration of the others to open up its own voice further.

In this context of a multiplicity of voices and at least six different genres nestled one within another, but uneasily and with friction and opposition between them, it becomes possible, we suggest, to glimpse a seventh genre and to see the *Symposium* not only as a multidimensional drama that calls itself into question but also as a form almost entirely new

12. See Chapter 7, passim.

to the development of human thought. For the seventh genre is the character of the work as a whole, a conversation into the middle of which we enter, which is played out through all the different genres, and through which the vanishing voice of the author himself, Plato, also addresses the reader. The *Symposium* is a whole greater than its parts, not in the sense of what Gilbert Ryle calls "Descartes' myth," that is, the view that the university is somehow more than the sum of its colleges or parts,[13] but rather in the sense of the complex dialectic that Plato (if Plato it really be) envisages in the *Seventh Letter*,[14] in which all the elements through which we seek to know anything—names, definitions, images, knowledges (*epistêmê, nous, orthê doxa* [342a–c])—even in repeated use by ascent and descent scarcely yield proper knowledge (343e): "Barely [*mogis*] when each of these things—names, definitions, and sights and perceptions—have been rubbed against one another and refuted in well-meaning refutations [*en eumenesin elegchois elegchomena*] by means of questions and answers without envy—only then, did wisdom and intellect [*phronêsis, nous*] shine out straining at the very extremity of human power" (344b).[15]

The *Symposium* implicitly distinguishes between defective science (in the Lesser Mysteries), which unsuccessfully attempts to remedy an endless brain drain on the level of serial succession, from more authentic science (in the Greater Mysteries) whose focus is not slavish attention to the beauty of a single instance (210c8–d1) but an entry to the great sea of beauty, animated as it were by the single science of dialectic (which also on these terms, as in the *Republic,* describes the whole ascent), which is the science of the beautiful itself (210d2–7). The *Seventh Letter* outlines a similar distinction: names, definitions, images, and knowledge fail to express only the being of

---

13. Ryle 1973, 13–25.

14. The *Seventh Letter* has been regarded as nonauthentic (1) for reasons of style (e.g., Levinson, Morton, and Windspear 1968), (2) for lack of Platonic philosophical content (e.g., Edelstein 1968; Müller 1986), and (3) on the grounds that the "philosophical digression" was not known by the early Middle Platonists and is therefore a later Thrasyllan insertion (Tarrant 1983, 1993). Against (1), see Morrow 1962; Ledger 1989; and Sayre 1995. Against (2) and (3), see Fritz 1971 and Gonzalez 1998. Although the question will never be decided conclusively, (1) if the style is consistent with that of later Plato, (2) if the philosophical content is strikingly in tune with what we know from the dialogues (esp. the "middle" dialogues), and (3) if the supposed "later" additions are not later (which cannot be part of our argument here), then there is perhaps good reason to suppose that the *Letter* was written either by Plato or by a mind equal to Plato (i.e., Plato).

15. The emphasis of this passage makes dialectic a risky business, for the heart of this activity is not a simple testing, but *refutation* in order either to corroborate or to annihilate. This "negative" aspect is mitigated by the context of essential friendship: "well-meaning" and "without envy" (cf. *Symp.* 212), as well as (343a2–3) a proper natural affinity for the subject (*eu pephykotos eu pephykoti;* cf. 344a), but the refutation of "these things" (*onoma, logos, eidôlon, epistêmê* [342b]) seems to involve their destruction and transformation.

things, but rather, because of the weakness of discourse (*to tôn logôn asthenes* [343a]), express the quality or likeness of the thing.[16] Each of them is "unclear" (343b–c), an image that conceals its opposition to the real being of anything. This is ultimately, it would seem, a defect of language, of word, and of discourse, since the word can only be replaced by other words, and there is no stable correspondence between word and thing (343a–c). As we have seen in the *Symposium*, for this reason no ideal or original language is possible (cf. 343a; and the *Cratylus*).[17] Yet all four elements are necessary to any participatory knowledge in the fifth, that is, the *being* of the thing (342d–e). But authentic science requires something more: the rubbing together of these elements in disruptive, but well-meaning, discourse. As in the *Symposium*, the plasticity of language involves destruction and yet it also yields transformation, for in "being rubbed together" and "refuted"— like sticks for the combustion of fire[18]—they also make possible the light of authentic understanding.

All the voices, persons, and genres in the *Symposium* are not unlike the four "elements" in the *Seventh Letter* rubbed together in a dialogue that call them fundamentally into question;[19] but they are also perhaps even more like the characters, chapters, and styles in a novel that reflect and address one another on their own terms, in friction, yet also in well-meaning reflexive discourse. Only in their proximity and friction of address can illumination take place. The *Symposium* is the space of this dialectical friction that seeks illumination, in the sphere of the beautiful, from the Good that declares its presence largely by its absence or, as we argued, by its afterimage behind, or together with, the revelation of the beautiful, since together with the pun on Agathon's name and the implicit distinction between the good and the beautiful early in Diotima-Socrates' conversation, Agathon's speech represents the shadow of the fifth step on the ladder of love.[20] To the degree that the Good is absent—and in the context of the *Republic*, the *Symposium* strongly suggests such an absence—the mutual address and friction of characters and genres that is the *Symposium* as a whole are in search of that point outside themselves, namely, the virtually absent Good. So, the voice

---

16. *Seventh Letter* 342e2–343a1.

17. This is strictly beyond the scope of the present inquiry, but the point is simply that language cannot reach the supposed "bedrock" of things by means of language (*Cratylus* 422b ff.). The battle of names has to be decided in a different manner (438d–439b).

18. The process of "being rubbed against one another" seems to be equivalent to "the *diagôgê* through all of them, moving up and down," an ascent and descent in constant motion that destroys them and yet transforms them into something else. Cf. *Rep.* 4.435a1.

19. See section 8.4, ad fin., below, on this issue.

20. See section 6.2, above.

of the "other" we sought earlier is ultimately the silent Good, which like the beautiful and the other "forms," is beyond the capacity of language, character, or genre to represent it.

In other words, for the first time in the history of thought, a new genre emerges, which is *conscious* of its function as an image, as of its special representative powers, and of its *difference* from all other literary and rhetorical genres, which turns thought into living speech and character in an open-ended, inconclusive way, and which brings even the purported distance of heroic events into the intimate proximity of everyday conversation in which every reader is included. Friedrich Schlegel regarded the Socratic dialogues as "the novels of their time" and Mikhail Bakhtin thought that the dialogues together with other seriocomical literature, as we shall see later, were "the authentic predecessors of the novel." In one way, Friedrich Nietzsche went further than Bakhtin and Schlegel, for he regarded the Platonic dialogues as the "lifeboat" in which all the older poetic genres were saved from "shipwreck": "Plato has furnished for all posterity the pattern of a new art form, the novel, viewed as the Aesopian fable raised to its highest power." Yet Nietzsche appears to view this new art form in an essentially nondialogical way, as an intensified form of fable in which all the older genres, including poetry, are forced to obey the procrustean direction of their "helmsman Socrates."[21] But if it is characteristic of the novel as a genre that it be essentially dialogical and that, if dialogical, it also be aware of itself as dialogical and aware also of its difference from other kinds of voice (epic, drama, lyric, and so on), then the *Symposium* in the strict sense (by contrast even with the earlier dialogues) is the first novel in history, and certainly the first philosophical novel as well as the first to articulate a complete poetics. True it is that the earlier and even contemporary dialogues set the scene for the emergence of the novel in the strictest sense, especially the *Republic*, with its critique of the arts through the firsthand narrative of Socrates. But it is only in the *Symposium* that the arts and sciences speak for themselves as individual players in a larger chemistry of presence and absence by which art and philosophy come together in the new form of the novel, which is specifically conscious of itself as a new genre among genres.[22]

21. Bakhtin 1981c, 22. Friedrich Wilhelm Nietzsche, *The Birth of Tragedy from the Spirit of Music* (1872), section 14, cited here from Richter 1989, 414.

22. Craig (1985, 158–73) argues for a very different and much more general position regarding the tragicomic novel and for Plato's commitment to realism (which is simply mistaken or too ambiguous to be helpful). José Ortega y Gasset, however, realized that something much more specific and new was taking place in the *Symposium*, though he restricts this to the *"tragic-comic synthesis* at the end of the *Symp."* (*Hudson Review* 10 [1957]: 40).

8.2 Bakhtin and the Dialogical Character of Novelistic Discourse

This claim can be brought into sharper focus against the background of Bakhtin's analysis of discourse in the novel.[23] For Bakhtin, Socrates serves already "as an image employed for the purposes of experiment" and in this "experimental guesswork . . . the image of the speaking person and his discourse become the object of creative artistic imagination." This process of "experimenting by turning persuasive discourse into speaking persons" becomes particularly important when one is striving to liberate oneself from the influence of such an image and its discourse by means of objectification or to expose the limitations of both image and discourse," for by objectifying that discourse, one gets "a feel for its boundaries."[24] By contrast with some forms of rhetoric, whose words become things and die as discourse, or whose double-voicedness is just diversity of voices and not real dialogue pervaded by the speech of the other (*heteroglossia*), real novelistic discourse essentially involves the other's voice:

> "Rhetoric is often limited to purely verbal victories over the word; when this happens the word itself is diminished and becomes shallow . . . words grow sickly, lose semantic depth and flexibility, the capacity to expand and renew their meanings in new living contexts; they essentially die as discourse, for the signifying word lives beyond itself, that is, it lives by means of directing its purposiveness outwards. . . . Within the arena of almost every utterance an intense interaction and struggle between one's own and another's word is being waged, a process in which they oppose or dialogically interanimate each other. The utterance so conceived is a considerably more complex and dynamic organism than it appears when construed simply as a thing that articulates the intention of the person uttering it, which is to see the utterance as a direct, single-voiced vehicle of expression."[25]

Successful novelistic discourse, on Bakhtin's account, is essentially multivoiced (polyglossial) and dialogical (heteroglossial). In Dostoevsky's writings, for instance, "there is nothing merely thing-like, no mere matter, no

---

23. Apart from Bakhtin 1981c, see also 1981b and 1984a. "On Bakhtin generally, see Morson 1981 and 1986; and Morson and Emerson 1990, 60 n. 23 on Bakhtin's favorable view of the Socratic dialogues as opposed to what he regards as Plato's later monologization of dialogue (but see also Bakhtin's qualification of this view in Bakhtin 1984a, as cited by Morson and Emerson [1990, 476 n. 23]).
24. 1981b, 347–48.
25. 1981b, 353–54.

object (*niet nichego veshnogo, niet predmeta, objekta*); there are only subjects. Therefore there is no word-judgement, no word about an object, no second-hand referential word; there is only the word as address, the word dialogically contacting another word, a word about a word addressed to a word (*slovo, dialogicheski soprikasay sheesya s drugim slovom, slovo o slove, obrashennoe k slovu*)."[26] The very first sentence of the *Symposium* is a perfect, self-aware example of "a word about a word addressed to a word," insofar as the work opens on one side of a conversation already initiated and therefore requires the voice of another. But Bakhtin tends to see the classical period and its relation to epic with remarkable insight and yet with less depth perception than does Plato himself. Building on the work of Erwin Rohde,[27] Bakhtin pays detailed attention to what he calls "the authentic predecessors of the novel" especially in seriocomical literature, such as the plotted mimes of Sophron, the bucolic poems, the fable, early memoir literature (e.g., the *Epidêmiae* of Ion of Chios, the *Homilae* of Critias), the Socratic dialogues (as a genre), Roman satire, *Symposia* literature, Menippean satire, and dialogues of the Lucianic type. Here, rather than in the so-called Greek novel as such, Bakhtin locates the important beginnings of a decisive shift toward the formation of the novel and its essential dialogical nature:

> "The authentic spirit of the novel as a developing genre is present in them to an incomparably greater degree than in the so-called Greek novels. . . . the serio-comical genres . . . anticipate the more essential historical aspects in the development of the novel in modern times, even though they lack that sturdy skeleton of plot and composition that we have grown accustomed to demand from the novel as a genre. . . . These serio-comical genres (especially the Socratic dialogues, and Menippean satire [including the *Satyricon* of Petronius]) were the first authentic and essential step in the evolution of the novel as the genre of becoming."[28]

What, on Bakhtin's account, are these "essential historical aspects" and how do they differ from epic and other genres? For Bakhtin, the emergence of the novel is the emergence of a historical struggle of genres, because the novel "parodies other genres . . . precisely in their role as genres" and "exposes the conventionality of their forms and their languages." In what becomes, therefore, the novelization of other genres, these genres "become

---

26. 1984a, 237; cf. 1981b, 349.
27. Rohde 1960.
28. Bakhtin 1981c, 22. Further page references to this work will appear in the text.

dialogized, permeated with laughter, irony, humour, elements of self-parody and finally . . . the novel inserts into these other genres an indeterminacy, a certain semantic open-endedness, a living contact with unfinished, still-evolving contemporary reality (the open-ended present)" (7). So the novel is the most fluid of genres, whose roots are ultimately to be found in folklore (21 ff.), whereas a genre like epic has a frozen, canonized, already completed quality to it insofar as it describes a national epic past based upon tradition, rather than personal experience, and memory, rather than knowledge, and separated from contemporary reality by an "absolute" distance. The novel, by contrast, (1) is three-dimensional; (2) possesses a multivoiced consciousness or polyglossia; (3) permits the image or voice to be examined, laughed at, poked, or taken seriously from every angle and in every tense; and (4) consequently, brings the literary image into a zone of maximal contact with the present in all its indeterminacy, indecision, and open-endedness. Here epic distance disintegrates and the possibility of "an authentically objective portrayal of the past as the past" emerges: "every great and serious contemporaneity requires an authentic profile of the past, an authentic other language from another time" (30). But this sense of the past arises out of a noncanonized view of the present as an unconcluded process: "The temporal model of the world changes radically: it becomes a world where there is no first word (no ideal word), and the final word has not yet been spoken. . . . Through contact with the present, an object is attracted to the incomplete process of a world-in-the-making, and is stamped with the seal of inconclusiveness" (30). This absence of internal conclusiveness has, for Bakhtin, the following consequences: first, it creates a sharp increase in demands for an *external* and *formal* completedness, especially in regard to plot; second, whereas in distanced images we have the whole event, the novel speculates in the unknown so that, on the one hand, the boundaries separating fiction and nonfiction, literature and nonliterature start to shift and become blurred, while, on the other hand, there is both a new authorial *surplus* knowledge (the author has a surplus of knowledge which the hero does not know or see, to be exploited in a host of different ways) and each figure or mask has "a happy surplus" of its own (36): the epic or tragic hero is nothing outside his destiny, which is both his strength and limitation, whereas one of "the basic internal themes of the novel is precisely the theme of the hero's inadequacy to his fate or his situation." The hero may be greater than his fate, but if he coincides absolutely with it, then he becomes a generic secondary character. So the inconclusive present inevitably tends to the future or to the "more" in all its different forms: "There always remains an unrealized surplus of humanness"; and in the absence of wholeness a crucial tension develops between the external and the internal man, so that "the subjectivity of the individual becomes an object of experimentation and representation" (37).

Finally, does the novel then subordinate other genres to itself in taking them over and transforming them? Bakhtin argues against this view. The novel, in his view,

> "is plasticity itself. It is a genre that is ever questing, ever examining itself and subjecting its established forms to review. Such indeed is the only possibility open to a genre that structures itself in a zone of direct contact with developing reality. Therefore the novelization of other genres does not imply their subjection to an alien generic canon; on the contrary, novelization implies their liberation from all that serves as a brake on their unique development, from all that would change them along with the novel into some sort of stylization of forms that have outlived themselves." (39)

8.3 The *Symposium* as the First "Novel" of Its Kind in History

Bakhtin's analysis, we suggest, permits us to sharpen our view of the *Symposium*. We have argued that the *Symposium* is demonstrably the first novel in human history, not in the sense that novelistic elements cannot be found in all of the earlier dialogues or in earlier literature, but rather in the strict sense that it is the first work of its kind to be demonstrably aware of itself as a new dialogical genre among genres and to dramatize and give individual voices to those genres in a philosophical struggle to see beyond the incomplete and sometimes fractured images represented. Plato has often been taken to task for subordinating art to philosophy, or eliminating mimetic poetry from serious consideration, or again for canonizing Socrates at the expense of a Thrasymachus or a Gorgias. Yet it is noteworthy that the *Symposium,* like the *Seventh Letter, includes everything* from mimetic art to philosophy, and recognizes the necessity of such art as well as its limitations. The philosophical dimension of the work (in myth, structure, and argument)[29] is, of course, the most authoritative element, but like other elements it is only part of a larger whole which is itself a represented plastic image in which philosophy, art, and everyday life come together in a new artistic form, undoubtedly under the aegis of what Socrates calls "the philosophical muse" in the *Republic.*[30]

---

29. On this, see section 8.6, below.
30. *Rep.* 499d; *Phaedo* 61a.

But the spirit of the *Symposium* is opposed to canonization, for it calls the typical canonization of Socrates into question and annuls the transferral of the world into an absolute epic past of archetypal beginnings by bringing the dialogical problem into the present, where such transferral and canonization are parodied (in different ways in the figures of Apollodorus, Aristodemus, and Alcibiades) and therefore excluded. In his very first words, Socrates himself eliminates the possibility either of an absolute epic past or of a primordial first word, by pointing to the destructive creativity of Homer, in the first case, and, in the second, by suggesting the plasticity of dialogical language and leaving the folkloric proverb unsaid. So the claim to have access to a completed event by means of memory literally undermines itself in its very inception: the endless destructive transformation of dialogue, the disruption of thought, and the generosity of the good appear to be the only provisional landmarks in a world of coming-to-be. So in the multidimensional structure and plot of the *Symposium* (more like Joyce's *Ulysses* or even *Finnegan's Wake* than Tolstoy's *War and Peace*) the present tense of immediate address unfolds into a mimetic past that carries as its first moment the radical incompleteness and interdependence of all speech, based on *absence* of foundation in the past and, in the figure of Agathon, *absence* finally of the good in the future. In just this sense, the dialogue is an enigma or experiment in search of itself, and as we have suggested, the image of Socrates "standing seeking" (an image of motionless movement or soul's self-motion, which Plato will develop in the *Phaedrus*) is in some measure an emblem of the dialogue itself in the figure of the hero, transformed by the beautiful, in search of the absent good.

But quite apart from the multidimensional structure and plot, and the essentially polyglossial discourse, what is also striking about the *Symposium*, in relation to Bakhtin's theory of novelistic discourse, is its transmutation of genre into character, its conscious shifting of the boundaries between fact and fiction, clarity and truth, and its recognition of a kind of extrafactual form of address, which is intelligible in the prismatic context of the work as a whole, but has a disruptive accidentality to it in its immediate context. By this extrafactual form of address we refer to the way Diotima "comments on" each of the earlier speeches and how Alcibiades corroborates, tests, tries, and develops the Socrates-Diotima speech. The clash and corroboration of speeches as of genres consciously destroys the simple distinction between fact and fiction, for imitative "fact" plainly does not get to the heart of the matter and yet it still comprehends the whole of the *Symposium*, on the one hand, while apparent fiction (for example, Diotima and the ascent to the beautiful), on the other hand, arguably gets closer to the deeper significance of so-called factual reality and yet is always just begging to be exploded by the raucous, physical entrance of Alcibiades and the revelers.

Bakhtin is, above all, the theorist of the carnivalesque, who likens Socrates to the ironic jester or clown. But he simultaneously emphasizes the serious purpose of laughter, and his words in this context unconsciously, but exactly, describe a part of Alcibiades' role in the *Symposium*. In the folkloric and popular-comic development of the novel, "laughter destroyed epic distance: it began to investigate man freely and familiarly, to turn him inside out, expose the disparity between his surface and his centre, between his potential and his reality. A dynamic authenticity was introduced into the image of man, dynamics of inconsistency and tension between various factors of this image; man ceased to coincide with himself, and consequently men ceased to be exhausted entirely by the plots that contain them."[31] Alcibiades devotes himself to turning the tables comically on Socrates and thereby to displaying the disparity between his surface and his center. Indeed, Socrates is the one character who "exhausts" everyone else (even Aristodemus), but remains inexhaustible himself. So Socrates exhibits that surplus of character and discourse in the true hero that Bakhtin considers essential to the novelistic form. But in its transmutation of genre into character, the *Symposium* also exhibits "that happy surplus" in each of its characters, and not just in the fact that millenia of readers and critics find Phaedrus, Pausanias, or Aristophanes or Alcibiades endlessly fascinating and endlessly new.

As we observed earlier, it is an essential feature of this polyglossial world that each character says more than he can mean, or ever could mean, in a world of facts considered as merely objectified things or states of affairs. Apollodorus and Aristodemus recount a story that they plainly understand and take delight in, *yet could never have composed* (except by divine accident).[32] Each speaker says much more about language, reality, and himself than he means, so that we, the readers, get to glimpse the characters from many angles, as do the actual participants themselves, at least to judge from the "chance," double-voiced remarks in the interludes and speeches. "Diotima" cannot comment on the earlier speeches, except again by divine accident, yet the "more" in those speeches, which they literally do not mean, is taken up and received, as we have suggested, into the free play of the movement to the beautiful. Alcibiades cannot even hear Socrates' speech, much less bear it, yet his love of those speeches and of that wondrous head permits him to address it with

---

31. Bakhtin 1981c, 35.
32. The phrase we have in mind is that employed by Socrates in *Rep.* 6.493a: *theou moiran* (cf. 492a: *ean mē tis autēi boēthēsas theōn tychēi*); 592a8–9: *theia tychē*.

new meanings. No voice in the *Symposium* is hermetically sealed off from the address of its neighbor. We overhear, as it were, not only the conversation of voices and genres, but also the free play and address of ideas.

In short, for Bakhtin the novel is to be distinguished by the following features:

1. by dialogical self-consciousness of itself and other genres,
2. by the transmutation of the problematics of event and genre into character on an experimental and testing basis,
3. by the potential multidimensionality of structure and plot,
4. by the radical intersection of the past with the everyday reality and problems of the present for the future, and
5. by the unconcludedness and incompleteness of the literary image in that intersection.

If these are the major distinguishing features of what is admittedly a fluid genre, then we may meaningfully claim that the *Symposium* is the world's first novel in this strict sense.

8.4 Plato's Dialectic at Play: Art, Reason, and Understanding

This view, however, plainly poses some deeper problems about Plato's thought. What precisely is the relation between the dialogue as a whole and the speeches and other genres that constitute it, if language has no foundation but is ultimately only plastic? If discourse is propositional, for instance, but any authentic understanding of the good is apparently nonpropositional and nonlinguistic, what role does "reasoning" or "philosophy," in any sense intelligible to our modern ear, play in such dialogues? Is the *Symposium* even an anti-intellectual dialogue by comparison with the by-and-large straight, hard discursive work of the *Republic* or the *Theaetetus* or *Sophist*? In other words, how precisely do structure, myth, and argument hang together in a distinctly rational, philosophical way? And in what philosophical sense can a "novel" be described as dialectic or even dialectic at play? Surely, everything that Plato has to say about art from the *Ion* to the *Laws,* and then too, the *Seventh Letter,* would suggest that the very phrase "dialectic at play" is an oxymoron?[33] Yes, one might agree, "play" is important and often underacknowledged perhaps in the dialogues,[34] but how can

---

33. Cf. *Laws* 7.816d–e (and following); also *Laws* 1, esp. 643b ff.; *Seventh Letter* 344c1–d2.
34. See, e.g., Sallis 1996, 21–22.

we meaningfully link "dialectic," that is, the infinitely serious *mathêma* of the *Republic* (and earlier dialogues), with playfulness? And in this precise sense of "dialectic," how can such a serious method apparently add nothing distinctively rational or philosophical, beyond playfulness, to our understanding of the *Symposium?*

These are difficult questions, because a proper answer requires extensive analysis of major passages in other dialogues that have proved problematic for generations of critics, but here we can at least sketch an answer in the following way. The *Symposium* is dialectic at play in a sense that matches exactly, but in dramatized form, the movement of dialectic in *Republic* 6–7. This is a major claim, and we have no wish to insist (along the lines of *Quellenforschung*) that these books of the *Republic* are a "source" for the *Symposium* in any mechanical sense. Our claim is rather to be understood thus: the *Symposium* is a complex dramatization not only of the dialectic of speech genres, but also of the play of "children" in whose apparently thoughtless games the material of dialectic is already unconsciously present, waiting as it were to be jolted into the structure of philosophical conversation by the destruction and transformation of images, and also needing to be tested in well-meaning and not so well-meaning "refutations." In order to show this hidden design, we shall start with the divided-line simile and then briefly examine the argument of *Republic* 6–7 before drawing specific conclusions about the *Symposium*.

In *Republic* 6, Plato visualizes a line divided into four sections, representing in order of ascent, first, *eikasia*, "image-making"; then *pistis* or *doxa*, "opinion"; then *dianoia*, "reasoning"; and finally, *noêsis*, "understanding." *Eikasia* and *pistis* constitute the sections of the "visible," but the section of the "intelligible" is divided according to two different procedures: on the level of *dianoia*, the soul uses sensible things as images and is compelled to seek by means of hypotheses, making its way not to a first principle, but to a conclusion;[35] on the level of understanding, or *noêsis*, the soul proceeds from a hypothesis, but without using sensible images, in the sense that its hypotheses do not limit her as assumptions, but serve as "under-positions" in the literal sense (*hypo-theseis*), that is, as stepping stones and starting points, from which she can reach what is "beyond hypothesis"[36] and then

---

35. [O]*uk ep' archên . . . all' epi teleutên* (*Rep.* 6.510b4–6), which involves presumably reaching a conclusion on the basis of its assumptions (*hypotheseis*) and premises.

36. [T]*o ep' archên anypotheton ex hypotheseôs iousa kai aneu peri ekeino eikonôn . . .* (510b6–9). The precise distinction between the two methods is a vexed question but, to simplify matters, we suppose that the difference is not that one method uses hypotheses and the other dispenses with them, but rather in the way each employs hypotheses. According to the first method, hypotheses determine entirely the conclusions reached from them, that is, reasoning is restricted to the hypothesis or image adopted so

"touching upon it, and in turn again holding to the things which hold to that principle,"[37] descend to a conclusion by means of forms themselves, through forms, and to forms" (511b3–c2; 510b8–9).

Exactly what Socrates is talking about has been the subject of extensive debate: what exactly is dialectic, hypothesis, and so on? Many commentators see this deeper sense of dialectic rightly as emerging out of the Socratic method of question and answer, a step-by-step procedure based on mutual refutation and agreement, but now becoming the hypotheticodeductive method in science[38] or something equivalent to "what we would call purely abstract reasoning."[39] As evidence for this sort of interpretation, Socrates' claim that the dialectician is able to give an account (*didonai logon*) of these hypotheses can be adduced.[40] To give an account, it would seem, is equivalent to giving a formal proof of one's hypotheses. Moreover, the descent through forms or Forms[41] to a conclusion that is also a Form would seem to necessitate an abstract, hypotheticodeductive method.[42]

However, there are major objections to this sort of interpretation. *Dianoia* is reasoning, *noêsis* understanding. If the "forms" are coordinate with understanding, then they are beyond the capacity of reasoning to do

---

that one cannot get behind the hypothesis, as it were, to give an account of it (510c2–d3). According to the second method, the image or hypothesis is not blinkered or solid in this way (510d5–511a), but a means by which to see beyond "visible forms" and *logoi* (cf. 511b ff.).

37. [*H*]*apsomenos autês, palin au echomenos tôn ekeinês echomenôn* (511b7–8). This may well involve a chain of reasoning, in the sense that reasoning may be called *noêsis,* or "understanding," later in *Rep.* 7 (on which see below in the main text), but there is a *gap* between the grasp of the first nonhypothetical principle and the "things" that hold to it insofar as such reasoning seems to depend (1) upon an *experience* of the principle (sc. understanding), and (2) upon reasoning not directly from the principle but from the "things" that depend upon it. See also Gonzalez 1998, 241–43 (Gonzalez is excellent throughout).

38. For a review of the various theories and difficulties, see Robinson 1953, 146ff., but, above all, the brilliant work of Gonzalez (1998, 220–42).

39. Grube 1974, 183 n. 13.

40. *Rep.* 6.510 c–d, 7.533 b–c, 534b.

41. Cf. Grube 1974, 165–66.

42. Or some other theory which will make sense for a modern scientific paradigm. Robinson (1953) gives four such examples, while Gonzalez (1998) gives seven (synthesis theory, analysis, axiomatization, "Phaedo," intuition, coherence, abstraction, and his own theory [220–44]). Neat divisions of "theories" in this way may, of course, obscure more than illuminate. Nonetheless, Gonzalez's whole approach is genuinely illuminating and represents an infinite improvement over that of Robinson. We might add that Plato's scientific paradigm is not "objective" in the modern sense (such as we find in most major thinking from Descartes, Locke, Berkeley, Hume, and on, and that is predominant in a great deal of contemporary philosophy). This is in no way to depreciate the complexity of contemporary scholarship on Plato's later thought, for instance, about *epistêmê* and *logos* (see, e.g., Nehamas 1989, 267–92), but rather to emphasize the difference between *dianoia* and *noêsis,* on the one hand, and the doubleness of *noêsis* itself, on the other, insofar as *noêsis* comes to include even in the *Republic dianoia, anôthen,* as it were (on which see below in this chapter).

more than represent them in images. But the "Good" is beyond even understanding and being, and so is to be coordinated with no system.[43] Rather, it is the cause and medium of anything intelligible being seen and so is at once beyond both sections of the intelligible and yet something glimpsed in the activity of thought itself.[44] But one cannot give a "formal proof" in this context, as if one were dealing with an object or set of objects, since the nature of the Good is essentially reflexive. Instead, in the immediate context of book 6, and later in book 7, "to give an account" is not the constitutive aspect of understanding or science, but rather a consequence of such understanding.[45] Understanding, then, is not opposed to reasoning; the *ability* to give an account or argument flows from understanding and occurs in the context of conversation: the sciences "are not able to go out beyond the hypotheses" (511a5–6), and so are restricted to their assumptions, that is, reasoning, or *dianoia,* whereas "the other section of the intelligible (*noêsis,* or understanding) is that which argument itself grasps by the power of conversation" (*hou autos ho logos haptetai tê tou dialegesthai dynamei* [511b4]). Neither understanding nor conversation is formal deductive science; conversation is a reflexive activity that demonstrates in the activity itself that it has genuine understanding by answering questions, replying to objections, giving explanations, revising its assumptions, and so on. This may well include formal proofs, but people do not normally restrict hypotheticodeductive claims of reasoning to "conversation." So understanding can be nonpropositional in the sense that it goes beyond the fractured limits of language to express it and yet, at the same time, can be rational and propositional in that it can be tested, revised, and so forth in provisional, but pragmatic, ways. In this light, the descent through "forms" may perhaps reflect a superdialectician's progress through "Forms," but *eidê* should not be capitalized in translation, for it could well refer also to the formal images about which dialectic comes to have a new understanding in the context of its ascent to the Good.[46] But we can only determine if there is this ambiguity in the word by watching how Socrates develops the meaning of this dialectic in *Republic,* book 7.

So to get a sense of dialectic in this broader context, which in an important way, we suggest, directly reflects the structure of the *Symposium,* let us

---

43. *Rep.* 6.509b6–10.

44. Cf. *Rep.* 490a1–b7, 508a1–509b10; *Symp.* 212a1–7.

45. Cf. 531e4–5: giving a *logos* is a sign that one knows; 534b3–c 5: giving a *logos* of the *ousia* of each thing and distinguishing the "form" of the Good by *exclusion* (*aphelôn*) certainly involves discursivity (*hôsper en machei dia pantôn elegchôn diexiôn*), and in this light is surely a form of understanding (discursive or propositional understanding), but it is still a representation of understanding.

46. *Rep.* 529d, 532c, 533b–d.

trace significant parts of Socrates' argument through book 7, paying particular attention to the two notions of "clarity" and "truth," which distinguish mnemonic imitation, on the one hand, and Socratic elenchus and dialectic, on the other, in the *Symposium*. At the end of book 6, Socrates affirms the principle that, in proportion, as each of the four cuts in the divided line—from *eikasia* to *noêsis*—participates in truth, so does each participate in clarity (511e2–4). What this turns out to mean, in the subsequent argument, is that even *eikasia* has a kind of dimmed clarity and truth, if we can put it in this way, but no truth in the strict philosophical sense, for such truth requires the reorientation of "the whole soul" to being (518c–d; 519b4: *eis ta alêthê;* b8); and so the turning of soul to the "true" day (in the continuation of the cave-emergence analogy) is the upward path to being, "which we in fact call true philosophy" (521c6–8). Truth and clarity, then, are gradational terms, even in the arts, but by contrast with a *mathêma*, which leads to the Good, "there is no truth" in them (522a2–b1). Roughly speaking, this corresponds to the view of the *Symposium*.

But the crucial question (for both the *Republic* directly and the *Symposium* indirectly) is how the notion of truth itself emerges, and for both dialogues this happens only when an opposition appears in "the same thing"[47] and forces one to call it into question by asking for the first time what it really is. In the *Symposium*, Socrates compels Agathon to agree that the truth must be the opposite of what he had supposed. In the *Republic*, Socrates argues that just as when sense-perception yields contrary impressions, for example, when something appears simultaneously both hard and soft, light and heavy, one and two, and so on (523a ff.),[48] and this experience rouses up thought and discriminating intelligence, so in the whole range of studies those experiences that affect the senses in contrary ways call on reasoning to discriminate, while those that do not so affect the senses possess no ability to wake up thought (*noêsis* [524d]). We recall vividly in the *Symposium* how each of the early speeches in its different way fails to spur—except indirectly in the reader or listener—the explicit emergence of truth or thought, because each tends to reflect only the self-composed face of each speaker rather than the illogicalities, self-serving qualities, and flickering oppositions that remain hidden in each speech; and we recall later how these speeches reach a crescendo of implicit oppositions in Agathon's speech before this "crescendo" is first made explicit by Socrates. What the *Republic* unfolds didactically in argument, the *Symposium* enacts dramatically in a complex practical image. The implicit oppositions of an unselfcritical tradition

---

47. Cf. *Rep.* 524a3, 8, d9–525a7.
48. Cf. *Phaedo* 10b ff.

summed up and embodied in Agathon's speech are made explicit by Socrates in the elenchus and become recognized in an explicit self-conscious way by Agathon himself.

So at the point when the object appears no more one thing than another, Socrates goes on to argue in the *Republic,* then the soul is in need of "one to judge" (*tou epikrinountos*) and the soul moves a conception (*ennoia*) in herself and asks what the thing is (524e2–525a).[49] This is the "ascent to truth" (525b1). Questioning what is presented, therefore, is the beginning of dialectic and this is to start treating sensible images as images, not as the truth, and to awaken understanding of what is not expressed in images (526a8–b3), since images or expressions (*logoi*) contradict science (for example, geometry) insofar as they express action, whereas study tends to pure thought (527a–b). Consequently, Socrates argues that the various sciences should be studied in order to break through sensible images or expressions, that is, to use them as "paradigms" through which to study intelligible things (529d7–8; cf. d1–3), and to awaken the eye of the soul "by which alone truth is perceived" (527e2–3). Dialectic, therefore, is not just a particular form of discourse or abstract reasoning about intelligible "objects" (and even less so in the case of the form of the Good)—at least as Socrates outlines its features here, but an activity seeing and seen in the act of seeing itself, not as an object but reflexively, and not as only one's own face, but as a "method" opened up by question and answer in friendly conversation to the "community" and "kinship" of all the sciences, a method that can therefore give an "account" of itself (531e4–5). Such a "science" both of itself and of other sciences had been envisaged as early as the *Charmides* and *Laches,*[50] but here in the *Republic* its essential features are outlined and in the *Symposium* transposed into dramatic, novel form; for, in the latter work, dialectic is not simply Diotima-Socrates' speech (as we shall see further below), but all the elements of the dialogue as a whole rubbed together in the presence of the beautiful and the absent good. And just as in the *Symposium,* so in the *Republic,* all of this—as Socrates insists—is still only an image (*eikôn*), and not the truth (533a2–3). So no matter how perspicacious or exalted, philosophical art is still not the real thing, in Plato's view, but *perhaps* an adequate image.

At this point in the *Republic,* we come even closer to the intricate design of the *Symposium.* The journey upward out of the cave has this unfortunate

---

49. Cf. *Seventh Letter* 342e2–343a, 343b8–c 1.

50. *Charmides* 165c–166e. If temperance is an *epistemê* that intrinsically involves self-knowledge, and self-knowledge is a knowledge of a knowledge—a knowing of knowing in which self-knowing and object known are not distinct—then temperance appears to be a metaknowledge, though Socrates and Critias have difficulty pinpointing how it can be "useful." This thought in developed form remains part of the *Republic* (see 531c6–7; as of Aristotle's *Metaphysics,* bk. 12: *noêsis noêseôs*).

consequence, Socrates affirms, that we cannot look at things themselves but only at *divine phantasms* of them (*phantasmata theia*) in water (532c1), which of course if we fall short of dialectic we take to be real things in themselves. In fact, all the other arts (*technai*), in Socrates' view, make these images the whole sphere of their concern (533b) and even "the remaining arts," such as geometry and those that follow her, are unable to provide a waking vision "as long as they make use of hypotheses and leave them unmoved and cannot give an account of them" (533b–c). "Dialectic alone travels the road to the origin itself" by *destroying* (*anairousa*) the hypotheses and gently draws the eye of the soul upward using the "arts" or, as Socrates goes on to specify, the inauthentic "sciences" as helpers (533c7–d6).[51] So in using the inauthentic arts or sciences in this way, the dialectician "destroys" them as hypotheses that prevent one from seeing through, or beyond, them and instead transforms them into stepping stones (cf. 511b) on the ascent. There is then a *destruction* of images but a *collection* of forms (cf. *Phaedrus* 265c–e; *Republic* 532a; *anamnêsis* [*Phaedrus* 249b–c]), followed by a methodical division of forms themselves ending up in forms (*Rep.* 510a6; 511b–c; *Phaedrus* 273d–e; 277b–c).

What, then, is the result of dialectic? The result is not the abandonment of hypothetical thinking, since all thinking—even dialectic—is necessarily "hypothetical." The result is rather the division of forms through a transformation of hypothetical thinking that thereby comes to recognize, first, that its images are *only images* and, second, that what it sees through those images is a greater truth and that this truth, as a function of its self-reflexive seeing, is a part, as it were, and the best part of itself.[52] It can hardly be accidental that after Socrates has completed this portion of the argument in book 7 he refers to *both higher sections* of the divided line as *noêsis* (543a)—a difference from his initial treatment in book 6—and the lower sections as *doxa*. In the light of dialectic, reasoning genuinely becomes a form of understanding. Let us turn now to the *Symposium,* for the connection between these two works is of major importance, but not immediately obvious.

With humor, pathos, and dramatic irony, the *Symposium* both conceals and enacts this vision of dialectic in the *Republic.* What is the fundamental assumption of each of the first five speakers? In each case, except that of Aristophanes, it is a *divine image* of love that the speaker takes to be an

---

51. These "sciences" are said to be "clearer than opinion but dimmer than science" (533d). See also 533c7–d1: *ep' autên tên archên hina bebaiôsêtai*. "Stability," "fixity," sometimes translated as "certainty" (e.g., Grube 1974), is a function of the *archê* rather than the movement of dialectic as such. Cf. *Philebus* 59b. *Bebaiotês*, however, is a gradational term (cf. *Politicus* 289d4). See also *Phaedo* 85d3, 90c9; *Timaeus* 37b–c; and Pausanias *Symp.* 184b; Diotima, 209c6.

52. See *Rep.* 532a ff., 586d–e, 589a–592b; and *Alc.* 1.132e ff.

unshakeable hypothesis and that determines the linear progression of his artistic or scientific thinking. Only in the case of creative art is there a more complex design, since the writer of the *Republic* (as well as the *Ion* and *Phaedrus*) and the lover of the mimes of Sophron, as well as of Homer, Hesiod, and the dramatic poets, was only too well aware of the power of art to get beyond its images, to examine objects from many different angles, but also to capture the "truth" in the adulation of its audiences, and thus to parody and distort the truth. So powerful did Plato consider such art to be that he dramatized its ascendancy even over the sciences because of its very *disruptive physicality* (as in Aristophanes' hiccups) and wove into his own version of that power the motif of the inverted dialectic, at the same time recognizing the power of philosophical art *as dialectic,* which he also wove as a motif into the fourth step of Diotima's ladder of ascent and embodied in the design of the *Symposium* as a whole.[53] The fundamental images of Aristophanes' art appear not to be provisional, that is, they are all-too-solid monstrous human beings and self-seeking gods, and in one way, of course, they grossly limit and distort any reality they purport to represent; yet the sheer power of art to capture something deeper in life, and something that transcends life itself, effectively shatters—but without being aware of or responsible for it—the limitations even of its own gross paradigms.

Here, then, in these early speeches, we hear the living voices of those inauthentic arts or sciences that take divine images to be sensible things or gross parodies of sensible things. And for Agathon, Plato creates a masterpiece of a new sort in that he conjures up in an ornamented, yet bathetic way—in the very best mode of traditional education that money can buy—a speech that flickers with opposition, as it were, and that is consequently, for this and other reasons, an "anticlimactic climax" to these voiced genres, for it is so filled with opposition that it "stirs up intelligence," and is in need of a "judge" to cross-examine it. This cross-examination, conducted by Socrates, is—on the terms of the *Republic*—the beginning of dialectic in the proper sense. And this starts not with a sensible image to limit its focus, but a psychic image, that is, self-reflexivity itself (Diotima through Socrates) and a mixed image of love (human and divine), to open up a shared landscape in which both *mythos* and *logos* illuminate each other.[54] This dialectic "destroys" the hypotheses of the inauthentic arts and sciences, but gathers their forms together and uses them as stepping stones in the ascent

---

53. See Chapter 7.

54. See Chapter 5 and sections 8.6 and 8.8. Once the "apparent" but absent "good" (i.e., Agathon) acknowledges that he *is* just that, in other words, only apparent, not "true," then the house of Agathon disappears and we enter (in Socrates-Diotima's speech) into a placeless, "timeless" dialogue of ideas.

to the beautiful, so that form can address form in the development of understanding in ways that individually limited speeches could not.

This is not, as A. W. Price puts it, "rather to characterize certain roles in an abstract way than to convey what it is like for a subject to fill them"[55] or "abstract reasoning," as Grube has it, or "impersonal," as Vlastos argues, but the heart of self-reflexivity in the conversation between friends or lovers with very practical consequences in each case.[56] Yet as in the *Republic,* it remains an image; it is not dialectic itself, as generations of critics have unfortunately assumed in supposing somehow that the image is solid reality or that Socrates has "the last word," or, again, that this speech expresses once and for all the essence of "Platonic love," or that Plato, at least momentarily, was so satisfied with himself that he was entirely unaware that he had to finish the rest of the *Symposium* or even needed to write the *Phaedrus!*

Instead, the entry of Alcibiades is fundamental to the structure of the work, not just to remind us forcefully that Socrates' speech is only an image, and a strange one at that, but literally *to divide* the climax of the ascent—simultaneously with humor, and poignancy—*from, and in, the figure of Alcibiades himself.* Among other things, Alcibiades is a vivid example of that love of the individual for his or her own sake that essentially characterized Aristophanes' speech; and in the destructive madness of his passion, as we soon find out, he is almost directly a "token" (*symbolon*) of the pathetic state of one of Aristophanes' original globular creatures immediately after division! He is disoriented, is led in, calls out with a monstrous Dionysiac-animal voice, is at first unconscious of the presence of Socrates, then, in Socrates' ironic mock, but perhaps also serious, protest, appears to threaten a "jealous," "grudging," violent *embrace* (213d: *zêlotypôn . . . phthonôn . . . tô cheire mogis apechetai;* cf. 219b–c: *peribalôn tô cheire toutô tê daimoniô*), and finally, in his own poignantly divided way, reveals his wholehearted fixation on Socrates, but in a fashion altogether different from the indiscriminate fixations of Aristophanes' divided halves. Alcibiades may have been divided from *this* dialectic, that is, Socrates' speech in the *Symposium,* but he has known "this" dialectic on many previous occasions, and consequently, he knows how to make his way through "forms" and end up with "forms," even if the contrary emotions of love and hatred and the irruption of destruction in him are threatening to destroy both him and everyone

---

55. Price 1989, 55. The language is that of T. Nagel (1974): what it is "like" to be a bat. To be "like" in this sense is the reverse of what we commonly mean by *like,* in the sense of the "comparative" *like.* Here we appeal to the "reflexive" *like,* that is, from the viewpoint of a reflexive subject. But little or nothing of this reflexive sense touches Price's treatment.

56. Grube 1974, 183 n. 13; Vlastos 1973, 3–34.

around him. Alcibiades' hypotheses or images (*di' eikonôn*) are, like those of Socrates, *semidivine* and *provisional*. He knows that Socrates is not Marsyas or a Silenus, but that the essential character of the image is not to blinker the reality one wishes to portray, but to see through and in it to the deeper truth; that is, to see within rather than to stop at the surface. And so the "conclusion" of Alcibiades' speech is not a sense image, but a *form:* the *placelessness* (*atopia*) and the *unlikeness* of Socrates.

However, as we have seen, Alcibiades' love is also deeply divided against itself: the very qualities for which he seeks to praise Socrates are those hated compulsive forces he wants dead. Of course, he means well, but his praise is a form of trial and his corroboration of the "truth" of Diotima-Socrates' speech its ironically well-intentioned refutation. He is, in short, the dramatic embodiment of the double-edged character of that famous phrase of the *Seventh Letter:* dialectic with "well-meaning refutations." The best intentions may have divided effects and, tragically, the most compelling form of corroboration (one function of *elenchus*) may lead to the refutation (another function of *elenchus*) or destruction of what one corroborates. Philosophical conversation is a risky business, and its offspring cannot be compelled or predicted.

Alcibiades' images in the concluding paragraphs of his speech, therefore, bear an intense, cumulative ambivalence. Yes, they literally "open up" (cf. 222a1) into "intellect within" (a2), and show images that are "most divine," possess multiple "statues" of excellence, and have "the most comprehensive reach"—even for a gentleman's practical education (a3–6)! But Alcibiades dramatically enacts the effect of dialectic on hypothetical thinking by the very pain he manifests in the destruction but transformation of his "hypotheses." Instead of the beloved "head" he wants to embrace more closely and more dearly than his own life, and from which he is forever severed, he nonetheless captures through his provisional images, so inadequate to the original, something of that "sea of beauty" Diotima had spoken about as being at the very threshold of the "sudden" appearance of the beautiful (210d–e). Just as love, however, may also be permeated by hate—for surely the state of dividedness from both oneself and the object (in the *Republic*) may be either the beginning, or the death, of dialectic—so too faithful images may also distort and even destroy. Alcibiades' final words, therefore, strongly suggest his "faithful" destruction of Socrates: "This, gentlemen, is what I say in praise of Socrates; and again I have also mixed in with it what I blame him for, what outrages he has committed against me" (222a7–8). But they also foreshadow his abandonment of "well-meaning" dialectic, as he cites the cases of Charmides and Euthydemus, among others, who will support him in his accusation but who have also given their names to

Platonic dialogues of significance in the development of dialectic:[57] "But not only me, I should say, has he done this to, but also Charmides, son of Glaucon, Euthydemus, son of Diocles, and very many others, whom this man deceives." Furthermore, the final motif of Alcibiades' speech ironically reflects the first motif of Socrates' opening words in Aristodemus's prologue, as Alcibiades explicitly, though no less offhandedly returns to the proverbial or folkloric sediment of speech itself: "So in fact I am warning you too, Agathon, not to be deceived by this man, but to beware by learning from our sufferings and not—as the proverb has it—to learn by suffering like a fool" (222b4–7). Socrates takes folklore and destructively transforms it into conversation and dialectic. Alcibiades finally, though he sees the beauty of dialectic, can only focus on the destructive deception itself and, for him, like Socrates, there is no path back to the supposed "bedrock" of the folkloric world. Alcibiades is exactly in the predicament of the golden child in the closing pages of *Republic* 7, who does not discover true principles that he makes "his own," but who in the eternal opposition of contrary *beliefs* (538d9), finds no path back to the now vanished bedrock of those unexamined, but perhaps worthy, beliefs handed on to him by his parents and family (537e–539a): "he will in fact, I think, from law-abiding have become law-less" (539a3).

Let us then draw the following conclusions. The *Symposium* dramatizes the dialectic of the *Republic,* in two precise ways. First, the *Symposium* implicity, like the *Republic* explicitly, points to the philosophical need to read and to enact the dialogue form not only in its parts, but also as a whole. As Socrates says at the conclusion of the argument about dialectic in *Republic* 7, immediately after he recognizes explicitly that he and Glaucon have been dealing throughout with an image rather than the reality, "the one who sees as a whole is a dialectician; the one who doesn't, isn't" (*ho men gar synoptikos dialektikos* [537c7]). The synoptic view has already been a fundamental part of the Socrates-Diotima dialectic, but even this speech remains, as we have argued, an image of dialectic, and by far the greater challenge, at least in the estimation of the *Seventh Letter,* is to embark on the reality rather than the image, since language is too plastic, it is argued extensively

---

57. We see in the *Euthydemus* the implicit difference between philosophical dialectic and eristic, though the two appear to be superficially similar, a fact that brings philosophy into disrepute (305a), and in the *Charmides* we have to confront the gap between, on the one hand, the conclusion that the knowledge of knowledge is empty and nonbeneficial, and, on the other hand, the eagerness of Charmides and Critias to follow Socrates, despite this, which indicates that such knowledge must in some sense be beneficial; yet even Charmides' eagerness contradicts the theme of the entire dialogue in a sinister fashion, since he and Critias want to acquire temperance or self-control by violence (*biazein* [176c–d]) without, as Socrates himself says, giving him *the first forms of law* (176c; Liddell, Scott, and Jones 1940, s.v. "anakrisis").

in the *Phaedrus, Cratylus,* and elsewhere, to bear the true weight of reality. Consequently, the answer in search of a question where the *Symposium* started and where we, the first or hundred-time readers, gradually find ourselves becoming conscious of the reflexivity of any question so addressed, is ultimately a challenge to leave the image behind—that is, to "destroy" it—and simultaneously to transform it "in seeing it whole."

Second, the *Symposium* as a whole is the dramatic enactment of dialectic at play in the precise sense this is indicated toward the end of *Republic* 7. Authentic art, for Plato, is not the challenge of command or violence, but of internal persuasion, as Bakhtin rightly puts it, and internal persuasion begins and develops in *free play*. "I forgot we were playing," Socrates says toward the end of *Republic* 7, when he thinks of the ridicule brought upon philosophy by its sham students and gets a little hot-tempered. So how should we teach students? he then goes on to ask. Not by compulsion, he replies, for "no free person should pursue any study like a slave" (536e1–2). Children should be instructed, that is, nourished, brought up, or fed, instead of by force, *by play* (*paizontas trephe* [537a1]).[58] At a later stage, he goes on to insist, this free play should be given structure by bringing all its unconscious pursuits together into a comprehensive, multidimensional view so that their kinship with one another and with reality can be seen. In precisely this sense, the *Symposium* is Plato's dialectic in free play gradually disclosing its synoptic character and finally posing its own synoptic challenge, just as in the *Republic:* the challenge of living dialectic.[59]

---

58. Cf. *Symposium* 216e5. A similar view is formulated toward the end of the *Phaedrus* at 278b–d: the dialogue and written word generally are "play," but what they are based on is "serious"; for the *Laws*, see note 33, above. On the theme of play in Plato, see generally Wilamowitz 1919,1:453–55; Gundert 1965, 188–221; Szlezàk 1985, 331–36; Guthrie 1975, 59–65; Vries 1969, 18–22; Sallis 1996, 21, 178–79, 527–29; Sprague in Gerber 1984. Gadamer (1960) makes much of play in Plato and ancient philosophy but little or nothing of this fundamental aspect we have outlined here. By contrast, Derrida (1981, 156–72) simply gets Plato wrong on this subject. See also Freydberg 1997 (our book was completed before this work came to our attention).

59. The *Symposium* perhaps also gives articulate voice to four kinds of image such as we find in the *Seventh Letter:*

1. Names (*onomata*): mimetic narrative (Apollodorus's prologue);
2. Definition-speeches (*logoi*): Socratic destructive-transformative narrative (Aristodemus's prologue and the framed narrative-interludes within the narrative);
3. Images (*eidôla*): the five early speeches;
4. Knowledge (*epistêmê, nous,* and *orthê doxa*);
5. Socrates' speech as a whole: collection and dialectic;
6. Alcibiades' entry and speech as division, that is, free, but divided "well-meaning refutations"; and an image of the relation of dialectic to hypothetical thinking, as well as a confirmation of the view that even this dialectic is an image, though a potentially distorting, even dangerous one.

In this book, the case we have presented for seeing the *Symposium* as an intimate companion piece to the *Republic* has been a cumulative one. It is tempting to suppose, however, if the *Symposium* is a dramatic enactment of dialectic at play, that most of the *Republic* must have been written before the composition of the *Symposium*. But the nature of the evidence does not permit us to draw such a conclusion with any confidence, since the *Symposium* could equally have been written before the *Republic* or, much more likely, during the composition of the *Republic*. At any rate, the real conclusion of our work in this respect is that the two dialogues were essentially conceived and articulated together.

8.5 Plato's Positive View of Art

In this context of dialectic as free play, it makes sense to ask what the *Symposium* suggests about the position of poetry and of art in general. The question itself is problematic, since the *Symposium*'s apparently more positive view of poetic composition seems to contradict not only the critique of mimetic art in the *Republic*, and later in the *Laws*, but also the radical skepticism about any form of writing expressed strongly at the end of the *Phaedrus* and in the *Seventh Letter*.[60] The *Symposium* seems more in tune with the positive assessment of artistic inspiration in the early dialogue, *Ion*, and for this reason too the dialogue has been regarded as early.[61] Two features of the *Symposium* are particularly problematic: first, Socrates' compelling Agathon and Aristophanes to the conclusion that one man might write both tragedies and comedies appears to contradict both the *Republic* and the *Laws*;[62] second, the idea that poetic composition is only one branch of *poiēsis* and that spiritual begetting through poetry, laws, and institutions is, in the words of one critic, "the truest and most beautiful thing Plato has to say about [poetry] in all his works," but unfortunately yields "no echo ... in anything he says about poetry anywhere else."[63] So what are we to make of this question?

We do not here intend to argue for a simple one-on-one correspondence (in a letter that, if genuine, was written some twenty-five years or more after the composition of the *Symposium*), but rather for an important overall yet precise similarity. These four images, nestled one within the other, call one another into question, first implicitly, and then when opposition as such emerges, explicitly. So they rub against one another uncomfortably and, in the dialogue of the whole, in which the reader, also at first unconsciously, walks together with the author, this friction itself is also in search of understanding.

60. *Phaedrus* 275d ff., esp. 277e–278b; *Seventh Letter* 344c–d.
61. Cf. Else 1986, 12.
62. *Rep.* 3; *Laws* 7.816d ff.
63. Else 1986, 12.

A more positive view of art, even in the *Republic,* has long been noticed. Adam, for instance, in a note to *Republic* 598a1, points to art's capacity to portray the ideal, rather than the photographically real, in several passages of the *Republic:* "Elsewhere throughout the Platonic writings there are not wanting indications of a juster estimate of the artistic faculty and its possibilities (see, for example, 3.401b–403c and especially 5.472d)."[64] Our reading of the *Symposium* demonstrates the truth of this judgment, but in a much more complex literary and philosophical setting than has usually been acknowledged. Mimetic art is only one layer of a complex series of images, *all of which* would seem to be essential for the understanding of the composition as a whole. Plato's theory of poetic composition is therefore *essentially* multidimensional. In this sense, the *Symposium* embodies and enacts the view that all forms of *poiêsis* find their reflection and transformation in philosophical poetry.[65]

Another way of looking at this might be as follows. A key criticism of mimetic art in the *Republic* is that it imitates the "lower" rather than awakens the "higher" nature in the audience and the artist, because the "highest" is most difficult to imitate and is, in fact, not suited for realistic representations. In the words of the Stranger in the *Statesman,* "the highest things can be shown only by means of examples [*paradeigmata*]" (277c), not by any form of direct representation. Mimetic art, by contrast, is simply unaware of the gulf between image and reality, so that it supposes either naively or even with considerable sophistication that what is depicted is the real. So in the *Symposium,* the personality of the artist either disappears into a caricature of individual identity, that is, into a generic type who receives an "original" material uncritically and uncreatively (for example, Apollodorus and Aristodemus), or who assumes predominant significance himself insofar as the parameters of his own generic identity become the boundaries of his own artistic possibilities (for example, the early speakers, for the most part). This limited personal identity (effectively individualized personality types) captivates and subjects the audience to a vision that bears little intellectual scrutiny, for it tends to make the world more or less in the image and likeness of its own limited "face." Even the greatest poetry, such as that of Homer, recounts stories about the gods—apparently uncritically—which cannot withstand philosophical analysis. It is for this reason, namely, because such art cannot go beyond its natural limitations, that Socrates argues in the *Republic* that the same artist cannot compose a tragedy and a comedy at the same time.

64. Adam 1965, 2:393.
65. For different, but cognate, views of this issue, see esp. Kosman 1992, 73–92 and Halperin 1992, 93–129.

The *Symposium* points to a complementary, but rather different understanding of art. Great art, even that of Homer, is creative, that is, destructive and transformative of its poetic material. But transformative *into* what? The Socrates-Diotima speech, as we have seen, is emblematic of a vision and conversation that is not patterned solely on Socrates' personal preferences, but is creatively shared, in a critical fashion, and animated by something beyond the "faces" of both interlocutors. It is in this context that Socrates argues at the end of the dialogue, against not only Aristophanes and Agathon, but also against his own earlier position in *Republic* 3, that there can be a form of artistic composition that goes beyond the natural limitations of the tragic and comic genres.

This conclusion (to a missing argument) reflects what we earlier called Plato's vanishing signature: that is, it is *Plato* who aspires to such art, but in the dramatic *persona* of someone who wrote nothing, namely, Socrates, and who is pictured both above and yet in the middle of "the whole tragicomedy of life" in which "pains are mixed with pleasures," as the *Philebus* will later put it (50b). The "signature" is erased as soon as it is suggested. In another way, the *Symposium* is itself the "missing argument," the embodiment of just such a tragicomedy (as we have shown particularly in relation to Alcibiades' speech and the conclusion of the dialogue) but in a new literary-philosophical form.[66] Here, then, we have the most striking *enactment* of Plato's most positive view of art, and yet it is a view that is only expressed by forms of *indirection,* that is, by an unexpressed argument, on the one hand, and by the *gap* between the actual power of the poets' speeches and their dialectical potential on the ladder of ascent, on the other hand.

So it would seem that this positive, but complex, enactment of philosophical art overcomes the specific critique of mimetic art in the *Republic* and contrasts strongly with the repudiation of any form of *mimetic* tragicomedy in the *Laws;* for in the latter case, when the Athenian stranger discusses this question at *Laws* 6.816d–e, he is certainly *not* talking about philosophical art, but initiating a discussion about the burlesque comedy of "ugly bodies and thoughts."[67] We cannot learn serious things (*ta spoudaia*) without comic things (*ta geloia*), he argues, or any one of a pair of contraries without the other, if one is to be wise (*phronimos*). But "to make" both serious and comic things is impossible, he continues, in the sense that the *imitation* of the burlesque should give rise to serious concern (*spoudê* [816e]). So there is no path to wisdom *from* such comedy; nor is imitative tragedy, the stranger goes on to argue, any match for the "fairest and best tragedy" of

---

66. See sections 8.1–3, above.
67. [*T*]*a de tôn aischrôn sômatôn kai dianoêmatôn* (*Laws* 816d5–6).

which he and his interlocutors are the *poiêtai* (817b), namely, the *Laws* themselves. So the notion of philosophical conversation as *poiêsis* is prominent in the *Laws,* but the context is entirely different from that of the *Symposium.* Yet for both works, neither mimetic comedy nor mimetic tragedy can serve as a model for philosophical art; only when "funny things" are for the sake of the truth, as Alcibiades puts it, can there be the possibility of a philosophical *poiêsis* that makes of comedy and tragedy a new form.

By contrast with the *Republic* and *Laws,* in which political or other necessities define the parameters of art, then, the *Symposium* is in many ways the primary example of a dialogue in which art is able to speak freely, but always indirectly, on its own behalf. This is also perhaps because the *Symposium* is a contemplative, festive dialogue celebrating a graceful occasion beyond utility or necessity, that is, the sheer beauty of successful art (Agathon's victory) in all its different shades and dimensions (the *synousia* or "get-together"). We read the dialogue not for this or that specific purpose, but simply to *see* what happens and take delight in it. This is not to say that beauty or art has nothing to do with everyday practical necessities, but that the sphere of the beautiful is not determined by these utilities or necessities. As Kant was to argue many centuries later (developing his own distinctive theory with an ever watchful eye on the horizon of the "supersensible"), imagination and understanding, in aesthetic reflective judgments, enter into a harmony of "free play" in the sense that they function without the limiting condition of a determinate concept.[68] In this sense, Kant argued that "poetry strengthens the mind" by freeing it up to experience its ability to probe nature in new ways and "to use nature . . . as a schema of the supersensible." By contrast with rhetoric, which Kant regarded "as deceiving by means of a beautiful illusion,": "[p]oetry plays with illusion, which it produces at will, and yet without using illusion to deceive us, for poetry tells us itself that its pursuit is mere play, though this play can still be used purposively by the understanding for its business."[69] The conception underpinning Plato's art is very different from Kant's conception of aesthetic judgment, but Kant's positive assessment of poetry as "play" partially fits the *Symposium*'s indirect enactment of philosophical tragicomedy poetry, except, of course, for (at least) one crucially important point: the "subjectification" of art in Kant is opposed to its dialogical open-endedness to the beautiful in all its different "forms" in Plato.

Moreover, the "indirect" art of the *Symposium* is by its very nature at every point disruptive and yet inclusive, in a way wholly consistent with

---

68. Kant 1908, 220–2.
69. Kant 1908, 326–27; 1987, 197.

the radical critique of *all* writing in the *Phaedrus* and *Seventh Letter*. As we read the dialogue forward in serial succession, the mimetic audio-video reportage that seeks to freeze-frame an "original" event is "destroyed" by the endless fluidity of speech, which looks forward "on the way" into the dialogue and flows, as it were, into the interludes between the "speech images," the "dialectic," and the "legal-historical test and trial of praise." In other words, the pure liquidity of speech destroys the "original" freeze-framing and pervades the rest of the dialogue. However, when we stop reading the dialogue simply in serial succession, but read it backward and sideway, we are forcibly struck, even from this "destructive" perspective, by the realization that the mimetic, narrative level itself is pervaded by the reflection of a "truth" that it cannot grasp on its own terms. Gadamer's view, then, that Plato's critique of poetry involves primarily a critique of the moral consequences of aesthetic consciousness (*aesthetisches Bewusstsein*) vastly oversimplifies what we actually find in the *Symposium* and other works: Plato criticizes *all* forms of consciousness that seek to enshrine the beautiful in their own "image" and likeness, but this critique at the same time brings a new positive focus to bear on even aesthetic consciousness.[70]

So the onion-skin form of narration also has this effect, to emphasize that all the layers in the dialogue—from Apollodorus-Aristodemus's mimetic narrative to Socrates-Diotima's dialectic—are *images,* simultaneously disrupted and yet included by one another. As we have argued above, this is the "destructive" yet "inclusive" function of images in dialectic (for both the *Republic* and the *Seventh Letter*), which nonetheless—even given the provisional character of all examples, images, propositions, and representations—has this positive result, that it can lead the soul to living dialectic and to understanding precisely because the images are always inadequate and can thus point beyond themselves. The *Symposium* as a whole, therefore, is Plato's enactment of an authentic, inclusive poetry, but it is also itself an image in search of understanding. For Plato, even the highest art, like all the different forms of philosophy and all other imagistic media, has to be left behind, but what art is as a living activity, as opposed to what it is like as a qualified image,[71] can be a genuine stepping stone to thought and reality, so authentic in fact that Plato parodies his own thought to signify the destructive side of this potential transformability in the voice of Aristophanes.

There always remains a doubleness, then, in Plato's view of poetic art. The highest form of art is the living dialectic of the true philosopher. This

---

70. Gadamer 1980, 65.
71. Cf. *Seventh Letter* 342e3–343a1, 343b6–c5.

is least of all an enclosed subjective world (as perhaps in Kant), or imitation, or simple self-expression, because it is radically open to the inspiration of the beautiful and the good. Yet if we are to believe Alcibiades in the onion-skin framework of the *Symposium*, it is a living art in which the self is most *uniquely* and yet most *comprehensively* expressed. In both the *Republic* and the *Phaedrus,* such a life is truly *musical.* The *Phaedrus* sums up the thought of all three dialogues with their very different emphases (*Republic, Symposium, Phaedrus*): the best life is that of the "philosopher or lover of beauty or a musical and erotic person" (*philosophou ê philokalou ê mousikou tinos kai erotikou*). However, the life of the mimetic poet *as such* is well down the scale in each dialogue; in the *Phaedrus* it is sixth in order (after the philosopher, lawful king or commander, politician or businessman, trainer or doctor, and prophet or conductor of rites), but it is still a life inspired by a form of "divine madness," although it is the lowest of the four types of such madness: love, prophecy, ritual, and poetry (244a–248e). As we have seen in the case of Aristophanes (and Agathon), inspiration is no guarantee of enlightenment.

All things considered, we are surely justified in saying of the *Symposium* what Alcibiades says of Socrates: the dialogue, even as a fractured image, is a *unique* example of an authentic musical art. By the same token, an expression often used by critics to designate the Platonic "Form," namely, the "ideal type," would surely have been for the author of the *Symposium* an oxymoron. Socrates is not a "type," and neither is the *Symposium* or, indeed, any "Platonic Form," in this sense, typological.[72]

8.6 Structure, Myth, and Argument

Our analysis of the Socrates-Diotima speech and of the structure of the *Symposium* as a whole suggests strongly that both *mythos* and *logos* are essentially included in Platonic dialectic. But this rather strange conclusion poses many problems for traditional Platonic scholarship as well as several questions of the *Symposium* that the dialogue may provoke, but clearly cannot answer. What is the respective function of each, if both have a philosophical purpose? Is one ultimately subordinate to the other? How can rationality be safeguarded if *logos* should prove accessory to *mythos?* Or are there many different kinds of *mythoi* and *logoi* in the dialogues that frustrate the critic's attempts to classify them? Here we shall simply attempt to suggest a line of approach on the basis of the *Symposium* itself without exploring the

---

72. See Chapter 6.

diversity of genres in all the dialogues, which a proper study would require. But first let us briefly take up the question of traditional scholarship.

Typically, Plato's use of myth has been explained in various ways:

1. as an evasion of rationality (a view that can be traced back to Paul Natorp)[73] or an embarrassment to it (Karl Popper, and others, have tended to see myth as just another form of totalitarian, dogmatic indoctrination combined with a false historicism);[74]
2. as an adjunct of, or support for, rational argument in different ways. For Friedländer, myths cannot be expressed in any other form; they thus pave the way to philosophy.[75] So again, for Hegel, the content of myth is elevated when it is expressed in a concept: *Vorstellungen*, "picture" presentations, are to be superseded by *Begriffe*, "concepts" or "notions."[76] Alternatively, myth may be regarded as having a literary justification insofar as it is a persuasive device that does not necessarily commit Plato to what he says mythically.[77]
3. as "Dreams expressive of Transcendental Feeling, told in such a manner and such a context that the telling of them regulates, for the service of conduct and science, the feeling expressed," according to the neo-Kantian view of Stewart,[78] a view that might be unpacked either as mystical intuition or rationalist idealism, but that in either case emphasizes a feeling or aesthetic consciousness that goes beyond the capacity of *logos* to express.[79]
4. or simply as distinguished by form: sustained discourse is myth; dialogue is dialectic.[80] (Hirzel)

---

73. Natorp (1921) takes a generally negative view of anything that does not fit into an analytic frame of thought, and the *Symposium* and *Phaedrus*, for instance, do not fare so well as compared with other dialogues in this narrow (Kantian) perspective.

74. Popper 1950. This was a powerful view in the twentieth century, echoed by Russell (the purpose of the *Republic*, for instance, is to "preserve the *status quo* as the ideal state in heaven does" [1950, 17]), Crossman (1937), Fite (1934), Toynbee (1972), and even Trevor-Roper (for whom the essence of Platonism is its abstract idealism, that is, "its determination to identify the universal spirit which informs matter and, having identified it, to disengage it from the bewildering variety, the inert machinery, the practical compromises in which, in practice, it is trapped and buried" [1985, 35]). Exactly the opposite is true.

75. Friedländer 1958, 176, 189.
76. Hegel 1988.
77. Rowe 1996, 8; 1993, 10–11.
78. Stewart 1960, 67.
79. In this way too myths have been thought to provide a religious foundation for philosophy (Baur) or to bring together mystery religion and natural philosophy (Kant 1908); see generally Frutiger's (1930, 147–77) survey.
80. Myths constitute "une rhétorique moralisatrice"; see Frutiger 1930, 157ff. (on Hirzel, Teichmüller, and Couturat). Cf. also Elias 1984, 95.

There is probably *some* truth in these explanations, but at the same time (1) is unfair to the basic spirit of Plato's work (open-ended, free inquiry). (2) has the obvious difficulty that myths are not always adjuncts to, or precursors of, rational inquiry. They may "conclude" rational arguments, as in the *Phaedo*,[81] or help to frame a conversation, as in Socrates' speech in the *Symposium*. Indeed, as Schelling argued, myths are not pictures or fictions; nor can they be transformed into some species of rational language. Rather, they spring from a preconscious, nonrational potency of the soul, as science and rational discourse spring from different potencies of the same soul, so that they stand together as expressions of different potencies and cannot supplant one another.[82] As for (3), Stewart's view, while some myths do possess the quality of a waking vision (*hypar* as opposed to *onar*) and while this may bring with it a heightened sense of feeling, myths can be perfectly rational, as well as distinctly *nonaesthetic,* and the line between myth and argument hard to draw, as in the *Timaeus*. While mythical accounts might not have the *accuracy* (*apêkribômenous*) of other accounts, on the "view" of the *Timaeus,* nonetheless if they have sufficient *probability,* we may accept "the probable story" and "search no further" (*Timaeus* 29c4–d3). So *mythos,* just as much as *logos,* may represent the "*end*" or conclusion of a particular line of inquiry. Finally, (4) fits neither the *Symposium,* nor the *Timaeus,* nor again the *Laws,* to mention but the larger picture.

Consequently, the works of scholars such as Frutiger and Elias have attempted to distinguish conscious from preconscious myth, to classify the many types of different myth in Plato, and to define myth in such a way that it does not get swallowed up by *logos,* or vice versa. Frutiger, in particular, is sensitive to the harmonic unity of Plato the philosopher and Plato the poet, and recognizes in the symbolic, free, and tentative characteristics of myth the relativity of myth and dialectic to each other. In myth, Plato deals with topics that "surpass his competence as a philosopher." So what cannot be rigorously demonstrated by dialectic is treated mythically.[83] The obvious problem with this view is that Plato often treats mythologically things that are also the subject of rational argumentation (for example, the divided line and the ascent to beauty), as Elias points out.[84] So Elias wants to go beyond a "weak defence of poetry" (according to which myth is pedagogical and supported by knowledge of a more formal kind)[85] to a "strong defence" (according to which, because the ultimate principles are insusceptible of

---

81. See section 8.7, below, on the *Phaedo* myth.
82. Schelling 1966, 1:108–31. On this, see Nicholson 1999.
83. Frutiger 1930, 36–37.
84. Elias 1984, 36.
85. Elias 1984, 226.

demonstration, they can only be shown by "examples," and so myths are Plato's ultimate defense of both poetry and philosophy).[86]

However attractive this hypothesis may be, it is unfortunately not true, unless we extend the meaning of myth to cover rational argument, account, and so on. The indemonstrability of axioms has as much to do with argument as it does with myth. Plato's strongest defense of poetry is not myth, but the dialogue form, and the *Symposium,* above all, as we have argued; but even this "defense" is too sophisticated and necessarily indirect, given Plato's critique of all images, for him to hang his hat on this one group of images rather than on any other. If Plato hangs his hat anywhere, it is on the image of dialectic itself, and this includes both myth and argument. We cannot adopt Schelling's view of the interaction of rational and nonrational potencies in the creation of the artwork, partly because art and myth, in Plato's dialogues, will not submit to the tag *pre-* or *non*rational and partly because the theory depends on other notions in Schelling's work, such as "genius," "imagination," and "the unconscious," which merely make the issue unwieldy. But the idea that myth, science, and philosophical argument stand together without being reducible to one another makes good sense in the context of the *Symposium* (and other works).

The whole of the *Symposium,* like the *Timaeus,* is a "myth," but it is pervaded by a host of different sorts of philosophical and scientific argumentation. The Socrates-Diotima dialectic is a "myth," but it is framed by, and comprises, both rational argumentation and "myths," from "tales" to "examples." *Mythos* and *logos* work together and are pervaded to a certain extent by each other, as they are in ordinary speech, but they are both images, though different. An argument ties together chains of reasoning and attempts, with more or less success, to achieve a certain clarity and certainty about the truth of things. But scientific certainty can be a cul-de-sac, if it is applied to the wrong domain of human experience or to all human experience, as we can see in the case of Eryximachus. Such certainty takes itself to be the whole of reality (with just a few things "left out," to be picked up by Aristophanes), so that not a glimmer of thought can penetrate its scientific solidity.

Myth, however, does not "put things together" in a scientific way, so that it forces the viewer to look all round the story and through the "words" to see its "meanings." Myth presents a "world," or a "landscape" in an example, which demands that it be filled with thought. Aristophanes' "myth" is a case in point, at the same time so brilliant and so thoughtless that it *requires* logical analysis for it to be seen as the muddle it really is, and yet it

---

86. Elias 1984, 357.

also *provokes,* by means of that analysis and as a voice *addressed* by Diotima, a new *understanding* of its double-edged character. To put such a myth "together" in propositional chains would be to destroy it utterly and to leave nothing but "Orphic soot" for the mind to reconstruct, which the human mind, at least, is not up to. In this sense, myth cannot be translated into argument; yet it needs argument as a means whereby its potential can be *understood.*

So the many different sorts of myth function freely within and around, both "above" and "below," the many different sorts of argument in Plato's conversations and in dialectic.[87] Sometimes they initiate, sometimes punctuate; very often they deflate or "destroy" a mood, frequently conclude. Sometimes they look up, sometimes down, but most often "around" or "through." And argument fulfills its own proper functions, equally, always by rubbing together with other images and dissolving their illusion of self-contained solidity. Indeed, as we argued in Chapters 4 and 5, since dialectic is not a mimetic art, its images, suppositions, examples, axioms, and so on require a new use of *image,* in which *mythos* and *logos* work together to "destroy" physical or psychic solidity and to open up a pathway to the mutual address of "ideas."

8.7 Soul-Body and Human Identity

In this context of the dialogue as a whole, the question of the soul-body relation in Plato's thought also emerges in rather a different way. We argued earlier that the view of the *Symposium* on the question of immortality and the soul-body relation is not incompatible with the view of earlier and contemporary dialogues; but it does provide a significant difference of emphasis. Let us sketch out the implicit findings of this study:

1. A simple distinction or separation between soul and body, such as that envisaged by Pausanias, is insufficient, because it makes of the soul the only criterion of its own moral excellence. So any authentic attempt to grapple with the problem has to go beyond the soul itself.

2. Plato starts here, as in the *Phaedo* and *Phaedrus,* with the obvious fact that soul and body are "fused together" in the world of appearance. The verb used to describe this relation in the *Phaedrus* is *pêgnysthai:* "soul and body

---

87. One example of myth is prayer. Socrates' beautiful prayer at the end of the *Phaedrus* is a little *mythos* that just "happens" to sum up the essence of what the *Republic, Symposium,* and *Phaedrus* have to say about the proper ordering of soul and body: "Dear Pan and all the other gods here, grant that I may become beautiful within and that there may be friendship between the external things I have and what is within. May I count the wise person wealthy and may I have as much gold as the wisely temperate person can carry or take with him" (279b–c). On this, see section 8.7 and note 94, below.

solidified" (246c). In the *Symposium,* body and soul are not yet distinguished in the world of appearance, and even when the distinction emerges, it is effectively a distinction between ego-consciousness and sex (for example, in Pausanias's speech). The problem in ordering life for Plato is to awaken the proper distinction, that is, in the language of the *Phaedo,* to "separate" soul from body, so that thought can start to discriminate between opposing appearances and become aware of itself as an agent.[88]

3. This means, in fact, that the soul/body distinction has to emerge out of "opposition" or opposing appearances in the sense-object.[89] So opposition itself must characterize this emerging relationship, insofar as a new self-consciousness annuls the body as a self-sufficient object, makes self-organization an essential feature of human life, and yet finds itself in some way uneasy with or opposed to itself, since the soul has to negate its own supremacy in order to be able to judge truly. So, according to Alcibiades' speech, implicitly, we look into the soul not so much in order to find a determinate, graspable "self" as to find "divinities," a world animated by something real outside of herself.

4. So the soul-body relation cannot be understood without a point of reference beyond the soul herself and without self-awareness. But this surely requires that soul and body cannot be related as two different "things" or even "substances" in the later language of thinkers such as Descartes, for instance,[90] since if reflexivity and self-knowledge characterize what it means to be a soul, then to understand how the soul is properly related to the body (not just "sunk" in it as in a stupor)[91] involves not just reflexivity of soul but the inclusion of the body in that reflexivity. In this perspective, even the body ceases to be a mere object. So Socrates "beautifies" his body in relation to something beyond himself. Or again, the movement of ascent necessarily includes not just "my" or "your" body, but the recognition—through the discriminate experience of bodies—that body is a dialogical channel open to a transcendent beauty.

5. Consequently, the soul-body relation itself cannot be understood without all five steps on the ladder of ascent. Another way of putting this would be to say that there is no single mind/soul-body relation in Plato's thought (at least not in the *Symposium*), but rather five different ways of configuring a relation that is *(a)* inherently dialogical in character, *(b)* genuinely

---

88. Cf. *Phaedo* 64a ff., and the emphasis prior to the beginning of the "argument" is upon recollected awareness rather than forgetfulness (64b5, 7–9).

89. Cf. *Rep.* 522c ff.; *Phaedo* 96e ff.

90. There is no evidence to suggest that Plato uses the word *ousia* in anything even vaguely analogous to this in his description of the different *ousiae* that go into the making of the world soul of *Timaeus* 35a.

91. Cf. *Phaedo* 81b ff.

open, in the development of its authentic character, to the "world" (the world of experience, learning, and study), *(c)* personal, practical and experimental (as dialogical it necessarily involves friendship; and it can test its offspring), and *(d)* always open ended in the direction of the transcendent. In other words, for Plato the mind-body relation is not just a "given," something fixed and frozen waiting to be found, but a relation to be experienced and realized on different levels.

6. It is also a relation that is so unlike a "thing" that it is pervaded by different dimensions. Just as there is no "original" foundation for language and reality in the flux of ordinary life, so is there no anchor for the soul-body relation in things, even if those "things" are mental constructs or solid chunks of science. And bodily or psychic identity constructed out of things is pervaded by their nothingness, their fleetingness. Ironically, wisdom does flow out of the soul but not into the head of the new disciple or student! The soul on her own with her libraries of bits of information is a very leaky vessel. So, on the one hand, the soul can be so buried in the body that no glimmer of self-consciousness can even be discerned, and on the other hand, even a dialogically self-conscious soul-body relation, if only dependent on the market value of things (and even noble things such as science, glory, and honor), is still subject to the eternal brain drain of opposites. Pausanias's proposed vertical exchange of wisdom for sex simply masks another version of the horizontal exchange of opposites.

But the real situation, according to Socrates-Diotima, is more alarming still: even lives far less selfishly defined, lives of honor and discovery, are still, in themselves, putting up a losing battle against destruction and death. Not only the unconsciously self-seeking body-soul relation (for example, Pausanias), but also the "political" and various types of "timocratic" soul-body relation are ultimately bundles of fleetingly associated thinglike entities that cannot prop up any sustainable identity or agency. Not only, then, must the soul-body relation be genuinely pervaded by the "world"; it must also be grounded on the search for the transcendent beautiful and the absent good. Only in this perspective, Diotima insists, a perspective that is not just "spiritual" but has been *tested* by intelligent experience, can there be the possibility of immortality: "and . . . when he has given birth to and nurtured true virtue, it belongs to him to be god-beloved, and to him, if to any human being, to be immortal" (212a5–7). Immortality, identity, and even the soul-body relation depend not on a world of things but on the gift of the beautiful. If this is so, then the most authentic body-soul relation can only be realized from this perspective.

7. In the *Symposium,* then, several rather different views of the soul-body relation sit uneasily in the same space. The body is "mortal nonsense"

(211e3), yet its "small beauty" (210c6) has to be included in the search for the beautiful. This means that the "body" as a solid impenetrable image that prevents thought has to be "destroyed" or left behind, while the "body" as an image through which to see the universe is included as a stepping stone on the moving ascent to the beautiful. But the same in its own way is also true of the soul, for if the soul becomes an end in itself, thought has nothing to grapple with beyond its own face. The soul, therefore, has to be opened out into the meaning of the world (in pursuits, studies, and so on) to avoid making the self the only criterion of "truth" and also to escape the fate of the generic *type* (Pausanias, Eryximachus, and so forth) who remains entirely bound by the qualitative genres of sociological, political, or scientific life. So the soul has to be stretched even further out into the attempt "to see things whole," which it cannot do on its own in the way someone might survey discrete parcels of information. The soul sees things whole through the medium of light or beauty or goodness that animates its vision transcendentally.[92] In the metaphor of the *Phaedo,* the boat or raft may have to be driven "hypothetically" by oars in the absence of the good, but the "best" method is to sail by means of the "wind."[93] And again, the only guarantee that this is a true vision—beyond the apparently self-authenticating character of such self-reflexivity—is that its consequences, or its offspring, can be cultivated and tested in a dialogue of friendship under the guidance of some "director," whether this be a teacher or the "good" itself. Such "poetry" is least of all "a private concern."[94]

8. "To see as a whole" in such a manner apparently is, in one way, to leave behind or go beyond the "mortal nonsense" of the body; but it is also to include and to see through the body so that the whole of empirical life has a proper order to it. So the effects of the synoptic view (in the *Republic*) or the single study of the beautiful (in the *Symposium*) for embodied life, at least according to the testimony of Alcibiades, are the proper ordering of soul and body in Socrates and the achievement of a unique identity: "he is not like anyone else." Socrates is not a *type.* He's the "real stuff," not "the qualified thing," to use the language of the *Seventh Letter,* or as close as any embodied being can come to the "real stuff." This more authentic soul-body relation or more unified, more integrated way of being incarnate is what the *Republic* picks up and emphasizes at the end of book 9 as the *result* of true dialectic. The person "who has *nous*" will not give up "the disposition and nurture of the body" so that he does not give it away "to the irrational pleasure" of

---

92. See note 104, below.
93. *Phaedo* 99c ff.
94. Cf. Asmis, in Kraut 1992, 344.

the beast. Instead, in looking after his body, health or beauty will not be his chief aim unless they bring moderation with them. The rule for the proper order of the body, then, is this: "he will always be found to attune the harmony in the body for the sake of a harmony in the soul" (591c–d).[95] And Glaucon replies, "By all means it must be so, if he is to be truly *musical* [*têi alêtheiai mousikos*])." The highest form of art does not neglect the body, but knows exactly how to articulate it properly and why. So later, in a famous passage of the *Phaedrus,* Socrates extends the principle to the "body" of speech: "every discourse ought to be organized, like a living being, with its own body so as to be neither handless nor footless, but to have a middle and extremities, composed as to be fitting for one another and for the whole work" (*Phaedrus* 264c). It is perhaps strange to think of the mind-body relation actually changing in a philosophical person, but since the essence of philosophy is the capacity for mindful *self*-organization, it would be even stranger if there were not to be such a change as a result of dialectic.

9. "To see as a whole," however, also involves a transformation in the soul. In previous forms of "seeing," the human being only sees things partially, and this is reflected in the soul so that her "parts" are out of their proper alignment,[96] or so that she cannot get beyond her own egotistical interests even when she sincerely believes that she acts for the highest altruistic motives (as perhaps in Pausanias). But "to see as a whole" means to see with the whole soul, that is, *to become whole.* Again, at the end of *Republic* 9, for the person who is on the way to the recovery of *nous,* "his whole soul [*holê hê psychê*] returns to its best nature" (591b). The soul that sees bit by bit, then, has a fragmented, inferior nature. Such a soul-state is that of an image—whether that image be characterized by sense-perception, the pure flow of discourse, or the limitations of inauthentic science and art (in the terms of the *Seventh Letter* or *Republic* 7). The soul is qualified and limited in a definite way and, therefore, on its own terms can only achieve the specious immortalities of propagation by progeny, prodigious psychic output, or glory—as the *Symposium* has it. In the *Republic,* this is a "little soul" (*psycharion*) with a sharp sense of its own interests (*Rep.* 519a).[97] "The whole soul," by contrast in the *Phaedo* and *Republic,* is immortal precisely because of its wholeness, which depends essentially on the Forms and the Good.

---

95. It is surely not accidental that Socrates' beautiful prayer to Pan and the other gods that concludes the *Phaedrus* exactly enshrines this principle (279b–c). See note 86, above.

96. Cf. *Rep.* 443c–444c.

97. In the *Phaedo* (91a1–b1), at one of the dramatic pivots of the dialogue after Simmias's and Cebes' objections, Socrates himself fears that he will not reply "philosophically," but speak instead like "very uneducated, victory-loving" people, who want only what *they* suppose to be the case to be accepted without any regard for the truth. This is what the "little soul" means in practice.

This wholeness, it is not unreasonable to suppose, is that of the dialectician's soul, but it is an *embodied wholeness,* as we see vividly represented in Alcibiades' speech and as Diotima's final words clearly intimate: "and to him, if to any *human being,* to be immortal" (212a5–6).[98]

So Plato's thought is not "dualist" in any simplistic sense of that term. The soul has to be "separated" from body if any "sensible" life is to occur—indeed if there is to be any beauty at all and not the sheer mind-numbing boredom of serial succession. But the "separation," despite the birth pangs of opposition and friction, which are never overcome, can give way to a new form of incarnation in which the body is ordered to a new way of living. In Plato's view, at least, this was not to be merely another disguised form of hierarchical totalitarianism, but *living, "truly musical" art,* in which the body is not subjected to the soul, as one "thing" to another "thing," but rather articulated naturally by the genuine self-reflexive, dialogical harmony of the soul.

10. "To see as a whole," then, involves a more authentic soul-body relation. The prisoner liberated from the cave and with his eyes blinded from the light of the Good must return to the cave to liberate and care for his imprisoned fellows. Wholeness involves responsibility and compassion for the whole. This may well be *the* (or one) meaning of that enigmatic, much debated, and much emended sentence at *Phaedrus* 246b: *pasa hê psychê [hê psychê pasa* or *psychê pasa] pantos epimeleitai tou apsychou* (the entire soul [or every *soul*] cares for everything that is without soul).[99] Wholeness of soul involves, in some way, a closer, more intimate relation to the world than partiality could ever attain. And in this sense, while body for Plato is certainly subordinate to soul, the *meaning* of body properly ordered and "beautified" seems to be coextensive with soul. As soul or the human being moves up the ladder of ascent, the flux, decay, and detritus of body is left behind, but its meaning and its beauty are somehow retained.

One may object, of course, together with Nietzsche, Derrida, and others, that this is no more than a covert and illicit transfer of the physical to the mental or spiritual, a transfer that then covers its illicit tracks by pretending to erase them.[100] But Plato knew all about such "transfers" long before Nietzsche or Derrida, and he was equally ready to puncture his most artistically contrived sacred icons (Socrates, by Alcibiades) as to point to the inadequacy of his own images. But there are many different ways of puncturing

---

98. On this passage, see Rowe 1998, 201; and on the "whole soul" in this context, see also *Phaedrus* 253e–254a: *pasa . . . hê psychê.*

99. On this passage, *Phaedrus* 246b6–7 (and 245c), see T. M. Robinson 1970, 114; Rowe 1996, ad loc.

100. Nietzsche 1974, 180; Derrida 1971, 51–55.

an image—a spiritual image, for instance, can be effectively shattered by a strong physical presence or a rather abstract argument by a perceptually vivid myth. The first type occurs at the end of the *Symposium* with Alcibiades' entry. The second type occurs at the end of the *Phaedo* in what many commentators have taken to be a sort of apocalyptic appendix, in the "otherworldly" style, to the extraordinarily difficult final "argument" that crowns the "philosophical" portion of the dialogue.[101] This is not a very satisfactory way of looking at the matter, for the myth is in some sense an integral part of the whole philosophical development of that dialogue, and to some degree, it concludes the "argument." But here we want to make a rather different point, which is crucial to understanding Plato's use of images as well as the contrast between the *Phaedo* and the *Symposium* on the soul-body question. The concluding myth of the *Phaedo* both punctures the prolonged "mood" of abstract argumentation leading up to it and is in some measure at the same time the *logical* consequence of that earlier argument.

The myth presents a holistic view of body lifted up into the perspective of soul and a series of body-soul relationships in the afterlife, culminating in a pure life "without bodies" and in the arrival at "dwellings still more beautiful" (114c2–6; cf. 109c–110b; 110c1–6; 111a3 ff., 111a4: *anthrôpous*). For the more purified of these relationships the afterlife is not a pallid, shadelike existence: it is as if the earth emerges with pristine *aesthetic* grace in a new intelligible way, communicating its own beauty, and the locus also of more intimate conversation between gods and men. The myth, then, presents a picture of an earth, which includes several possible relations of soul to body, from the dimmest sort of life sunk in the "hollows" of the earth to the purely separated soul that arrives at an even greater "perceptual" beauty; and these are mediated by the purified, but embodied, soul that experiences direct conversation between gods and human beings, from a perspective in which the full beauty of *sensible* things only emerges as such for the first time. Because of this, the myth sits uneasily with the final argument of the *Phaedo* insofar as it transposes into vivid aesthetic embodiment what the final argument had apparently tried to approach by means of thought.

But how are we to take this myth? Bostock thinks we should not take the *Phaedo* myth seriously, and Robinson, not unwisely, objects that it is as illusory to look for an organised body of "religious" truth in one myth as to search for a totally coherent philosophical system in another.[102] By

---

101. For a variety of very different views, see Archer-Hind 1894; Burnet 1911; Bluck 1955; Hackforth 1955; Loriaux 1969; Gallop 1975; Dorter 1982; Burger 1984; Geddes 1985; Bostock 1986; Dixsaut 1991; Rowe 1996.

102. Bostock 1986, 28–29; T. M. Robinson 1970, 131.

contrast, Robin, Friedländer, and Guthrie[103] hold that the *Phaedo* myth does present a serious scientific picture ("an attempt to adapt the Ionian conception of the earth as a concave-surfaced disc to the more recent hypothesis that it is spherical") interwoven with distinctly eschatological Platonic strands such as the contrast between the hollows and the surface, in Guthrie's view, perhaps mistakenly, "the unstable objects of sensation and opinion and the immutable Forms that are the objects of knowledge."[104] But if we accept Friedländer's literal scientific basis, how metaphorical can the metaphorical level be? Hackforth holds that the myth presents metaphorically "the immaterial in a material form,"[105] Dorter, that it shows "the timeless in a temporal form or the implicit present in an explicit future,"[106] which is to say that it shows "what in our present embodied existence we make of ourselves for all time." Dorter also notes the metaphoricity of the whole corporeal description: the circulation of the stream of Hades is equivalent metaphorically to the circulation of blood with Tartarus as the heart.[107] But the precise interpretation even of this metaphysical body is in doubt. For Burger, by contrast, the final myth is not a vision of the fate of souls after death, but rather an allegorical description of the relationship between soul and body, and the earth is a gigantic Corpse![108]

There seems little doubt that the myth is in some sense or other a serious attempt to express in metaphorical or imagistic terms something of a realistic, sensual *idea* of the earth as a whole and the soul's journey in relation to it. In fact, the image brings together into apparently impossible proximity the literal and the ideal as part to the whole. The literal interpretation was common in antiquity. Aristotle criticizes the myth (*Mete* 2.2.355b32–356a14) without even considering Socrates' own warning that this or something like it is true (114d2–3). Certainly, later Platonist

103. Robin, 1926; Friedländer 1964, 261ff.; Guthrie 1975, 361–63; Cf. Edelstein 1949, 463–81.

104. Guthrie 1975, 362.

105. Hackforth 1955, 186 (cf. 171–75). Cf. also Geddes 1985: "Plato here considers the Earth as a platform of life midway between the two others: one, beneath, in the sea, where all the forms are, from the thickness of the element, low and coarse; the other, in the ether above, where the forms are pure and noble, our air being to them as dense and inimical to life as water is to our respiration" (165). Cf. also D. White's (1989) comment on Geddes in the light of his own degrees of reality interpretation: "Geddes thus makes explicit the fact that the myth incorporates the Forms, with the upper and lower worlds in the myth displaying different degrees of reality depending on their respective exemplification of the Forms" (20; cf. 258–60).

106. Dorter 1982, 165.

107. Dorter 1982, 165.

108. Burger 1982, 194.

interpreters regarded it as "true," whether literally or allegorically. Damascius, for example, in his commentaries on the *Phaedo* distinguishes two schools of interpretation. One, represented by a certain Democritus and by Plutarch of Athens, held that the earth of 108c5–110b1 was incorporeal, Democritus maintaining that it was the Form (108b9), Plutarch that it was Nature Plato intended. Representing the other school, Harpocratio, Theodorus of Asine, Proclus and Damascius all held, in different ways, that the earth intended was corporeal, Harpocratio maintaining that it was the whole world, Theodorus and Proclus that it signified the sublunary world, and Damascius that "it is the earth of our geography books."[109] Damascius's arguments are worth briefly considering: against the incorporeal earth interpretation he urges "that Socrates thinks of its inhabitants as having bodies and [possessing the faculty of sense perception] and further says that animals have a longer span of life."[110] Against the view that the earth is Form or Idea, Damascius asks further how it could be "whiter than chalk" if it were an Idea; and if it were Nature, how could it be "an abode of blessed souls" and "inhabited by gods"? Here, then, we seem to meet the later Neoplatonic belief in astral bodies developed undoubtedly with reference to Plato's myths and Aristotle's conception of *pneuma* and parallelled in the "perfect body" (*sôma teleion*) of the Mithras liturgy, the "immortal body" (*athanaton sôma*) of *Corpus Hermeticum* 8.3, and the Gnostic "garment of light."[111] The references to "vehicles" in the Platonic dialogues (*Phaedo* 113d; *Phaedrus* 247b; *Tim.* 41e, 44e, 69c) could not, as Dodds has pointed out, "by themselves suggest to the most perverse mind a theory of astral bodies."[112] The only passage that does propose a fiery or aerial body is the late *Laws* 898e ff. Against the corporealist tradition, however, would seem to be Socrates' explicit avowal that he will speak of "the idea of the earth" (108d9) and his statement that no man of sense would take it literally (114d). Certainly too, Plotinus interprets the myth of the *Phaedo* (and also the *Phaedrus*) to refer to the intelligible world of Being.[113]

How then are we to interpret this? Socrates' *caveat* acts like a healthy negative theology precluding us from taking either our affirmations or our negations too seriously. The myth presents a picture of the immediate fate of the souls after death. As Gregory of Nyssa later understands it, this

---

109. Westerink 1977, vol. 2, Damascius I, sections 503–4, 254–55.
110. Section 505 (n. 406).
111. Dodds 1971, appendix 2: "The Astral Body in Neoplatonism," 313–21.
112. Dodds 1971, 315.
113. See, e.g., *Ennead* 5.8.4 (Plotinus refers to both the myths of the *Phaedo* and *Phaedrus* in this chapter).

involves reincarnation[114] whether into the grosser bodies of animals or the more purified, perhaps even ethereal ones of (apparently) *human* beings. Damascius's view that the earth in question is "the earth of our geography books" seems plausible, but this does not exclude other metaphorical or allegorical interpretations, for in the picture of the myth Socrates provides us with the eyes of a Lynceus, as it were, to see into the living reality of the earth, with all its hollows and heights suddenly revealed and illuminated by a light that ultimately springs from a higher world of being, altogether without body. The myth, then, certainly prepares the reader to understand by analogy, and in terms accessible to the ordinary mind, that the ultimate abode of the purified soul, the immaterial realm of Forms, is one not of pallid emptiness, but of abundant, if ineffable, richness. The vision of an intermediate, purified body-soul relationship, foreshadowing the depiction of the world's body in the *Timaeus,* is a radical transformation of a detail from popular belief into the philosophical argumentation of the *Phaedo,* but it is also a positive exemplar of an integrated soul-body relation lived out by purification or separation of soul from body. Thus the *Phaedo* presents a positive view of body in its concluding myth as the logical extension of the positive notion present in the final argument, namely, that it is soul as form-bearer that gives life, content, and meaning to body, and therefore that the significance of body only begins to emerge properly when the active, causal nature of the soul and the source of this causality, soul's affinity with the Forms, provide the essential background to the understanding of even the most simple, physical substance.[115] But the myth itself is, again, a disruptive and transformative image for the *soul,* but by means of the *body;* and part of the point is surely that the myth refuses to be resolved into either a literal or an ideal interpretation, for it remains a "tale" as an image, just as the whole line of *argumentation* or *logos* on its own terms is introduced by Socrates as a form of "tale-telling" (*diamythologein*) at 70b.[116]

---

114. Gregory of Nyssa, PG 46 (Migne) *De Anima et Resurrectione* 108b–109b: "*(psychên)* . . . *metendyomenên ta sômata, kai pros to areskon aei metabainousan, ê ptênon, ê enydron, ê chersaion ti zôon ginomenên* . . ." Gregory in this and other passages, of course, has the *Phaedrus* myth more in mind. Gregory argues that even the pagan philosophers agree about corporeal resurrection, the difference being that the pagans hold that the soul returns to a different body, the Christians that it returns to the same body.

115. The complexity and difficulty of the "final argument" are notorious, but there is no room here for a separate treatment of this.

116. This does not diminish the status of rationality, but rather points to the need for intelligent balance. Misology, in Socrates' view, is a fate worse than his own death. Excessive trust inevitably passes into its opposite: excessive distrust. What rational argument needs is an intelligent, human balance that recognizes its strength as well as its limitation (cf *Phaedo* 89d1 ff.).

At any rate, the upshot of our discussion of the *Phaedo* myth is the following. In its conclusion, the *Phaedo* presents a positive "intermediate" view of the soul-body relation, a view that is rooted in the reflexivity of direct conversation between gods and human beings and that points mythically to the purified state of the separated soul in which the positive meaning and beauty of body is not subtracted. To have a pallid afterlife existence is the fate of souls sunk in the hollows of the earth; for those who can see as a whole (cf. 111c4 ff.), the whole form of earth is their dwelling; and for those purified sufficiently by philosophy, their dwellings are "fairer still than these" (114c4–5). In the *Phaedo* the central question, even in the context of death, appears to be the need for soul to put on her own, not an alien, beauty (114e4–5); and here too Socrates *bathes* his body before embarking on that final journey (116a). In the "life" of the *Symposium,* Socrates also bathes for the journey to the beautiful, and the transformation that occurs in that perspective results both in the positive ordering of soul and body in relation to all five "steps" on the ladder of ascent and in a unique identity that, under the influence of any other animating principle (art, politics, science, and so on), would have devolved into something more generic and, ultimately, herdlike or beastlike (in terms of the analogy Socrates and Thrasymachus employ in *Republic* 1 and 9).[117] This positive view of embodiment that we find, in different ways, in the *Republic, Phaedo, Symposium,* and *Phaedrus* surely means that there is something in the very essence of soul that has to do with body; and so it is not surprising that Plato should develop this authentic relation within the *ousia* of soul herself later in the *Timaeus.* The soul has an indivisible *ousia* and also an *ousia* to be divided about bodies (*Timaeus* 35a).

The *Symposium,* then, is suggestive of this larger picture of soul-body and human identity, and of this rather unfamiliar way of looking at the soul-body relation itself; but since the dialogue poses more questions than it answers, it evidently also addresses those dialogues both before and after it. If there is no "first" word, there is equally no "last" word.

8.8 "Platonic Love" and "Plato"

Two final questions: What is "Platonic love"? and Who is this author who addresses us so gracefully, so obliquely, and so disruptively? As we have shown, Platonic love is none of the things it is commonly thought to be: "abstract," "impersonal," "purely spiritual," "homoerotic," and so forth. In the light of this final chapter, it is also clear that such "love" embraces the

---

117. *Rep.* 1.343a ff., 9.588c ff.

movement of the whole dialogue, which is a dialectic, open to the transcendent beautiful and the absent good, and tested in the "well-meaning" and not so well-meaning "refutations" of Socrates' brilliant, but *divided,* interlocuter, Alcibiades. It is because it embraces the movement of the *whole* dialogue that Platonic love has so successfully over the centuries been identified with some of its more conspicuous parts, from Pausanias's and Eryximachus's distinction between a "heavenly" and "mundane" love, to Arisophanes' fragmented halves in search of their absurd globular "wholeness," and Alcibiades' Silenus image. Some of these identifications are genuinely crazy, but others, often despised by modern scholarship, are actually more sophisticated than the scholarship that despises them. For they have instinctively recognized that the *Symposium* is a complex dialectic and not an objective tableau of somewhat eccentric "facts."

The dialectic as such starts in the elenchus of Agathon, but effectively embraces all the previous speeches and prologues, by puncturing or destroying them as solid self-sufficient images but also including them as free ideas in mutual address. Such "love," therefore, is practical: it listens to and reaches into "ordinary" speech, from proverb to epic to Gorgianic jingle, and it starts, in the middle of things, with the chance meetings of everyday life between resourceful and not so resourceful people (Socrates and Aristodemus). It even finds its way uninvited into the house of the apparent, but always absent, "good." Here, in the mind-numbing flux of the pursuit of pleasure and avoidance of pain, there emerge—with all the artificial and potentially self-seeking displacements attached to such chance events—the at first so imposing "worlds" of individual, yet generic speech, in each of which the overwhelming force of Love flickers with a different face behind the apparently solid styles and types. But only when the apparent "good" (Agathon) acknowledges that the real "good" is absent (in the elenchus) do the present time and space drop away; and we find ourselves no longer in Agathon's house, but in a recollected placeless dialogue, which has occurred at no one time—in short, in a story of "ideas" whose "mother" is a woman, Diotima.[118] Love, it turns out, is the search for a different "good" reflected in all forms of desire throughout the universe, but its nature and birth are framed in a conversation between a resourceful women and a not so resourceful man (the "wise" and the "inferior"), a conversation that is always in movement between the poles of particular, immediate need (already in Agathon's elenchus) and the unique transforming disclosure of

---

118. We might even say that the Socrates-Diotima speech in the *Symposium* is a dramatic enactment of the "philosophical imperfect," that is, the imperfect tense (*ên*) we find in Aristotle's strange phrase for "essence," namely, *to ti ên einai,* or "the what *it was* to be," apparently derived from Antisthenes.

the beautiful. Unlikeness, defamiliarization, and pain are fundamental to such love, but so too is a different sort of awakening, likeness, and delight that beckons from the beautiful and that is part of the reflexive activity of the dialectical movement itself. But in the light and generative power of the beautiful, we return to the house of Agathon, to images, of which Socrates is persuaded, and to the real, sometimes unfortunate, consequences of the always necessary, well-meaning refutations (that is, benevolent *criticism*), whose precise emphasis we cannot control (Alcibiades). The successive waves of revelers, like historical disasters, succeed in destroying the social fabric of this "get-together," but not the spirit of dialectic or of the unique, impossible person who has "nous." And so when we consciously return to the outer skin of the narrative with Aristodemus's semifanatical eye for the "facts" of Socrates' life, the mimetic level is already transformed by our reading of the dialogue so that we unconsciously want to see, even if we have not yet learned to do it, what Socrates was *thinking* in this search for the absent good rather than what he was *doing*. The "Platonic love" of the *Symposium,* therefore, is a dialectic in search of an understanding beyond itself. Such "love" already needs the *Phaedrus* and, indeed, as Plato makes quite clear, a lot more besides.[119]

119. Cf. *Phaedrus* 278b–d. In this way, the *Symposium* (and the other "middle" dialogues) is a pivotal work for the reading of Plato's dialogues insofar as (1) Plato never writes anything quite like it again (the *Phaedrus* has many features in common with the *Symposium,* though an examination of this question is beyond the scope of the present work, but its overall structure and character are different) and (2) the implicit questions the *Symposium* provokes look forward to all the later dialogues. For example, (1) the question of speech as speech and the nature of rhetoric, as well as the issue of self-motion (and the "divine banquet" [on this especially, see Sallis 1996, 143–44, 178]) naturally anticipate the *Phaedrus,* as we have argued (Chapter 6, ad fin.); (2) the problem of form, unity, and multiplicity that is fundamental to portions of the *Republic* and *Phaedo,* as well as to the *Symposium* (from Pausanias and Aristophanes to Socrates' and Alcibiades' speeches) anticipates both "sections" of the *Parmenides* (where something of the *Symposium*'s structure is even refashioned); (3) the problem of authentic *epistêmê,* which is a pressing issue that arises out of the very structure of the *Symposium* (as well as from the treatment of dialectic in the *Republic* and the "second sailing" of the *Phaedo*), looks forward to the *Theaetetus* and its negative conclusion that *orthê doxa* plus a *logos* cannot simply be *epistêmê;* (4) the *Symposium*'s treatment of sophistry and dialectic (and its apparent inclusion of Diotima as a "Sophist"), a treatment reflecting the apparent indiscernibility between dialectic and eristic in much earlier dialogues (e.g., *Laches, Euthydemus,* etc.), and above all the inclusion of self-motion in (the approach to) being, necessitates, among other reasons, the examinations of the *Sophist;* (5) the question of "pleasure" in *Republic* 9 and implicitly on all five levels of ascent in the *Symposium* anticipates the five-level treatment of pleasure in the *Philebus;* (6) the continuing problematic of political life for Plato evinced in the *Symposium* against the background of free dialectical play and the unique *person* of Socrates looks forward to the *Politicus* and its dialectical pursuit of a "second best" course; and (7) among many other things, the essential connection with body *in soul,* which is an implicit part of all the middle dialogues, anticipates the more "positive" world soul-body account of the *Timaeus*. All in all, Plato never repeats himself. The *Laws,* for instance, is an *entirely* different work from the *Republic* (on this, see esp. Dixsaut 1985), though it is often wrongly assumed to be merely a form of philosophical arteriosclerosis. In such a context and given the uniqueness of the *Symposium* in the dialogues as a whole, it would be strange if the *"philosophical digression"* of

Since our author, Plato, seems to suggest his presence so often and since he also disappears beyond the text just at the point at which we come to suspect this presence, then it is perhaps reasonable to ask a rather strange question: who might Plato be *like?* The present work has been written in the conviction that Plato is less like a northern European or American scholar-gentleman than he is a clever, angular-thinking Greek. For the worlds of his dialogues, Plato is always either "ill" or "not at home," just like the Strangers of his later writings. Perhaps he is a little like Diotima, or even Aristodemus, but he is surely even more like that most "curved thinking" of all Greek hero vagabonds, Odysseus. This impression is not accidental, for Odysseus makes an appearance in all the middle dialogues, mostly by not being there. Only in the *Republic* does he make a command performance, as the last soul to choose his new life on the Plain of Truth in the myth of Er. Unlike all the previous souls, who choose tyrannies and the lives of various animals, Odysseus chooses the humblest human life with much discrimination: "and in memory of his former troubles [the soul of Odysseus] had thrown away his love of honor and went around for a long time *in search* [*zêtein*] of the life of a disinterested [*apragmonos*] private citizen, and with difficulty [*mogis*] found it lying somewhere disregarded by the rest" (*Republic* 10.620c5–d1). The quest that started in book 1 with the ordinary citizen's innocent definition of justice (that is, with Cephalus), and continued in the deceptively simple attempt to found a just city that might incorporate the principle of the nonmeddling, disinterested development of each person's own nature or task (*to heautou prattein*), is completed when that most long-suffering and intelligent Greek, Odysseus, becomes self-knowing in the humble manner prescribed by the Delphic commandment "Know thyself."[120] Although the story is told by Er, here in the *Republic* (just as tends to happen in the *Symposium*) the myth of Er addresses the *logos* of Socrates in its conclusion. "Odysseus" is therefore, mythically speaking, the first trueborn son of Socrates' *logos*—that is, the unsaid Plato.

In the *Phaedo, Phaedrus,* and *Symposium,* by contrast, "Odysseus" makes no direct appearance except obliquely in the "speech" of Simmias and Socrates. In the *Phaedo,* Simmias, an interlocutor from out of town (*xenos*)

---

the *Seventh Letter* (if this is really written by Plato, and in our view there are no compelling reasons against its authenticity) bore no relation whatsoever to *the* dramatic enactment in novelistic form of Plato's dialectic "at play," nonetheless "in earnest" for what is represented through it (cf. *all' eph' hois espoudaken ekeinôn* [written words or images are play; *Phaedrus* 278b–d]).

120. This is not so much an epistemic pronouncement but, as Wilamowitz (1932, 123), Nilsson (1948) and others have argued, a counsel to moderation and humility—to know one's place in life as subject to divine will.

and of penetrating intellect and whose name is first mentioned directly alongside that of the absent Plato (59b10–c1), states his belief that in the absence of an ability to learn the truth from others or discover it for ourselves (*ê mathein . . . ê heurein*), just as Socrates will be unable to discover (*out-'heurein*) or learn (*oute . . . mathein*) the nature of the good a little later in the dialogue (99c8–9), we should sail though life on the least refutable (*dusexelegktotaton*) account we can find: "as on a raft" (*hôsper epi schedias*) (85c8–d2). The infinitive *diapleusai*, "to sail through," used by Simmias (85d2) is picked up later by Socrates when he outlines his second-best, or "second sailing" (*deuteros plous*), hypothetical method, which, according to Eustathius on the *Odyssey*, is, when becalmed, to make progress by rowing rather than to be propelled by the "divine" wind.[121]

At the center of this dialogue, therefore, in the conversation between the Plato-like Simmias and Socrates, it is the unsaid Odysseus, who navigates the risky seas, somehow managing, in the absence of a "better" propulsion system, to steer a course between excess and defect. Again, in the *Phaedrus* (after the dialectic of the *Republic* and the *Symposium*) Socrates tells his interlocutor, Phaedrus, that the music of dialectic is the only means by which to steer clear of the bewitching song of the "Sirens" (259a) and gain the respect of the "cicadas" (cf. *Symposium* 191c2), who report to all the muses, but, above all, to Calliopê and Urania, about the noblest song, philosophy (259b–d).[122] In both these dialogues, the mantle of "Odysseus" implicitly embraces both interlocutors, whether Simmias and Socrates or Phaedrus and Socrates. But in the *Symposium*,[123] this mantle

---

121. Eustathius, in *Od.* 1453, 20.

122. In the *Symposium*, it is the divided Alcibiades who forcibly covers his ears against Socrates as if he were running away from the Sirens and instead conducts the business of the Athenians (sc. cicadas), so that he won't grow old on the rowing bench beside Socrates (216a4–7).

123. Cf. *Symp.* 205d2–3: *ho megistos kai doleros erôs* (in everyone), that is, Diotima, Socrates, the reader, Plato, and perhaps Odysseus, of whom the adjective *doleros* is conspicuously used at *Hippias Minor* 369c: *ton de doleron te kai polla pseudomenon*. In our view, it seems probable in the context we have outlined above that the *Symposium* reference bears a conscious reflection on this earlier dialogue. Plato could have well written *megas kai doleros*, so why did he actually write *megistos*? *Megistos*, we propose, among other things in situ, reflects the superlative quality of Odysseus's *supposed* ability to deceive in the *Hipp. Min.* This dialogue is undoubtedly of inferior quality, but since its authenticity is attested to by Aristotle, no one has been able to relegate it to the scrap heap of poor imitation. Generally too, this dialogue (quite possibly Plato's earliest, and certainly among the earliest; see Brandwood 1990 has been misunderstood (but for a different more positive treatment, see Zembaty 1989, 51–70), for it is more subtle (admittedly for an "off day" by Plato's standards) than scholars take it to be. Hippias claims that of Homer's heroes, Achilles is the "best," Nestor the "wisest," and Odysseus the "most wily" (*polytropos*), and that Achilles and Odysseus, the former is simplest (*haploustatos*) and truthful (*alêthês*), while the latter is wily and deceitful (*pseudês*). Under Socrates' questioning, Hippias comes to hold the principle that the person who is "capable" of knowing the truth is also the one who will best know how to deceive and that it is this person one prefers to have handy in a crisis rather than someone who deceives,

Conclusion

incongruously transfigures the diminutive Aristodemus as he and Socrates, in the "disruption" of an epic past, walk and talk together always "on the way," like Odysseus and Diomedes, although their names are never "said," but only suggested in the misquotation of *Iliad* 10.224. So in the diverse figures of Simmias, Phaedrus, Cephalus, Odysseus, and Aristodemus-Apollodorus, a rather new, angular-thinking "Odysseus," for the most part "unsaid" and always beyond our grasp, seems to beckon the reader into the middle of things.

---

lies, or makes a mistake out of ignorance. So *the same person* knows how to be truthful and how to be a liar (and Socrates then goes on to generalize the case for all the sciences). This principle Hippias holds as his own, but its consequences under Socrates' apparently eristic treatment in the closing portion of the dialogue lead to absurdity, that is, to the conclusion that it must be the good man who wittingly (*hekôn*) does wrong things who is to be preferred to the one who acts out of ignorance, and Socrates admits that he is *divided* against himself on this point. The real conclusion, then, appears to be purely negative and even moralistic insofar as Socrates points out that if not only *he* can go so astray but apparently "wise people" such as Hippias too, then things look pretty grim. Yet this is only the apparent conclusion, for the real "ironic" conclusion is a little more complex, so that it is not worth questioning Hippias any more, since he is obviously a fool if he cannot see for himself the "real" conclusion (Socrates emphasizes twice in the concluding portion that he stops questioning people when he realizes that he can really learn nothing from them). So what is the "real" conclusion? The real conclusion might be stated as follows: whether or not Hippias holds the view that Achilles is "the best," Nestor "the wisest," and Achilles "the most wily" (and he holds this view unshakably throughout the conversation), (1) on Hippias's own principle (cf. the oft repeated *kata son logon*) that the *same person* knows both the true and the false (the first half of the dialogue) and (2) on the basis of Socrates' divided conclusion—he is at sea literally "between opposites"—only the one who is capable of judging between opposites is the wisest and the best, and this is of course Odysseus, in other words, *not* the "simplest" man. So the "wiliest" turns out to be, on the basis both of Hippias's agreements and his disagreements, the "greatest": *Odysseus*. This interpretation, when put into its context here in the *Symposium*, supports our view of 205d2–3, namely, that it refers to an Eros of *opposites* insofar as the one *logos* knows both (cf. the "final argument" about the three lives of *Rep*. 9). We suggest that Plato refers to himself in *Hippias Minor* in the apparent "quotation" at *Symp*. 205d2–3 as well as to his negative treatment of Eros in the *Republic* (cf. also *Symp*. 188a7–8). So while the *Symposium* treats the positive anagogic aspects of Eros, it is aware of the much greater complexity of the problem.

SELECT BIBLIOGRAPHY

Editions, Translations, and Commentaries

Allen, Reginald E. 1991. *The Dialogues of Plato.* Vol. 2, *The Symposium.* New Haven: Yale University Press.
Anderson, Daniel E. 1993. *The Masks of Dionysos: A Commentary on Plato's "Symposium."* Albany: State University of New York Press.
Benardete, Seth, and Allan Bloom. 2001. *Plato's "Symposium."* Translated by S. Benardete. Commentaries by A. Bloom and S. Benardete. 1993. Reprint, Chicago: University of Chicago Press.
Bonelli, Guido. 1991. *Socrate Sileno: Dinamica erotica e figurazione scenica nel Convivo di Platone.* Turin.
Brisson, Luc. 1998. *Platon: Le Banquet.* Paris: Flammarion.
Burnet, John. 1901. *Platonis opera.* Oxford Classical Texts. Vol. 2. Oxford: Oxford University Press.
Bury, R. G. 1932. *The "Symposium" of Plato.* 2d ed. Cambridge: W. Heffer and Sons.
Calogero, Guido. 1928. *Il Simposio (versione a saggio introduttivo).* Bari: Laterza.
Cobb, William S. 1993. *The "Symposium" and the "Phaedrus": Plato's Erotic Dialogues.* Albany: State University of New York.
Dover, Kenneth J. 1980. *Plato: Symposium.* Cambridge: Cambridge University Press.
Hamilton, Walter. 1951. *Plato: The Symposium.* Harmondsworth: Penguin.
Hug, Arnold. 1884. *Platons Symposion.* Leipzig.
Lacan, Jacques. 1991. *Le seminaire: Livre VIII, Le Transfert.* Texte établi par Jacques-Alain Miller. Paris: Editions Kimé.
Menissier, Thierry. 1996. *Eros philosophe: Une interpretation philosophique du Banquet de Platon.* Paris.
Mitchell, R. L. 1993. *The Hymn to Eros: A Reading of Plato's "Symposium."* Lanham: University Press of America.
Nehamas, Alexander, and Paul Woodruff. 1989. *Plato: Symposium.* Indianapolis: Hackett.
Reale, Giovanni. 1993. *Platone: Simposio.* Milan.
Rettig, G. F. 1876. *Platonis Symposion.* Halle.
Riickert, L. I. 1829. *Platonis Convivium.* Leipzig.
Robin, Leon. 1966. *Platon: Oeuvres completes.* T. IV.2, *Le Banquet.* Paris: Les Belles Lettres.
Rosen, Stanley. 1968. *Plato's "Symposium."* New Haven: Yale University Press.
Rowe, Christopher. J. 1998. *Plato: Symposium.* Warminster, U.K.: Aris and Phillips.
Vicaire, Paul (with J. Laborderie). 1992. *Platon: Oeuvres completes.* T. IV.2, *Le Banquet.* 2d ed. Paris: Les Belles Lettres.
Waterfield, Robin. 1994. *Plato: Symposium.* World's Classics. Oxford: Oxford University Press.

Selected Works

Adam, James. 1965. *The "Republic" of Plato.* Edited with critical notes, commentary, and appendices with a new introduction by D. A. Rees. 2 vols. Cambridge: Cambridge University Press.
Allen, Reginald E., ed. 1965. *Studies in Plato's Metaphysics.* London.
Annas, Julia. 1985. "Self-Knowledge in Early Plato." In *Platonic Investigations,* edited by Dominic J. O'Meara, 111–38. Studies in Philosophy and the History of Philosophy, vol. 13. Washington, D.C.: Catholic University of America Press.
———.1996. "Plato's *Republic* and Feminism." In *Feminism and Ancient Philosophy,* edited by Julia K. Ward, 3–12. London: Routledge. .
Anton, John P., and George L. Kustas. 1971. *Essays in Ancient Greek Philosophy.* Albany: State University of New York Press.
Anton, John P., and Anthony Preus. 1989. *Essays in Ancient Greek Philosophy 3: Plato.* Albany: State University of New York Press.
Archer-Hind, R. D. 1894. *The "Phaedo" of Plato.* 2d ed. London: Macmillan.
Armstrong, Arthur Hilary. 1961. "Platonic Eros and Christian Agape." *Downside Review* 79:105–21.
Arendt, Hannah. 1996. *Love and Saint Augustine.* Edited and with an interpretive essay by Joanna Vecchiarelli Scott and Judith Chelios Stark. First copyright 1929. Chicago: University of Chicago Press.
Ast, Frederick. 1956. *Lexicon Platonicum Sive Vocum Platonicarum Index.* Leipzig, 1835. Reprint, Bonn.
Bacon, Helen. 1959. "Socrates Crowned." *Virginia Quarterly Review* 35:415–30.
Bakhtin, Mikhail. 1981a. *The Dialogic Imagination* (*Yoprosy literatury: Estetiki,* Moscow, 1975). Translated by C. Emerson and M. Holquist. Austin: University of Texas Press.
———. 1981b. "Discourse in the Novel." In *The Dialogic Imagination.* Translated by C. Emerson and M. Holquist. Austin: University of Texas Press.
———.1981c. "Epic and Novel: Toward a Methodology for the Study of the Novel." In *The Dialogic Imagination.* Translated by C. Emerson and M. Holquist. Austin: University of Texas Press.
———. 1984a. "Problems of Dostoevsky's Poetics." In *Problems of Dostoevsky's Poetics.* Edited and translated by C. Emerson. Minneapolis: University of Minnesota Press.
———. 1984b. *Problems of Dostoevsky's Poetics* (*Problemy poetiki Dostoevskogo,* Moscow, 1963). Edited and translated by C. Emerson. Minneapolis: University of Minnesota Press.
Bambrough, J. Renford. 1967. *Plato, Popper, and Politics: Some Contributions to a Modern Controversy.* Cambridge: Heffer; New York: Barnes and Noble.
Barnes, Jonathan. 1982. *The Presocratic Philosophers.* Boston: Routledge.
Barrachi, Claudia. 2000. "Another Apology." In *Retracing the Platonic Text,* edited by J. Russon and J. Sallis. Evanston: Northwestern University Press.
Belfiore, Elizabeth. 1980. *"Elenchus, Epode,* and Magic: Socrates as Silenus." *Phoenix* 34:128–37.
———. 1984. "Dialectic with the Reader in Plato's *Symposium.*" *Mafia* 36:137–49.
Benardete, Seth. 1993. *The Tragedy and Comedy of Life: Plato's "Philebus."* Chicago: University of Chicago Press.
———. 1994. *On Plato's "Symposium"/Uber Platons Symposion.* Munich: Carl Friedrich von Siemens Stiftung.

Blanckenhagen, P. H. von. 1993. "Stage and Actors in Plato's *Symposium.*" *Greek, Roman, and Byzantine Studies* 34:1–18.
Bluck, R. S. 1955. *Plato's "Phaedo."* London: Routledge and Kegan Paul.
Boardman, J. 1990. "*Symposion* Furniture." In *Sympotica: A Symposium on the "Symposion,"* edited by Oswyn Murray, 122–31. Oxford: Clarendon Press.
Bostock, David. 1986. *Plato's "Phaedo."* Oxford: Clarendon Press.
Bowery, A. M. 1996. "Diotima Tells Socrates a Story: A Narrative Analysis of Plato's *Symposium.*" In *Feminism and Ancient Philosophy,* edited by Julia K. Ward, 175–94. London: Routledge.
Bowie, A. M. 1997. "Thinking with Drinking: Wine and the Symposium in Aristophanes." *Journal of Hellenic Studies* 107:1–21.
Boyancé, P. 1963. "Note sur la phroura platonicienne." *Revue de Philologie,* 7–11.
Brague, R. 1985. "The Body of the Speech: A New Hypothesis on the Compositional Structure of Timaeus' Monologue." In *Platonic Investigations,* edited by Dominic J. O'Meara, 35–52. Studies in Philosophy and the History of Philosophy, vol. 13. Washington, D.C.: Catholic University of America.
Brandwood, Leonard. 1990. *The Chronology of Plato's Dialogues.* New York: Cambridge University Press.
Bremmer, J. M. 1990. "Adolescents, Symposion, and Pederasty." In *Sympotica: Symposium on the "Symposion,"* edited by Oswyn Murray, 135–48. Oxford: Clarendon Press.
Brink, C. O. 1958. "Plato on the Natural Character of Goodness." *Harvard Studies in Classical Philology* 63:193–98.
Brisson, Luc. 1977. "Platon 1958–1975." *Lustrum* 20:5–304.
Brisson, Luc (with Hélène Ioanidi). 1983. "Platon 1975–1980." *Lustrum* 25:31–320.
———. 1984. "Corrigenda à *Platon* 1975–1980." *Lustrum* 26:205–6.
———. 1988. "Platon 1980–1985." *Lustrum* 30:11–294.
———. 1989. "Corrigenda à *Platon* 1980–1985." *Lustrum* 31:270–71.
———. 1992. "Platon 1985–1990." *Lustrum* 34:7–330.
Brisson, Luc (with Fréderic Plin). 1999. *Platon 1990–1995: Bibliographie.* Paris: Vrin.
Brock, R. 1990. "Plato and Comedy." In *Owls to Athens: Essays on Classical Subjects Presented to Sir Kenneth Dover,* edited by Elizabeth M. Craik, 39–51. Oxford: Clarendon Press; New York: Oxford University Press.
Brown, Wendy. 1994. "'Supposing Truth Were a Women . . . ': Plato's Subversion of Masculine Discourse." In *Feminist Interpretations of Plato,* edited by N. Tuana, 157–80. University Park: Penn State Press.
Brumbaugh, Robert S. 1989. *Platonic Studies of Greek Philosophy: Form, Arts, Gadgets, and Hemlock.* Albany: State University of New York Press.
Burger, Ronna. 1984. *The "Phaedo": A Platonic Labyrinth.* New Haven: Yale University Press.
Burkert, Walter. 1987. *Ancient Mystery Cults.* Cambridge: Harvard University Press.
Burnet, John. 1916. "The Socratic Doctrine of the Soul." *Proceedings of the British Academy* 7:235–59.
———. 1911. *Plato's "Phaedo."* Oxford: Oxford University Press.
Burnyeat, Miles F. 1977. "Socratic Midwifery, Platonic Inspiration." *Bulletin of the Institute of Classical Studies* 24:7–17. Reprinted in Hugh H. Benson, ed., 1992, *Essays on the Philosophy of Socrates,* 53–65, New York: Oxford University Press.

Canto, M. 1994. "The Politics of Women's Bodies: Reflections on Plato." Translated by A. Goldhammer. In *Feminist Interpretations of Plato,* edited by Nancy Tuana, 49–66. University Park: Penn State Press.
Cherniss, H. 1959–1960. "Plato 1950–1957." *Lustrum* 4:5–308; 5:321–648.
Clarke, W. M. 1978. "Achilles and Patroclus in Love." *Hermes* 106:381–96.
Craig, D. 1975. "The Tragic and Comic Poet of the 'Symposium.'" *Arion,* n.s., 2:238–61.
Cobb, William S. 1993. *The "Symposium" and the "Phaedus": Plato's Erotic Dialogues.* Albany: State University of New York.
Cornford, Francis MacDonald. 1971. "The Doctrine of Eros in Plato's 'Symposium.'" In *Plato: A Collection of Critical Essays,* edited by Gregory Vlastos, 2:119–31. Garden City, N.Y: Anchor Books.
Corrigan, Kevin. 1985. "The Irreducible Opposition Between the Platonic and Aristotelian Conceptions of Soul and Body in Some Ancient and Mediaeval Thinkers." *Laval Théologique et Philosophique* 41:391–401.
———. 1986a. "Body and Soul in Ancient Religious Experience." In *Classical Mediterranean Spirituality: Egyptian, Greek, Roman,* edited by A. H. Armstrong, 360–83. Vol. 15 of *World Spirituality: An Encyclopedic History of the Religious Quest.* New York: Crossroad.
———. 1986b. "Ivan's Devil in *The Brothers Karamazov* in the Light of a Traditional Platonic View of Evil." *Forum for Modern Language* 22:1–9.
———. 1990. "The Function of the Ideal in Plato's *Republic* and Thomas More's *Utopia*." *Moreana* 27, no. 104:27–49.
———. 1995. "Ecstasy and Ectasy in Some Early Pagan and Christian Mystical Writings." In *Greek and Medieval Studies in Honor of Leo Sweeney, S. J.,* edited by William J. Carroll and John J. Furlong, 27–37. New York: P. Lang.
———. 1996. *Plotinus' Theory of Matter-Evil and the Question of Substance: Plato, Aristotle, and Alexander of Aphrodisias.* Leuven: Peeters Press.
———. 1997. "Some Notes Towards a Study of the 'Solitary' and the 'Dark' in Plotinus, Proclus, Gregory of Nyssa, and Pseudo-Dionysius." *Studia Patristica* 30:151–57
Cotter, J. 1973. "The *Symposium*: Plato's Title and Intent." In *Classics and the Classical Tradition: Essays Presented to Robert E. Dengler,* edited by E. N. Borza and R. W. Carrubba, 33–50. University Park: Penn State Press.
Cowling, W., and Nancy Tuana. 1994. "The Presence and Absence of the Feminine in Plato's Philosophy." In *Feminist Interpretations of Plato,* edited by Nancy Tuana, 243–69. University Park: Penn State Press.
Craig, R. 1985. "Plato's Symposium and the Tragicomic Novel." *Studies in the Novel* 17:158–73.
Craik, Elizabeth M., ed. 1990. *Owls to Athens: Essays on Classical Subjects Presented to Sir Kenneth Dover.* Oxford: Clarendon Press; New York: Oxford University Press.
Crombie, I. M. 1962. *An Examination of Plato's Doctrines.* 2 vols. London: Routledge and Kegan Paul.
Crossman, Richard, H. S. 1939. *Plato Today.* New York: Oxford University Press.
Dante Alighieri. 1995. *Vita nuova.* Italian text with facing English translation by Dino S. Cervigni and Edward Vasta. Notre Dame: University of Notre Dame Press.
Daux, George. 1942. "Sur quelques passages du *Banquet* de Platon." *Revue des Etudes Grecques* 55:236–71.
Derrida, Jacques. 1971. "La mythologie blanche." In *Rhêtorique et philosophie, poétique* 5. Paris.

———. *Dissemination.* 1981. Translated and with an introduction and additional notes by Barbara Johnson. Chicago: Chicago University Press.
des Places, Eduoard. 1981. *Etudes platonicennes.* 1929–1979. Leiden: E. J. Brill.
de Vogel, C. J. 1953. "On the Neoplatonic Character of Platonism and the Platonic Character of Neoplatonism." *Mind* 62:43–64.
Diels, Herman, and Walter Kranz. 1951. *Die Fragmente der Vorsokratiker.* 6th ed. Berlin: Weidmann.
Diès, Auguste. 1976. *Autour de Platon: Essais de critique et d'histoire.* Vols. 1 and 2. New York: Arno.
Dillon, John. 1977. *The Middle Platonists.* Ithaca, N.Y.: Cornell University Press.
Dixsaut, Monique. 1991. *Platon: Phédon.* Paris.
———. 1998. *Le naturel philosophe: Essai sur les dialogues de Platon.* Paris: Vrin.
Dodds, Eric Robertson. 1971. Proclus, "The Elements of Theology." 2d ed. 1963. Reprint, Oxford.
Dorter, Kenneth. 1969. "The Significance of the Speeches in Plato's *Symposium.*" *Philosophy and Rhetoric,* no. 2:215–34.
———. 1982. *Plato's Phaedo: An Interpretation.* Toronto: University of Toronto Press.
———. 1992. "A Dual Dialectic in the *Symposium.*" *Philosophy and Rhetoric* 25, no. 3:253–70.
———. 1996. "Three Disappearing Ladders in Plato." *Philosophy and Rhetoric* 29:279–99.
Dover, Kenneth J. 1964. "Eros and Nomos (Plato, *Symposium* 182a–185c)." *Bulletin of the Institute of Classical Studies* 11:31–42.
———. 1965. "The Date of Plato's *Symposium*" *Phronesis* 10:2–20.
———. 1966. "Aristophanes' Speech in Plato's *Symposium.*" *Journal of Hellenic Studies* 66:41–50.
———. 1974. *Greek Popular Morality in the Time of Plato and Aristotle.* Oxford.
———. 1978. *Greek Homosexuality.* Cambridge: Harvard University Press.
du Bois, P. 1994. "The Platonic Appropriation of Reproduction." In *Feminist Interpretations of Plato,* edited by Nancy Tuana, 139–56. University Park: Penn State Press.
Ebert, Theodor. 1974. *Meinung and Wissen in der Philosophie Platons.* New York: de Gruyter.
Edelstein, Ludwig. 1945. "The Role of Eryximachus in Plato's *Symposium.*" *Transactions of the American Philological Association* 76:83–103.
———. 1949. "The Function of the Myth in Plato's Philosophy." *Journal of the History of Ideas* 10:463–81.
———. 1966. *7th Letter.* Leiden: E. J. Brill
Elias, Julius A. 1984. *Plato's Defence of Poetry.* Albany: State University of New York Press.
Else, G. F. 1986. *Plato and Aristotle on Poetry.* Chapel Hill: University of North Carolina Press.
Erbse, H. 1966. "Sokrates und die Frauen." *Gymnasium* 73:201–20.
Farrell Smith, J. 1994. "Plato, Irony, and Equality." In *Feminist Interpretations of Plato,* edited by Nancy Tuana, 25–48. University Park: Penn State Press.
Fasce, S. 1977. *Eros: La figura e il culto.* Genoa.
Ferber, Rafael. 1989. *Platos Idee des Guten.* 2d ed. Sankt Augustín: Academia Verlag Richarz.
Ferrari, G. R. F. 1992. "Platonic Love." In *The Cambridge Companion to Plato,* edited by R. Kraut, 248–76. Cambridge: Cambridge University Press.
Festugière, A. J. 1970. *Proclus: Commentaire sur la Republique.* 3 vols. Paris: Vrin.

Ficino, Marsilio. 1956. *Commentaire sur le Banquet de Platon.* Texte presenté et traduit per Raymond Marcel. Paris: Les Belles Lettres.
Findlay, John N. 1974. *Plato: The Written and Unwritten Doctrines.* London: Routledge and Kegan Paul.
Fite, W. 1934. *The Platonic Legend.* Princeton: Princeton University Press.
Frede, Dorothea. 1993. "Out of the Cave: What Socrates Learned from Diotima." In *Nomodeiktes: Greek Studies in Honor of Martin Ostwald,* edited by Ralph M. Rosen and Joseph Farrell, 397–422. Ann Arbor: University of Michigan Press.
Frede, Michael. 1992. "Plato's Arguments and the Dialogue Form." *Oxford Studies in Ancient Philosophy,* vol. 10, 201–20. Oxford.
Freud, Sigmund. 1989. *Beyond the Pleasure Principle.* 1920. New York: Norton.
Freydberg, Bernard. 1997. *The Play of the Platonic Dialogues.* New York.
Friedländer, Paul. 1923. *Der Grosse Alkibiades: Kriische Erorterungen.* Bonn.
———. 1958/1964/1969. *Plato.* Translated by H. Meyerhoff. 3 vols. Princeton: Princeton University Press.
Fritz, Kurt von. 1971. "The Philosophical Passage in the Seventh Platonic Letter and the Problem of Plato's 'Esoteric' Philosophy." In *Essays in Ancient Greek Philosophy,* edited by John P. Anton and George L. Kustas, 1:408–47. Albany: State University of New York Press.
Frutiger, Perceval. 1930. *Les mythes de Platon.* Paris.
Gadamer, Hans-Georg. 1960. *Wahreit und Methode.* Tübingen: Mohr.
———. 1980. *Dialogue and Dialectic: Eight Hermeneutical Studies on Plato.* Translated by P. C. Smith. New Haven: Yale University Press.
———. 1986. *The Idea of the Good in Platonic Aristotelian Philosophy.* Translated by P. C. Smith. New Haven: Yale University Press.
Gagarin, M. 1977. "Socrates' *Hubris* and Alcibiades' Failure." *Phoenix* 31:22–37.
Gallop, David. 1975. *Plato's "Phaedo."* Oxford: Clarendon Press.
Geddes, W. D. 1985. *The "Phaedo" of Plato.* London.
Gerber, D. E., ed. 1984. *Greek Poetry and Philosophy: Studies in Honour of Leonard Woodbury.* Chico, Calif.: Scholars Press.
Gilbert, W. 1909. "Der zweite Teil des Logos der Diotima in Platons Gastmahl (Cap. 24–29, Pag. 204 C–212A)." *Philologus,* n.F., 22:52–70.
Gill, Christopher. 1990. "Platonic Love and Individuality." In *Polis and Politics: Essays in Greek Moral and Political Philosophy,* edited by Andros Loizou and Harry Lesser, 69–88. Brookfield, Vt.: Avebury.
———. 1995. *Personality in Greek Epic, Tragedy, and Philosophy.* New York: Clarenon Press.
Golden, M. 1984. "Slavery and Homosexuality at Athens." *Phoenix* 38:308–24.
———. 1985. "O Pais, 'child' and 'slave.'" *L'Antiquité Classique* 54:91–104.
Gomperz, Theodor. 1964. *Greek Thinkers: A History of Ancient Philosophy.* 4 vols. [1901–12]. Reprint, London.
Gonzalez, Francisco J. 1998. *Dialectic and Dialogue: Plato's Practice of Philosophical Inquiry.* Evanston: Northwestern University Press.
Gould, Thomas. 1963. *Platonic Love.* London: Routledge and Paul.
Greene, William Chase. 1938. *Scholia Platonica.* American Philological Association Monograph Series 8. Haverford, Pa.: Societas Philologica Americana.
Greifenhagen, Adolf. 1951. *Griechische Eroten.* Berlin.
Grube, G. M. A. 1935. *Plato's Thought.* London: Methuen.

———. 1974. *Plato's "Republic."* Indianapolis: Hackett.
Gundert, H. 1965. "Zum Spiel bei Platon." In *Beispiele,* edited by Ludwig Landgrebe, 188–221. The Hague: Nijhoff.
Guthrie, W. K. C. 1957. "Plato's Views on the Nature of the Soul." *Recherches sur la tradition platonicienne.* Fondation Hardt, Entretiens 3. Vandoeuvres-Genève.
———. 1962–81. *A History of Greek Philosophy.* 6 vols. Cambridge.
———. 1975. *A History of Greek Philosophy.* Vol. 4, *Plato: The Man and His Dialogues.* Cambridge: Cambridge University Press.
Hackforth, R. 1950. "Immortality in Plato's *Symposium*" *Classical Review* 64:42–45.
———. 1952. *Plato's "Phaedrus."* Cambridge: Cambridge University Press.
———. 1955. *Plato's "Phaedo."* Cambridge. Cambridge University Press.
Hadot, Pierre. 1995. *Philosophy as a Way of Life.* Edited by A. I. Davidson. Translated by M. Chase from *Exercices spirituelles et philosophie antique.* Paris, 1987. Cambridge, Mass.: Blackwell.
Halperin, David M. 1985. "Platonic Eros and What Men Call Love." *Ancient Philosophy* 5:161–204.
———. 1986. "Plato and Erotic Reciprocity." *Classical Antiquity* 5:60–80.
———. 1990. "Why Is Diotima a Woman? In *One Hundred Years of Homosexuality and Other Essays on Greek Love,* edited by David M. Halperin, 113–51, 190–211. New York: Routledge.
———. 1992. "Plato and the Erotics of Narrativity." In *Methods of Interpreting Plato and His Dialogues.* Supplementary volume of *Oxford Studies in Ancient Philosophy,* edited by James C. Klagge and Nicholas D. Smith, 93–129. Oxford: Clarendon Press; New York: Oxford University Press.
Hampton, C. 1994. "Overcoming Dualism: The Importance of the Intermediate in Plato's Philebus." In *Feminist Interpretations of Plato,* edited by Nancy Tuana, 217–42. University Park: Penn State Press.
Harris, Bluestone N. 1994. "Why Women Cannot Rule: Sexism in Plato Scholarship." In *Feminist Interpretations of Plato,* edited by Nancy Tuana, 109–30. University Park: Penn State Press.
Hegel, Georg Wilhelm Friedrich. 1988. *Lectures on the Philosophy of Religion: The Lectures of 1827.* Edited by P. C. Hodgson. Berkeley.
Heidel, William Arthur. 1976. *Plato's "Euthyphro": Pseudo-Platonica.* With introduction and notes. 1896. Reprint, New York.
Hirzel, Rudolf. 1914. *Die Person, Begriff und Name derselben im Altertum.* Munich: Verlag der Königlich Bayerischen Akademie der Wissenschaften.
Hussey, Edward. 1972. *The Presocratics.* New York: Scribner.
Irigaray, Luce. 1994. "Sorcerer Love: A Reading of Plato's *Symposium,* Diotima's Speech." Translated by E. H. Kuykendall. In *Feminist Interpretations of Plato,* edited by Nancy Tuana, 181–96. University Park: Penn State Press.
Irwin, Terence. 1995. *Plato's Ethics.* New York: Oxford University Press.
Isenberg, M. W. 1940. "The Order of the Discourses in Plato's *Symposium.*" Ph.D. diss., University of Chicago.
Kahn, Charles H. 1976. "Plato on the Unity of Virtues." In *Facets of Plato's Philosophy,* edited by William Henry Werkmeister, 21–39. Assen, Netherlands: Van Gorcum.
———. 1987. "Plato's Theory of Desire." *Review of Metaphysics* 41:77–103.
Kant, Immanuel. 1908. *Kants gesammelte Schriften.* Edited by Wilhelm Windelband. Akademie ed. Vol. 5. Berlin.

———. 1987. *Critique of Judgement*. Translated by W. S. Pluhar. Indianapolis: Hackett.
Konstan, D., and E. Young-Bruehl. 1982. "Eryximachus' Speech in the *Symposium*." *Apeiron* 16:40–46.
Kosman, L. A. 1976. "Platonic Love." In *Facets of Plato's Philosophy*, edited by William Henry Werkmeister, 53–69. Assen, Netherlands: Van Gorcum.
———. 1992. "Silence and Imitation in the Platonic Dialogues." *OMPH*, 73–92.
Krämer, Hans Joachim. 1990. *Plato and the Foundations of Metaphysics*. Translated by J. R. Catan. Albany: State University of New York Press.
Kranz, Walther. 1926. "Diotima von Mantineia." *Hermes* 61:437–47.
Kraut, Richard, ed. 1992. *The Cambridge Companion to Plato*. Cambridge: Cambridge University Press.
Kristeva, Julia. 1983. *Histoires d'amour*. Paris: Denoël.
———. 1984. *Revolution in Poetic Language*. New York: Columbia University Press.
Kruger, G. 1973. *Einsicht und Leidenschaft: Das Wesen des platonischen Denkens*. 4th ed. Frankfurt.
Kurke, L. 1997. "Inventing the Hetaira: Sex, Politics, and Discursive Conflict in Archaic Greece." *Classical Antiquity* 16:106–50.
Lear, Jonathan. 1990. *Love and Its Place in Nature: A Philosophical Interpretation of Freudian Psychoanalysis*. New York: Farrar, Straus and Giroux.
———. 1998. *Open Minded: Working Out the Logic of the Soul*. Cambridge: Harvard University Press.
Lasserre, F. 1944. "*Erotikoi logoi*." *Museum Helveticum* 1:169–78.
Ledger, Gerard R. 1989. *Re-counting Plato: A Computer Analysis of Plato's Style*. Oxford: Clarendon Press.
Levi, A. 1946. "Sulla demonologica platonica." *Athenaeum* 24:199–28.
Levin, Susan. 1975. "Diotima's Visit and Service to Athens." *Grazer Beitrage* 3:223–40.
———. 1996. "Women's Nature and Role in the Ideal *Polis*: *Republic* V Revisited." In *Feminism and Ancient Philosophy*, edited by Julia K. Ward, 13–30. London: Routledge.
Levinson, M., A. Q. Morton, and A. D. Windspear. 1968. "The Seventh Letter of Plato." *Mind* 77:309–25.
Levinson, Ronald B. 1953. *In Defense of Plato*. Cambridge: Harvard University Press.
Levy, D. 1979. "The Definition of Love in Plato's *Symposium*." *Journal of the History of Ideas* 40:285–91.
Liddell, Henry George, Robert Scott, and Henry Drisler Jones. 1940. *A Greek-English Lexicon*. 9th ed. Oxford.
Lissarague, F. 1995. "Un rituel du vin: La libation." In *In Vino Veritas*, edited by Oswyn Murray and Manuela Tecusan, 126–44. London: British School in association with American Academy at Rome.
Loriaux, R. 1969. *Le "Phédon" de Platon*. Namur, Belgium: Presses Universitaires de Namur.
Lowenstam; S. 1985. "Paradoxes in Plato's *Symposium*." *Ramus* 14:85–104.
Luce, J. V. 1952. "Immortality in Plato's *Symposium*." *Classical Review*, n.s., 2, no. 3/4: 137–41.
Marcel, R. 1956. *Marsile Ficin: Commentaire sur le Banquet de Platon*. Paris: Les Belles Lettres.
Markus, Robert A. 1955. "The Dialectic of Eros in Plato's *Symposium*." *Downside Review* 73:219–30. Reprinted in G. Vlastos, ed., 1971, *Plato: A Collection of Critical Essays*, 2:132–43. Garden City, N.Y.: Anchor Books.
Mattingly, Harold B. 1958. "The Date of Plato's *Symposium*." *Phronesis* 3:31–39.

Merlan, P. 1953. *From Platonism to Neoplatonism.* The Hague: M. Nijhoff.
Miller, Mitchell. 1985. "Platonic Provocations: Reflections on the Soul and the Goal in the *Republic.*" In *Platonic Investigations,* edited by Dominic J. O'Meara, 163–94. Studies in Philosophy and the History of Philosophy, vol. 13. Washington, D.C.: Catholic University of America Press.
Moravcsik, Julius M. E. 1971. "Reason and Eros in the "Ascent" Passage of the *Symposium.*" In *Essays in Ancient Greek Philosophy,* edited by John P. Anton and George L. Kustas, 285–302. Albany: State University of New York Press.
Morrison, J. S. 1964. "Four Notes on Plato's *Symposium.*" *Classical Quarterly* 14:42–55.
Morrow, Glenn R. 1962. *Plato's Epistles.* Indianapolis: Bobbs-Merrill.
Morson, Gary Saul, ed. 1981. *The Boundaries of Genre: Dostoevsky's Diary of a Writer and the Traditions of Literary Utopia.* Austin: University of Texas Press.
———. 1986. *Bakhtin: Essays and Dialogues on His Work.* Chicago: University of Chicago Press.
Morson, Gary Saul, and Caryl Emerson. 1990. *Mikhail Bakhtin: Creation of a Prosaics.* Stanford: Stanford University Press.
Müller, Gerhard. 1986. "Die Philosophie im pseudoplatonischen Brief." In *Platonische Studien,* edited by Andreas Graeser and Dieter Maue, 146–71. Heidelberg: Carl Winter Universitätsverlag.
Murray, Oswyn. 1990a. "The Affair of the Mysteries: Democracy and the Drinking Group." In *Sympotica: A Symposium on the "Symposion,"* edited by Oswyn Murray, 149–61. Oxford.
———. 1990b. "Sympotic History." In *Sympotica: A Symposium on the "Symposion,"* edited by Oswyn Murray, 2–13. Oxford: Clarendon Press.
———, ed. 1990c. *Sympotica: A Symposium on the "Symposion."* Oxford.
Murray, Oswyn, and Manuela Tecusan, eds. 1995. *In Vino Veritas.* London: British School in association with American Academy at Rome.
Mylonas, George E. 1961. *Eleusis and the Eleusinian Mysteries.* Princeton: Princeton University Press.
Nagel, T. 1974. "What Is It Like to Be a Bat." *Philosophical Review* 83, no. 4:435–50.
Nancy, Jean-Luc. 1982. *Le partage des voix.* Paris: Galilée.
Narbonne, J.-M. 2002. "The Origin, Significance, and Meaning of the *Epekeina* Motif in Plotinus and the Neoplatonic Tradition." In *Proceedings of the Boston Area Colloquium in Ancient Philosophy,* vol. 17, ed. J. J. Cleary and G. M. Gurtler, 185–206. Brill: Leiden.
Natorp, Paul. 1921. *Platons Ideenlehre.* 2d ed. Leipzig: F. Meiner.
Nauck, A. 1889. *Tragicorum Graecorum Fragmenta.* 2d ed. Leipzig.
Nehamas, Alexander. 1989. "*Episteme* and *Logos* in Plato's Later Thought." In *Essays in Ancient Greek Philosophy,* edited by John P. Anton and Anthony Preus, 267–92. Albany: State University of New York Press.
Neumann, H. 1965. "Diotima's Concept of Love." *American Journal of Philology* 86:33–59.
Nicholson, Graeme. 1999. *Plato's "Phaedrus": The Philosophy of Love.* Purdue: Purdue University Press.
Nietzsche, Friedrich Wilhelm. 1956. *Twilight of the Idols and the Anti-Christ.* Translated by Francis Colffing. Garden City, N.Y.
———. 1974. "On Truth and Falsity in their Ultramoral Sense (1873)." In *Works.* Vol. 2. New York.

Nightingale, Anne Wilson. 1995. *Genres in Dialogue: Plato and the Construct of Philosophy.* Cambridge.
Nilsson, Martin P. 1948. *Greek Piety.* Oxford: Clarendon Press.
Nussbaum, Martha C. 1986. *The Fragility of Goodness.* Cambridge: Cambridge University Press. Earlier version of chapter 6 published 1979, "The Speech of Alcibiades: A Reading of Plato's *Symposium,*" *Philosophy and Literature* 3:131–72.
———. 1990. *Love's Knowledge: Essays on Philosophy and Literature.* New York: Oxford University Press.
Nye, Andrea. 1994. "Irigaray and Diotima at Plato's Symposium." In *Feminist Interpretations of Plato,* edited by Nancy Tuana, 197–216. University Park: Penn State Press.
Nygren, Anders. 1969. *Agape and Eros.* Translated by Philip S. Watson. New York.
O'Brien, D. 1967–68. "The Last Argument of Plato's *Phaedo.*" *Classical Quarterly,* n.s., 17, no. 2:198–231; 18, no.1:95–106.
———. 1997. "L'Empedocle de Platon." *Revue des Etudes Grecques* 110:381–98.
O'Brien, Michael J. 1984. "Becoming Immortal in Plato's *Symposium.*" In *Greek Poetry and Philosophy: Studies in Honour of Leonard Woodbury,* edited by D. E. Gerber, 185–205. Chico, Calif.: Scholars Press
O'Meara, Dominic J. 1989. *Pythagoras Revived: Mathematics and Philosophy in Late Antiquity.* Oxford: Oxford University Press.
———., ed. 1985. *Platonic Investigations.* Studies in Philosophy and the History of Philosophy, vol. 13. Washington, D.C.: Catholic University of America.
O'Neill, William. 1965. *Proclus: Alcibiades I, a Translation and Commentary.* The Hague: Nijhoff.
Osborne, Catherine. 1994. *Eros Unveiled: Plato and the God of Love.* Oxford: Clarendon Press.
Osborne, R. 1985. "The Erection and Mutilation of the Hermai." *Proceedings of the Cambridge Philological Society,* n.s., 31:47–73.
Patterson, R. 1982. "The Platonic Art of Comedy and Tragedy." *Philosophy and Literature* 6:76–92.
———. 1991. "The Ascent in Plato's *Symposium.*" *Proceedings of the Boston Area Colloquium in Ancient Philosophy* 7:193–214.
Pender, Elizabeth E. 1992. "Spiritual Pregnancy in Plato's *Symposium*" *Classical Quarterly* 42:72–86.
Penwill, J. L. 1978. "Men in Love: Aspects of Plato's *Symposium.*" *Ramus* 7:143–75.
Pépin, Jean. 1971. *Idées grecques sur l'homme et sur dieu.* Paris: Les Belles Lettres.
Phillips, J. F. 1990. "Plotinus and the 'Eye' of Intellect." *Dionysius* 14:79–103.
Pickard-Cambridge, Arthur Wallace. 1968. *The Dramatic Festivals of Athens.* Revised by John Gould and David M. Lewis. London: Oxford University Press.
Plass, P. 1978a. "Anxiety, Repression, and Morality: Plato and Freud." *Psychoanalytic Review* 65:533–56.
———. 1978b. "Plato's 'Pregnant' Lover." *Symbolae Osloenses* 53:47–55.
Plochmann, G. K. 1971. "Supporting Themes in the *Symposium.*" In *Essays in Ancient Greek Philosophy,* edited by John P. Anton and George L. Kustas, 328–44. Albany, N.Y.
Popper, Karl. 1950. *The Open Society and Its Enemies.* Vol. 1, *The Spell of Plato.* Princeton: Princeton University Press.
Price, A. W. 1989. *Love and Friendship in Plato and Aristotle.* Oxford: Clarendon Press.
Rappe, S. 2000. *Reading Neoplatonism: Non-discursive Thinking in the Texts of Plotinus, Proclus, and Damascius.* Cambridge: Cambridge University Press.

Reeve, M. D. 1971. "Five Notes." *Classical Review*, n.s., 21:324–29.
Renehan, R. 1980a. "The Meaning of *Soma* in Homer." *California Studies in Classical Antiquity* 21:269–82.
———. 1980b. "On the Greek Origins of the Concepts of Incorporeality and Immateriality." *Greek, Roman, and Byzantine Studies* 21:105–38.
———. 1990. "Three Places in Plato's *Symposium*." *Classical Philology* 85:120–26.
Richter, David H. 1989. *The Critical Tradition: Classic Texts and Contemporary Trends*. Translated by Francis Golfing. New York.
Riedweg, Christoph. 1987. *Mysterienterminologie bei Platon: Philon and Klemens von Alexandrien*, New York: W. de Gruyter.
Rist, J. M. 1964a. *Eros and Psyche: Studies in Plato, Plotinus, and Origen*. Phoenix, Supplement 6. Toronto: University of Toronto Press.
Rist, J. M. 1964b. "Mysticism and Transcendence in Later Neoplatonism." *Hermes* 92, no. 2:213–25.
Robin, Leon. 1908. *La theorie platonicienne de l'amour*. Paris: Presses Universitaires de France.
———. 1926. *Platon: Phedon*. Paris: Les Belles Lettres.
Robinson, Richard. 1953. *Plato's Earlier Dialectic*. 2d ed. Oxford: Clarendon Press.
Robinson, T. M. 1970. *Plato's Psychology*. Toronto: University of Toronto Press.
Rohde, Erwin. 1925. *Psyche: The Cult of Souls and Belief in Immortality Among the Greeks*. Translated by W. B. Hillis. London: D. Paul, Trench, Trubner; New York: Harcourt, Brace.
———. 1960. *Der griechische Roman und seine Vorläufer*. Wiesbaden: Breitkopf and Härtel, 1914. Reprint, Hildesheim: Georg Olms.
Roochnik, David L. 1987. "The Erotics of Philosophical Discourse." *History of Philosophy Quarterly* 4:117–30.
Rosen, Stanley. 1987. *Plato's "Symposium."* 2d ed. New Haven: Yale University Press.
———. 1993. *The Quarrel Between Philosophy and Poetry*. New York: Routledge and Kegan Paul.
Rosenmeyer, T. 1951. "Eros-Erotes." *Phoenix* 5:11–22.
Rosler, W. 1995. "Wine and Truth in the Greek *Symposium*." In *In Vino Veritas*, edited by Oswyn Murray and Manuela Tecusan, 106–12. London.
Roux, J. 1961. "A propos de Platon: Reflections en marge du *Phedon* (62b) et du *Banquet*." Revue de Philologie, 207–24.
Rowe, Christopher J. 1993. *Plato: Phaedo*. Cambridge: Cambridge University Press.
———. 1996. *Plato: Phaedrus*. Warminster, U.K.: Aris and Phillips.
Runia, David T. 2003. "Plato's Timaeus, First Principle(s), and Creation in Philo and Early Christian Thought." In *Plato's Timaeus as Cultural Icon*, edited by Gretchen J. Reydams-Schils. Notre Dame: University of Notre Dame Press: 133–51.
Russell, Bertrand. 1950. *Unpopular Essays*. New York: Simon and Schuster.
Russon, John, and John Sallis. 2000a. *Retracing the Platonic Text*. Evanston: Northwestern University Press.
———. 2000b. "We Sense That They Strive: How to Read (the Theory of the Forms)." In *Retracing the Platonic Text*, edited by John Russon and John Sallis. Evanston: Northwestern University Press.
Ryle, Gilbert. 1966. *The Concept of Mind*. Harmondsworth, Middlesex: Penguin.
Sallis, John. 1996. *Being and Logos: Reading the Platonic Dialogues*. 3d ed. Bloomington: Indiana University Press.

———. 2000. "Traces of the *Chora*." In *Retracing the Platonic Text*, edited by John Russon and John Sallis. Evanston: Northwestern University Press.
Sallis, John, and John Russon. 2000. *Retracing the Platonic Text*. Evanston, Ill.
Santas, G. X. 1988. *Plato and Freud: Two Theories of Love*. Oxford: Blackwell.
Saxonhouse, A. W. 1984. "Eros and the Female in Greek Political Thought: An Interpretation of Plato's *Symposium*." *Political Theory* 12:5–27.
———. 1994. "The Philosopher and the Female in the Political Thought of Plato." In *Feminist Interpretations of Plato*, edited by N. Tuana, 67–86. University Park: Penn State Press.
Sayre, Kenneth. 1995. *Plato's Literary Garden: How to Read a Platonic Dialogue*. Notre Dame: University of Notre Dame Press.
Schelling, Friedrich Wilhelm Joseph von. 1966. *Philosophie der Mythologie*. 2 vols. Originally published in *Saemmtliche Werke*, Augsburg, 1856 (vol. 11), and 1857 (vol. 12). Darmstadt.
Schleiermacher, Friedrich E. D. 1973. *Introduction to the Dialogues of Plato*. Translated by W. Dobson. Cambridge, 1836. Reprint, New York.
Shaw, G. 1999. "Eros and Arithmos: Pythagorean Theurgy in Iamblichus and Plotinus." *Ancient Philosophy* 19:121–43.
———. 2000. "After Aporia: Theurgy in Later Platonism." In *Gnosticism and Later Platonism: Themes, Figures, Texts*, edited by J. D. Turner and R. Majerclk. Atlanta: Society of Biblical Literature: 57–82.
Skinner, Quentin. 1969. "Meaning and Understanding in the History of Ideas." *History and Theory* 8:3–53.
Smith, A. 1974. *Porphyry's Place in the Neoplatonic Tradition: A Study in Post-Plotinian Neoplatonism*. The Hague: M. Nijhoff.
Solmsen, F. 1971. "Parmenides and the Description of Perfect Beauty in Plato's *Symposium*." *American Journal of Philology* 92:62–70.
Souilhé, Joseph. 1960. *Lettres*. Vol. 13, pt. 1 of *Platon: Oeuvres completes*. Paris: Les Belles Lettres.
Spelman, E. V. 1994. "Hairy Cobblers and Philosopher-Queens." In *Feminist Interpretations of Plato*, edited by Nancy Tuana, 87–108. University Park: Penn State Press.
Sprague, Rosamund Kent. 1984. "Plato and Children's Games." In *Greek Poetry and Philosophy: Studies in Honour of Leonard Woodbury*, edited by D. E. Gerber, 275–84. Chico, Calif.
Stannard, J. 1959. "Socratic Eros and Platonic Dialectic." *Phronesis* 4:120–34.
Stenzel, Julius. 1940. *Plato's Method of Dialectic*. Edited and translated by D. J. Allan. Oxford.
Stewart, John Alexander. 1960. *The Myths of Plato*. London.
Stokes, Michael C. 1986. *Plato's Socratic Conversations: Drama and Dialectic in Three Dialogues*. New York: Routledge.
Strauss, Leo. 1983. *Studies in Platonic Political Philosophy*. Chicago: University of Chicago Press.
———. 2001. *Leo Strauss on Plato's "Symposium."* Edited by S. Benardete. Chicago: University of Chicago Press.
Szlezàk, Thomas Alexander. 1985. *Platon und die Schriftlichkeit der Philosophie*. New York: G. de Gruyter.

Taran, Leonardo. 1985. "Platonism and Socratic Ignorance." In *Platonic Investigations,* edited by Dominic J. O'Meara. Studies in Philosophy and the History of Philosophy, vol. 13. Washington, D.C.: Cornell University Press.
Tarrant, Harrold. 1983. "Middle Platonism and the Seventh Letter." *Phronesis* 28:75–103
———. 1993. *Thrasyllan Platonism.* Ithaca, N.Y.: Cornell University Press.
Taylor, Alfred Edward. 1960. *Plato: The Man and His Work.* 7th ed. London.
Tecusan, M. 1995. "Logos Sympotikos: Patterns of the Irrational in Philosophical Drinking—Plato Outside the Symposium." In *Essays in Ancient Greek Philosophy,* edited by Oswyn Murray and Manuela Tecusan, 238–60. London.
Thesleff, H. 1982. *Studies in Platonic Chronology.* Commentationes Humanarum Litterarum 70. Helsinki.
Tomin, J. 1987. "Socratic Midwifery." *Classical Quarterly* 37:97–102.
Toynbee, Arnold. 1972. *A Study of History.* New ed., revised and abridged by Arnold Toynbee and Jane Caplan. New York: Oxford University Press.
Trevor-Roper, H. 1985. *Renaissance Essays.* London: Seeker and Warburg.
Tuana, Nancy, ed. 1994. *Feminist Interpretations of Plato.* University Park: Penn State Press.
Tuana, Nancy, and William Cowling. 1994. "The Presence and Absence of the Feminine in Plato's Philosophy." In *Feminist Interpretations of Plato,* edited by Nancy Tuana, 243–69. University Park: Penn State Press.
Vernant, J. P. 1990. "One . . . Two . . . Three: *Eros.*" In *Before Sexuality: The Construction of Erotic Experience in the Ancient Greek World,* edited by Froma I. Zeitlin, John J. Winkler, and David M. Halperin, 465–78. Princeton: Princeton University Press.
Vlastos, Gregory. 1965. "Degrees of Reality in Plato." In *New Essays on Plato and Aristotle,* edited by J. Renford Bambrough. London.
———. 1981. "The Individual as an Object of Love in Plato." In *Platonic Studies,* by Gregory Vlastos, 3–42. 2d ed. Princeton.
———. 1987. "Socratic Irony." *Classical Quarterly* 37:79–96.
———. 1994. "Was Plato a Feminist?" In *Feminist Interpretations of Plato,* edited by Nancy Tuana, 11–24. University Park: Penn State Press.
Vries, G. J. de. 1969. *Spel bij Plato.* Amsterdam.
———. 1973. "Mystery Terminology in Aristophanes and Plato." *Mnemosyne* 26:1–8.
———. 1980. "Marginal Notes on Plato's *"Symposium."*" *Mnemosyne* 33:349–51.
Wallis, R. T. 1972. *Neoplatonism.* Indianapolis: Hackett.
Ward, Julia K., ed. 1996. *Feminism and Ancient Philosophy.* London: Routledge.
Warner, M. 1979. "Love, Self, and Plato's *Symposium.*" *Philosophical Quarterly* 29:329–39.
Wender, D. 1973. "Plato: Misogynist, Paedophile, and Feminist." *Arethusa* 6, no. 1:75–90.
Westerink, Leendert Gerrit, ed. 1976–77. *The Greek Commentaries on Plato's "Phaedo."* 2 vols. New York: North-Holland.
White, David A. 1989. *Myth and Metaphysics in Plato's "Phaedo."* Cranbury, N.J.: Associated University Presses.
White, F. C. 1989. "Love and Beauty in Plato's *Symposium.*" *Journal of Hellenic Studies* 109:149–57.
Whittaker, J. "Basilides on the Ineffability of God." *HThR,* 367–71.
———. 1969a. "Epekeina nou kai ousias." *Vigiliae Christianae* 23:91–104.
———. 1969b. "Neopythagoreanism and Negative Theology." *Symbolae Osloenses* 44:109–25.

———. 1973. "Neopythagoreanism and the Transcendent Absolute." *Symbolae Osloenses* 48:77–86.
Wilamowitz(-Moellendorff), Ulrich von. 1919 (2d ed., 1920). *Platon.* 2 vols. Berlin.
———. 1932. *Der Glaube der Hellenen.* Berlin.
Wilson Nightingdale, Anne. 1995. *Genres in Dialogue: Plato and the Construct of Philosophy.* Cambridge: Cambridge University Press.
Wippern, Jürgen. 1965. "Eros und Unsterblichkeit in der Diotima-Rede des Symposions." In *Synousia Festgabe,* edited by H. Flashar and K. Gaiser, translated by W. Schadewaldt, 123–59. Pfullingen.
Zanker, Paul. 1995. *The Mask of Socrates: The Image of the Intellectual in Antiquity.* Translated by Alan Shapiro. Berkeley and Los Angeles: University of California Press.
Zeitlin, Froma I., John J. Winkler, and David M. Halperin, eds. 1990. *Before Sexuality: The Construction of Erotic Experience in the Ancient Greek World.* Princeton: Princeton University Press.
Zembaty, J. S. 1989. "Socrates' Perplexity in Plato's 'Hippias Minor.'" In *Essays in Ancient Greek Philosophy,* edited by John P. Anton and Anthony Preus, 3:51–70. Albany: State University of New York Press.

INDEX

absence, 30, 32, 77, 158, 192, 195, 201, 209, 217, 226, 235–39. *See also* gap
    of visual clarity, 27–82
    missing speeches, 56, 100–101, 151–52
    silence, 16–17
accidentality, problem of, 1, 3, 23–28, 29–33, 36–37, 39–42, 202, 202 n. 32, 235, 237–39
account. *See logos*
Achilles, 52, 53, 55, 56, 115, 238 n. 123
acquisition/possession, 134, 135–36, 158, 172
Adam, J., 97 n. 65, 216 n. 64
address/addressee, 7ff., 12, 20, 76–77, 89, 189–203, 209–10, 224. *See also* reflexivity
    extrafactual, 201
Adeimantus, 8 n. 2, 52 n. 4
Admetus, 52, 53, 55
Aeschylus, 52, 72
Aesop, 72
Agamemnon, 14
agapê, 45, 106. *See also* love, *eros*
Agathon, 1, 4, 5, 8, 9, 13, 16, 17, 18, 22, 23, 26, 27, 30, 33, 33 n. 21, 34, 35, 37, 41 n. 42, 42, 46, 47–50, 55, 56, 62, 65 n. 23, 77, 82, 85–103, 108–11, 113, 114, 117, 119, 121, 122, 127, 130, 133, 135–37, 145, 146, 147, 151–62, 164, 170 n. 12, 173, 179, 184–85, 186, 188ff., 208, 220, 235, 236
Alcestis, 51, 53, 55, 56, 115
Alcibiades, 1, 8, 13, 26, 27, 30, 31, 39, 50, 52, 63, 97, 107, 112, 126, 145, 160, 161, 163–87, 188ff., 214 n. 59, 217, 219, 220, 229, 230, 235, 236, 238 n. 122
Alcman, 121
allegory (*hyponoia*), 121, 123, 125, 125 n. 47, 129, 233. *See also* myth, image
Allen, R. E., 15, 26 n. 8, 33 n. 23, 34 nn. 25, 28, 37 n. 33, 39 nn. 34, 36, 45 n. 7, 48, 48 n. 18, 57 n. 12, 69, 69 n. 33, 106 n. 3, 107 nn. 8–9, 109 n. 14, 112 n. 23, 113 n. 25, 120 nn. 39–40, 122 n. 44, 131, 131 n. 60, 132 nn. 61–62, 133, 133 n. 65, 162 n. 29, 163 n. 2, 164 n. 3, 174 n. 19
anachronisms, 18–20, 78–80, 111 n. 20
Anaximenes, 88
Anderson, D. E., 163 n. 1, 164 nn. 3–4, 173 n. 15
Annas, J., 83 n. 53, 118 n. 34
answer/question, 7, 19, 20, 29, 108, 134, 141, 184–87, 188ff., 201, 214. *See also* address, reflexivity
Antisthenes, 235 n. 118
Anton, J. P., 150 n. 11
Anytus, 70
Aphrodite, 25, 45, 55, 57, 58, 61, 62 n. 17, 64, 105, 116, 121, 127, 131 n. 57, 162
Apollo, 5, 14, 39, 72, 80, 163, 169 n. 11, 186
Apollodorus, 3, 4, 7–20, 21–42, 57, 77 n. 43, 145, 146 n. 88, 151, 166, 179, 181 n. 28, 185, 188ff., 214 n. 59, 216, 219, 239
appearance (versus truth/reality), 31, 54, 56, 60, 93, 100 n. 67, 171
apprentice, 1, 51ff., 129 n. 51, 148, 151, 155, 171
Apuleius, 133
Archer-Hind, R. D., 230 n. 101
archetype. *See* image, type
Archilochus, 175 n. 20
Arendt, H., 107, 107 n. 9
aretê (excellence, virtue), 33 n. 22, 34, 55, 57ff., 60, 86, 90–91, 100, 102, 144, 208, 208 n. 50, 212, 213 n. 57, 226
    Socratic, 64–65
argument, 5, 60–61, 71, 88, 89–90, 108–11, 124, 129, 129 n. 51, 146, 188ff., 200, 203–15, 217, 220–24, 225, 230–34. *See also* myth, structure, *logos*
Aristodemus, 3, 4, 7–20, 21–42, 56, 57, 100, 112, 113, 145, 151, 179, 185, 186, 188ff., 214 n. 59, 216, 235, 236, 239
Aristophanes, 1, 4, 14 n. 20, 18, 26, 27, 41 n. 42, 44, 45, 47–50, 62–63, 67, 68–85, 90–91, 93, 94, 100–103, 107, 116, 118 n. 35, 119, 121, 125, 127, 128 n. 50,

Aristophanes (*continued*)
    135–37, 151–62, 164, 167 n. 7,
    184–85, 186, 188ff., 220, 223, 235
Aristotle, 46, 83 n. 53, 89, 154 n. 17, 158, 162,
    208 n. 50, 231
Arkadians, 18 n. 22, 73
Armstrong, A. H., 79 n. 45, 129 n. 53
art(s), 2–3, 7, 12, 37, 41, 63, 84–85, 91, 102–3,
    104, 155–57, 159, 167, 184–85,
    189–203, 203–14, 215–20, 220–24,
    228, 229. See also *techne,* creativity
    criticism of (*Republic*), 3, 11–12, 18, 70,
        75–78, 103, 146, 154–55, 174, 185,
        215
    and dialectic, 159, 208–9
    inspiration, 215
    positive view, 3, 5, 157, 159, 215–20
    rhetorical/philosophical, 41, 210, 215–24
ascent, 2, 4, 10, 31, 42, 49–50, 101, 107,
    148–58, 174, 183, 188ff., 193, 204–9,
    234. See also ladder, love, movement
    steps/rungs, 31, 136, 148–58, 160, 192,
        194, 195, 195 n. 18, 209, 227, 234
Asclepiad, 63
Asclepius, 79, 79 n. 45, 185
Ast, F., 148 n. 6
Athena, 116
atopia/atopos, 170–72, 176, 181–83, 212. *See also*
    uniqueness, identity
    placelessness, 7, 26–28, 210 n. 54, 212
    timelessness, 210 n. 54
    unlikeness, 212
audio-video reportage, 17, 20, 186, 189, 193,
    219. *See also* narrative
Augustine, 105

Bakhtin, M., 3, 6, 196, 196 n. 21, 197–203,
    214
Bambrough, J. R., 36 n. 32
Barnes, J., 63 n. 19
Barth, K., 107, 107 nn. 6–7, 109, 161 n. 28
bathing, 14 n. 20, 22, 234
beast, 95, 103
beauty (*to kalon*), 1, 7, 23–26, 28, 31, 52, 53,
    57, 74–75, 87, 90, 94, 110, 111, 118,
    136, 141, 168, 174–75, 185, 192, 194,
    209, 211, 212, 218, 220, 225, 227,
    230–36
    beautiful itself, 105, 108, 109, 149, 209,
        225, 234–36
    as criterion, 57
    inner, 174–75

and good, 52, 136, 141
and procreation, 137–41
romantic catalogue, 53
and sufficiency, 23–26
being, 36, 36 n. 32, 115, 195, 232, 233, 236 n.
    119
belief, opinion (*doxa*), 204, 213
Benardete, S., 74 n. 41, 94 n. 62, 170 n. 12
Benci, T., 131 n. 57
Berkeley, G., 205 n. 42
between/middle, 7ff., 34, 136, 170, 192, 235,
    239
birth (procreation), 117, 118, 120, 121–30,
    137–40, 144–45, 145–58, 226, 235–36
Bluck, R., 230 n. 101
body, 7, 31, 36, 76, 81, 101–3, 139, 141,
    148ff., 182–83, 224ff., 236 n. 119
    astral, 232–33
    compassion/care, 182–83, 229
    dialogical channel, 225
    different views, 226–27, 230ff.
    inclusive view, 31
    and intelligence, 76
    organization, 76, 224 n. 87, 227, 234
    soul-body, 36, 57, 82, 90, 101–3, 118 n. 34,
        134 141, 143, 148–58, 226–34
    and speech, 228
Boethius, 114
Bonelli, G., 164 n. 3, 186 n. 35
Bostock, D., 230, 230 nn. 101–2
Bowery, A. M., 118 n. 34
Brandwood, L., 102 n. 69, 238 n. 123
Brisson, L., 9 n. 6, 15 n. 21, 19 n. 32, 27 n. 10,
    39 n. 37, 48, 48 nn. 18–19, 72 n. 40, 82
    n. 51, 111 nn. 19–20, 112 n. 21, 113 n.
    26, 148 n. 6, 149, 150 n. 12, 169 n. 12,
    178 n. 24
Burger, R., 230 n. 101, 231 n. 108
Burnet, J., 57 n. 12, 145, 230 n. 101
Bury, R. G., 8 n. 1, 8 n. 4, 15, 18 n. 22, 19 n.
    32, 26 n. 9, 33 n. 21, 43 n. 1, 47, 47 nn.
    11–14, 57 n. 12, 68 n. 26, 69, 69 n. 28,
    70, 70 n. 35, 87, 87 n. 57, 111 n. 19,
    148, 148 n. 4

Callias, 34
Callicles, 77 n. 42, 124
Callimachus, 72
Calliope, 238
Caricature, 11, 216
Cebes, 228 n. 97
Cephalus, 8 n. 2, 54, 237, 239

Index

chance. *See* accidentality
character, 3–5, 10, 11, 44, 51ff, 88, 96, 166–67, 188–96, 197–203. *See also* voice, genre
   atopia (extraordinary character), 170–72, 176, 181–83
   character and vision, 167
   surplus of, 202
Charmides, 8 n. 2, 212, 213, 213 n. 57
Chiasmus, 25
chronology, 19, 102, 102 n. 19, 190ff.
Cicero, 83 n. 53
clear/clarity, 17, 18, 27–28, 190, 207ff., 209. *See also* truth
   and truth, 18, 207ff.
collection, 209, 214 n. 59. *See also* division
comedy (and tragedy), 1, 23, 69–71, 88, 184–85, 189, 217
communication, 37, 120
communion/commonality, 145, 153, 154, 160, 208–9
compulsion, 180–81, 184, 189
conception (*ennoia*), 208
contest, 24–25
contradiction, 56, 61, 64, 66–67, 73–74, 103, 104, 111, 153, 190ff., 206, 212, 230, 234, 235, 238. *See also* opposition
conversation, 8–10, 11, 29, 30, 31, 114, 121, 130, 141 n. 81, 158
Cornford, F. M., 47, 47 n. 14, 112 n. 22, 131, 131 n. 58, 132, 133, 147 n. 2
Corrigan, K., 130 nn. 54–55
corruption, 95, 98, 157, 169, 177 181, 214–15
Cos, 62
Cowling, W., 118 n. 34
Craig, R., 196 n. 22
creativity, 2, 11, 32, 86, 91, 129, 134, 154–57, 167, 190–91, 197, 201, 210, 217
   as *poesis*, 91, 134
criteria/standard, 23–26, 58–60, 66, 74, 108, 111, 177
Critias, 198, 208 n. 50, 213 n. 57
Crito, 143 n. 84, 184
Cronos, 87, 125
Crossman, R., 221 n. 74
cut(s), 80–81, 135, 138 n. 76. *See also* division
Cydathenaeum, 9, 9 n. 6

daimon, 118ff. *See* also *eros*
Damascius, 232, 232 n. 109, 233
Dante, 131, 131 n. 59
date, 18–19 nn. 31–32, 158–59, 158 n. 23
death, 176ff., 226, 234

deconstruction, 61, 135 n. 69, 153. *See also* destruction
definition, 134, 135, 136, 194–95, 214 n. 59. See also *logos*
deliberation, 124–27
delusion (*atê*), 87–88
Democritus, 232
Derrida, J., 229, 229 n. 100
Descartes, 194, 205 n. 42, 225
desire (*epithymia*), longing, feeling, 12 n. 11, 30, 45, 61, 73, 102, 109, 118, 119, 126, 134, 135–36, 139–40, 161, 222, 235–36
destruction, 11, 14–15, 21–42, 98, 100, 162, 179, 191, 195, 195 n. 18, 201, 209, 210, 211, 212, 213, 214. *See also* image, transformation
   and transformation, 21–42, 212–14, 217, 219, 224, 226, 227, 235
diachronism, 18–19 n. 31. *See also* anachronism
dialectic, 29, 71, 80–84, 102–3, 124, 129 n. 51, 133–34, 137, 138 n. 76, 147, 155–56, 159, 161, 173–74, 183, 188ff., 192–96, 203–15, 220, 221, 222, 225–26, 235–37, 235 n. 119, 239. *See also* dialogue
   and art, 159
   forms of, 129 n. 51
   parody of, 80–82, 102
   at play, 203–15
   and rhetoric, 133–34
   synoptic vision, 155–56, 213, 227
dialogue, 2, 18, 19, 41, 104, 114, 118, 129–30, 146, 162, 171, 184–87, 188–203, 220, 221, 225–26, 235–36. *See also* dialectic, narrative, conversation, reflexivity
   levels of, 31, 37, 38–39, 41
   onion-skin layers, 18, 19, 220, 236
dialogues (Plato)
   Alcibiades, I 83 n. 53
   Apology, 70, 75
   Charmides, 208 n. 50, 213 n. 57
   Cratylus, 195 n. 17
   Crito, 143 n. 84
   Euthydemus, 213 n. 57
   Gorgias, 34, 77 n. 42, 117, 124, 134, 143
   Hippias Minor, 238 n. 123
   Laws, 39, 215, 217–18, 236–37 n. 119
   Lysis, 30
   Parmenides, 8 n. 1, 149 n. 9, 192, 236 n. 119
   Phaedo, 79, 107, 171, 225, 227, 228 n. 97, 230–34, 236 n. 119, 237–38

dialogues (*continued*)
  Phaedrus, 81, 123, 187, 201, 214 n. 58, 215, 219, 224–25, 228, 229, 236–37 n. 119
  Philebus, 186, 217, 236 n. 119
  Politicus, 236 n. 119
  Republic, 1–3, 36, 75–77, 82, 94–98, 102, 105, 123–25, 126, 135, 144, 154, 155–56, 159, 171, 180–81, 204–9, 213, 214–15, 216, 219, 227–29, 234, 236 n. 119, 237
  Seventh Letter, 194–95 nn. 14–16, 212, 214, 215, 219
  Sophist, 236 n. 119
  Timaeus, 133, 234, 236 n. 119
Diomedes, 24, 32, 239
Dione, 125, 127
Dionysus, 5, 37, 39, 162, 163–87
Diotima-Socrates, 1, 2, 10, 16, 19 n. 31, 23, 25, 41, 42, 43, 48, 49, 50, 55–56, 63, 68, 93, 104–62, 167, 183, 185, 188ff., 219, 220, 223, 226, 229, 235, 236 n. 119, 237
disciple, 11, 19
discourse, levels of, 31, 37, 38–39, 97, 148–58, 171, 197–203. *See also* speech, *logos*
  father of, 39–41, 54
  gendered, 139 n. 76
  immortal, 145
  mutual reflexivity, 188–96
discrimination, 74, 89, 152, 152 n. 15, 207ff., 225, 237
disorder, 63, 64, 67, 71, 85, 164. *See also* order, gap, interruption
disruption. *See* interruption, destruction
divine-human relation, 41, 54, 66, 67, 103, 84 n. 53, 120, 136, 140–41, 158, 164–65, 209–10, 225, 230, 234
  devaluation of, 74–75
  superabundance, 94, 126ff.
division/dividedness, collection, gatherer, 80–81, 102, 156, 209, 210, 211, 235
Dixsaut, M., 22 n. 1, 79 n. 45, 149 n. 7, 150 n. 12, 184 n. 33, 230 n. 101, 236 n. 119
Dodds, E. R., 232, 232 nn. 111–12
Dorter, K., 47–48, 47 n. 15, 48 nn. 16–17, 49, 52, 52 n. 7, 53, 53 n. 8, 61 nn. 15–16, 64, 64 n. 20, 88 n. 58, 230 n. 101, 231, 231 nn. 106–7
Dover, K., 8 n. 1, 13 nn. 13, 16, 14 nn. 18–19, 16, 16 n. 22, 19 n. 31, 23, 23 n. 2, 26, 26 n. 2, 26 nn. 8–9, 27 n. 11, 31 n. 18, 32 n. 19, 40 n. 39, 45 n. 4, 45 nn. 6–7, 46 nn. 9–10, 52 n. 5, 57 n. 12, 65 n. 22, 69–70, 69 n. 34, 71 n. 36, 71 n. 39, 72 n. 40, 73, 82 n. 51, 87, 104, 104 n. 1, 105, 105 n. 2, 106 nn. 3, 5, 107 n. 10, 109 n. 15, 111 n. 19, 112, 112 n. 24, 113 n. 26, 117 n. 30, 120 n. 38, 122 n. 43, 134 nn. 67–68, 135, 135 n. 20, 138, 138 n. 76, 139, 139 n. 78, 140–41, 140 n. 80, 145, 148, 148 n. 5, 158 n. 23, 167 n. 8, 168, 168 n. 9, 171 n. 13, 178 n. 24
doxa. *See* opinion, knowledge
drama, 113, 189ff., 196, 204–15
dream, 36, 221, 222
drinking party/get-together, 5, 11, 18, 179, 218
  rules of, 27, 34, 39
drunkenness/wine, 23, 37–38, 125–6, 163ff., 168, 173–74, 180, 184
dualism, 229
duBois, P., 118 n. 34, 138 n. 76

earth, 230–34
Ebert, T., 149 n. 8
Edelstein, C., 194 n. 14, 231 n. 103
education (*paideia*), 33–37, 61, 71–72, 74, 89, 95, 96, 103, 117, 212
  empty, ornamental, 95
  and poetry, 7
  sophistic, 103
  by touch, 33–37, 117
eikasia (imaging-making), 81, 204, 207
Eileithyia, 138
elenchus, 5, 94, 94 n. 62, 104, 108–11, 112, 192, 212, 214, 235
Eleusinian mysteries, 141, 176
Elias, J. A., 40 n. 38, 221 n. 80, 222, 222 nn. 84–85, 223 n. 86
Else, G. F., 215 nn. 61, 63
Emerson, C., 197 n. 23
Empedocles, 66, 70
enchantment, 130
encomium (praise), 39, 46, 408
epic, 32, 88, 190–91, 196, 199, 202, 239
epistêmê, 43, 64, 66, 91, 118–19 n. 35. *See also* science, knowledge
epistemology, 116, 118 n. 34, 127–28
  and intercourse, 116–17
Er, 237
Erasmus, 13
eros, 14, 16, 23, 30, 34, 39–40, 44–46, 55, 105, 110, 118–33, 137–43, 168, 169. *See also* love
  agapê, 45, 106

doleros, 110, 238 n. 123
ekstatikos, 130
energy, 132
eristic, 231 n. 57, 236 n. 119
eros-daimon, 54, 118–21, 132, 167, 176
  eros-lust, 45, 110, 126, 180–81
Eros-Phanes, 72 n. 40
erotic joust, 25
  erotika/love matters, 25, 65, 112, 167
  philia, 30
  platonic. *See* love
  sexual, 188–90
Erythrae, 61
Eryximachus, 22, 23, 26, 27, 38, 39, 40, 41 n. 42, 47–50, 56, 62–68, 69, 71, 73, 84, 85, 90–91, 92, 100–103, 116, 118 n. 36, 119, 127, 143, 144, 151–62, 163, 168, 169, 188ff., 223, 227, 235
Euripides, 39, 40, 41, 44, 52 n. 6, 116, 168
Eurydice, 53
Eusebius, 127 n. 48
Euthydemus, 212, 213, 213 n. 57
exchange (of opposites), 35, 36, 37, 38, 59, 172, 226

fable, 192, 196, 198
face, 49, 59, 67, 103, 163ff., 207, 209, 216 217. *See also* character, genre
fact (and fiction), 7, 19, 37, 90, 146, 188ff., 193, 201, 235
failure, 100
feast, 125, 130, 180, 187, 218 (*festive dialogue*), 236 n. 119 (*divine banquet*)
feminism, 118 n. 34, 138 n. 76. *See also* woman
Ferrari, G. R. F., 46 n. 9, 48 n. 19, 63 n. 18
Ficino, M., 20, 20 n. 33, 105, 131 n. 57, 161
fiction, 7, 19, 25 n. 5, 105, 108, 111, 115, 124, 140, 146, 162, 188ff., 193, 199, 201
filling (and emptying), 35–36, 65, 67, 99–100, 117–18, 119
Findlay, J. N., 69, 69 n. 30, 151 n. 14, 153 n. 16
Fite, W., 221 n. 74
flutes, 163ff., 177
forgetfulness, 126, 137, 151
form(s) (ideas), 7, 80, 148, 157–58, 182–83, 184, 196, 198, 204–6, 206 n. 45, 209, 211, 212, 216
  and sameness, 182–83
frame, 7–42, 188–96, 197–203, 219, 220. *See also* structure
Frede, M., 129 n. 51, 136 n. 72, 181 n. 1
Freud, S., 68, 69 n. 31, 106, 161, 161 n. 26

friction, dialectical, 194–95, 209
Friedländer, P., 8 n. 1, 16 n. 22, 30 n. 17, 33 n. 22, 39, 39 n. 37, 40, 40 n. 40, 83 n. 53, 122, 122 n. 44, 164 n. 5, 221, 221 n. 75, 231, 231 n. 103
friendship, 30, 66, 67, 116, 120–21, 130, 145, 158, 226, 227
Fritz, K. von, 194 n. 14
Frutiger, P., 40 n. 38, 128 n. 50, 221 n. 79–80, 222 n. 83

Gadamer, H. G., 214 n. 58, 219, 219 n. 70
Gallop, D., 230 n. 101
gap/rupture, 19, 27, 59, 67, 101, 153, 154, 156, 175, 216, 217
gatherer, 80–81. *See also* division/collection
Geddes, W. D., 230 n. 101, 231 n. 105
generosity, 32, 33 n. 21, 97, 191ff.
genre, 49, 103, 188–96, 197–203, 235–36. *See also* character, voice
genuine versus counterfeit, 21, 58, 154
Gerber, D. E., 142 n. 83, 214 n. 58
Gill, C., 107 n. 4
Glaucon, 8, 9, 10, 11, 16, 30, 52, 96, 115, 118 n. 34, 213, 228
god(s), 25, 52, 54, 65, 66, 75, 83, 86, 93, 96, 103, 111, 118–21, 122, 125, 126, 127, 148, 158–59, 163ff., 174–5, 178, 210, 216, 225, 230, 234
  god-belovedness, 149, 158–59
good (and beautiful), 7, 30–31, 32, 52, 61, 92, 94–98, 103, 109, 125, 129, 134, 135, 141, 145–46, 149, 178, 182, 191–92, 195, 201, 206, 206 n. 45, 207ff., 226, 227, 228, 235–36, 238
  absent, 157–58, 195, 201, 209, 226
  Agathon's name, 30, 32
  Agathon's portrait, 94–98
  distinguished from beautiful, 141
  gift, 158
  self-giving, 129, 182
  shadow of, 94ff.
Gonzalez, F. J., 194 n. 14, 205 nn. 37–38, 205 n. 42
Gorgias, 44, 77 n. 42, 93, 95 n. 63, 124, 200
gossip, 20 n. 35
Gould, T., 39, 39 n. 37, 46 n. 9, 69, 69 n. 31
grace, 90, 97, 100
Gregory of Nyssa, 105, 232, 233 n. 114
Grube, G. M. A., 96 n. 64, 105, 105 n. 2, 107 n. 3, 205 nn. 39, 41, 209 n. 51, 211, 211 n. 56

Gundert, H., 214 n. 58
Guthrie, W. K. C., 18 n. 22, 19 n. 32, 23, 24 n. 3, 36 n. 32, 42, 42 n. 43, 47, 47 n. 14, 63 n. 19, 69, 69 n. 27, 71 n. 37, 80 n. 48, 214 n. 58, 231, 231 nn. 103–4
Gyges, 52

Hackforth, R., 140, 140 n. 79, 142 n. 83, 158 n. 23, 230 n. 101, 231, 231 n. 105
Hadot, P., 39 n. 36, 164 n. 6, 173 n. 15, 176 n. 21
Halperin, D. M., 8 n. 1, 12 n. 11, 20 n. 35, 25 n. 5, 28 n. 12, 112, 116 n. 28, 146 n. 88, 216 n. 65
Hamilton, W., 58 n. 13, 107 n. 4, 128 n. 49
happiness, 141
harmony, 228
Harpocratio, 232
Hegel, G. W. F., 173, 221, 221 n. 76
Heidel, W. A., 83 n. 53
Hephaestus, 73, 82
Heraclitus, 63–65, 119, 144
Hercules, 34, 46
herd instinct, 141
herms, 169, 178
Herodotus, 74 n. 41
Hesiod, 44, 72, 85, 87, 90, 123, 144, 179, 210
heteroglossia, 197
heterosexuality, 61, 112 n. 21
hiccups, 62–63, 67, 68, 71, 85, 101, 102, 164, 210
Hippias, 34, 238 n. 123
Hippocrates, 70
Hirzel, R., 221, 221 n. 80
holy (piety), 60, 90–91
Homer, 11, 13, 14, 15, 22, 28, 29, 30, 31, 32, 44, 85, 87, 105, 123, 144, 175 n. 20, 179, 190, 191, 201, 210, 216, 217, 238 n. 123
homosexuality, 39, 48, 51, 61, 66, 71, 112 n. 21, 117, 128, 114–45
honor, glory, 142–43, 226
hubris (outrage), 13–15, 16, 28–33, 36, 37, 67, 163, 172, 177–79, 181, 190
human being/nature, 72–75, 116, 154–55, 199–200, 201, 202, 224–34
　embodied wholeness, 229
　form of, 80
　identity, 6, 82–84
　male, female, androgynous, 72
　surplus, 199, 202
Hume, D., 105, 143, 205 n. 42

Hussey, E., 63 n. 19
Hyginus, 41 n. 41
hypothesis/nonhypothetical, 84, 102, 123, 181, 204, 204 nn. 35–36, 205, 205 n. 37, 209–10, 212, 238

Iamblichus, 83 n. 53
idea(s), 5, 19, 38, 42, 128–29, 130, 139–40, 145–6, 159, 216, 220, 224, 231, 235–36. *See also* form
　clash/play, 38, 128, 146
　ideal, 216, 220
　myth as, 128–29
identity, 7, 82–84, 134, 143, 144, 181–84, 216, 224–34
　bundle, 143, 181
　diversity/uniqueness, 181–83, 212
　form, 7, 84 n. 53, 182, 184
　gender, 118 n. 34
　horizontal/vertical dimensions, 83, 83 n. 53
　human/ individual, 82–84, 134, 181–83, 216
　material, 82, 84 n. 53, 144, 182
ignorance, 112, 118, 122, 127
illusion, 218
image, 5, 42, 50, 73–74, 81, 84, 88, 90, 102, 103, 114–15, 117, 124, 125, 139–40, 149–50, 155, 156, 159, 181, 192–93, 194–95, 202, 205ff., 208–14, 216–20, 223, 228, 229–30, 236. *See also* art, narrative, destruction
　and dialectic, 124, 173–74
　divine, 209–10, 212
　eikasia, 81, 207
　eikôn, 159, 170–72, 200
　fractured, 220
　psychic, 115, 139–40, 192–93, 210
　token/*symbolon*, 211
imagination, 15, 55, 89, 114
imitation (*mimesis*), 10–12, 12 n. 12, 19, 28–33, 37, 75–78, 137, 146, 185, 192, 215, 216–20. *See also* art, narrative, representation
　different kinds, 12 n. 12
　of imitation, 11–12, 19, 189ff.
　mimetic narrative, 19, 29, 28–33, 236
immortality, 55, 56, 132–33, 137–41, 145, 158–59, 167, 224, 226, 228, 229
inconclusiveness, 199, 201, 203
indirection, 217–18
inferior versus superior theme, 14–15, 22, 25, 57ff., 75, 94, 190–91, 235, 239

instinct, 141, 161
  drives, 161, 161 n. 26
intelligence, mind (*nous, phronesis*), 59, 74, 76, 82, 94, 102, 194, 213–14, 213 n. 59, 226, 227, 228, 237–39. *See also* thought, understanding, reason
interruption/disruption, 150 n. 12, 191, 194–95, 210–11, 219, 233, 239
intersubjectivity, 82, 84 n. 53, 160
intertextuality, 29, 48–49
invited/uninvited, 22, 25, 191
Ion of Chios, 198
Irigaray, L., 118 n. 34, 138 n. 76
irony, 9, 14–15, 25, 89, 94, 112, 169, 191
Isenberg, M. W., 63 n. 18
Isocrates, 57 n. 11
Japetus, 87
journey/method, 7ff., 10, 26, 29, 31–32, 124, 153, 208–9, 234, 238–39
Joyce, J., 201
Jung, C., 68
justice/injustice, 59–60, 80, 91, 124, 237
Kafka, F., 105
Kallone, 138, 139, 140
Kant, I., 218, 218 nn. 68–69, 220, 221, 221 n. 79
Kierkegaard, S., 164 n. 3
kinship, 63, 73, 97, 98, 99, 100, 135, 153, 208–9. *See also* science
  of sciences, 65, 208–9
knowledge (*epistêmê*), 34–37, 84 n. 53, 117, 118–19 n. 35, 148, 194–95, 213, 213 n. 57, 236 n. 119. *See also* science
  and account (*logos*), 118–19 n. 35
  and opinion (*doxa*), 118–19 n. 35, 194, 236 n. 119
  self-knowledge, 187
  surplus, 199
Kosman, L. A., 12 n. 12, 216 n. 65
Kraut, R., 227 n. 94
Kristeva, J., 170 n. 12

Lacan, J., 57 n. 11, 71 n. 39, 88 n. 58, 113 n. 26, 138 n. 76, 164 n. 3, 169–70 n. 12
lack. *See* need
ladder of love, 1–5, 42, 49–50, 106, 114, 148–58, 171, 210, 234. *See also* ascent
language, 5, 30, 32, 103, 116, 120, 134, 135–36, 194–95, 201, 203ff., 206. *See also* speech, *logos*
  limits of, 206–7
  plasticity of, 30–32, 195, 201, 203

laughter, 199, 202. *See* comedy
law (*nomos*), 57, 58, 61, 148–49
Lear, J., 161 n. 26
Ledger, G. R., 194 n. 14
Lenaea, 18
Levin, S., 118 n. 34
Levinson, M. A., 194 n. 14
liberality, 33 n. 22, 91, 97. *See also* generosity
Liddell, Scott, and Jones, 45 nn. 3, 5, 108 n. 13, 110 n. 16, 213 n. 57
like (*homoios*)/unlike, 30–31, 90, 127, 147, 212, 236, 237–39. *See also* identity, uniqueness
Locke, J. 205 n. 42
logos, 12 n. 12, 20, 40, 71, 97, 114, 118–19 n. 35, 123, 124, 135, 183, 194–95, 205, 206, 206 n. 45, 208, 210. *See also* speech, reason, account, myth
  account/definition, 71, 124, 135, 205ff., 206 n. 45
  argument, 124
  conversation, 206
  and gossip, 20 n. 35
  logical analysis, 234–35
  and *mythos*, 5, 40, 123, 220–24
  opened up, 183
  rational discourse/reason, 107, 109, 124, 142
  representation, 12 n. 12
  speech/discourse, 23, 30, 40, 97
  story/tale/myth, 20, 40, 105, 123, 124, 135, 230–34
Loriaux, R., 230 n. 101
love, 44–46, 163ff., 174ff., 183, 234–36. *See also eros*
  abstract, 69, 107
  comprehensive power of, 100, 101, 136
  daimon, 54, 118–21, 130–33, 167, 176
  doleros, 110, 238 n. 123
  god-belovedness, 149
  and hate, 166ff., 211–12
  of individual, 69, 105, 120–21, 152 n. 15, 165, 165 n. 7, 174–75, 174 n. 20, 211
  lust, 110
  passionate, 60, 166
  Platonic, 105–7, 109, 136–37, 234ff.
  relation or substance, 130–33
Luce, J. V., 159 n. 24
Lucian, 198
Lyceum, 38
Lycourgos, 144
Lyncaeus, 233

lyric poetry, 19, 192, 196
Lysias, 57 n. 11

madness, 11, 15–16, 220
malakos/manikos (soft/mad) 11, 15–18
Mantinaea, 111
Mantineans, 18 n. 22, 79
Marsyas, 39, 164, 171, 172, 173, 181, 212
mathêma, 101, 150, 155, 156, 204, 207
Mattingly, H. B., 18 n. 22, 158 n. 23
medicine, 38, 39, 63–68, 69, 70, 84, 101, 102, 153
Medusa, 93
Megalopolis, 62
Melannipe, 40, 41, 41 n. 41, 53
Meletus, 70
memory, 7–20, 80–81, 190, 237
Menelaus, 14, 23, 24, 25
Menissier, T., 25, 25 n. 5, 57 n. 11
Metamorphosis. *See* transformation
Metapontus, 41 n. 41
Metis, 121
metonymy/metaphor, 138 n. 76, 231
Meyer, C. F., 176, 176 n. 21
middle/ between, 7ff., 34, 136, 170, 235, 239
mimesis. *See* imitation
Mitchell, R. L., 164 n. 3
Mithras, 232
moira, 138
morality, 35, 56, 60–61, 135, 148–58, 160, 161, 219
  versus self-interest, 60–61, 160
Moravczik, J., 107 n. 11
Morrison, J. S., 142 n. 83, 158 nn. 22–23
Morson, G. S., 197 n. 23
Moschion, 72
movement/motion, 29, 32, 100, 120–21, 137, 148–58, 191ff., 236 n. 119
  dialectic, 29
  versus frozen past, 32
Müller, G., 194 n. 14
Murray, O., 8 n. 3, 174 n. 19
muse(s), 65, 65 n. 23, 71, 86, 137, 185, 220, 238
  philosophical, 84–85, 137, 156, 185, 200, 220, 228
  tragic/comic poet, 1ff., 86, 185–86, 215–20
music, 64, 64 n. 21, 220, 228, 229, 239
mysteries, 48, 80, 107, 108, 112, 118 n. 34, 141–45, 147–62
  greater, 108, 114, 147–62
  lesser, 141–45, 147

myth (and *logos*), 40–41, 51, 52, 87, 88, 101, 102, 104, 105, 121–30, 146, 192, 203–15, 220–24, 230–34
  aetiological, 72
  as idea, 128
  master/slave, 33 n. 22. *See also* tyranny, slavery
  and prayer, 224 n. 87
  story, 122–30
  theories of, 221–23

Nagel, T., 211 n. 55
names, 194–95, 214 n. 59, 239
Nancy, J-L., 189 n. 1
narrative, 3–6, 7, 9, 10–12, 14–20, 27–28, 28–33, 38–39, 41, 102, 112, 146, 171, 185, 188–96, 197–203, 236. *See also* genre, voice, art, *logos*
  and character, 3, 15
  destruction/transformation, 28–33
  erotics of, 12 n. 11
  frame, 4, 7–42, 188–203
  mimetic, 10–12, 19, 28–33, 41, 146
  mimetic/hubristic/dialogical, 28–33
  notions/temperaments, 14–15
  reported speech, 17, 28
  thrice removed, 9, 12, 17, 20, 189ff.
  types of, 102, 188
Natorp, P., 221, 221 n. 73
need/ lack, 28, 73–74, 77, 84, 91, 92–94, 97, 122–23, 127, 129, 136, 235–36. *See also* poverty
Nehamas, A., 205 n. 42
Neoplatonism, 83 n. 53, 129ff., 162
Nestor, 238 n. 123
Nicholas of Cusa, 105
Nicholson, G., 222 n. 82
Nietzsche, F., 6, 79 n. 45, 105, 164 n. 3, 196, 196 n. 21, 229, 229 n. 100
Nilsson, M. P., 237 n. 120
nomos (law, rule, convention), 57
novel, 196, 200–203, 208. *See also* narrative, genre, voice
  novelistic discourse 197–203
Nussbaum, M., 105, 105 n. 2, 106 n. 3, 109 n. 15, 152 n. 15, 164 n. 3, 165 n. 7, 174 n. 20
Nye, A., 118 n. 34, 138 n. 76
Nygren, A., 107, 107 n. 6

O'Brien, M. J., 142 n. 83, 159 n. 24
Odysseus, 24, 25, 32, 237, 238, 238 n. 123, 239

Index

oikeios (belonging to oneself), 30, 82, 98, 213
Olympiodorus, 68, 83 n. 53
opinion/appearance (*doxa*), 43, 194–95, 204, 213, 231, 236 n. 119
   right opinion, 118–19 n. 35, 194
opening up, 174, 183, 212, 218, 224, 226
opposition/opposites, 15 n. 20, 38, 64, 67, 68, 75, 93–94, 100, 103, 119, 127, 147, 179, 207ff., 213, 215 n. 59, 225, 226, 238, 239 n. 123
   coincidence of, 93–94, 100, 103
   claim of, 37
   cycle of, 37–39
   necessity of, 127
   pleasure and pain, 15 n. 20, 35, 38, 217
order, 26–28, 29, 39, 42, 43–50, 63ff., 71, 85, 100–103, 113, 180. *See also* disorder
   ascent, 4–5, 101
   and body, 31, 76
   ordering/soul and body, 224 n. 87
   past versus future, 32
   scientific, 39, 63ff., 85
   spatial, 26–28
   speeches, 28, 42, 43–50, 100–103
origin/bedrock/source, 28–33, 40, 41, 55, 190–92, 195, 209, 213, 216, 226
Orpheus, 53
Ortega, y Gasset., 196 n. 22
other, 118, 189–203
Ouranos, 125

Pan, 224 n. 87, 228 n. 95
pantagruelism, 68
paradigm, 125, 208, 210, 216
   divine, 125
   triple male-female, 127ff.
Parmenides, 87, 90
parody, 11, 64 n. 21, 65, 70, 77, 80–82, 172, 219
Patroclus, 52, 55, 142
Pausanias, 18, 23, 26, 27, 34, 38, 41 n. 48, 47–50, 56–62, 63, 64, 73, 82 n. 52, 89, 92, 100–103, 115, 125, 143, 144, 145, 151–62, 163, 172 n 14, 175, 181 n. 28, 188ff., 209 n. 51, 224, 225, 226, 227, 228
Pentheus, 168
Pépin, J., 83 n. 53
perception/senses, 207ff., 228, 230, 231, 232
personal/impersonal, 105–6, 211, 226
personality, 44, 171, 216 (of artist). *See also* character, voice, self

persuasion, 89, 214
Petronius, 198
Phaedrus, 3, 18, 20, 23, 26, 27, 38, 39, 40, 46–50, 51–56, 87, 88, 100–103, 108, 115, 142, 145, 151–62, 188ff., 238, 239
Phalerum, 8
philosophical/nonphilosophical discourse, 1, 10, 20 n. 35, 41–42, 47, 54, 142, 203–15, 216, 230ff.
philosophy, 7, 10, 20 n. 35, 21, 44, 54, 78, 95–97, 98, 103, 114–15, 153, 156–57, 159, 177, 188, 200, 203–15, 216, 219, 220–24, 236–37 n. 119, 238
Phoenix, 8, 12, 16
Piraeus, 8, 10 n. 2
Plato, vanishing signature, 19–20, 57, 78–80, 184–85, 194, 217
play (and seriousness), 1–2, 5, 16, 22, 42, 56, 89, 102, 128, 146, 172, 189, 193, 203–15, 235–36, 235 n. 119
   of ideas, 128, 146
pleasure and pain, 15 n. 20, 35, 38, 217, 236 n. 119
Plenty (*Poros*), 2, 92, 97, 116–17, 121, 122–30
Plochmann, G. K., 150 n. 11
plot, 188–203
Plotinus, 33 n. 21, 105, 129, 129 nn. 52–53, 131, 131 n. 57, 132, 133, 138, 162, 162 n. 30, 162 n. 32, 232, 232 n. 113
Plutarch of Athens, 232
poet, writer of both comedy/tragedy, 1ff., 86, 185–86, 215–20
poetics, 196, 216–20
poetry, 1, 13–20, 23, 55, 75–78, 86, 87, 91, 92, 100, 134, 169, 184–85, 196, 215–20
   comedy, 71ff., 86, 100, 184–85, 215
   and education, 72
   epic, 13–20
   and imitation, 75–78, 220
   lyric, 91
   philosophical, 216
   poiesis, 91, 134, 215, 216
Polemarchus, 8 n. 2
political dimensions, 78–80, 82, 144, 169, 176ff., 226, 236 n. 119
Polus, 124
polyglossia, 197
Polyhymnia, 65
Popper, K., 162, 221, 221 n. 74
Poseidon, 41 n. 41
Poverty (*Penia*), 3, 10, 75, 82, 92ff., 105, 116, 121, 122–30, 136

prayer, 224 n. 87
Price, A. W., 39 n. 34, 107 n. 4, 211, 211 n. 55
Proclus, 83 n. 53, 232
procreation/pregnancy, 117, 118, 125, 137–41, 144–45, 148–58, 173. *See also* birth
Prodicus of Ceos, 34
prologues, 7–20, 21–42
Protagoras, 34, 44
proverb, 22, 29ff., 190–91, 213
Pseudo-Dionysius, 130, 130 nn. 54–55
Pythagoras, 144

question (and answer), 7, 108, 134, 162, 188ff., 193

Rabelais, 68
reality, 3, 30, 36, 43, 81, 99, 111, 168, 171–72, 190–2, 213, 214, 235–36, 239 n. 123. *See also* truth
  degrees of, 33, 33 n. 32
reason. *See* reasoning, *logos*
reasoning (*dianoia*), 204, 205, 205 n. 42, 206 n. 45, 209. *See also* narrative, image
receptivity, 15–18, 113–15
recollection, 80–81, 112–13, 112 n. 25, 145–46, 170, 225 n. 88
recognition/misrecognition, 153, 169–70 n. 12, 193
refutation, 194–95, 204, 212, 214, 214 n. 59, 236, 238
Renehan, R., 30 nn. 15–16
religious observance, 37–39
  religion and myth, 221 n. 79, 230
representation, 12, 12 n. 12, 28, 191, 205–7, 216
  expression veresus content, 87
rest, 172–73, 184
  stability, 209 n. 51
revelation (sudden), 116, 148, 160, 164, 179–80, 212
revellers, 164, 179–80, 236
rhetoric, 7, 57 n. 12, 33–34, 57, 59, 60, 89, 91, 101, 103, 104, 133–34, 167, 189 n. 1, 192
  positive, 33–34, 41, 134
  sophistic, 60, 101, 134 n. 66
Rhode, E., 198, 198 n. 27
Richter, D. H., 196 n. 21
Rist, J. M., 107 n. 6, 121 n. 42, 124 n. 46
Robin, L., 15, 42, 42 n. 43, 47 n. 14, 57 n. 12, 69, 69 n. 32, 78, 80, 131, 131 n. 58, 132, 133, 149 n. 10, 150 n. 11

Robinson, R., 205 nn. 38, 42
Robinson, T. M., 229 n. 99, 230, 230 n. 102
Rosen, S., 14 n. 18, 24, 24 n. 4, 25, 33 n. 21, 34 nn. 25, 29, 47 n. 14
Rösler, W., 174 n. 19
Rowe, C. J., 8 n. 1, 8 n. 4, 13 n. 16, 15 n. 21, 16 n. 24, 18 n. 31, 25 n. 7, 28 n. 12, 30 n. 16, 39 n. 37, 48–49, 49 nn. 20–21, 64 n. 21, 65 n. 23, 72 n. 40, 79 n. 45, 109 n. 15, 111 n. 19, 116 n. 27, 138 n. 75, 142 n. 83, 148 n. 6, 151 n. 13, 159 n. 24, 163 n. 1, 169 n. 12, 174 n. 19, 178 n. 24, 184 n. 33, 221 n. 77, 229 nn. 98–99, 230 n. 101
Russell, B., 221 n. 74
Ryle, G., 194, 194 n. 13

Sallis, J., 10 n. 2, 22 n. 1, 130 n. 56, 203 n. 34, 214 n. 58
satire, 198
satyr, 13, 171–73, 178, 182
Sayre, K., 194 n. 14
Schlegel, F., 196
Schleiermacher, F. E. D., 83 n. 53
Schelling, F. W. J., 222, 222 n. 82, 223
science (*epistêmê*), 39, 43, 63–68, 84, 85, 101, 102, 103, 118–19 n. 35, 143, 149–57, 185, 194–95, 205, 205 n. 42, 208, 214 n. 59, 223, 226, 228, 236 n. 119. *See also* knowledge, thought, understanding
self, 134, 153, 174–75, 174 n. 20, 182–83, 220, 225–34, 237. *See also* identity, uniqueness
  characteristics on ascent, 160
  divided, 177, 235, 239 n. 123
  self-consciousness, 200–203, 208, 225, 237
  self-deception, 62, 160
  self-disclosure, 159, 235–36
  self-knowledge, 237
  self-motion, 236 n. 119
  self-reflexivity, 210–11, 210 n. 55, 225, 229
seriousness (and playfulness), 204–15, 217–20, 236–37 n. 119
sex/sexuality, 13, 25, 45–46, 51, 56, 62, 69, 73ff., 116, 119, 138–41, 145, 153, 168, 172, 173, 225, 226
shadow, 42, 94–98, 103, 115, 178, 186
shame/guilt/and honor, 52, 54–55, 58, 59, 94, 143, 173, 176–77, 192, 235–36, 235 n. 119
Silenus/Sileni, 164, 172–73, 182, 183, 212
Simmias, 107, 228 n. 97, 237, 238, 239

Sirens, 238
slave(ry), 33, 33 n. 22, 97, 100, 108, 118 n. 34, 153, 179, 214. *See also* tyranny
Socrates *passim. See also* Diotima-Socrates
　external appearance, 31–33, 234
　figure, 164–65
　hubris, 13–15, 31
　identity, 181–83
　Silenus, 1, 163ff.
　standing seeking, 184–87, 191, 201
softness, 11, 15–18, 88, 92. See also *malakos*
Solon, 144
Sophist(s), 34, 36–37, 57, 89, 92ff., 96, 101, 104, 142, 152, 236 n. 119
Sophocles, 44, 74 n. 41
Sophron, 198, 210
soul (*psyche*), 7, 36, 57–60, 69, 73, 74, 75, 88, 101–3, 117, 118, 130, 132–33, 139, 143–44, 148–58, 174–75, 174 n. 20, 187, 204ff., 224–34, 236 n. 119, 237
　and community, 153ff.
　excellence/ well-being of, 60, 161
　eye of, 155, 208
　immortality, 158–59
　love of, 58
　philosophical, 95ff.
　pregnancy of, 118
　principle of discrimination, 74–75
　self-mover, 130, 187
　tripartite, 99, 131, 228
Spartans, 73, 79
speakers. *See also* speech
　insight/ limitations, 44, 51ff., 55, 166–67, 207
speech, 38, 43ff., 51ff., 89, 100–3, 180, 201, 228, 237. See also *logos*, conversation
　common versus private, 114–15
　correlation/gap, 156, 159, 166–67, 201, 207
　everyday/ordinary, 30, 74, 103, 223, 235
　missing, 56, 100–101, 151–52
　and structure, 148–58
spiritual voice, 120
Sprague, R. K., 214 n. 58
Stenzel, J., 107 n. 12
Stewart, J. A., 221, 221 n. 78, 222
story. See *mythos, logos*
stranger, 111ff., 237
Stobaeus, 127 n. 48
Stokes, M., 94 n. 62, 109 n. 15
structure, 7–20, 21ff., 147–62, 183–84, 188ff., 203–15, 235–36, 235 n. 119

five-stage subdivision, 148–50
style, 42, 194 n. 14
substance (*ousia*), 130–33, 191ff., 206 n. 45, 225, 234
sufficiency, 23–26, 39, 186. *See also* criterion
symposium, 8 n. 3
synousia, 130
Szlezàk, T., 214 n. 58

Tarrant, H., 194 n. 14
Tartarus, 231
Taylor, A. E., 56, 56 n. 9, 68, 68 n. 25, 147 n. 2, 151 n. 14
teaching/education (*paideia*), 33–37, 61, 71–72, 108, 111, 135, 137, 167
techne (skill, craft, art), 87, 209
Tecusan, M., 174 n. 19
test (and trial), 118, 160, 163ff., 168, 189, 194–95, 194 n. 15, 200–203, 219, 226
　of praise, 168–76
Teuffel, 33 n. 21
Thebes, 62
Theognis, 175 n. 20
theology, 85–100, 101, 103, 121, 129–30, 232
Thesleff, H., 83 n. 53
thought/understanding (*noesis*), 31, 118–19 n. 35, 148, 152 n. 15, 167, 168, 172–73, 186–87, 203–15, 225, 230, 237–38
　self-moving, 187
　waking up, 207–9
Thrasymachus, 8 n. 2, 162, 200
Thucydides, 174
Tolstoy, L., 201
Toynbee, 221 n. 74
timocratic ideal (honor), 142, 226
transformation (metamorphosis), 1, 18, 21–42, 118, 128, 153, 168, 185, 190–92, 200–203, 214, 217, 219, 234, 238–39. *See also* destruction
　of factual reference, 21ff., 201
　journey, 26, 153
transmission, 12, 13, 17, 34–37
　of wisdom, 34–37
Trevor-Roper, H., 221 n. 74
trial, 163ff., 168, 200–203, 219
　of praise, 176–79
truth (reality/*aletheia*), 7, 18–20, 42, 43, 69, 77, 77 nn. 42–43, 84, 90, 94–95, 97, 111, 113–14, 143, 146, 155, 159, 165, 170, 174, 178, 192, 207, 218, 232, 237
　and anachronism, 18–20
　thrice removed from, 20

truth (*continued*)
    indifference to, 71
    and fiction, 113
Tuana, N., 41 n. 42, 118 n. 34
type, 97, 216, 220, 227, 235–36. *See also* genre, individual
tyranny, 28–29, 36, 58, 95, 97, 98, 102, 103, 180–81

understanding/thought (*noesis*), 118–19 n. 35, 195, 203–15, 219, 224, 236
uniqueness, 181–83, 220, 234, 230 n. 119
unity, 73, 82–84, 89, 100, 101, 149, 149 nn. 7–9, 156, 227, 236 n. 119
    material versus spiritual, 73ff., 83–84
    globular fusion, 74–76
    general concepts, 80
    abstract, 89, 90, 100
Urania, 238

Vicaire, P., 47, 47 n. 14, 78, 80, 148 n. 6
violence, 168, 213 n. 57, 214. See also *hubris*
vision, 44, 150, 155–56, 167, 192, 213, 226–27
    and character, 167
Vlastos, G., 36 n. 32, 105, 105 n. 2, 106 n. 3, 118 n. 34, 136, 136 nn. 71, 73, 137, 152 n. 15, 165 n. 7, 211, 211 n. 56
voice, 188–96, 197–203. *See also* character, genre, speaker
    erased, 41
Vries, G. J. de, 214 n. 58

Ward, J., 41 n. 42, 118 n. 34

Waterfield, R., 174 n. 19
Westerink, L. G., 232 nn. 109–10
White, D., 110 n.17, 157 n. 20, 231 n. 105
wholeness, 67–85, 100, 101, 147, 156, 214, 228–34, 235–36
    embodied, 229
Wilamowitz, U. von, 18 n. 30, 24 n. 3, 107, 107 n. 12, 134 n. 66, 214 n. 58, 237 n. 120
Wilson-Nightingale, A., 164 n. 3, 165 n. 7, 189 n. 1
wisdom (*sophia, phronesis*), 34–37, 57, 58, 59, 65, 75, 91, 94, 115, 117, 118, 120, 149, 172, 191–92, 194
    repletion/evacuation, 65
    for sex, 172
woman, 40–41, 53, 58, 111–18, 118 n. 34, 138–41, 146, 192, 235
    Melanippe/displacement of, 40–41, 116
    Alcestis/displacement of, 53, 115
    Diotima, 111–18, 192
    chiastic balance, 116–17
    male-female paradigm, 127ff., 138–41
word, 197–203
writing, 215

Xenophon, 45, 57

youth/old age, 94ff., 143, 179ff., 180, 192

Zembaty, J., 238 n. 123
Zeus, 72, 75, 78, 80, 102, 105, 111, 121, 125, 127, 156

www.ingramcontent.com/pod-product-compliance
Lightning Source LLC
Chambersburg PA
CBHW031547300426
44111CB00006BA/207